Medieval into Renaissance

Professor Helen Cooper by June Mendoza. University College, Oxford

Medieval into Renaissance

Essays for Helen Cooper

EDITED BY
ANDREW KING
AND
MATTHEW WOODCOCK

D. S. BREWER

© Contributors 2016

All Rights Reserved. Except as permitted under current legislation
no part of this work may be photocopied, stored in a retrieval system,
published, performed in public, adapted, broadcast,
transmitted, recorded or reproduced in any form or by any means,
without the prior permission of the copyright owner

First published 2016
D. S. Brewer, Cambridge

ISBN 978 1 84384 432 7

D. S. Brewer is an imprint of Boydell & Brewer Ltd
PO Box 9, Woodbridge, Suffolk IP12 3DF, UK
and of Boydell & Brewer Inc.
668 Mt Hope Avenue, Rochester, NY 14620–2731, USA
website: www.boydellandbrewer.com

A catalogue record for this book is available
from the British Library

The publisher has no responsibility for the continued existence
or accuracy of URLs for external or third-party internet websites
referred to in this book, and does not guarantee that any content on
such websites is, or will remain, accurate or appropriate

This publication is printed on acid-free paper

Contents

List of Illustrations	vii
List of Contributors	viii
Acknowledgments	ix
Abbreviations	x
Introduction ANDREW KING AND MATTHEW WOODCOCK	1
Unknowe, unkow, Vncovthe, uncouth: From Chaucer and Gower to Spenser and Milton ALEXANDRA GILLESPIE	15
Armour that doesn't work: An Anti-meme in Medieval and Renaissance Romance R.W. MASLEN	35
'Of his ffader spak he no thing': Family Resemblance and Anxiety of Influence in Fifteenth-Century Prose Romance MEGAN G. LEITCH	55
Writing Westwards: Medieval English Romances and their Early Modern Irish Audiences AISLING BYRNE	73
Penitential Romance after the Reformation JAMES WADE	91
The English Laureate in Time: John Skelton's *Garland of Laurel* MARY C. FLANNERY	107
Thomas Churchyard and the Medieval Complaint Tradition MATTHEW WOODCOCK	123
Placing Arcadia NANDINI DAS	143
Fathers, Sons and Surrogates: Fatherly Advice in *Hamlet* JASON POWELL	163

'To visit the sick court': Misogyny as Disease in *Swetnam the Woman-Hater*
JOYCE BORO   187

The Monument of Uncertainty: Sovereign and Literary Authority in Samuel Sheppard's *The Faerie King*
ANDREW KING   209

Mopsa's Arcadia: Choice Flowers Gathered out of Sir Philip Sidney's Rare Garden into Eighteenth-Century Chapbooks
HELEN VINCENT   235

Bibliography   251

Index   273

A Bibliography of Helen Cooper's Published Works   279

Tabula Gratulatoria   285

Illustrations

Frontispiece Portrait of Professor Helen Cooper by June Mendoza. University College, Oxford. Reproduced with kind permission of the artist, and the Master and Fellows of University College, Oxford.

Figure 1 Etienne Dupérac, *Vestigi dell'antichita di Roma* (Rome, 1575), Plate 7. (c) The British Library Board. Shelfmark: General Reference Collection C.108.k.3. 148

Figure 2 Map 'Tabula Europae X' showing Arcadia in the Peloponnesus. Giacomo di Gastaldi, *La Geografia di Claudio Ptolemeo* (Venice, 1548). (c) The British Library Board. Shelfmark: Maps C.1.a.3. 157

Figure 3 Map 'Tierra Nueva' showing Arcadia in the New World. Gastaldi, *Geografia*. (c) The British Library Board. Shelfmark: Maps C.1.a.3. 158

Figure 4 *Viaggio fatto nel 1524 all'America settentrionale*: copy of the long-lost Verrazano letter to Francis I, fol. 5r. Reproduced with permission of the Pierpont Morgan Library, New York. Shelfmark: MA 776. 160

The editors, contributors and publishers are grateful to all the institutions and persons listed for permission to reproduce the materials in which they hold copyright. Every effort has been made to trace the copyright holders; apologies are offered for any omission, and the publishers will be pleased to add any necessary acknowledgement in subsequent editions.

Contributors

Joyce Boro	University of Montreal
Aisling Byrne	University of Reading
Nandini Das	University of Liverpool
Mary C. Flannery	University of Lausanne
Alexandra Gillespie	University of Toronto
Andrew King	University College Cork
Megan G. Leitch	University of Cardiff
R.W. Maslen	University of Glasgow
Jason Powell	St Joseph's University, Philadelphia
Helen Vincent	National Library of Scotland, Edinburgh
James Wade	Christ's College, Cambridge
Matthew Woodcock	University of East Anglia

Acknowledgments

Risking the charge of naïveté, the editors feel that the most obvious, and the most necessary, acknowledgment for this essay collection must be made to Professor Helen Cooper herself. All of the contributors to the present volume are Helen's sometime research students. This volume is a token of the most affectionate esteem as well as the profound intellectual respect in which she is held, and has grown out of the contributors' individual delight at supervisory sessions with Helen in Oxford or Cambridge (in which the word 'nice' was the highest accolade for a student's work).

    The editors would like to thank Leanne O'Sullivan, Sarah Elsegood, Sue Hedge, Rob Kinsey, Rohais Haughton, Nick Bingham, Tom Roebuck and Cian O'Mahony, together with the anonymous publisher's reviewers, for their help during the preparation of this book. We are also indebted to Caroline Palmer, Editorial Director at Boydell and Brewer, for her longstanding interest in and support for this project. We are grateful to the Winchester Excavations Committee for granting permission to use the image of King Arthur from the Winchester Round Table for the cover of our volume. We are delighted to have been able to use June Mendoza's recent portrait of Helen as our volume's frontispiece, for which our thanks go to the artist and to the Master and Fellows of University College, Oxford.

Abbreviations

BL	British Library, London
Cooper, *Pastoral*	Helen Cooper, *Pastoral: Mediaeval into Renaissance* (Cambridge, 1977)
Cooper, *Romance*	Helen Cooper, *The English Romance in Time: Transforming Motifs from Geoffrey of Monmouth to the Death of Shakespeare* (Oxford, 2004)
CSPD	*Calendar of State Papers: Domestic*
EETS	Early English Text Society
ELH	*English Literary History*
ELR	*English Literary Renaissance*
ES	Extra Series
ESTC	*English Short Title Catalogue*
HLQ	*Huntington Library Quarterly*
ITS	Irish Texts Society
JMEMS	*Journal of Medieval and Early Modern Studies*
LRB	*London Review of Books*
MED	*Middle English Dictionary*
MP	*Modern Philology*
NQ	*Notes & Queries*
NS, n.s.	New Series
ODNB	*Oxford Dictionary of National Biography*
OED	*Oxford English Dictionary*
OS	Original Series
RES	*Review of English Studies*
Riverside Chaucer	Geoffrey Chaucer, *The Riverside Chaucer*, gen. ed. Larry D. Benson, 3rd edn. (Oxford, 2008)
SEL	*Studies in English Literature*
SP	*Studies in Philology*
Spenser, *Faerie Queene*	Edmund Spenser, *The Faerie Queene*, ed. A.C. Hamilton, 2nd edn., with Hiroshi Yamashita and Toshiyuki Suzuki (Harlow, 2001)
SQ	*Shakespeare Quarterly*
TLS	*Times Literary Supplement*
YLS	*Yearbook of Langland Studies*

Unless otherwise stated, quotations from medieval and early modern texts and manuscripts modernise i/j and u/v spellings and expand all contractions and ampersands.

Introduction

⊰ ANDREW KING AND MATTHEW WOODCOCK ⊱

The reign of Henry VII marks the end of the Middle Ages. These were succeeded by an age of daring discoveries, such as when Capornicus observed the Moon while searching the skies with a telescope, thus causing the rotation of the Earth, crops, etc. [...] The greatest of these discoverers, however, was St Christopher Columba, the utterly memorable American, who, with the assistance of the intrepid adventurers John and Sebastian Robot, discovered how to make an egg stand on its wrong end. (Modern History is generally dated from this event.)[1]

Sic. The more glaringly erroneous and nonsensical claims made about the transition between the medieval and Renaissance periods in W.C. Sellar's and R.J. Yeatman's pithy, parodic *1066 and All That: A Memorable History of England* (1930) are sandwiched between more coherent bold pronouncements of a sort that commonly elicit expressions of scepticism, scorn or caution from scholars of English literature produced before 1600. That is to say, the claim that the Middle Ages ended in 1485, and the implied suggestion that Tudor history and the discovery of the Americas are essentially 'modern' – if only early modern – stories, are troublesome in a different way. As Helen Cooper makes plain, 'the people of England did not wake up the day after the Battle of Bosworth, which saw the end of the long-ruling Plantagenets and the establishment of the parvenu Tudors, to find themselves in a new and modern world'.[2] Moreover, we would need to propose another set of working dates were we to be writing of the advent of the Renaissance in, say, Italy, Scotland or Eastern Europe, or if we were considering disciplines other than literature. Histories of the Renaissance in 'natural philosophy' and scientific enquiry, for example, usually begin by discussing the publication of works by Nicholas Copernicus ('Capornicus') and Andreas Vesalius during the 1540s and then concentrate on later sixteenth – and seventeenth-century sources. There is, however, a certain admirable simplicity to the kind of boldness and cleanness of line exhibited, albeit in an exaggerated form, in that opening quotation. These are the kind of certainties to which a freshman student of literary history might

---

[1] W.C. Sellar and R.J. Yeatman, *1066 and All That: A Memorable History of England* (London, 1930), p. 52.
[2] Helen Cooper, *Shakespeare and the Medieval World* (London, 2010), p. 4.

cling, and that a sympathetic instructor might grudgingly concede are useful starting points for further, more nuanced exposition and enquiry. C.S. Lewis maintained that 'though "periods" are a mischievous conception they are a methodological necessity'.[3] James Simpson, in the conclusion to his landmark *Reform and Cultural Revolution* (2002) – a work that has stimulated renewed debate about literary periodisation for well over a decade – admits that his initial intention when writing the book had been to dissolve the boundary lines between medieval and Renaissance, though he ultimately came to recognise that to do so would be a 'misrepresentation of history'. As he argues throughout his book, there *was* a distinct, perceptible disjuncture between the two periods that occurred as a result of the sudden 'concentrations of cultural and political power' taking place during the first half of the sixteenth century as a consequence of the Henrician Reformation.[4] Simpson and others have shown that drawing lines or pinpointing particularly significant dates or moments, and generally thinking with and around the concept of periodisation, can still prove a fruitful exercise if it prompts new questions or routes of analysis.

The borderline between the periods commonly termed 'medieval' and 'Renaissance', or 'medieval' and 'early modern', has long been one of the most hotly, energetically and productively contested faultlines in literary history studies. Nomenclature employed to identify these periods can itself prove contentious and we are fully aware of how loaded a term 'Renaissance' is when we use it (for reasons discussed below) in the title of our collection and throughout this introduction. Literary periodisation remains a compelling concern for scholars working on both sides of the perceived divide, and for the growing number of those with cross-chronological interests. Critics attempting to characterise what makes the medieval distinct from the Renaissance have continued to demonstrate not only the complexity of the task before them, but just how much is at stake when one establishes a historical point of demarcation and declares that this represents a moment of transition, transformation or cessation. Margreta de Grazia has examined the different epistemological and teleological implications of this line-drawing process: 'Whether you work on one side or the other of the medieval/modern divide has relevance to the present; everything before it is irrelevant.'[5] For the great nineteenth-century thinkers and historiographers Hegel, Burckhardt and Marx (writes de Grazia), the Renaissance was to be separated off from the medieval and valorised as constituting the 'inaugural epoch of the modern'.[6] It was the historical moment – for Burckhardt situated during the fourteenth century, for Hegel during the

---

[3] C.S. Lewis, *English Literature in the Sixteenth Century, Excluding Drama* (Oxford, 1954), p. 64.
[4] James Simpson, *Reform and Cultural Revolution* (Oxford, 2002), pp. 1, 558–9.
[5] Margreta de Grazia, 'The Modern Divide: From Either Side', *JMEMS* 37.3 (2007), 453.
[6] De Grazia, 'Modern Divide', 459–61.

sixteenth – at which many recognisable fixtures and attributes of 'our' modern world, such as individuality, interiority and freedom of consciousness, are first articulated or made manifest.[7] As one of the more recent treatments of medieval and Renaissance literary history puts it, the 'cultural investments' in maintaining the divisions of period remain exceptionally powerful even if we have become more hesitant about identifying where the crucial boundary markers lie:

> None of [the] claims for a profound historical and cultural break at the turn of the fifteenth into the sixteenth centuries is negligible. But the very habit of working within those periodic bounds (either medieval or early modern) tends, however, simultaneously to affirm and to ignore the rupture. It affirms the rupture by staying within standard periodic bounds, but it ignores it by never examining the rupture itself. The moment of profound change is either, for medievalists, just over an unexplored horizon; or, for early modernists, a zero point behind which more penetrating examination is unnecessary.[8]

The recognition that medieval and Renaissance studies entail tracing patterns of both continuity and change, looking both backwards and forwards, and paying attention to specificities of genre, region, class, language and medium, places a particular premium upon the micro-historical approach and individual case-studies, such as one finds in Brian Cummings and James Simpson's 2010 *Cultural Reformations* collection (quoted above) or, indeed, in the present volume. As discussed below, our book is dedicated to a scholar who has long been committed to exploring the complex connections and interactions between the medieval and Renaissance, and to both periods' treatment of the classical past.

As if to confirm all of those narratives that see the roots of the modern in the Renaissance period, it is to the Renaissance itself that we must turn to first see the drawing of our periodic boundary lines. In sixteenth-century England (as James Wade observes at the beginning of his essay in this volume), periodic

---

[7] David Aers and Lee Patterson have shown that such arguments have lingered on in contemporary studies of sixteenth-century subjectivity, interiority and self-fashioning: David Aers, 'A Whisper in the Ear of Early Modernists; or, Reflections on Literary Critics Writing the "History of the Subject"', *Culture and History, 1350–1600: Essays on English Communities, Identities and Writing*, ed. David Aers (Detroit, 1992), pp. 177–202; Lee Patterson, 'On the Margin: Postmodernism, Ironic History and Medieval Studies', *Speculum* 65 (1990), 87–108, and 'The Place of the Modern in the Late Middle Ages', *The Challenge of Periodisation: Old Paradigms and New Perspectives*, ed. L. Besserman (New York, 1996), pp. 51–66. In a special issue of *JMEMS*, Sarah Beckwith and James Simpson re-examine the relationship between the so-called 'premodern' and modernity: *JMEMS* 40.1 (2010). See also James Muldoon, ed., *Bridging the Medieval-Modern Divide: Medieval Themes in the World of the Reformation* (Farnham, 2013).

[8] Brian Cummings and James Simpson, 'Introduction', *Cultural Reformations: Medieval and Renaissance in Literary History*, ed. Brian Cummings and James Simpson (Oxford, 2010), p. 3.

boundaries served to distinguish the era of the newly Reformed church from what was perceived as centuries of ignorance and misguidance of the Roman Catholic church that preceded. For Simpson, the Reformation is the motive force behind the cultural revolution he examines in his 2002 study: 'A sudden, politically driven break in history will prize novelty because a new dispensation must legitimate itself, and must, therefore, redescribe the repudiated order as "old" and depleted.'[9] Simpson's opening chapter (on John Leland and John Bale) demonstrates just how inexorably connected English literary history, and the writing of that history, is to the unification of church and state during the 1540s, and how the first articulation of a national literary tradition is underpinned by the drive on Bale's part to recover and preserve a specifically Protestant tradition. For Jennifer Summit too the dissolution of the monasteries and dispersal of monastic libraries from the 1530s onwards marks the effective start of the 'Middle Ages' as a temporal and intellectual concept; the dissolution 'enabled the Middle Ages to emerge as a distinct chapter in English history as well as an object of study.'[10] Of course, boundary lines were being drawn long before the English Reformation as writers and scholars as far back as the fourteenth century sought to mark the advent of an age of humanist learning in which there was a greater consciousness of the temporal otherness of the classical past. For many critics of Renaissance culture it is that recognition of temporal distance from the medieval past, and between the medieval past and classical antiquity, together with an enhanced appreciation of the concept of anachronism, that is the signal moment or defining characteristic of the Renaissance.[11] Martin Heidegger made much the same point in his 1938 essay 'The Age of the World Picture' when writing of how an age views or conceptualises itself, and the part this plays in the development of mankind seeing itself as a valid subject of study and improvement: 'The world picture does not change from an earlier medieval to a modern one; rather, that the world becomes picture at all is what distinguishes the essence of modernity. [...] To be "new" belongs to a world that has become picture.'[12] This defining sense of temporal and diachronic consciousness is at the heart of Thomas Greene's study of dialectical imitation and Renaissance perceptions of what had been lost from the classical period, and it also plays a vital part in A.C. Spearing's

---

[9] Simpson, *Reform*, p. 1.
[10] Jennifer Summit, *Memory's Library: Medieval Books in Early Modern England* (Chicago, 2008), p. 8.
[11] Margreta de Grazia, 'Anachronism', *Cultural Reformations*, ed. Cummings and Simpson, p. 28.
[12] Martin Heidegger, 'The Age of the World Picture', *Off the Beaten Track*, ed. and trans. Julian Young and Kenneth Haynes (Cambridge, 2002), pp. 68–9.

cross-chronological *Medieval to Renaissance in English Poetry* (1981).[13] As Spearing maintains: 'What is most characteristic of the Renaissance, then, is not a rediscovery of lost material, but a new sense of the historical distance and difference inherent in classical texts, most of which had never been lost, together with a sense of the possibility of overcoming that distance and difference by creative imitation.'[14]

Critical interest in tracing how sixteenth-century English writers negotiated that temporal distance between themselves and the classical past, and the persistent fascination with reading forward from the Renaissance to try and perceive the roots of modernity, has meant that comparatively less emphasis is placed on how Renaissance texts and authors exhibit continuity with medieval forms, ideas and modes of representation. As Cooper observes, 'like the humanists, we take most interest in the new'.[15] Literary histories spanning the fourteenth to sixteenth centuries usually focus more on change and transition, on the agents and exemplars of political and cultural transition, and on the task of tracing the first shoots of the perceived 'flowering' of English literature during the later sixteenth century. Lewis famously divided his *English Literature in the Sixteenth Century, Excluding Drama* (1954) – and the Tudor century – into three eras, which he delineates with great force and conviction. The Late Medieval, he writes, can be extended to the end of Edward VI's reign and is characterised by metrical irregularity and contortions, and a proclivity for allegory. Thereafter, we find ourselves in the stylistic wasteland of the Drab Age, lasting until the late 1570s. In this period 'poetry has little richness either of sound or images. The good work is neat and temperate, the bad flat and dry. There is more bad than good. Tottel's *Miscellany*, "Sternhold and Hopkins", and *The Mirror for Magistrates* are typical Drab Age works.'[16] (Sir Philip Sidney would have disagreed with Lewis about these hugely popular mid-century works, though he too made the point that there was obviously a gulf between his own 'clear age' and the 'misty time' in which Chaucer wrote.)[17] Finally – at last – we get to the Golden Age: 'the unpredictable happens. With

---

[13] Thomas Greene, *The Light in Troy: Imitation and Discovery in Renaissance Poetry* (New Haven, CT, 1982); A.C. Spearing, *Medieval to Renaissance in English Poetry* (Cambridge, 1981).
[14] Spearing, *Medieval to Renaissance*, p. 13.
[15] Cooper, *Shakespeare and the Medieval World*, p. 4.
[16] Lewis, *English Literature*, p. 64. Lewis's view of the mid-Tudor period took a long time to displace but renewed critical attention has recently been paid to the major 'Drab' works he identified: see, for example, J. Christopher Warner, *The Making and Marketing of Tottel's Miscellany, 1557* (Farnham, 2013); Stephen Hamrick, ed., *Tottel's Songes and Sonettes in Context* (Farnham, 2013); Beth Quitslund, *The Reformation in Rhyme: Sternhold, Hopkins and the English Metrical Psalter, 1547–1603* (Aldershot, 2008); Scott Lucas, *A Mirror for Magistrates and the Politics of the English Reformation* (Amherst, 2009).
[17] Sidney's *'The Defence of Poesy' and Selected Renaissance Literary Criticism*, ed. Gavin Alexander (London, 2004), p. 44.

startling suddenness we ascend. Fantasy, conceit, paradox, colour, incantation return. Youth returns. The fine frenzies of ideal love and ideal war are readmitted. [...] Nothing in the earlier history of our period would have enabled the sharpest observer to foresee this transformation.'[18] As the use of 'to' rather than 'and' in his title indicates, Spearing too is interested in thinking across periodic boundaries and asking questions about what characterises and facilitates transition. Indeed, he posits an idiosyncratic model of continuity between the medieval and Renaissance by proposing that Chaucer's contact with contemporary Italian culture, experienced first-hand during the 1370s, furnished him with that all-important new appreciation of the relationship between the past and present, and of his own place in literary history, which thus transformed him into England's first Renaissance man.[19] But does that moment in *Troilus and Criseyde*, for example, when Chaucer translates and incorporates sonnet 132 of Petrarch's *Canzoniere* as the 'Canticus Troili' really see the English poet recognising that the Italian writer was doing or saying something especially radical or game-changing?[20] When examining Chaucer's fifteenth-century imitators, Spearing himself demonstrates that the poet's prodigious achievements represented something of a false dawn for English literature.[21] Like Lewis before him, Spearing productively decouples the idea of Renaissance qualities or attributes from a rigid progressivist chronology and the positing of signal dates for the medieval and Renaissance periods. Simpson also readily admits that what he calls the 'reformist' practice of medieval literatures did not end in 1485 or even 1547, the terminus of his study; writers of the 'Renaissance' could be found composing (in his terms) 'medieval' works, and vice versa.[22]

The literary history of the fourteenth to sixteenth centuries starts to look different if we continue to investigate the elasticity or (switching the metaphor) the porousness of periodic boundary lines, and if we concentrate rather less on transition, novelty and the conscious effacing of the past, and pay attention to continuity, inheritance, preservation and memory. Over the last four decades these latter concepts have persistently underpinned and informed

---

[18] Lewis, *English Literature*, p. 1.
[19] Spearing, *Medieval to Renaissance*, pp. 15–58, 89.
[20] On the continued interrogation of the impact of Chaucer's use of Petrarch, and Petrarch's putative status as the definitive Renaissance man, see David Wallace, *Chaucerian Polity: Absolutist Lineages and Associational Forms in England and Italy* (Stanford, 1997), pp. 9–64; Paul Strohm, *Theory and the Premodern Text* (Minneapolis, 2000), pp. 80–96; James Simpson, 'Subjects of Triumph and Literary History: Dido and Petrarch in Petrarch's *Africa* and *Trionfi*', *JMEMS* 35.3 (2005), 489–508; William T. Rossiter, *Chaucer and Petrarch* (Cambridge, 2010), pp. 109–31. As Richard Helgerson reminds us, Roger Ascham considered Chaucer and Petrarch to be medieval, counting both among what he called the 'Gothians'; see *Forms of Nationhood: The Elizabethan Writing of England* (Chicago, 1992), p. 306n5.
[21] Spearing, *Medieval to Renaissance*, ch. 3.
[22] Simpson, *Reform*, pp. 2–3.

the scholarship and teaching of this essay collection's dedicatee. Professor Cooper's work, it should be stressed, is rarely unconcerned with processes of change, development and transformation in medieval and Renaissance literature, but such processes are repeatedly shown to have involved later writers looking backwards, recalling earlier genres and authorities, or maintaining and adapting older traditions. The subtitle of Cooper's first monograph, *Pastoral: Mediaeval into Renaissance* (1977), offers a subtle and, for its author, characteristically playful means of conceiving how the medieval relates to the Renaissance within a particular genre. Cooper's use of the word 'into' here speaks not only to the broad period encompassed by her study, but to the more complex ways in which the Renaissance takes up and incorporates aspects of the medieval, and to the interpenetration of the one in the other (as in moments like that mentioned above where we find Chaucer adapting Petrarch). As she writes, 'the change from mediaeval to Renaissance styles of pastoral is clear and unmistakable, but there is no break in tradition; and while a few poets are concerned to create an almost entirely new kind of pastoral, the tools of every writer had been forged in the Middle Ages'.[23] Cooper's book not only returned the medieval to the history of the pastoral genre but served as a methodological exemplar of how to analyse literary continuities and traditions.[24] Memory, Cooper emphasises, has a hugely significant part to play in thinking about periodisation and in examinations of how the medieval connects and interacts with the Renaissance. One of the most resonant lines in all of Cooper's scholarship, which is rephrased and expanded upon on many subsequent occasions, can be found on the first page of *Pastoral*, describing Elizabethan writers' treatment of both earlier and contemporary traditions: 'They used everything and forgot nothing.'[25] Cooper revisits the importance of retrospection in the introduction to *Shakespeare and the Medieval World* (2010) when juxtaposing the value judgements associated with the medieval. It is frequently perceived that

> the early modern, the modern, and the post-modern are progressive and look forward; the medieval is unpleasant, regressive and anything we don't like. Consciousness, however, works with memory much more than with prediction. The Elizabethans knew what was there in their world and what had been there

---

[23] Cooper, *Pastoral*, p. 100.
[24] Cooper's earlier essay, 'The Goat and the Eclogue', *Philological Quarterly* 53 (1973), 363–79, takes in a similarly impressive broad chronological sweep when tracing the formal eclogue tradition in classical, medieval and Renaissance poetry.
[25] Cooper, *Pastoral*, p. 1.

before, not what was going to happen next, and their own memories were supplemented by what their parents had told them.[26]

Cooper's 2004 study of English romance had earlier used the language of genetic memory to characterise how generic motifs (or 'memes') survive, mutate and adapt between the medieval and Renaissance periods.[27] Her scholarship has long demonstrated just how many different ways the medieval is remembered or preserved during the sixteenth century and beyond, be it through imitation, adaptation, translation, continuity of ideas and practices, or through the printing and re-appropriation of medieval texts. Reception history is shown to be a species of memorialisation. For Cooper, the Renaissance was certainly not the sudden, 'unpredictable' or unforeseeable event that Lewis described.

Sixteenth-century authors were themselves interested in acts of remembrance and in how the medieval past was preserved in and for their own age. Edmund Spenser, for example, depicted memory as a vast library within the body-house allegory in Book II of *The Faerie Queene*, and in doing so offered a representation of how his great poem itself was made – the process of re-membering and rehearsing old stories and books, the 'matter of just memory', as he calls it.[28] Sites of memory were, of course, prone to deterioration; witness the 'worm-eaten' records in Eumnestes's library, the 'untimely breach' that abruptly curtails the 'Briton moniments' or the reworked fragments of Chaucer incorporated into Book IV that project the anxieties of both poets about the deleterious effects of 'cursed Eld the cankerworme of writs'.[29] Deteriorated and ruined structures are found throughout Spenser's works serving as reminders of the past that were still there in the present, albeit now perhaps more as sites for contemplation about change and mutability.[30]

The present essay collection is itself an act of remembering as it responds to and commemorates Cooper's contribution to the study of medieval and

---

[26] Cooper, *Shakespeare and the Medieval World*, p. 4. Cooper's book is one of several recent studies that explore Shakespeare's medievalism and use of native dramatic and poetic traditions, and the impact of the medieval on the playwright's conceptions of language, theatre and culture: see Kurt A. Schreyer, *Shakespeare's Medieval Craft* (Ithaca, 2014); Helen Cooper, Ruth Morse and Peter Holland, eds., *Medieval Shakespeare: Pasts and Presents* (Cambridge, 2013); Curtis Perry and John Watkins, eds., *Shakespeare and the Middle Ages* (Oxford, 2010); Martha W. Driver and Sid Ray, eds., *Shakespeare and the Middle Ages: Essays on the Performance and Adaptation of the Plays with Medieval Sources or Settings* (London, 2009).
[27] Cooper, *Romance*, pp. 3–4.
[28] Spenser, *The Faerie Queene*, II.proem.1. See Andrew King, *The Faerie Queene and Middle English Romance: The Matter of Just Memory* (Oxford, 2000); Summit, *Memory's Library*; Lucy Munro, *Archaic Style in English Literature, 1590–1674* (Cambridge, 2013), pp. 80–5.
[29] Spenser, *Faerie Queene*, II.ix.57; II.x.68; IV.ii.33.
[30] See King, *Faerie Queene*, esp. pp. 69–73; Rebeca Helfer, *Spenser's Ruins and the Art of Recollection* (Toronto, 2012).

Renaissance literature, literary history and periodisation. Named in homage to the subtitle of Cooper's first book, this volume comprises essays written by scholars taught and supervised by our dedicatee during her career teaching at Oxford and Cambridge. Each contributor to this collection takes up ideas, authors or genres addressed in Helen's work, or otherwise speaks to topics spanning the medieval and Renaissance, to acknowledge her sustained interest in forms and traditions that resist neat or formulaic divisions of period.

Alexandra Gillespie opens this collection with an essay that exhibits an appropriately 'Cooperian' texture and breadth of reference – taking in Chaucer, Gower and the pseudo-Chaucerian *Plowman's Tale*, as well as Spenser's *Shepheardes Calender* and Milton's poetry – and immediately poses questions about the realities and complexities of authorship and literary tradition. Through detailed exploration of the reworking, misquoting or (strategic?) misremembering that lies behind E.K.'s attribution of the phrase 'Uncouthe unkiste' to 'the olde famous Poete Chaucer', Gillespie reveals a more unstable, haphazard, fragmentary reception of Chaucer in the sixteenth century than is often assumed. The inauthentic lurks within E.K.'s mannerist attempts to assert the authenticity and authority of the 'new Poete'. In his Epistle to Gabriel Harvey, E.K. plays fast and loose with who and what is known and unknown, couth and uncouth, just as Spenser does directly when he asks wryly or perhaps ironically of another (un)couth 'swain' at Mount Acidale 'who knowes not Colin Clout?'[31]

R.W. Maslen's essay is the first of several contributions to this volume focusing on medieval and Renaissance romance. His wide-ranging investigation into armour that does not work adopts the meme-based methodology of Cooper's *English Romance in Time* as well as a titular allusion to Helen's chapter (and earlier article) on 'magic that does not work', and explores how romance narratives repeatedly interrogate both the material trappings and readers' expectations of the genre.[32] Moving between *Sir Gawain and the Green Knight*, Chaucer, Malory, Spenser and *Troilus and Cressida*, with glances to Italo Calvino and T.H. White, Maslen examines the paradoxical relationship between armour and the body in romance – how each element is opposed to and yet protective of the other – and he reveals how successive authors deliberate upon the tensions and oppositions between armour's functional and symbolic role within the genre. Megan G. Leitch looks to a different, often neglected form of native romance as she proposes a framework within which we can read the English prose romances of the fifteenth century. Many of the

---

[31] Spenser, *Faerie Queene*, VI.x.16. See also Andrew Hadfield, *Literature, Politics and National Identity: Reformation to Renaissance* (Cambridge, 1994), pp. 170–2.

[32] Cooper, *Romance*, ch. 3; 'Magic that does not work', *Medievalia et Humanistica* 7 (1976), 131–46.

essays in this volume touch upon, to some degree, the matter of tradition and inheritance between generations and literary periods. Leitch too explores similar ideas in her treatment of generational and generic anxiety, instability and betrayal in prose romance, concentrating on *Huon of Burdeux*, *The Siege of Thebes*, *Valentine and Orson* and *Melusine*. As Leitch reveals, family resemblance is a source of tension within each narrative but there is also a perceptible anxiety of influence within the sub-genre itself as the authors and author-translators of these works seek to distance themselves from the preoccupations and perspectives of their verse-writing forebears.[33]

Aisling Byrne takes up another strand of the reception and publication history of medieval romance and moves our discussion about the continued longevity and adaptability of the genre and its motifs into new territory. Offering a critical outline of how English metrical romances circulated in Ireland between the fifteenth and seventeenth centuries, Byrne's essay discusses the adaptation and readership of works including *Fierabras*, *Octavian*, *William of Palerne*, *Guy of Warwick* and *Bevis of Hampton*. It not only makes the case for a more extensive 'archipelagic' study of medieval romance, but demonstrates the necessity of a cross-chronological approach when considering how Middle English texts were received and read in early modern Ireland, a country where the 'Renaissance' is commonly perceived to have taken little hold. Staying with romance, James Wade's essay begins by considering further the difficult, yet nevertheless permeable and thus negotiable, division of the medieval and Renaissance periods in English. The importance of establishing a recognisable division between England's Catholic past and the era of Reformed Christianity had serious implications for the reception of Middle English romance, texts that were easily pilloried for their seemingly Popish elements by figures such as Roger Ascham and John Foxe. Nevertheless, as many of our contributors continue to show, romance remained popular well into the seventeenth century, moving from manuscript to print. Most surprising for Wade is the survival and, indeed, growth of the so-called penitential romances such as *Guy of Warwick*, *Sir Isumbras* and *Sir Gowther*. Crucial to the survival of works such as these (and many others) is that they tend to focus on the individual's spiritual struggles and supplication to God, rather than the agency of the church. The continued interest in penitential romance during the sixteenth century manifested not only in the reworking of older verse romances like *Sir Gowther* into euphuistic prose in Thomas Lodge's *Robert the Devil* (1591), but in the enduring vogue for dramatised romance on the early modern popular stage. The

---

[33] Cooper herself explores anxieties of family resemblance in 'Choosing Poetic Fathers: The English Problem', *Medieval and Early Modern Authorship*, ed. Guillemette Bolens and Lukas Erne (Tübingen, 2011), pp. 29–49.

essay concludes forcefully with *King Lear*, enlightening this play anew through a consideration of its relationship to penitential romance.

It is perhaps a given that there will always be a place for John Skelton in any discussion of periodisation and the relationship between the medieval and Renaissance. Exactly where we should place Skelton is, however, far less obvious and his works continue to raise questions about how we draw periodic boundaries, and on which side of the line are we to locate this apparently 'maverick' poet.[34] What are we to make of this conservative figure who (as Spearing discusses) rarely aligned himself with the more progressive intellectual currents of early Tudor humanism concerning translation of the Bible, grammatical instruction and the teaching of Greek, and the imaginative reconstruction of pagan antiquity?[35] George Puttenham twice distinguished Skelton's 'rude', 'ridiculous' work from the achievements of other early Tudor courtly makers like Wyatt and Surrey.[36] And yet here too was a man whose projection of a distinct self-reflexive identity and propagation of personal fame anticipate all of the 'self-crowned laureates' (to borrow Richard Helgerson's term) of the later sixteenth century.[37] For Andrew Hadfield, Skelton represents an evolutionary dead-end in English literary history through his advocacy of 'a particular brand of Englishness [that] ceased to exist after the inauguration of the Reformation'.[38] More recently, Dan Breen writes of how Skelton has come to represent the outer limit of 'a discrete narrative of history': 'Rather than become absorbed into the discussion of how the current boundary between the Middle Ages and the early modern period might be reconfigured, Skelton has in a limited way *become* that current boundary.'[39] Hadfield and Breen contemplate Skelton's place in literary history by focusing on *The Garland of Laurel*, in which the speaker is enjoined to adopt a Janus-like temporal perspective looking both backwards and forwards. Mary C. Flannery's essay on the *Garland* plays upon the title of Cooper's romance monograph as it examines Skelton's self-conscious location of the laureate's position 'in time' and picks up on the concept of memorialisation that runs through many essays in the present volume. As Flannery shows, the laureate in Skelton's *Garland* occupies a peculiar position in time: he is absorbed with acts of remembrance

---

[34] Jane Griffiths, *John Skelton and Poetic Authority: Defining the Liberty to Speak* (Oxford, 2006), pp. 1–2.
[35] Spearing, *Medieval to Renaissance*, pp. 225–30.
[36] *Sidney's 'The Defence of Poesy'*, ed. Alexander, pp. 104, 125.
[37] Richard Helgerson, *Self-crowned Laureates: Spenser, Jonson, Milton and the Literary System* (Berkeley, 1983); Dan Breen, 'Laureation and Identity: Rewriting Literary History in John Skelton's *Garland of Laurel*', *JMEMS* 40.2 (2010), 349.
[38] Hadfield, *Literature*, p. 24.
[39] Breen, 'Laureation', 347.

and memorialisation but these are undertaken with posterity in mind and an eye to whatever place the poet might occupy in the future.

Mid-way through this collection attention returns to the pastoral genre and the imaginative landscape of our dedicatee's first monograph, a work that showed that Virgil and Spenser by no means held the monopoly on inaugurating a successful career by writing of shepherds and goatherds. Matthew Woodcock's essay says little about shepherds – though there are passing references to sheep – but it does reflect the way in which more recent studies of pastoral have broadened conceptions of the genre to include the writing of rural labour more generally, and to place the notion of work, rather than *otium*, at its heart.[40] Complementing Mike Rodman Jones and Katherine Little's cross-chronological studies of polemical and reformist pastoral, Woodcock examines how the Tudor soldier-author Thomas Churchyard adapts medieval traditions of satirical complaint, particularly those associated with the figure of Piers Plowman, to speak to the economic and social ills of the 1550s. Nandini Das's essay 'Placing Arcadia' looks to the more familiar locus of classical and early modern pastoral, a place so widely imagined, evoked and recollected by writers and artists that it has become a literary commonplace. But what lay behind the collective fashioning of Arcadia in particular into the exemplary site of pastoral fiction? Taking in classical pastoral, and medieval and early modern topography, mythography, cartography and poetry, Das explores how Arcadia is both spatially and temporally difficult to locate, and possesses a memorial as much as a geographic presence – it is somewhere more to be remembered than visited or accurately mapped.

With the essays by Jason Powell and Joyce Boro the focus of this volume shifts to the early modern stage and its relationship with medieval literature. Over the last twenty years critics have been steadily dismantling the notion that non-professional traditions of medieval and early Tudor drama were simply dismissed, supressed, rejected or otherwise forgotten about in the age of Elizabeth and/or Shakespeare. As John Watkins writes, we are 'no longer obliged to narrate the transition from Mankind to Marlowe in triumphalist or even evolutionary terms'.[41] Theresa Coletti has shown, for example, how Biblical cycle drama performed at Chester continued to reflect institutions of sixteenth-century religious culture across the perceived medieval and early modern divide.[42] Cooper's own *Shakespeare and the Medieval World* and

---

[40] See Mike Rodman Jones, *Radical Pastoral, 1381–1594: Appropriation and the Writing of Religious Controversy* (Farnham, 2011); Katherine C. Little, *Transforming Work: Early Modern Pastoral and Late Medieval Poetry* (Notre Dame, 2013).

[41] John Watkins, 'Bedevilling the Histories of Medieval and Early Modern Drama', *MP* 101 (2003), 69.

[42] Theresa Coletti, 'The Chester Cycle in Sixteenth-Century Religious Culture', *JMEMS* 37.3 (2007), 531–47.

co-edited collection *Medieval Shakespeare* demonstrated that we must move beyond looking solely at continuity of theatrical traditions to fully appreciate the indebtedness of early modern drama to the Middle Ages. It is to earlier traditions of romance, folk-tale, chronicle and – as Powell argues here – advice literature that we must also turn. Powell's essay on the presentation and function of fatherly advice in *Hamlet* begins by reconsidering the sources for the scenes of paternal instruction or *institutio* in the play, focusing on fifteenth – and sixteenth-century courtesy books and their antecedents. The earlier traditions of precept literature are shown to have underpinned a significant, though frequently ignored, source of tension in the play generated by the opposition of Claudius's injunction that Hamlet should forget his father with Old Hamlet's insistent demand to the prince: 'Remember me.' It is not just literary historians who must grapple with the difficult relationship between memory and inheritance. Boro's essay on *Swetnam the Woman-Hater* (first performed 1617–19) discusses a different form of inheritance and shows how the anonymous play, although dramatising the eponymous seventeenth-century English pamphleteer and misogynist, adapts the fifteenth-century Spanish romance *Grisel y Mirabella* by Juan de Flores. Entering into similar territory as the essays by Byrne, Wade, Andrew King and Helen Vincent, insofar as it deals with the afterlife and cross-cultural transmission of romance, Boro's contribution here explores how the play continues the long-running *querelle des femmes* and takes the plot of *Grisel* in new directions through investing it with references to the Jacobean Swetnam controversy and with contemporary theories and dramatic conventions of melancholy.

The final two essays of this volume each examine how sixteenth-century romance was revisited, reimagined, redeployed and reshaped during the seventeenth and eighteenth centuries. In so doing they move beyond Cooper's work on the afterlife and transformation of medieval and Renaissance romance found in the closing portions and appendix of *The English Romance in Time*, and reveal how Spenser's *Faerie Queene* and Sidney's *Arcadia* were repeatedly taken up by new generations of readers and audiences who were themselves interested in historical and literary continuities, ruptures and transformations.[43] Both Andrew King's treatment of Samuel Sheppard's *The Faerie King* and Helen Vincent's essay on chapbook versions of Sidney's Argalus and Parthenia story compel us to continue questioning exactly what continuity really means when it comes to adapting a story, text or genre to fit new historical conditions or literary tastes. Although Sheppard's poem has recently been seen as an act of forgetting or denial, deliberately obscuring or effacing the realities of civil war and the death of Charles I, King's detailed reading of *The Faerie King* reveals a more anxious and ambivalent relationship between the poet and both

---

[43] Cooper, *Romance*, ch. 8, and Appendix.

his literary forebear Spenser and his ostensible subject Charles.[44] Just how was Sheppard supposed to locate himself in the literary and political history of the Interregnum? King's essay also addresses another recurrent concern of this volume: the transformation of literary genres during the medieval and Renaissance periods. It considers how *The Faerie King* modulates between romance and tragedy – arguably following the direction of Spenser's own unfinished poem – and reveals, moreover, how Sheppard seems haunted by fears that the subject of his work might render the poem obsolete.

Vincent looks at a very different kind of literary inheritance and examines how the Argalus and Parthenia story finds its way from the *Arcadia* to eighteenth-century chapbooks via seventeenth-century verse adaptations. Not only does she revise the textual history of the story's transmission but she challenges the commonly received, largely negative view that the chapbook versions were little more than debasements or vulgarisations of Sidney's language and narrative. Vincent proposes that the changes made by the people who turned this particular Sidneian narrative into one of the most popular stories of the long eighteenth century capture the continuities and transformations at the moment when the discursive romance narrative was evolving into the novel. In translating the tale of Argalus and Parthenia into a prose narrative with popular appeal, the authors of the chapbooks and histories bring Sidney's idealised notion that romantic love was the preferred basis for marriage to an ever-widening range of social classes. The compass of Vincent's essay raises again a familiar set of issues about lines and labels. Just how far forward do we want to extend the early modern period? What sort of criteria or terminology should we use to establish and designate its *terminus ad quem*? As Lewis, Simpson, Cooper and others demonstrate, the act of contemplating and drawing borderlines can be immensely productive and generative, the starting point in a debate or 'consciousness-raising exercise' rather than the object or end-point of literary-historical enquiry.[45] In a volume offering a series of new investigations into the fundamental continuation of ideas, forms, activities, methods and practices between periods, that seems an entirely appropriate concept to keep in mind. Like the speaker in Skelton's *Garland*, the essays in this collection are all engaged in drawing upon the authoritative models and precedents of those who came before – our dedicatee included – but also look onwards and to the future: to new and emerging critical debates about periodisation, memorialisation and the value of making bold claims about literary history.

---

[44] Kirsten Tranter, 'Samuel Sheppard's *Faerie King* and the Fragmentation of Royalist Epic', SEL 49 (2009), 94–101.
[45] Cooper, *Shakespeare and the Medieval World*, p. 8.

Unknowe, unkow, Vncovthe, uncouth

From Chaucer and Gower to Spenser and Milton[*]

ALEXANDRA GILLESPIE

My discussion, which owes a great deal to the work of Helen Cooper, begins with E.K.'s remarks on the 1579 edition of *The Shepheardes Calender*.[1] Edmund Spenser is not named in this book, but he is in subsequent early editions and in modern editions.[2] The first substantive point that E.K. makes in his Epistle, which is directed to Gabriel Harvey, is that once the anonymous, 'vncovthe' author of the poem to follow is 'covthe' he will be irresistibly attractive to readers. The passage in question is well known, but because my analysis of it will be detailed, I reproduce it at length:

> To the most excellent and learned both Orator and Poete, Mayster Gabriell Haruey, his verie special and singular good frend E.K. commendeth the good lyking of this his labour, and the patronage of the new Poete.
>
> VNCOVTHE VNKISTE, Sayde the olde famous Poete Chaucer: whom for his excellencie and wonderfull skil in making, his scholler Lidgate, a worthy scholler of so excellent a maister, calleth the Loadestarre of our Language: and whom our Colin clout in his Æglogue calleth Tityrus the God of shepheards, comparing hym to the worthines of the Roman Tityrus Virgile. Which prouerbe, myne

---

[*] An early draft of this essay was presented at a 2008 conference at Harvard University: my particular thanks to Maura Nolan and James Simpson for their insights at that time; to Laura Mitchell and Taylor Cowdery for assistance; and to Jeff Espie, the publisher's anonymous reader and the editors of this volume for their helpful comments on my final version.

[1] Cooper, *Pastoral*, is especially important to what follows. It was at Helen's suggestion that I first examined sixteenth-century printed editions of Chaucer's *Works* as a way to approach my topic of Spenser's indebtedness to Chaucer. This essay is a tribute to a wonderful advisor, mentor and friend.

[2] See Richard A. McCabe, '"Little booke: thy selfe present": The Politics of Presentation in *The Shepheardes Calender*', *Presenting Poetry: Composition, Publication, Reception*, ed. H. Erskine-Hill and R.A. McCabe (Cambridge, 1995), pp. 15–40.

owne good friend Ma. Haruey, as in that good old Poete it serued well Pandares purpose, for the bolstering of his baudy brocage, so very well taketh place in this our new Poete, who for that he is vncouthe (as said Chaucer) is vnkist, and vnknown to most men, is regarded but of few. But I dout not, so soone as his name shall come into the knowledg of men, and his worthines be sounded in the tromp of fame, but that he shall be not onely kiste, but also beloued of all, embraced of the most, and wondred at of the best.[3]

The word 'covth', shunted aside here by the prefix 'vn-', is an archaism, one of the 'olde and obsolete words [...] most vsed of country folke' that Spenser draws upon for the poetry of the *Calender*, in order, E.K. says, to bring 'auctoritie to the verse'.[4] The word appears elsewhere. It describes Colin's piping in the 'Januarye' eclogue (10) where E.K. gives a lengthy gloss – it 'commeth of the verbe Conne, that is, to know or to haue skill. As well interpreteth the same the worthy Sir Tho. Smitth in his booke of gouerment: wherof I haue a perfect copie in wryting, lent me by his kinseman, and my verye singular good freend, M. Gabriel Haruey: as also of some other his most graue and excellent wrytings'. Colin uses it himself to describe his singing ('June', 41) and the unknown, buried maid he mourns in 'November', she who 'couth the shepherds entertayne' (95). Thomalin uses it; so does Diggon, when he says that 'To leaue the good, that I had in hande,/ In hope of better, that was vncouth' ('September', 59–60: E.K. glosses this use of the word 'vnknowen').

Of particular relevance here is the reuse of the word in description, rather than quotation, of the old poet Chaucer. Spenser writes that Chaucer-Tityrus, the god and sovereign leader of shepherds,

> Well couth he wayle hys Woes, and lightly slake
> The flames, which loue within his heart had bredd,
> And tell vs mery tales, to keepe vs wake,
> The while our sheepe about vs safely fedde. ('June', 85–8)

'[C]outh' is here a modal verb in the third person and the past tense; it has the second sense that E.K. gives it in his gloss for 'Januarye': 'to have skill' ('Well could he wail'). In the Epistle, in contrast, 'Vncovthe' is a past participle, and it is associated with E.K.'s first sense in his 'Januarye' gloss: 'to know'. It means what it means when E.K. glosses the word in the 'September' eclogue: 'vnknowen'.

---

[3] Edmund Spenser, *The Shorter Poems*, ed. Richard A. McCabe (New York, 1999), p. 25. All references to the *Calender* in the text are from this edition. Since it is important to the case I am advancing in this essay, the orthography of the sixteenth-century printed editions of Spenser and Chaucer has been preserved here.

[4] For instance in Nathan A. Gans, 'Archaism and Neologism in Spenser's Diction', *MP* 76 (1979), 377–9.

Annabel Patterson, Jennifer Richards and Jeff Espie have noted that the use of the word in both these ways in the *Calender* is particularly suggestive in light of E.K.'s use of Thomas Smith's *De Republica Anglorum* in one of his glosses.[5] E.K. draws upon an etymology that Smith gives for the Old English word 'cyning'.[6] The etymology in question is false, but Smith does correctly identify descendants of Old English verbs which, in the present participle, superficially resemble 'cyning'. These are '*cen* or *ken* which betokeneth to know and understand', that is, OE *cennan* (cf. Middle English 'kenning' for 'knowledge'); and '*kan* or *kon* which betokeneth to be able or to have power', that is, OE *cunnan* (cf. ME 'cunning' for 'knowing' and also 'skillful'). As Espie observes, E.K. further recognizes in the *Calender* that the semantic range covered by words derived from OE *cunnan* overlaps with that covered by words derived from OE *cennen*. ME *connan* means both to have skill *and* to have knowledge.[7] E.K. is thus able to derive two senses and two grammatical functions for 'couth' from the 'verbe Conne'. 'Couth' is both an old and obsolete orthographic variant of 'could', and an old and obsolete word for 'known'. 'Vncovthe' is thus a word to describe and simultaneously to *be* 'vnknown to most men'.

Espie argues persuasively that the complex uses of '(un)couth' in the *Calender* conflate the royal power and the literary authority with which Chaucer was associated by Spenser's contemporaries in Renaissance England. Smith's etymology for king 'explains and legitimizes a title that Colin gives to Chaucer in June. Chaucer can be here deemed the "soveraigne head" of love poetry because the name given to a display of Chaucerian aesthetics (couth) and the name given to a sovereign (king) may be traced to a common range of meanings.'[8] I think this is right. I also think that E.K. and Spenser put the multiple meanings and associations of the word 'couth' into play in the *Calender* in order to approach a topic that is a matter of playful concern to Chaucer too. What is an author, or a 'Poete'? How are authorship and textual authority established and maintained? For what reward, and at what cost?

In the Epistle, the word 'covthe', used in 'vncovthe', is first designed to draw attention to Spenser's anonymity. Its dual sense – known and could – is also

---

[5] Patterson, *Reading Between the Lines* (Madison, 1993), p. 54; and Richards, *Rhetoric and Courtliness in Early Modern Literature* (Cambridge, 2007), pp. 158-9. I am particularly indebted to Espie's '(Un)couth: Chaucer, *The Shepheardes Calender* and the Forms of Mediation', *Spenser Studies*, forthcoming.

[6] [Thomas Smith], *De Republica Anglorum, A Discourse on the Commonwealth of England*, ed. L. Alston (Cambridge, 1906), I, 9 (pp. 18-19).

[7] See *MED*, s.v., 'kennen' and 'connan'; and for useful discussion, Hannah Crawforth, *Etymology and the Invention of English in Early Modern Literature* (Cambridge, 2013).

[8] Espie, '(Un)couth'. On the connection between Chaucer and royal power, for example that of Henry VIII, see Greg Walker, *Writing Under Tyranny: English Literature and the Henrician Reformation* (Oxford, 2005), pp. 56-99; and Alexandra Gillespie, *Print Culture and the Medieval Author: Chaucer, Lydgate, and Their Books, 1473-1557* (Oxford, 2006), ch. 4.

evoked as E.K. draws attention to the entirely well-known author Chaucer and his 'wonderful skil' in poetic making. E.K. goes on to remark upon the lines of literary descent by which authors come to be known: the praise of Chaucer's 'skil' comes from 'Lidgate'. This emphasis on reception makes sense, given that E.K.'s goal is to claim the authority of an 'olde famous Poete' in order to argue for a happy ending to the anonymity of a 'new Poete'. If Chaucer is 'famous' still, and Chaucer's example is followed in the *Calender*, then Chaucer brings 'auctoritie to the verse' by supplying a precedent for the adulation of the uncouth new author Spenser.

And yet something like the opposite is also true. 'Vncovthe unkiste' is not, in fact, what Chaucer 'sayde'. As many scholars have remarked, it is E.K.'s own invention – a translation of line 809 of Book 1 of *Troilus and Criseyde*.[9] In manuscripts and printed editions of Chaucer's text up to 1579 the line appears as it does to most modern readers in *The Riverside Chaucer*: 'Unknowe, unkist, and lost that is unsought.'[10] The new word 'covth' enables a skilful E.K. to address a very Chaucerian problem. 'Disblameth me if any word be lame', the narrator of *Troilus* asks his future readers: 'Ye knowe ek that in forme of speche is change' (2.17, 22). By the time of the 1579 *Calender*, time has indeed undone some of Chaucer's words, including one from the line E.K. is quoting. 'Unknowe' now lacks the sturdy, voiceless velar stop, /k/ that preceded its nasal /ɛn/ in fourteenth-century Middle English usage.[11] 'Vncovthe' restores the sound, but it does so at the expense of the line's visual rhetoric. The consistent orthography of extant versions of Chaucer's original text, 'Unk [...] unk', is replaced by the much less satisfying 'Vnc [...] vnk'. The *Calender*'s prefatory material suggests that this c/k substitution is introduced not by accident but by design. The Epistle occupies the right side of the first full opening of the 1579 edition. On the left and facing page are verses addressed 'TO HIS BOOKE' itself. These too begin with something Chaucer 'sayde': 'Goe little booke: thy selfe present,/ As child whose parent is vnkent'. The 'Go little book' motif is another borrowing from Chaucer's *Troilus*. The significance of its use has often been discussed, in terms relevant to but beyond the scope of the present discussion.[12] Here it is sufficient to notice the word 'vnkent'. It is a past participle derived from OE *cennan*, and E.K. could have used it for Chaucer's sense, unknown; for Chaucer's

---

[9] See William Kuskin, *Recursive Origins: Writing at the Transition to Modernity* (Notre Dame, 2013), pp. 51–87.

[10] *Troilus and Criseyde*, ed. Stephen A. Barney, *Riverside Chaucer*. All references to *Troilus* in the text are from this edition.

[11] James Daniel Gordon, *The English Language: An Historical Introduction* (New York, 1972), p. 177.

[12] R.J. Schoek, '"Go Little Book"—A Conceit from Chaucer to William Meredith', *NQ* 197 (1952), 370–2.

sound, /k/; *and* for the Chaucerian line's visual repetition of 'k'. He could have, and he must have known he could have, but he did not.¹³

The cumulative irony of these few opening lines is almost oppressive. Posterity may preserve and protect the work of a poet who is 'olde' and 'famous' but as it does so it will change the form of that poet's original speech. In at least that sense the author himself will be unknown – 'Vncovthe vnkiste'. In other senses too: the reader who goes on with the *Calender* finds it stuffed with authors in more or (more often) less 'vncovthe' forms. They include Tityrus as Virgil and as Chaucer, and Virgil and Chaucer as themselves. Lydgate is, as usual, merely 'a worthy scholler of so excellent a maister'. Gower is missing from the early modern Chaucer-Gower-Lydgate triumvirate, but featured obscurely as 'J. Goore' in a gloss.¹⁴ Colin is an invention of Skelton and Marot; Skelton and Marot are also named as themselves; and the reader is told that it is Colin 'under whose person the Author selfe is shadowed'. There are a few ancients, including 'Alceus', the Greek poet of Mytilene, whose works had been recovered and printed in several continental editions by Spenser and E.K.'s time but only in fragments, alongside the work of other little known Greek lyric poets.¹⁵ 'Petrarque', 'Boccace [and] Sanazarus' are named; 'diuers other excellent both Italian and French Poetes' (152–3) are not. Finally, elided and elusive, underscoring the muddle, are Spenser and/as E.K. himself.¹⁶

Slightly later in the Epistle, E.K. suggests that the obsolete diction of Spenser's *Calender* may 'elumine' its grave topics and glorious words, just as a background scene of 'rude thickets and craggy clifts' set off a portrait of great beauty: '[F]or oftimes we fynde ourselues, I knowe not how, singularly delighted with the shewe of such naturall rudenesse, and take great pleasure in that disorderly order' (65–7). E.K.'s brief gesture to the limits of his understanding – 'I knowe not' – is important here. The 'disorderly order' he describes is 'vncovthe' in that it contains unfamiliar, rude, or old words, but it is also 'vncovthe' because it is beyond knowing. A 'disorderly order' is an impossible one. Disaggregated by the negative force of that prefix, 'dis-', it is order no more. Surrounded by the uncouth, unable to put his finger on what he likes about it, E.K. locates literature's positive affect, the experience of 'pleasure'.

In doing so, he points back to one more meaning for the old Chaucerian

---

¹³ There are other reasons why 'vnkent' appears on one side of the opening but not on the other. In 'TO HIS BOOKE', the use of 'vnkent', which is more obscure and archaic than any form of uncouth, is justified metrically: it completes a rhyme. 'Vnkent' also allows the writer to hint at and then pun upon a toponymic surname for Spenser, the otherwise/still unnamed author, as noted by Louise Schleiner, 'Spenser's "E. K." as Edmund Kent (Kenned/ of Kent): Kyth (Couth), Kissed, and Kunning-Conning', *ELR* 20 (1990), 374–407.
¹⁴ 'Julye', to 177.
¹⁵ James S. Easby Smith, ed., *The Songs of Alcaeus* (Washington, 1901).
¹⁶ The best argument for Spenser as E.K. (an argument I subscribe to, though I treat the two as separate persons here) is that of Schleiner, 'Spenser's "E. K."'.

saying 'Vncovthe vnkiste' that opens his Epistle – the last that will concern me in this part of my discussion. The proverb serves this new poet, E.K. tells Harvey, just as it 'serued well Pandares purpose, for the bolstering of his baudy brocage'. Pandarus deploys the saying to persuade his friend Troilus to make himself known to Criseyde, confident that once he does, neither lover nor beloved will remain 'vnkiste' for long (nor, hopefully, will their helpful broker Pandarus). E.K. imagines fame for the anonymous author of the *Calender* in similar terms: many scholars have discussed his representation of literary reception as a kind of homosocial 'brocage'. In the forms of the 1579 printed edition, Spenser, 'vnkist, and vnknown to most men', is 'regarded' only by a 'few' – presumably coterie readers who are already his intimates.[17] When 'his name shall come into the knowledg of men' he will 'be not onely kiste, but also beloued of all, embraced of the most, and wondred at of the best'. But E.K. establishes a hierarchy as well as an erotics of reception here. He draws distinctions between the 'all' and the 'most', who will love and embrace Spenser, and the 'best', who may offer their share of kisses, but whose affective response will also be one of wonder. This wonder is the counterpart of the delight E.K. says he gets – 'I knowe not how' – from that which remains 'vncovthe'. That is, he identifies himself (of course) as the *best* sort of reader: one who knows that the pleasure to be had from literature is the joy of not knowing, but enjoying all the same.

My argument is that from the first, the *Calender*'s play on the word 'uncouth' involves its authors in this kind of wonder: it activates this affect of the inexplicable. E.K. and Spenser suggest that the 'best' response to the question 'What is an author?' is not really an answer at all. It is instead the pleasure of an endlessly productive 'game of writing' in which the shifting positions occupied by a writer are part of literature's play.[18] This in turn constitutes a sometimes overlooked aspect of Chaucer's reception in the Renaissance. I would argue that part of what Chaucer models for early modern writers is a complex, self-reflexive, relentlessly ironizing mode of literary authorship. Part of what his example further teaches is that even as they seek to stabilize it, imitators, scribes, printers and readers may disrupt the authority of a venerable writer's texts. Chaucer thus serves Spenser and E.K. not only as a father and fount of literary excellence, but as evidence that the author of any text is an unruly confection – of allusions, ascriptions and apocrypha; of false etymologies and enlightening glosses; of manuscript books and printed ones, and the variant words arranged within them. Chaucer also models a suitable response to all the disorder. What is a new author to do on wondering about the uncertain

---

[17] As argued by McCabe, '"Little booke"'.
[18] 'Game of writing' here is a nod to Michel Foucault, 'What is an Author?', *Textual Strategies: Perspectives in Post-Structuralist Criticism*, ed. Josué V. Harari (Ithaca, 1979), pp. 141–60.

fate of old authors but follow his master Chaucer and offer such uncertainty to readers as an affectively powerful and intellectually engaging aspect of any author's art?

Earlier in this discussion I state that 'in manuscripts and printed editions of Chaucer's text up to 1579 the line appears as it does to most modern readers in *The Riverside Chaucer*' (that is, 'Unknowe, unkist, and lost that is unsought'). This statement requires qualification. I have seen all the manuscripts and a large number of copies of the twelve editions that were printed between Caxton's first edition of 1483 and 1579 when the *Shepheardes Calender* appeared. The books I have seen all have this line, but accidentals vary. Final 'e's on the participial adjectives come and go; 'v' appears where we would now expect 'u'; not every scribe or compositor has punctuated in the same way; and so on.

Like most of Spenser's students I am inclined to think that he and E.K. read Chaucer in John Stow's 1561 edition (printed by John Kyngston in three issues, two for John Wight, one for Henry Bradsha).[19] There, at least in the copies I have examined, the line begins 'Unknowe'. But I have not seen *all* the surviving copies of this or several of the other early printed editions of *Troilus*. As Joseph A. Dane and Seth Lerer have demonstrated, copies of the 1561 edition, like copies of all sixteenth-century editions of Chaucer's texts, are replete with minor variants that attest to mid-run press corrections, resettings, the replacement of pieces of broken type and other vagaries of production. There is universal truth in this finding: a single line from a single edition of the handpress period may not want for a variant. Or, two copies of the same early printed book are never quite the same.[20]

With Dane's caveats about 'meagre returns and the finitude of life' in mind, I have not tried very hard to fill the gaps in my record of pre-1579 witnesses to Book 1, line 809 of *Troilus and Criseyde*.[21] However, even as I have comforted myself that the copy or copies that Spenser and E.K. read are likely lost, I have wondered if those books contained suggestive variants. New York, Pierpont Morgan Library MS M 817 is a fifteenth-century copy of Chaucer's *Troilus*. There, Book 3, line 1797 has the phrase 'in so vnkow wyse' for other manuscripts' and *The Riverside Chaucer*'s 'in so unkouth wise'.[22] The Morgan

---

[19] *ESTC* 5076.
[20] 'Press-Variants in John Stow's Chaucer (1561) and the Text of "Adam Scriveyn"', *Transactions of the Cambridge Bibliographical Society* 11 (1999), 468–79. Dane makes similar observations of Thynne's 1532 edition in 'On "Correctness": A Note on Some Press Variants in Thynne's 1532 Edition of Chaucer', *The Library*, 6th series, 17 (1995), 156–67.
[21] 'On "Correctness"', 158n6.
[22] Fol. 36v. See Stephen A. Barney, 'Chaucer's *Troilus*: Meter and Grammar', *Studies in Troilus: Chaucer's Text, Meter, and Diction*, rpt. *Essays on the Art of Chaucer's Verse*, ed. Alan T. Gaylord (London, 2001), pp. 167–8 on his *Riverside* gloss to the 'difficult' sentence in which the phrase appears, which concerns Troilus's bearing as a lover: 'And moreover, he knew so well

manuscript's 'vnkow' looks very much like an orthographic error for 'vnknow'. However, M 817 is an early and accurate copy, one that was made for or at least belonged to Henry V when he was Prince of Wales. *MED* treats the variant as authoritative and gives it its own entry – as a unique, shortened form of 'uncouth'.

Would Spenser or E.K. have noticed variant forms of derivatives of OE *cnawen, cunnen,* or *connan* if they came across them in old books containing Chaucer's texts? Would they have expected contemporary readers to notice their own variant in the *Calender,* 'vncouthe', or wonder if there was a source for it? I know of at least one Elizabethan reader who was drawn to the proverb when she or he encountered it in Chaucer's text. Houghton Library at Harvard University holds a copy of Thynne's 1532 edition Chaucer's *Works* (the shelfmark is its *ESTC* number, ESTC 5068). Someone with a reasonably distinctive, informal sixteenth-century secretary hand makes annotations throughout the book, including one that dates the activity loosely: 'god preserve oure noble queen Elyzabeth' on sig. B1r. Another note appears on sig. HH6v in the upper margin, above Book 1, line 809 of *Troilus*. This copy of the 1532 edition has 'Unknow'; the Elizabethan annotator writes it out again with a spelling variant, 'unknowe'.

These are not very consequential findings, but they do illustrate some of my claims. The 'Chaucer' to whom Renaissance readers and writers responded was not bibliographically or textually coherent. Scholars have noticed that Spenser's Chaucer was not ours; that the sixteenth-century literary canon contained many texts ascribed to Chaucer that we now consider apocryphal, including some that associated him with Lollardy; that Stow's 1561 edition made Chaucer's *Works* a space within which to publish texts attributed to John Lydgate.[23] Spenser and E.K.'s Chaucer was a sixteenth-century Chaucer, that is. But what was that? A Henrician assemblage of courtly poems by John Clanvowe and Thomas Usk as well as Chaucer himself? An English reformers' collection of proto-Protestant pieces? Master to his (worthy?) 'scholler Lidgate' and friend of 'Goore'? A collection of texts misread and miscopied, or corrected and understood?

My answer is that Chaucer was sometimes one or another, sometimes all and sometimes none of these things. In this way he provided an example to later English authors of the ennobling and deleterious effects of the preservation

how to order (devyse) all his behavior (array) feelingly (Of sentement) and in so striking a way (uncouth wyse) that lovers thought all was well done, whatever he said or did.' Barney's translation of uncouth – 'striking' – misses something of its meaning of strikingly different or strikingly new. Whatever Troilus is doing to attract lovers' approval, that it is 'uncouth' may suggest that it is not what they are used to; see *MED*, s.v. 'uncouth'.

[23] See for example Glenn Steinberg, 'Spenser's *Shepheardes Calender* and the Elizabethan Reception of Chaucer', *ELR* 35 (2005), 31–51.

of literary works and the spread of literary fame. Chaucer anticipates E.K. and Spenser's interest in these matters. The Chaucer they find in bits and pieces of old books intersects in complex ways with the Chaucer who dreams, narrates, records, appears in and disappears from the texts borne *by* those books. This is evident when E.K. begins the *Calender* with 'vncovthe vnkiste'. By ascribing the words to Chaucer, he contributes to the veneration of the old poet. By choosing a proverb and translating its advice for lovers to the domain of literary making, he associates lovers' and authors' pursuit of fleeting worldly rewards. And by misquoting that proverb, he raises Chaucerian questions about time, change and the fate of little books.

E.K. is very insistent that the words he begins with are Chaucer's. He assures readers that 'vncovthe unkiste' is what Chaucer 'sayde' immediately upon citing it, and again in the very next sentence: 'who for that he is vncouthe (as said Chaucer) is vnkist'. The repetition of the assurance and its proximity to the word 'vncouthe' are part of the Epistle's knowing joke: the best reader is meant to realize that this is not what Chaucer said.

E.K.'s insistence that the proverb is Chaucer's is further complicated if the reader remembers two more things about the text. Firstly, Chaucer insists that *Troilus and Criseyde* is not his own, that he writes only after a Latin source, '[a]s writ myn auctour called Lollius' (1.394). Chaucer did indeed translate much of *Troilus*, but from Giovanni Boccaccio's *Il Filostrato*. His deliberate misrepresentation of his text's history works in much the same way that E.K.'s misquotation of 'unknowe' works. The careful reader's attention is drawn to questions about authorship, but she or he is offered error and subterfuge in place of answers. The likely source for Chaucer's Lollius is an Epistle of the Roman poet Horace which begins 'Troiani belli scriptorem, Maxime Lolli', or 'Maximus Lollius, I have been reading the writer of the Trojan war'. This is straightforward enough: Horace has been reading Homer. But a few medieval scribes made a muddle of the line, read 'scriptorem' as 'scriptorum', and gave the Middle Ages 'Lolli[us], the greatest of the writers of the Trojan war'. Who knows if Chaucer understood all of this when he chose Lollius as a foil for his narrator, but the irony is rich. Lollius is a mistake, a mistake that proves even the work of the 'the greatest of writers of the Trojan war' will be subject to the vicissitudes of time and the depredations of copyists.[24]

Secondly, 'Vncouvthe vnkiste' is a proverb. It is voiced not by the narrator of *Troilus* but by Pandarus, who draws it from common stock of such sayings. It is one of the 'ensample[s]' (*Troilus*, 1.232) that he puts to work in his 'baudy brocage'. Chaucer's is the first written record of the saying and it could be his invention. But after he (or more precisely Pandarus) says it, and before E.K.

---

[24] George Lyman Kittredge, 'Chaucer's Lollius', *Harvard Studies in Classical Philology* 28 (1917), 47–133 (76 for quotation of Horace's Epistle 1.2.1).

ascribes it to him, it tends to turn up unattributed, as an 'old saw'. It is meaningful because no one and therefore everyone is the author of its meaning. It appears in a fifteenth-century collection of courtly poems in British Library MS Harley 682; in a c.1500 copy of a Christmas carol; in two Tudor collections of proverbs gathered by John Heywood; and in *Friar Daw's Reply* to the antifraternal treatise *Jack Upland*.[25]

There are two exceptions to this trend towards anonymity aside from Chaucer's *Troilus* itself. The first seems to build on E.K'.s case that the saying should be treated as Chaucer's. In Usk's *Testament of Love*, Book 3, at lines 846–8, Love tells the narrator that he must speak plainly because,

> he that lyst nat to speke but stylly his disease suffre, what wonder is it tho he come never to his blysse? Who that traveyleth unwist and coveyteth thyng unknowe, unwetyng he shal be quyted and with unknowe thyng rewarded.[26]

The *Testament* develops Pandarus's sentiment here; the passage is analogous to E.K'.s own account of wonder and unknowing in the Epistle and can be considered a second Chaucerian source for that account, given that the *Testament* was printed as Chaucer's in every sixteenth-century edition of Chaucer's *Works*. It can be considered an added source of wonder in another way. Would readers as mindful of Chaucer's style, diction and intellectual preoccupations as Spenser and E.K. really take Usk's overwrought prose and at times 'hopelessly confused' ideas as Chaucer's own? [27]

The proverb also appears in John Gower's *Confessio Amantis*. Spenser and E.K. certainly knew their Gower. In the 'July' Eclogue, E.K. glosses '*glitterand, glittering*' as 'a Participle vsed sometime in Chaucer, but altogether in I. Goore'. Gower uses the word 'glisterande' only three times in the 33,000-line *Confessio*,

---

[25] *The English Poems of Charles of Orleans*, ed. Robert Steele and Mabel Day, EETS OS 215, 220 (London, 1941 and 1946; rpt. 1970), no. 22, line 642, 'Let me not goon as oon unknowe unbast [sic]'. On the modern attribution of the poems in this book to Charles D'Orleans, see Mary-Jo Arn, 'Charles of Orleans and the English Poems of Harley 682', *English Studies* 74 (1993), 222–35. Richard Leighton Green, ed., *A Selection of English Carols* (Oxford, 1962), no. 346, line 1, 'An old-said sawe, "Onknowen, onkyst"'. John Heywood, *Works and Miscellaneous Short Poems*, ed. Burton A. Milligan (Urbana, 1956), *Dialogue*, 233 and *Epigrammes*, 104. The formulation in *Friar Daw's Reply*, which survives in only one manuscript, is 'On old Englis it is seid "unkissed is unknowun"'; *Jack Upland* was ascribed to Chaucer when first printed in 1536 (Bale thought it was Wycliffe's; Foxe attributed it to Chaucer). See *Friar Daw's Reply, Six Ecclesiastical Satires*, ed. James Dean (Kalamazoo, 1991), p. 232; and Gillespie, *Print Culture*, pp. 195–7.

[26] Thomas Usk, *The Testament of Love*, ed. R.A. Shoaf (Kalamazoo, 1998), 3.846–8.

[27] Usk, *Testament*, p. 7. The description of the content as 'hopelessly confused' is Shoaf's. On Chaucer and the printing of the *Testament*, see Anne Middleton, 'Thomas Usk's "Perdurable Letters": The *Testament of Love* from Script to Print', *Studies in Bibliography* 51 (1998), 63–116. The lady's promotion of plain speaking is part of the confusion: the text itself is extremely, perhaps deliberately, certainly knowingly convoluted: 'In this boke be many privy thinges wimpled and folde' (3.1105–6).

so E.K. has read 'Goore' rather thoroughly. Spenser and E.K. had access to Gower's text in one of two sixteenth-century editions; the second, printed 1555, was a column-for-column reprint of the first, printed in 1532.[28] As noted above, Chaucer's *Works* were also first printed in 1532; the printer of *Confessio*, Thomas Berthelet, used the same monumentalizing folio format, a similarly distinctive continental typeface and a similarly worded dedication to Henry VIII for Gower's work. Berthelet, a Stationer and King's Printer, may have financed or distributed part of the 1532 Chaucer edition. He notices the book favourably when citing Chaucer's allusion to 'moral Gower' (*Troilus*, 5.1856) in his preface to *Confessio*:

> The whiche noble warke, and many other of the sayde Chausers, that neuer were before imprinted, and those that very fewe men knewe, and fewer hadde them, be nowe of late put forthe together in a fayre volume.[29]

All this is to say, as others have said before, that Gower was closely associated with Chaucer in the early printed books and in the literary imagination of the sixteenth century.[30]

This in turn provides a context for thinking about the use that 'moral Gower' makes of Pandarus's proverb in *Confessio*:

> And for men sein unknowe unkest,
> Hire thombe sche holt in hire fest
> So clos withinne hire oghne hond,
> That there winneth noman lond;
> Sche lieveth noght al that sche hiereth,
> And thus fulofte hirself sche skiereth
> And is al war of 'hadde I wist'.[31]

In *Troilus*, Pandarus uses the words 'unknowe, unkist' to argue for action: if you do not speak your beloved Criseyde cannot know you or kiss you and you will not know her. She will be 'lost' because 'unsought'. Gower has something quite different to say. 'Unknowe unkest' is something Amans's lady knows because it is common knowledge: it is what 'men sein'. Envious Amans infers that this includes the men who are in pursuit of her. They press her with their proverbs about love all day. For the lady, the proverb is thus an incentive for

---

[28] See *The English Works of John Gower*, ed. G.C. Macaulay, EETS ES 81-2, 2 vols. (Oxford, 1900-1, rpt. 1969), *Confessio Amantis*, 1.1138, 7.815, 5.3734, 3743, for forms of *glisteren*.
[29] Gillespie, *Print Culture*, pp. 134-6, and Joseph A. Dane, *Who Is Buried in Chaucer's Tomb? Studies in the Reception of Chaucer's Book* (East Lansing, 1998), p. 68-72. Text cited is ESTC 12143, sig. AA3v.
[30] See Andrew Higl, 'Printing Power: Selling Lydgate, Gower and Chaucer', *Essays in Medieval Studies* 23 (2006), 57-77; and Espie, '(Un)couth'.
[31] *The English Works of John Gower*, ed. Macaulay, *Confessio Amantis*, 2.461-73.

inaction. It teaches her to trust nothing she hears, to close her thumb in her fist, defend her 'lond' and remain 'unkest'. 'Unknowe unkest' is useful because it puts her in mind of another kind of knowing entirely, one personified by that looming figure for self-reproach, 'hadde I wist' – 'had I known' (what the result of this sort of carnal knowing might be).

Gower's reading of the proverb thus also serves as a reading of *Troilus* itself, one that misses some of the irony of the original, but does take Chaucer's hint that Pandarus's proverbial advice is not to be trusted. It does Troilus no good. He spends most of Book 1 in his chamber, wanting to know Criseyde but not knowing what that means. 'I noot', he cries, at the exact midpoint of that famous Petrarchan song (1.410). He tells Pandarus, as soon as his friend arrives, to leave him 'unknowe' (1.616). But Pandarus's image of him 'unknowe, unkist' and his reconfiguration of it – he sees himself, dead from love, and Criseyde's not knowing this ('his lady naught to wite' (1.825)) – eventually prompts Troilus to ask his friend for help. Troilus does not want his lady's kiss; he does not even want to live. But nor does he want to die 'unknowe'. From this comes the poem's fatal and foreknown 'sorwe' (1.1). In ways that prompt much Boethian searching for Christian consolation, Troilus's desire to be known by Criseyde and Pandarus's advice that he should seek her out will bring him precisely the ending he did not desire. He *will* die for his love. His gains will all become losses: his double sorrow is that he will be kissed and know his Criseyde, and she will be untrue, and he, unknown to her, will lie 'slen' (1.823) on the fields of the always already lost battle for his city.

This is the wisdom that Chaucer's *Troilus* offers at the last, and it offers it in direct contradiction of Pandarus's proverb, 'unknowe, unkist'. Gower's lady seems to realize this: the end of men's worldly striving to know what is 'unknowe' will always be sorrow. And for E.K. and Spenser's purposes, it matters that in *Troilus*, this advice – that it might be better to stay unkissed after all – applies explicitly to authors and their works as well as to lovers. 'Go litel book' (5.1786), writes the old, famous Chaucer. 'So prey I God that non myswrite the' (5.1795). He says this, well aware that 'in forme of speche is chaunge/ Withinne a thousand yeer, and wordes tho/ That hadden pris, now wonder nyce and straunge/ Us thinketh hem' (2.22–5). Someday, someone like E.K. *will* 'myswrite' or misread or mis-say or simply cease to read what he has said. When E.K. uses 'unknowe unkist' to introduce the *Calender* and argue that its author, once known, will be loved by all, and when he misquotes his source, the 'wonder' is that he both misses and gets Chaucer's point completely.

E.K. has a figure for the 'vncovthe', archaic diction of the *Calender*. He derives it from Cicero: 'As that worthy Oratour sayde [...] [j]ust as, when walking in the sunshine [...] the natural result is that I get sunburnt, even so, after perusing those books [...] I find that under their influence my discourse takes on a new complexion.'³² Such, E.K. tells the reader, is the case in the *Calender*. Given that the new poet 'bene much traueiled and throughly redd, how could it be, [...] but that walking in the sonne although for other cause he walked, yet needes he mought be sunburnt' (31–4)? The literary past is imagined as a strange country: travelled and 'thoroughly redd', it leaves its mark on the author. This author is himself 'vncovthe', and now that word takes on new significance. In Middle English, the range of meanings for 'uncouth' includes unknown, unfamiliar, unpredictable, wonderful, foreign and finally barbarous or uncivilized. From the last of these develops the sixteenth- and seventeenth-century usage, in which the uncouth are uncultured, 'rude and rustical' Northerners, uplanders, labourers, or swains.³³

In this use of the word, the 'vncouthe' author is a pastoral poet, who tends his sheep and sings rustic songs in a far-off land under a strange 'sonne'. From here it is a short step to another of the *Calender*'s bookish and Chaucerian beginnings. The sunburned metaphor in E.K.'s Epistle has been much discussed. In one relatively recent study, for instance, it is described as an aspect of a Renaissance or early modern refiguring of classical tradition.³⁴ But E.K. does not lose sight of one old author (Chaucer) as he turns to another (Cicero). The figure he chooses is a way to refer to both. The compound 'sun-burnt' that E.K. uses to translate Cicero's text is also used in *The Plowman's Tale* to describe an uncouth ploughman who joins Chaucer's Canterbury pilgrimage unexpectedly:

> Our Hoste behelde wele all about,
> And sawe this man was sun ybrent.
> He knewe well by his senged snout,
> And by his clothes that were to-rent,
> He was a man wont to walke about,
> He nas nat alway in cloystre ypent;
> He coulde not religiousliche lout,
> And therfore was he fully shent.
> Our Host him axed, 'What man art thou?'³⁵

The Plowman's Tale is a Lollard dialogue, composed in the early 1400s. It was

---

³² Cicero, *De Oratore*, ed. and trans. E.W. Sutton, 2 vols. (Cambridge, MA, 1948), 2: 14.60.
³³ MED and OED, s.v., 'uncouth'. For a full discussion of the relationship between the word, the idea of the untutored, and education and the forms of social distinction, see Patterson, *Reading*.
³⁴ E. Armstrong, *A Ciceronian Sunburn: A Tudor Dialogue on Humanistic Rhetoric and Civic Poetics* (Columbia, 2006). John N. King notes the connection to the Chaucerian Plowman in 'Spenser's *Shepheardes Calender* and Protestant Pastoral Satire', *Renaissance Genres: Essays on Theory, History, and Interpretation*, ed. Barbara Kiefer Lewalski (Cambridge, MA, 1986), pp. 380–1.
³⁵ *Six Ecclesiastical Satires*, ed. Dean, pp. 9–17.

given its Chaucerian prologue by a Tudor redactor in the 1530s and printed by Thomas Godfray at about the time he printed the 1532 edition of Chaucer's *Works*. It was then included in the *Works* when they were reprinted by Richard Grafton (for William Bonham and John Reynes) in 1542. It remained a part of the Chaucer canon until it was removed on the evidence of manuscripts by Thomas Tyrwhitt in 1775.[36]

The *Calender*'s debt to *The Plowman's Tale* has been noted by other scholars. It supplies a great part of that text's archaic diction, the 'rude and rustical' terms which E.K. says are the legacy of the new poet's reading.[37] The *Tale*'s representation of the corruption of the Roman Church is a model for Spenser as he turns old anticlerical debates into pastoral dialogue. The *Calender* makes the *Tale* a part of a claim – akin to that made by the early modern collectors and printers of Anglo-Saxon and Middle English Biblical writings and medieval writings on the independent English Church – that the new religion is an older one revived.

The *Calender*'s relation to *The Plowman's Tale* thus establishes the sometimes overlooked importance of late medieval thought to early modern institutions and the process by which writers such as Chaucer and Wycliffe were singled out as different from the medieval culture to which they belonged – a process that has not ended in modern criticism, where Chaucer especially is still sometimes treated as a proto-modern poet who makes his contemporaries and many of his successors seem positively medieval.

However, I have just argued that the *Calender* does not simply use the literary past for Reformation purposes. Its literary achievement depends upon the unsettling effects of that past, and *The Plowman's Tale* has some share in this process. It is to the 'Ploughman' that the *Calender* returns at the end of the book:

> Goe lyttle Calender, thou hast a free passeporte,
> Goe but a lowly gate emongste the meaner sorte.
> Dare not to match thy pipe with Tityrus hys style,
> Nor with the Pilgrim that the Ploughman playde a whyle:
> But followe them farre off, and their high steppes adore,
> The better please, the worse despise, I aske nomore. (Envoy, 7–12)

Chaucer's is the original of the motif here, as noted above. In his *Troilus*, the steps to follow are those of ancient and Latin writers: the little book is told to

---

[36] For a fuller account, see Gillespie, *Print Culture*, pp. 195–201; and Joseph A. Dane, 'Bibliographical History versus Bibliographical Evidence: The Plowman's Tale and Early Chaucer Editions', *Bulletin of the John Rylands University Library of Manchester* 78 (1996), 47–61.

[37] His debt is first noted by Percy W. Long, 'Spenser and the *Plowman's Tale*', *Modern Language Notes* 28 (1913), 262; see also John N. King, *Spenser's Poetry and the Reformation Tradition* (Princeton, 1990).

'kis the steppes where as thow seest pace/ Virgile, Ovide, Omer, Lucan, and Stace' (5.190–1). The *Calender* follows Chaucer's wording and imagery closely, and then adds another layer, giving the Virgilian 'Tityrus'-Chaucer for the elder poet's own *auctores*.

It is the slightly unexpected 'Pilgrim that the Ploughman playde a while' that interests me here, however. In bibliographical terms, it is true that the Plowman's turn as a pilgrim is not one of long duration – just a 'while'. There is a Plowman in the General Prologue of *The Canterbury Tales*, but he tells a tale in only one surviving manuscript of the texts, and there his contribution to the apocryphal Chaucerian canon is a Marian hymn rather than an anticlerical dialogue.[38] Spenser might have seen *The Plowman's Tale* printed as Chaucer's in 1542, 1550 and 1561 editions of his *Works*; but he might also have seen editions of the *Tales* from 1476, 1483, 1494, 1498 and 1526, or a copy of the 1532 *Works* in which *The Plowman's Tale* is missing. The appearance and disappearance of the text from the Canterbury collection was noted by contemporary readers. It is a problem that the antiquary John Leland takes pains to explain away in the bio-bibliography for Chaucer that he compiled in the 1530s:

> *Petris Aratoris* fabula, quae communi doctorum consesu Chaucero, tanquam vero parenti, attribuitur, in utraque editione, quia malos sacerdotum mores vehementer increpavit, suppressa est
>
> [The Tale of Piers Plowman, which by the common consent of the learned is attributed to Chaucer as its true author has been suppressed in each edition, because it vigorously inveighed against the bad morals of the priests].[39]

Leland's unnamed 'learned' men may agree that a Plowman's tale belongs in the *Works*, but the text that Leland names, *Petris Aratoris*, seems to be Langland's *Piers Plowman*, rather than *The Plowman's Tale* (whose Plowman has no name). It is possible that the edition of *The Plowman's Tale* that was printed by Godfray in about 1532 with its Chaucerian prologue was originally intended for Thynne's 1532 edition of Chaucer's *Works* but was suppressed, although in 1532 England was still two years off its break with Rome. But Leland takes the argument further than this. There is no reason to think that earlier editors or printers of Chaucer's *Tales* – William Caxton, for instance, whose edition Leland refers to elsewhere – took any tale of any ploughman to be Chaucer's, for none of the manuscripts upon which their editions are based include such

---

[38] See *The Ploughman's Tale* in *The Canterbury Tales: Fifteenth-Century Continuations and Additions*, ed. John Bowers (Kalamazoo, 1992).
[39] John Leland, *De Viris Illustribus*, ed. and trans. James P. Carley with Caroline Brett (Toronto and London, 2010), pp. 160–1.

a text. Leland, carried away by thought of pre-Reformation religious practices and those prevented from reforming them, imagines this scenario anyway.

The Plowman's Tale also had an unhelpful tendency to wander about in print. The text was the only one of *The Canterbury Tales* published as a part of that work, but separately in the early modern period. It was printed on its own in 1548 and again in c.1606.[40] Its status within the *Works* was uncertain too. The compilers of the 1542 editions of the *Works* tacked the text onto the end of *The Canterbury Tales*, after 'The Parson's Tale'. In 1550, perhaps noticing that this position for the text made a complete nonsense of the structure of *The Canterbury Tales* (where the Parson says he will 'knytte up' the tale-telling competition, X.47), a new printer and group of publishers had it tucked back in behind the Parson's. In this 1550 edition, the arguments of a pilgrim who 'coulde not religiousliche lout' are thus 'shent' by an orthodox, medieval cleric who certainly 'coulde'. The Parson's text thus ends the *Tales* with an exercise in penitential orthodoxy in copies of the 1550 edition, just as it does in most more or less complete books made of the *Tales* before the Reformation.

Let us go back, then, to the implications of the question 'What man artow?' that the Host poses to this bibliographically bewildering, well-'traveilled', uncouth, sun-burned pilgrim. That question is asked of Chaucer in the *Tales* themselves, when the Host demands a tale from him (VII.695). At that point in the Canterbury pilgrimage, it alerts the reader to series of questions raised by the narrative presence of Chaucer the pilgrim/author. Who is the pilgrim who tells the tales of Thopas and Melibee? Is he the metrically challenged 'Chaucer' mentioned by the Man of Law (II.47)? Why does he fail to give his name (here or anywhere in his writings except as 'Geffrey' in the *House of Fame*, 729)? Does he mean to make the point that the medieval conditions for writing were not secure ones for self-naming – that scribally copied books tend to loosen texts from authorizing contexts? Or that political and religious controversies make authorship perilous when writers are readily identifiable?[41] Perhaps this is just a little Chaucerian humble-brag. After all, the decision taken by the writer of all of these dazzling tales to hide behind the fat form of an inept pilgrim actually draws witty attention to the fact that he has done so. 'What man artow?' The author, of course.

All this is part of the wonder and brilliance of Chaucer's *Tales*. In combination with the strange bibliographical history of *The Plowman's Tale*, it frames the appearance of a 'Ploughman' who is also a 'pilgrim' alongside Tityrus-Chaucer in the envoy to the *Calender*. Spenser's Ploughman could be Piers Plowman,

---

[40] See Gillespie, *Print Culture*, pp. 200–1 for details.
[41] See Kathryn Kerby-Fulton, 'Langland and the Bibliographic Ego', *Written Work: Langland, Labour, and Authorship*, ed. Kathryn Kerby-Fulton and Steven Justice (Philadelphia, 1997), pp. 67–143.

and his envoy would thus be a paean to those medieval greats Chaucer and Langland who appear here in allegorical guise. Critics have already written persuasively upon Langland's importance to Spenser's writing.[42] However, the 'Pilgrim' that this ploughman 'playde awhile' sounds less like Langland than he sounds like the pilgrim-ploughman of *The Plowman's Tale*.

If the apocryphal Chaucerian Plowman is indeed the ploughman to which Spenser and E.K. allude, or at least one of the possibilities they want to keep in play, he is still – appropriately – uncouth. In the sixteenth century, the teller of *The Plowman's Tale* was sometimes configured as a character of Chaucer's devising. In that sense the pilgrim-ploughman of the *Calender* is another guise for Tityrus himself. However, Chaucer's narrative framework for the *Tales* and the editorial history of *The Plowman's Tale* also separate the teller of this tale from Chaucer. The early modern prologue to *The Plowman's Tale* links an obviously older, Middle English text to *The Canterbury Tales*, but it does so very awkwardly. This text is then fitted into some of Chaucer's books, but not all of them and only for a 'while'. As he comes and goes from this or that part of the Canterbury pilgrimage, the Plowman directs attention to the space Chaucer left in his own text for precisely this sort of treatment. There is a connection and conversely quite a gap between the Plowman and the old famous author Chaucer in the sixteenth century. Both are the result of an unstable textual and bibliographical tradition. Both are also of Chaucer's own making. Both serve Spenser and E.K., as they bring the *Shepheardes Calender* to its close.

I want to end this essay with a coda rather than a conclusion. In his 1981 essay, '*Lycidas*: A Poem Finally Anonymous', Stanley E. Fish argues that it is in the impossible strains of what E.K. calls 'disorderly order' that the music of John Milton's poem *Lycidas* is to be heard.[43] It is heard in the voices that interpose and puncture 'the illusion of independence and control' for which the speaker has struggled from the first (338). It is in the tangle of syntax and tense and of these voices, which include the pastoral poet who ironizes his chosen form, Apollo, the Triton whose plea is also 'Neptune's', a chorus, the Galilean Pilot perhaps as Christian type, a new voice of Christian consolation which may be the Archangel Michael's, a singing Swain, and an anonymous narrator. The poem succeeds as it erases the author and his struggle and leaves only startling, compelling discontinuities for the reader to work with.

My interest here is the 'uncouth Swain' who arrives at the very end of the poem to disrupt what has come before:

---

[42] Beginning with A.C. Hamilton, 'Spenser and Langland', *SP* 55 (1958), 533–48.
[43] Cited from C.A. Patrides, ed., *Milton's Lycidas: The Tradition and the Poem* (Columbia, 1983), poem at pp. 3–11; Fish's essay at pp. 319–40.

Thus sang the uncouth Swain to th'Okes and rills,
While the still morn went out with Sandals gray,
He touch'd the tender stops of various Quills,
With eager thought warbling his Dorick lay:
And now the Sun had stretch'd out all the hills,
And now was dropt into the Western bay;
At last he rose, and twitch'd his Mantle blew:
To morrow to fresh Woods, and Pastures new. (186–93)

Fish observes that '[t]he last eight lines of *Lycidas* have always been perceived as problematic, because they insist on a narrative frame that was not apparent in the beginning, because the frame or coda is spoken by an unidentified third-person voice, because that voice is so firmly impersonal', and being impersonal 'unidentified' (339). He notes that his reading of the text removes the problem. The poet is unidentified because the poetic space he has created is not one in which he is able to assert his coherent identity.

My purpose here is to notice that the history of the 'uncouth Swain' is vital to a reading in which *Lycidas* is thus, finally, untethered. He is a descendent of the uncouth swain of Spenser and E.K.'s *Calender*, as other commentators have noted. Because he is 'uncouth' he is also descended from the work of Chaucer, Gower, Usk, from medieval proverbs, and even a medieval ploughman (or two).[44] He has been marked by his past – by Chaucer and Spenser's ironic mode of poetic self-representation, and by those textual histories of error and anonymity that inform it.

The poem *Mansus*, Milton's panegyric to the Italian humanist, patron and literary biographer Giovanni Battista Manso, whom he met in Naples in 1638, also features a song-making swain. Apollo himself features, resting from his labours 'rura Pheretiade' (57), the farm where, according to Apollodorus, he tended flocks for Admetus, King of the Pherae. There are some ploughmen, whose noise Apollo wishes to avoid ('clamosos placuit vitare bubulcos' (59)). And Chaucer shows up in his Spenserian guise as Tityrus, as a fellow traveller to Italian shores.[45] In *Mansus*, Milton's figuring of famous authors is certainly

---

[44] On Milton's debt to *The Plowman's Tale*, see Mike Rodman Jones, *Radical Pastoral, 1381–1594: Appropriation and the Writing of Religious Controversy* (Farnham, 2011), p. 94n21.

[45] Cited from John Milton, *The Complete Shorter Poems*, ed. Stella P. Revard (Oxford, 2009). Chaucer did indeed make it to Italy, but Milton's belief that he did so is based on literary evidence and the guesswork of Thomas Speght, who in his 1598 edition of the *Workes* raises the possibility of a meeting between Chaucer and Petrarch (probably working from notes by John Stow). Helen Cooper describes Chaucer's role in *Mansus* in 'Choosing Poetic Fathers: The English Problem', *Medieval and Early Modern Authorship*, ed. Guillemette Bolens and Lukas Erne (Tübingen, 2011), p. 43. The further connection to Spenser is recorded in Thomas Warton's *Observations on The Fairy Queene of Spenser* (London and Oxford, 1754), p. 88. I owe these references to the generosity of Jeff Espie, who first drew my attention to *Mansus*.

– indeed hopefully – self-reflexive. But the poem steers away from what is unruly, deleterious or relentlessly ironizing about the bookish process by which poets earn renown. Milton praises Manso's work because through it the poet may still be seen, 'smiling from […] bronze' ('arridentem […] ex aere poetam' (16)), his name and Mansus's own 'inscribed […] on everlasting pages' ('aeternis inscripsit […] chartis' (8)). A well-known writer lives forever.

That simple trope yields in *Lycidas* to something much more diffuse and unsettling, less obviously and yet more subtly engaged with its literary antecedents. The poet-swain who sets himself apart from rowdy (and in that sense 'uncouth') labourers in *Mansus* is now himself uncouth. His 'Quills' are not pens, ready to inscribe his name so that it might last forever. They have been selected by Milton to call that idea to mind, but only as they substitute for it things much vaguer and more ephemeral. The swain's pipes are touched not by breath, but by thought. And whereas in *Mansus*, Apollo's song soothes some spotted lynxes, the swain of *Lycidas* warbles his lay to unresponsive 'Okes and rills'.

Unnamed, unanticipated and unheard, Milton's swain is indeed 'finally anonymous', as Fish puts it. He is perennially *unknown*. He is also, ironically, Milton's tribute to his best known English forebears, Chaucer and Spenser. The word he chooses to describe his inheritance, 'uncouth', is theirs, and so is the understanding of literary history it evokes. The rewards of poetry may be cast in memorial bronze, but its pleasures are more disorderly – fleeting, uncertain and wonderful.

Armour that doesn't work
An Anti-meme in Medieval and Renaissance Romance

⊰ R. W. MASLEN ⊱

One of Helen Cooper's finest essays concerns the function of magic that doesn't work in medieval and Renaissance romance.[1] Bringing together her impish sense of humour, her astonishing range of reading and her infectious delight in tracing the mutations of genre in response to cultural change, the essay is a scholarly tour de force, perhaps the most memorable chapter in her celebrated monograph *The English Romance in Time*. It is particularly suggestive where it draws attention to the moments in medieval romance when the presence of magic serves to focus the reader's attention on some peculiarly human quality: on selfless love, for instance, as when the imperilled teenage lovers Floris and Blancheflour compete over which of them will bestow on the other the magic ring which is said to preserve its owner's life; or on stubborn courage, as when an anonymous lover in a tale by Marie de France refuses to drink the magic potion that would help him carry his beloved up a mountain, an act of heroic obstinacy that kills them both.[2] The chapter is not about a 'meme', Cooper explains – an idea or theme that survives from generation to generation, mutating in response to the changing pressures of the times. Instead it concerns what she calls a 'meme that got out of hand', that of the magical object.[3] All too easily magic can get boring, operating in too predictable a fashion, providing too easy an escape route from a tricky situation. The magic that doesn't work revitalizes the magical narrative by introducing a crucial element of surprise, disorder, or emotional crisis; and as such it resists replication, since the whole point of it (when well used) is to unsettle the romance reader's expectations.

I would like to consider in this essay another recurring theme that has given us some of the most striking passages in medieval and Renaissance romance: that of armour that doesn't work. For a modern reader, armour is the ultimate emblem of chivalric romance, especially the full plate armour of the fifteenth

---

[1] Cooper, *Romance*, ch. 3: 'Magic that doesn't work'.
[2] Cooper, *Romance*, pp. 148–51.
[3] Cooper, *Romance*, p. 138.

and sixteenth centuries, as fetishized in the paintings of John William Waterhouse, John Boorman's film *Excalibur*, or the BBC TV series *Merlin*. For the late medieval reader, too, armour or harness that worked was romance incarnate. Someone in the fifteenth or sixteenth century wearing splendid harness instantly displayed his gender, his status, his affiliations (if he wore a coat armour, or if the steel itself bore heraldic devices), and his physical attributes (think of Henry VIII's expanding girth as recorded in his successive sizes of battle dress). Armour stood for the chivalric code; praying over it was an integral part of a squire's induction into knighthood. What you wore in the Middle Ages was, in theory, who you were; and fine armour was at the very apex of the sartorial pyramid.[4]

For all these reasons – because it is so instantly readable in so many ways – armour can be a boring object in romance, especially when its bearer is vying for the position of Number One Knight, so to speak, in the chivalric standings. Under these conditions the armour bearer is like a machine, whose limited functions are always predictable and whose victory always assured. The ultimate example of an armour-bearing machine is of course Sir Galahad, who gallops through the landscape of Malory's 'Tale of the Sankgreal' fulfilling prophecies left and right without any emotional engagement with the men and women he encounters. Galahad is the embodiment of spiritual commitment; he has no personality or history, and when all his deeds have been accomplished his soul is carried up to Heaven by a team of adoring angels, leaving little physical trace behind on the earth he barely touched.[5] In some ways, then, he is the worthy forebear of Spenser's mechanical man Talus, the metallic dispenser of justice in Book V of *The Faerie Queene* who signals the poet's uncomfortable commitment to the Tudor project of subjugating Ireland by force. Talus's status as what can anachronistically be termed a self-propelled suit of armour conveniently sets him apart from human beings in such a way as to make that project seem (barely) defensible, since though devised by men it is executed by an agent without a soul. Nevertheless, the iron man's association with the animated statues of Virgilius the Sorcerer or Cornelius Agrippa confirms his ambiguity as a representation of justice. Virgilius derived his power from the devil and Marlowe assumed, in *Doctor Faustus*, that Agrippa too was

---

[4] My knowledge of medieval armour depends largely on two sources: Claude Blair's *European Armour circa 1066 to circa 1700* (London, 1958); and the kindness of Dr Ralph Moffat, Curator of European Arms and Armour at the Kelvingrove Museum, Glasgow. Warm thanks to Ralph for showing me round the museum's remarkable collection and providing me with an invaluable reading list.

[5] 'And so suddeynly departed hys soule to Jesu Cryste, and a grete multitude of angels bare hit up to hevyn evyn in the sight of hys two felowis': Sir Thomas Malory, *Works*, ed. Eugène Vinaver (Oxford, 1977), p. 607, lines 6–8. All references are to this edition.

in cahoots with the fiend.⁶ Given that Talus is simply an allegorical machine, unsullied by magic, he can in theory be employed by Spenser's knight of justice, Sir Artegal, without tainting his employer with infernal associations. But the memory of other moving statues would have been hard to shake off for an early modern reader. And there remains the fact that Talus is impossible to like, with his remorseless efficiency, his predictable reactions to every situation, and his utter indifference to the Christian quality of mercy.

This problem of the perfect knight as a soulless machine is brilliantly addressed by Italo Calvino in *The Non-existent Knight* (*Il cavaliere inesistente*, 1959), his sparkling tribute to Ariosto and Cervantes.⁷ The book's protagonist, a full-body harness that comes to life by an act of sheer will-power, makes himself universally unpopular with his fellow paladins by his rigid adherence to the rules of military and chivalric good conduct. As the book proceeds, however, the knight's increasing sensitivity to other people's views of him makes him increasingly likeable, and his posse of followers – the fool Gurduloo, the idealistic female warrior Bradamante, the confused young squire Raimbaud – endows him by proxy with the flesh and emotions he lacks. He becomes the focus of their dreams and passions, the anchor of their identities, no longer merely a metal container for the regulations by which these dreams are rendered manageable by the authorities. Armour requires the flesh to make it move, both emotionally and physically speaking; and codes of conduct, however impractical, give direction to the undirected yearnings of the flesh. Calvino's story beautifully captures the awkward symbiosis between the organic and the inorganic which is the late medieval and early modern knight.

Flesh, then, is the essential adjunct to the carapace of protective steel, as late Victorian painters such as Waterhouse acknowledged when they surrounded their gleaming knights with voluptuous temptresses. Men, of course, can display their fleshly qualities in romance by defeating powerful opponents without the benefit of armour; this is the homosocial equivalent of the amorous encounters, chaste or unchaste, with which romance women have been traditionally associated. A fine example of such an unarmed hero is the young Sir Perceval de Gallys in the Middle English metrical romance, whose lack of armour serves at first merely to underline his lack of education in chivalry.⁸ Wearing only goatskins, young Perceval's first heroic act is to transfix his father's killer, a fully armoured knight, with a light Scottish throwing-spear, when the man is foolish

---

⁶ See [Anon.], *Virgilius* (Antwerp. 1518), sigs. A5v–A6v; Marlowe, *Doctor Faustus*, ed. David Bevington and Eric Rasmussen (Manchester and New York, 1993), A-Text, I. i. 102–68. For Agrippa's moving statues, see *Three Books of Occult Philosophy Written by Henry Cornelius Agrippa*, trans. J.F. (London, 1651), pp. 77–8.

⁷ Italo Calvino, *Our Ancestors*, trans. Archibald Colquhoun (London, 1980), pp. 285–382.

⁸ *Sir Perceval of Galles*, in *Middle English Metrical Romances*, ed. Walter Hoyt French and Charles Brockway Hale, 2 vols. (New York, 1930), 2: 530–603.

enough to raise his visor. But Perceval is an adolescent at the time, and every reader knows from the old stories that he will soon acquire some armour and join his fellow knights at the Table Round. For Perceval, the acquisition of his harness from the slaughtered body of his enemy makes it an emblem of his power and skill, a natural extension of the unusual muscularity of his right arm and torso, his easy mastery over the objects and people he meets on his travels. But I am concerned in this essay with the knights whose harness proves useless in one way or another *after* its acquisition; either because the adventure they are on cannot be achieved with the help of steel, or because they are caught without armour through trickery, neglect or betrayal, or because their armour provides inadequate protection – or even because their harness itself is a kind of trap. For these heroes, armour is a difficult affair, never at hand when you need it, not fulfilling its prescribed function when you have it, brittle, permeable or imprisoning rather than impervious, encumbering rather than enabling. And in the adventures they take part in, armour often becomes intriguing in its own right, for a variety of unpredictable reasons.

One twentieth-century embodiment of this difficult relationship with armour is King Pellinore in T.H. White's novel *The Sword in the Stone* (1938). Pellinore is an errant knight who is perpetually engaged in the rather pointless pursuit of a friendly creature called the Questing Beast. When the future King Arthur, here known as the Wart, first encounters Pellinore, the boy quickly learns a great deal about the inconvenience of closed helmets for those who wear spectacles (the lenses get 'completely fogged'[9]), and of armour generally. As the knight explains:

> All this beastly amour takes hours to put on. When it is on it's either frying or freezing, and it gets rusty. You have to sit up all night polishing the stuff. Oh, how Ay do wish Ay had a nice house of my own to live in, a house with beds in it and real pillows and sheets. [...] Then Ay would [...] throw all this beastly armour out of the window, and let the beastly Beast go and chase itself, that Ay would.[10]

In this passage King Pellinore is a kind of human snail, whose metal shell serves as an uncomfortable substitute for the nice warm house he yearns for. His armour has little value as a means of defence, since the Questing Beast is far too friendly to attack him. Instead it tends to erase the distinction between its bearer and the animal world through which he wanders, exaggerating the limitations of the King's body by fogging up his spectacles and fraying his temper to the extent that he keeps referring to his equipment as *beastly*. When the Questing Beast turns up a page or so later, the King's animal passions get

---

[9] T.H. White, *The Sword in the Stone* (London, 1959), p. 26.
[10] White, *Sword in the Stone*, p. 30.

further excited and he promptly forgets the allure of sheets in the thrill of the chase. An unsuccessful fusion of animal unruliness and rigid artifice, of chaos and convention, White's knight is a direct descendant of Carroll's White Knight and Cervantes' Quixote, both of whom are always damaging their elderly bodies precisely *because* they insist on wearing protective steel. For all three, the harness they wear underscores the limitations of the flesh it encases, as well as the eccentric relationship between that flesh and the code of conduct that the harness represents.

In this as in other ways, armour that doesn't work has a similar function to magic that doesn't work, as Cooper describes it. If full plate armour is a kind of meme in late chivalric romance – like the meme of the magic object – then the armour that doesn't work is designed to circumvent the narrative problems posed by that meme: an 'anti-meme', in other words. The romance hero is nearly always one of the greatest fighters of his time, and in full armour his fighting prowess must necessarily render him as indestructible as the owner of an effective charm or talisman – and hence as dull, in terms of the narrative possibilities to which he gives rise. For such a knight to retain his stature as a combatant while engaging in properly perilous adventures he must be stripped of his protective exoskeleton, deprived of the tools of his trade by one means or other – or those tools must be turned against him, like King Pellinore's fog-inducing helmet. And the effect of this process of stripping down, deprivation or armorial recalcitrance is to draw attention to the fragile humanness of the romance's male protagonist.

This may be the central difference between the magic that doesn't work and the armour that doesn't work. Cooper's examples of non-functional magic (and she includes under this rubric magic that might well work but isn't used, just as the present essay includes functional armour that gets left aside at crucial moments) often serve to demonstrate the spectacularly *exceptional* nature of the people who fail to use it. It is the exceptional strength of Floris and Blancheflour's love that prompts a sympathetic king to urge their captor, the Admiral or Emir of Babylon, to spare them. In Marie de France's tale, it is the refusal of the lover to drink the magic potion that exhibits the exceptional potency of his love, since love alone gives him strength to achieve what no other man has managed by carrying his lady unassisted up a mountain. Armour that doesn't work, by contrast, tends to underscore the vulnerability of the person it fails, or who fails to wear it. For this reason it becomes one of the defining themes of the late chivalric tradition, when the best writers (Chaucer, Malory, Shakespeare) chose to produce 'works designed to question their own generic assumptions' in response to the 'strong self-consciousness of a genre now passing into its fourth century', as Cooper reminds us.[11]

[11] Cooper, *Romance*, p. 363.

These comments on late chivalric romance come from the final chapter of *The English Romance in Time*, 'Unhappy Endings', and armour that doesn't work is strongly represented here among the romances that choose to resist the genre's assumption that all its narratives must end well. But like magic that doesn't work, non-functional armour can be comic too. Inevitably it is Chaucer who provides the best examples of both the comic and tragic aspects of this 'anti-meme' (Cooper was always pointing out to me in tutorials that Chaucer provides the best examples of almost *anything* before the late sixteenth century). In *The Canterbury Tales*, Sir Thopas exhibits his own and his narrator's ignorance of the romance tradition by getting caught without his armour when he meets a giant. Any medieval reader would have known that an errant knight should be wearing armour when he seeks adventure, and that if he happens not to be wearing it he should defeat his antagonist regardless, as Perceval beats the Red Knight dressed only in goatskins. But for Chaucer's narcissistic protagonist, wearing the wrong clothes for any given deed is inexcusable; he must hurry home to arm himself before he can even think of engaging in combat. When he does so, it is in an elaborate metal and fabric confection which again violates romance conventions, both by its placement in the wrong part of the narrative (he should have armed himself at the beginning) and by the sheer weight of clichés that cluster round it (his coat armour is 'whit as is a lilye flour', his fine cypress spear 'bodeth werre, and nothyng pees', and so on).[12] The belatedness of Sir Thopas's arming also confirms his inverted understanding of the chivalric code, which has already been signalled by his plan to marry an elven queen because no mortal woman is worthy of him. After reading this poem it is hard to imagine anyone taking another metrical romance entirely seriously.

At the tragic end of the spectrum, 'The Knight's Tale' provides an example of a yet more radical inversion of the proper order of the chivalric romance narrative and the code to which it theoretically adheres; and it does so largely through the difficult relationship it sketches out between a man and his armour. Like a true romance hero, the protagonist Arcite defeats his friend and rival Palamon in combat, and the tournament in which he achieves this is stuffed to bursting with allusions to armour: from the frantic 'devisynge of harneys' that precedes the fighting (line 2496) to King Theseus's prohibition of certain weapons from the contest itself ('ne polax, ne short knyf [...] Ne short swerd, for to stoke with poynt bitynge', lines 2544–6). As it turns out, however, neither harness nor prohibition offers much protection to the contestants. 'The helmes they tohewen and toshrede,' the poet tells us with unnerving relish; 'Out brest the blood with stierne stremes rede;/ With myghty maces the bones

---

[12] *Sir Thopas*, in Geoffrey Chaucer, *Works*, ed. F.N. Robinson, 2nd edn. (Oxford, 1977), p. 166, lines 867 and 882. All references are to this edition.

they tobreste', and it is by the merest chance that no one dies in the melee (lines 2609–11). When the tournament is over, Arcite takes off his helmet to salute the woman who inspired his triumph; and at once his horse falls over and fatally crushes him. The calamitous effect of this fall on Arcite's flesh is described in lurid detail, as if to stress the limitations of his strong young body: 'The pipes of his longes gonne to swelle,/ And every lacerte [muscle] in his brest adoun/ Is shent with venym and corrupcion' (p. 44, lines 2752–4). In this narrative, then, armour and the rules that govern its use represent men's feeble attempt to take control in a world full of insidious poisons, from the venom of corrupted wounds to the contagion of desire, from the disease of jealousy that sets the knights at odds to the poisonous rivalry of the gods who sponsor each combatant. Theseus does his best to reimpose a sense of order after Arcite's accident, declaring the tournament a draw and delivering a speech that affirms the continuing stability of creation. But Arcite's death was not in fact accidental. It was engineered by Venus (or rather by Saturn acting on her behalf), and intended to benefit Palamon, her devoted acolyte. Arcite, by contrast, was an acolyte of Mars, the god of war, who also happens to be Venus's lover. So the pantheon of pagan gods would seem to be as violently competitive as the knights they sponsor, and as capable of circumventing regulations and breaking alliances. The armour that doesn't work here serves to point up the limitations of the structures that bind us: above all the kind of structure represented by traditional stories and comforting fictions, the imaginative armour with which we defend to ourselves such slippery concepts as honour and friendship.

The works of Malory, too, offer fine examples of both the comic and tragic aspects of non-functioning armour. On the tragic side, there is the tale of the brothers Balin and Balan, who hack each other to death because each is wearing unfamiliar harness. The final section of 'The Knight with the Two Swords' begins with Balin accepting a shield from a stranger knight in place of his own, whereupon a mysterious damsel warns him that 'ye have put yourself in grete daunger, for by your sheld ye shold have ben knowen' (p. 56, lines 22–4). His brother meets him shortly afterwards wearing unmarked red armour, and in the fight that follows both men dismantle each other plate by plate until 'their hawberkes [were] unnailed, that naked they were on every syde' (p. 57, lines 12–13). Mortally wounded, Balan crawls to his brother and takes off his helmet; but he cannot recognize him at first because of the damage he himself inflicted in the battle: he 'myght not knowe hym by the vysage, it was so ful hewen and bledde' (p. 57, lines 22–3). As Cooper has argued, part of the power of this denouement springs from the fact that it forms part of a larger narrative with which the medieval reader was well acquainted – the Arthurian cycle – while the knights themselves have no idea what forces drive their fate.[13]

---

[13] Cooper, *Romance*, pp. 367–9.

Throughout his adventures, the invincible Balin is helplessly propelled by the machinery of story, unwittingly setting up riddles, problems and conundrums that will only be resolved long after his death by the machine-man Galahad. The armour that destroys him, then, embodies his entrapment in structures he cannot understand because of his limited vision – the restricted view you get from inside a closed helmet (think of Pellinore's spectacles). The fact that he cannot recognize his brother, and that his brother cannot recognize him, sums up his condition as an ignorant tool of dispassionate supernatural forces – as represented at Balin's burial by the sorcerer Merlin, who laughs sardonically as he makes further predictions about the tragic fate of Balin's sword.

Malory's Lancelot, meanwhile, furnishes us with examples of both the comic and tragic aspects of armour that doesn't work. Of all the knights in Malory's pantheon apart from Galahad, Lancelot stands in greatest danger of becoming boring, since he is the best knight in the world and we know in advance the likely outcome of every battle – and hence of every narrative – in which he is involved. For this reason Malory is careful to vary the scenes he selects for inclusion in the parts of his work he devotes to Lancelot; and an inordinate number of these episodes involve non-functional armour. In 'A Noble Tale of Sir Launcelot du Lake' the hero is forced to don another man's armour if he wants adventures; wearing his own means he is avoided like the plague. But some of his best adventures occur when he wears no armour at all. On one occasion, for instance, he finds a pavilion in the forest, lavishly prepared for the reception of a guest. In many romances such a discovery would signal the presence of the supernatural: the pavilion would belong to a fairy or enchantress, as in *Sir Launfal*, and Lancelot would have to deploy all his knightly self-control to resist the seductions of its owner. It seems only natural, then, to the reader that on finding the tent he should remove his armour, lie down in the bed and go to sleep; this is what you do in enchanted pavilions. Later, the knight who owns the pavilion comes home and gets into bed. Finding Lancelot between his sheets and assuming him to be his lover, he 'toke hym in his armys and began to kysse hym', scratching the sleeping hero with his 'rough berde' (p. 153, lines 27–8). This leads to a brief, fierce swordfight between the two warriors – presumably naked – during which Lancelot wounds the stranger 'sore nyghe unto the deth' (p. 153, line 33). At this point, the men pause to explain themselves to each other. Lancelot then takes the stranger indoors to tend his injuries, and the knight's lady arrives. The lady is naturally inclined to blame Lancelot for her husband's injuries; but she soon comes up with a means for him to make amends. He must use his influence at court, she insists, to procure her man a place at the Round Table. In this way Lancelot's nakedness leaves him exposed to the lady's judicial expertise, to the extent that he must set aside the usual procedure for admitting knights to that exclusive company and offer a seat at the Round Table to an unproven stranger. What began as an encounter with potential enchantment ends not with a dazzling display of unmatchable swordsmanship but with an out-of-court settlement, a legal compromise; and in this way the episode exposes the absurdity both of chivalric convention and of the narrative traditions Lancelot lives by.

Later in the same book, Lancelot is tricked into removing his armour and climbing a tree to rescue a lady's falcon. Once he is safely in his breeches and astride a branch, the lady's husband leaps out of a bush 'all armed' (p. 169, line 44) and explains that this was all a plot to get Lancelot into a state of undress so as to enable him to be summarily dispatched. Lancelot disarms the knight with a stick and kills him with his own weapon; but the episode neatly illustrates one of the perils of being a romance hero, which is that the landscape gradually fills up with people who hold a grudge against you, and whose only hope of besting you is by trickery. As a hero you can only trust that your own wiles, or the wiles of some well-disposed passing damsel, will permit you to escape from the tricks to which these grudgers are prepared to resort. And in the last two books of Malory's work, a deadly web composed of grudges and trickery binds together all the major episodes that feature armour that doesn't work.

Lancelot's relationship with armour in these last two books becomes increasingly difficult, as if to emphasize the increasing difficulty of reconciling his duty to King Arthur with his devotion to Arthur's wife. In the tale of the Fair Maid of Astolat, Lancelot plays his old trick of borrowing armour in order to participate in a tournament. But the armour fails him – he is pierced through the side by his cousin Bors while wearing it; and during his long period of convalescence, necessarily unclothed, his body attracts the devotion of his nurse, the Maid of the title. The borrowed armour has meanwhile got him into trouble with Guinevere, since to complete the disguise he wore a token on his helmet, a red sleeve lent him by the Maid. The sleeve misleads the Queen into thinking he has transferred his affections to another woman, while encouraging the Maid to believe he might eventually fall in love with her. In 'A Noble Tale of Sir Launcelot du Lake', Lancelot's appropriation of Sir Kay's armour had no serious consequences; it was a game, as were the fights he undertook while bearing it. In the last two books, games turn to earnest, and borrowing armour becomes a problem, which interweaves itself with the personal and political problems that accumulate around the adulterous couple.

Armour is yet more problematic in 'The Knight of the Cart'. The villain here is a kind of anti-Lancelot, Sir Melliagaunt, who shares his alter ego's obsession with Guinevere but none of the chivalric qualities by which he justifies that adulterous passion. The difference between the two men can be summed up by their attitudes to armour. Melliagaunt captures the Queen while she is out a-maying with some unarmed knights, who are seriously wounded trying to defend her against the villain's armed retainers. Lancelot sets out to rescue her, but his horse is shot dead by Melliagaunt's archers, and as a result his armour ceases to assist him and becomes a burden. He cannot get at the archers because it weighs him down, and when he tries to continue his journey he finds himself 'sore acombird of hys armoure, hys shylde, and hys speare' (p. 653, lines 41–2). Worse still, when he finally arrives at Melliagaunt's castle – travelling in the requisitioned transport of the title like a prisoner carted off to punishment – the villain refuses to fight him, throwing himself on Guinevere's mercy. The Queen grants him her protection, and as a result all Lancelot's skills, as embodied in his harness, are rendered useless. At the end of the first part of this story, Lancelot has been reduced to a state of helpless jealousy, all his efforts to act as the conventional romance hero having been thwarted either by his enemy or by his lover, neither of whom plays by the rules a knight's harness represents. There could be no more devastating exposure of the many chinks in Lancelot's emotional and physical defences.

Next Melliagaunt succeeds in underscoring the *moral* link between himself and Lancelot, thus breaking down any clear distinctions that might have been signalled by their different attitudes to armour. The night after arriving at Melliagaunt's castle, Lancelot disarms himself and slips into Guinevere's bed, leaving blood on her sheets from a minor injury to his hand. Melliagaunt finds the blood, and accuses Guinevere of infidelity with one of the unarmed knights who were wounded defending her. Lancelot's discarding of his harness here endangers his knightly colleagues and he seeks to make up for this lapse by resorting to the chivalric rules of engagement by which he has always lived: rules that require full body armour for their fulfilment. He challenges the villain to trial by combat, as if Lancelot remains the impregnable entity he has always been thanks to his hitherto unquestioned identity as a top romance hero. But God is the ultimate judge in any such trial, ensuring that the fighter with the best cause will emerge triumphant; and in this case, the hero is saddled with a cause which is decidedly questionable. Guinevere has indeed committed adultery, as Melliagaunt asserts, and Lancelot is forced to equivocate in order to place himself on the side of justice. He therefore challenges his alter ego on the basis not that Guinevere *has not been unfaithful* but that she *has not slept with any of the knights who were wounded in her defence*. This is a blatant prevarication, and its problematic moral status is reflected in the peculiar nature of the trial itself. After a brief bout of hand-to-hand fighting, Melliagaunt surrenders tamely to Lancelot, and chivalry dictates that his opponent must accept his surrender. But Guinevere signals to the hero that her accuser must die, and if Lancelot is to obey her he must once again find a way to circumvent the rules of the judicial game. He persuades Melliagaunt to fight on by offering to disarm his own head and left side to make the contest more even; and he kills the villain, of course, despite this handicap. But the half-armoured state in which he does so confirms his morally compromised position, his susceptibility to the corruption his opponent embraces. And the disarming of his body on the left side in particular, where the heart is, may be taken to demonstrate the extent to which the desires of that body are undermining his role as a knight. The whole adventure, in fact, foreshadows the part that will be played by armour in the final book, which tells how Lancelot's adultery with Guinevere brings about the dissolution of the Round Table and the fall of Arthur.

In this last book, the 'Morte Arthur', it is the lack of armour that takes centre stage rather than its failure. When Lancelot is finally caught *in flagrante delicto* in Guinevere's bedroom, he blames his resulting predicament on his unarmed state: 'Alas,' he complains, 'in all my lyff thus was I never bestad that I shulde be thus shamefully slayne, for lake of myne armour' (p. 676, lines 24–5). The sentence recalls the wording of his earlier complaint when trapped up a tree in the story of the falcon: 'Alas […] that ever a knyght sholde dey wepynles!' (p. 170, line 17). But on that occasion Lancelot could have been taken as a representative 'knyght', the equivalent of any romance hero trapped by treachery. In Guinevere's room, by contrast, his situation is unique: he considers it only in the context of his private misfortunes ('in all *my lyff* thus was I never bestad'), and sees the situation as 'shameful' to himself, not to those who have trapped him. The contrast between the two laments underscores his increasing alienation both from honour or worship and from his fellow knights. He succeeds, of course, in escaping; but he does so by killing one of his comrades of the Round Table, Sir Colgrevaunce, then donning his armour and fighting his way to freedom. The echo here of the many past occasions on which Lancelot borrowed armour serves only to underscore the extent to which what was once a game has become a disaster. And a lack of armour plays a yet more tragic role in the events that unfold in the wake of this episode.

Another knight killed at the door of the Queen's chamber is Sir Agravain, brother of Gawain, Lancelot's best friend. It is a measure of Lancelot's worth that Gawain does not resent his killing. Indeed, Malory fills these late books with loyal friends who refuse to begrudge the hero his unfortunate propensity for causing the deaths of those who love him: the faithful horse in 'The Knight of the Cart' which is shot full of arrows by Sir Melliagaunt's archers, yet continues to follow its master with its guts hanging out; the Maid of Astolat, who dies for love of Lancelot, and her brother Lavayne, who understands why she chose to do so – 'for sythen I saw first my lorde sir Launcelot I cowde never departe frome hym' (p. 639, lines 13–14). Gawain's younger brother Gareth is another of these paragons of loyalty, who never forgets that Lancelot was the man who made him knight. He switches to Lancelot's side in 'The Great Tournament' and fights against his brothers on his mentor's behalf; and when Arthur orders him to accompany Guinevere on her final journey to execution as an adulteress, he refuses to wear his 'harneyse of warre' as a token of solidarity with her absent lover (p. 683, line 41). Inevitably Lancelot rides to her rescue; and inevitably Gareth is killed with his brother Gaheris in the confusion, 'for they were unarmed and unwares' (p. 684, line 26). At this point in the story Lancelot is once again the most efficient of killing machines, as he was before things got complicated. But his repeated compromising of the chivalric code means that his mechanical efficiency is no longer simple. Instead of being deployed in the service of some good cause, his force gets visited on the vulnerable flesh of the men he loves. Even Guinevere suffers from its effects, since the enmity brought about by Gareth's death – the falling out it occasions between Gawain and Lancelot – is responsible both for her husband's downfall and for her penitent demise.

Lancelot himself claims it is the brothers' missing armour that was responsible for their deaths. 'God wolde,' he says at one point, that Gareth and Gaheris 'had ben armed [...] for than had they ben on lyve' (p. 695, lines 41–2). He duly offers to make reparation by forgoing his warrior status, as embodied in his harness, and walking from end to end of the kingdom 'in my shearte', founding religious houses along the way to sing masses for the dead men's souls (p. 696, line 14). But Gawain, too, has by this stage become machine-like – welded, so to speak, into his martial persona. War against Lancelot is the only reparation he will accept. And since everyone knows by now that Lancelot will be victorious in any conflict, the reader sees at once that this mechanical insistence on revenge will usher in the end of Arthur's reign. Malory has reversed the machinery of the romance narrative so that it destroys its most efficient components, the iron-clad knights; and it is the armour that doesn't work which is largely responsible for changing the function of the armour that does, from protective covering to engine of (self-) destruction.

Interestingly, what brings about this major change in the function of armour is a change in the form of Malory's evolving Arthurian narrative. Many of his earlier works consist of a succession of largely disconnected episodes, such as 'A Noble Tale of Sir Launcelot du Lake', with its errant structure neatly but loosely bound together by certain recurrent themes: the tricks Lancelot has to play to get a fight, the tricks played on him to render him vulnerable. But the episodes in the later 'Book of Launcelot and Guinevere' are woven together by tangled chains of cause and effect. The consequences of each episode get played out in the next; and the final book, the 'Morte Arthur' itself, is more tightly woven still, with each tale emerging organically from its predecessor. It is as if armour can only remain impervious in episodic narratives. Where one adventure has few links to the next, the simplicity of armour's function as an emblem of the knightly ideal can be sustained, or can readily be recovered when that function has been compromised. But where competing allegiances – to friend and lover, to King and Queen, to knightly honour and a jealous mistress – get carried over from one episode to the next, armour too becomes permeable. In Malory's interlinked narratives, harness loses its singular purpose and becomes instead, in its uneasy relationship with the flesh it covers (or fails to cover), an increasingly sophisticated device for undermining its bearer's pretensions to honour, for exposing the fissures and flaws in his logic, the anarchic passions he seeks to hide or suppress.

The most sophisticated medieval study of the armour that doesn't work is *Sir Gawain and the Green Knight*; and here too it is the structure of the narrative that renders that armour problematic, as it accumulates associations through the successive sections or 'fits' of the poem. In the opening scene at Arthur's court, where the mysterious Green Knight invites one of the king's champions to strike off his head with an axe, the poet makes much of the stranger's unarmed status: 'Wheþer hade he no helme ne hawbergh nauþer,/ Ne no pysan ne no plate þat pented to armes'. The Green Knight's armourlessness is notable because he possesses a body so eminently suited to martial exploits ('Hit semed as no mon myȝt/ Under his dynttez dryȝe'), and because the giant axe he carries underscores the violent nature of the strange game he proposes.[14] The relationship between flesh and steel, then, is implicitly foregrounded from the moment he rides into the court; and when Sir Gawain takes up his challenge, the blow he aims at the Green Knight's neck constitutes perhaps the most graphic encounter between flesh and steel in English literature: 'þe scharp of þe schalk schyndered þe bones,/ And schrank þurȝ þe schyire grece, and schade hit in twynne,/ Þat þe bit of þe broun stel bot on þe grounde' (lines 424–6). And flesh and steel continue to dominate the poem. The Green Knight survives the blow, by supernatural means, and leaves the court; Gawain sets off to find him the following year, as the game dictates; and his journey begins, as in all proper romances (though not that of Sir Thopas), with a ritual arming, described in loving detail as the knight's servants assemble his harness piece by piece around his torso, limbs and head. But even as this physical armour is assembled the reader is aware that it will prove useless, since the encounter Gawain has agreed to entails exposing his own 'naked' neck to the Green Knight's axe. And that approaching moment of nakedness is recalled again and again throughout Gawain's journey.

It is invoked in the physical rigours of his passage through wintry landscape, during which armour provides no protection against the cold: 'Ner slayn wyth þe slete he sleped in his yrnes/ Mo nyȝtez þen innoghe in *naked rokkez*' (my emphasis) (lines 729–30). It is recalled, too, in the Christmas game Gawain plays while staying at Bertilak's castle. Each day Bertilak goes hunting while his guest remains at home, and at the end of the day they agree to exchange whatever they have obtained in their respective activities. This second contest, like the Green Knight's, involves the conspicuous juxtaposition of flesh and steel: the lavish descriptions of Bertilak's wife, who seeks to seduce her

---

[14] *Sir Gawain and the Green Knight*, ed. J.R.R. Tolkien and E.V. Gordon, 2nd edn., ed. Norman Davis (Oxford, 1979), lines 201–4. All references are to this edition.

guest in her husband's absence, being interlaced with passages that describe the mangling and butchering of animal flesh with steel on Bertilak's hunting expeditions. And as the game goes on, the final encounter between flesh and steel at the Green Knight's chapel draws steadily closer, until it hardly seems surprising when on his final day at the castle Gawain succumbs – not to the lady's seduction, but to her offer of additional armour. The armour, however, is not metal, since we already know that metal is useless. Instead she offers him a girdle, whose virtue, she claims, is to protect its wearer so that 'no haþel under heven tohewe hym þat my3t,/ For he my3t not be slayn for sly3t upon erþe' (lines 1853–4). Gawain accepts the gift and does not declare it to Bertilak that evening, thus violating the terms of the game they have been playing; and next morning he ties it on over his harness like an extra layer of proofing. He never, however, wholly trusts in its protection – witness the flinch he gives when the Green Knight raises his axe. After all, the green girdle represents the love of the body, which is intimately connected through food, drink, desire and clothing with the beasts and growing plants in the world around it; and flesh is frail as grass, as the Bible reminds us.[15] The body's frailty could not be better suggested than by the contrast between the soft silk girdle and the iron plates it binds, or between the fatty tissue of a man's exposed neck and the steel blade that nicks it. The girdle confirms Gawain's humanity, and as such it serves a similar purpose to the armour that doesn't work which he is wearing, and which he knows full well will do him no good when he meets his enemy.

In tying on the girdle over his harness, as Cooper points out in *The English Romance in Time*, Gawain compromises the symbolic function of that armour in an effort to supplement its function as protection.[16] This symbolic function is indicated by the device he wears on his coat armour: a pentangle that stands for five interlinked virtues, each virtue possessing five aspects, together making up the combined qualities to which a knight is expected to aspire. In tying on the girdle, Cooper points out, Gawain obscures the 'endeles knot' of the pentangle with a lace which has two distinct ends ('pendauntez', line 2038) and which is also tied in a 'knot' (line 2376). As a man who knows he has an end – the death that awaits all mortals – Gawain shares with his readers the wish to defer it for as long as possible. He is not made of metal, and metal in any case has been inescapably connected with mortality throughout the poem. Most commentators agree with the Green Knight that Gawain's love of life, as embodied in the girdle, makes him more, not less, attractive.[17]

Gawain's useless armour, which gets trumped by a band of green silk, foreshadows the many varieties of non-functioning armour in the sixteenth

---

[15] Isaiah 40:6 and 1 Peter 1:24.
[16] Cooper, *Romance*, p. 160.
[17] Cooper, *Romance*, p. 52.

century. Spenser, whose iron man Talus embodies the grimmer connotations of fully functional armour, opens *The Faerie Queene* with the portrait of a young knight whose ancient armour does not quite suit him, as if to alert us to the complex relationship between physical, spiritual and political struggle that the poem explores. In the first stanza we read about the 'cruell markes of many a bloody fielde' with which Redcrosse's arms are covered, together with the paradox that 'armes till that time did he never wield'; and Redcrosse certainly does not find it easy to acclimatize himself to his antique equipment.[18] At the half-way point of the first book we find him cavorting with the sorceress Duessa, 'Pourd out in loosnesse on the grassy grownd' (I.vii.6), just at the moment when a ferocious giant happens by. Sir Thopas, too, met a giant when he was unarmed, but unlike Chaucer's hero Redcrosse never gets time to dress for the occasion. 'Ere he could his armour on him dight' the knight finds himself the giant's prisoner (I.vii.8), and has to be rescued by a better-furnished hero, Prince Arthur, whose worth is signalled by his 'glitterand armour' (I.vii.29). This hero, too, has something in common with Sir Thopas – he serves a fairy queen – but fortunately his excellent dress sense is better matched by his prowess and he slays the giant with ease. (Sir Thopas never even gets close to his.) The whole of Spenser's poem, in fact, is populated by people whose outward garb bears a difficult relationship with their inward qualities, or lack of them, and by the time the reader meets Redcrosse's rescuer Arthur she has become well used to scrutinizing the verbal and emblematic context of each character's first appearance in the poem before passing judgement on them.

Even after his rescue by Arthur, who ought to have furnished him with a good example of a knight whose inward qualities match his harness, Redcrosse's armour remains a problem to him. His climactic fight sees him face a dragon whose scales resemble a 'plated cote of stele' (I.xi.9), and whose weaponry (the fire he breathes, his claws, the stings in his tail) render armour a hindrance rather than a help to his antagonist. Finding himself 'seard' through his metal covering (I.xi.26), Redcrosse seeks to remove it and unlace his helmet. Soon afterwards the monster pierces his shoulder with its stings, then grips his shield so fiercely he is forced to cut off its claw, which remains attached to the shield, much to the knight's annoyance. In his 'Letter to Ralegh' Spenser explains that the ancient armour Redcrosse wears is the armour of Christ described by St Paul in Ephesians 6:10–18; but its emblematic associations (the breastplate of righteousness, the shield of faith, the helmet of salvation) keep breaking down in this encounter, and the steel has to be reinforced with further injections of allegory – water from the well of life, balm from the tree of life – whose exact significance (baptism? Eucharist?) has never quite been settled. The intense pain Redcrosse endures in his battle with an enemy who is as well armoured

---

[18] Spenser, *Faerie Queene*, I.i.1. All references are to this edition.

as himself tends to overwhelm the allegorical function of his harness, and only the spiritual remedies applied to his scorched and damaged flesh can restore him to his symbolic identity as the champion of holiness.

Lorna Hutson has written brilliantly about how the feats of physical combat that had been central to medieval romance were displaced in many Tudor romances by verbal combat, in which the hero displays his prowess through eloquence rather than force.[19] It is for this reason, perhaps – the widespread emphasis on debate, and in particular the orator's skill in arguing on both sides of any given question – that there are so many examples of armour that doesn't work throughout the period: from the armour borne by Parthenia in Sidney's *New Arcadia*, which she dons not to avenge her dead husband but to share his fate; to the borrowed armour worn by the hero to hide his identity in Robert Greene's *Gwydonius*, which means that he nearly kills his own father in the romance's climactic fight; or the poisoned helmet put on by Duke Brachiano in John Webster's tragedy *The White Devil*. In each of these cases the tools of defence are transformed into agents of destruction – much as Redcrosse's armour becomes a furnace when he fights the dragon. The analogy with the way a skilful orator could deploy the same material to argue against a cause he had just been defending is irresistible.

The most sophisticated post-medieval treatment of this anti-meme occurs in Shakespeare's most knotty play, *Troilus and Cressida*. Like *The Faerie Queene*, the play can be read as a response to Chaucer, though it also recalls the other English-language versions of the Trojan War that had circulated since the Middle Ages. By the sixteenth century Troy was best known, perhaps, as the focus of a conflict about which radically different accounts had been written, some biased towards the Greek perspective, others towards the Trojan. Debate, then, and many forms of falsification were inseparably attached to the Trojan myth, as we learn from the early fifteenth-century romance *The Destruction of Troy*: 'sum poyetis full prist þat put hom þerto/ With fablis and falshed fayned þere speche,/ And made more of þat mater þan hom maister were.'[20] And armour was the theme of one of the most celebrated debates of the conflict: the quarrel between Ulysses and Ajax over which of them should inherit the arms of Achilles, as described by Ovid in the thirteenth book of the *Metamorphoses*. Ulysses won those arms with his crafty tongue, a result that led to the suicide of Ajax; and in the process Ajax's claim that Ulysses was dedicated to undermining his Greek comrades as much as his Trojan enemies was lent a large measure of credibility.

Shakespeare's play is full of similar debates, between purported friends as

---

[19] See *The Usurer's Daughter: Male Friendship and Fictions of Women in Sixteenth-Century England* (London, 1994).

[20] *Middle English Metrical Romances*, ed. French and Hale, p. 811, lines 33–5.

well as deadly enemies. The Trojans squabble over whether they should continue to keep Helen from the Greeks; the Greeks contend over whether she is worth fighting for, and over how to maintain discipline in the ranks of the pan-Hellenic army. Caught up in these controversies, armour finally loses the chivalric connotations it possessed in romance, becoming instead a potent weapon in the war of words, fought out in a period of stalemate between the Greeks and Trojans when other forms of fighting have been temporarily suspended. Shakespeare punctuates this, one of his most verbally inventive plays, with allusions to armour, and these become increasingly contaminated by the anxieties and inconsistencies of the armour-bearers as the play wears on.

The performance opens with a 'Prologue arm'd', who delivers his speech clad in protective steel. His appearance may have resembled that of the actors illustrated in Henry Peacham's near-contemporary sketch of a scene from *Titus Andronicus*: a peculiar fusion of ancient and modern costume, with Elizabethan vambraces and leg-harness tacked on to Graeco-Roman cuirasses.[21] The Prologue's harness is, however, no sign of heroism, as it was for Shakespeare's Henry V when he wore it at Agincourt. Instead it betrays his lack of 'confidence' in the play itself, an uncertainty that stems in part from his ignorance about which side the audience will favour in this particular version of the Trojan War: 'Like, or find fault,' he tells us, 'do as your pleasures are:/ Now good, or bad, 'tis but the chance of war' (Prologue, 30–1).[22] In these lines, as in the play that follows, values have become contingent, the quality of 'goodness' being assigned to whichever side emerges victorious from the conflict, while 'badness' is used to brand their defeated enemies regardless of any merits they might have had. Under such circumstances, armour is a political weapon, a means of gaining the upper hand in the confusion of battle. Its links with knightly honour have been severed, and with them the romance presumption that a common code of conduct binds together the men who sport it.

The first scene of the play confirms the central part that will be played by armour in the action that follows. Angered, we learn, by a recent defeat at the hands of Ajax, the Trojan hero Hector has 'chid' his wife that morning and 'struck his armourer' before going to battle (1.2.6). His chiding of Andromache, taken together with the blow against a nameless technician, points to the culture of violence that underpins the Trojan claim to be waging war for the best of reasons: in defence of honour and the women they love. Helen may be the official cause of the Trojan War, but she is in reality no more than an excuse to engage in the testosterone-fuelled grapplings that define a young

---

[21] The sketch is reproduced in *The Norton Shakespeare*, ed. Stephen Greenblatt, et al., 2nd edn. (London, 2008), p. 89.
[22] All references to *Troilus and Cressida* are taken from Kenneth Palmer's edition for the Arden Shakespeare (London, 1982).

man's standing in a warrior culture. To drive the point home, Shakespeare later makes Hector use Andromache as an excuse for a return match against Ajax, offering to engage in single combat with any Greek who refuses to acknowledge her as 'a lady wiser, fairer, truer,/ Than ever Greek did couple in his arms' (1.3.274–5). The terms of this challenge effectively explode the Trojan claim that Helen is worth fighting for (if Hector is right, she is neither as 'fair' nor as 'true' as his Trojan wife). This fact, however, is mentioned by nobody; and this is because everyone knows full well that the claim for Andromache's pre-eminence among women has been swiftly cooked up for the single purpose of restoring Hector's pre-eminence among fighting men. The real motive for the single combat is made clear when Hector enters the Greek camp, as enemies on both sides eye up each others' muscles and embrace with more than soldierly enthusiasm. Men are far more interested in their own masculinity than in the women they claim as prizes; and this fact is reflected in the tendency of that most masculine of costumes, armour, to get caught up in the rampant infidelities of its bearers.

Ulysses, for instance, deploys armour prominently in his bid to set his fellow Greeks against each other, while ostensibly inciting them to honourable action. When he informs the Greek commanders that Achilles and Patroclus have been undermining their authority among their men, he reinforces the claim by re-enacting one of the scenes Patroclus is supposed to have acted for Achilles' pleasure: a mocking imitation of the aged warrior Nestor 'Arming to answer in a night alarm', where the coughing and spitting old man 'with a palsy fumbling on his gorget/ Shake[s] in and out the rivet' (1.3.171–5). Whether or not Ulysses is telling the truth about Patroclus, his performance in front of Nestor of Nestor's own ineptitude with his armour is clearly more subversive of the old man's authority than any performance that may have taken place in Achilles' tent. Later, when Ulysses urges Achilles himself to return to military action after an extended hiatus, he tells him that only 'Perseverance' will maintain his heroic status in the public eye: 'to have done is to hang/ Quite out of fashion, like a rusty mail/ In monumental mockery' (3.3.150–3). In saying so, Ulysses encourages Achilles to break his promise to the Trojan princess Polyxena, whom he loves and who has made him swear he will not harm her fellow citizens. This is, then, another treacherous invocation of armour on Ulysses' part. And when Achilles' 'rusty mail' does indeed go to war, first enclosing the body of Patroclus (who dies in it), then on Achilles' own body as he seeks revenge for Patroclus's death, it is more a monument to his serial faithlessness than to his valour. Achilles has betrayed Polyxena with his male lover Patroclus, betrayed the Greeks by making a promise to Polyxena, and betrayed Polyxena by going to war and breaking his promise. When he finally fights Hector in Act Five, the Greek hero is out of condition and unused to wearing armour or carrying weapons ('my arms are out of use', 5.6.16), and it is this that leads him to his final act of betrayal: to have the 'unarm'd' Hector slain by his men-at-arms, the Myrmidons, instead of fighting him hand to hand (5.8.9).

Hector, meanwhile, has a passion for armour that amounts to infidelity, not only to his wife Andromache but to the values he purports to be defending. In the central scene of the play, Act 3 scene 1 – our only extended encounter with Helen, the woman whose 'worth' is cited by both Greeks and Trojans as justification for their conflict – Paris exhorts his purloined lover to encourage Hector to keep fighting by indulging in a little erotic dalliance with his equipment:

> Sweet Helen, I must woo you
> To help unarm our Hector. His stubborn buckles,
> With these your white enchanting fingers touch'd,
> Shall more obey than to the edge of steel
> Or force of Greekish sinews: you shall do more
> Than all the island kings – disarm great Hector. (3.1.145–50)

Paris's request links the act of disarming with a whole sequence of infidelities: Helen's to her husband Menelaus; his own to Helen in encouraging her to seduce his brother; and Hector's to Andromache in being aroused by Helen's 'white enchanting fingers'. Later, it is Hector's armour that points up his forgetfulness of the value he earlier attached to his wife Andromache. When she begs him 'Unarm, unarm, and do not fight today' (5.3.3) – convinced by many omens that he will die if he ignores her warning – he threatens to 'offend' her, for the second time in the play, if she does not lay off (5.3.4). It seems appropriate, then, that armour should also prove his undoing. His last act of war is to pursue a weaponless soldier because he admires his harness ('I like thy armour well', 5.6.28). This is another mark of Hector's inconsistency; he earlier told Troilus that he would never kill a helpless enemy because of his commitment to the rules of 'fair play'. When he kills the fleeing soldier for the sake of his outer covering he describes him as a 'putrefied core' concealed in 'goodly armour' (5.8.1–2); and it is not entirely clear here whether he means that all mortal flesh is effectively putrid or that this soldier in particular was diseased, perhaps with syphilis, another mark of infidelity. There is certainly something rotten about Achilles' actions when he catches Hector 'unarm'd' beside the victim's body. The Greek hero orders his Myrmidons to kill him, which is bad enough; but he then dresses up the unequal contest in a garb of 'fair play', by ordering them to spread the word that Achilles killed the Trojan champion in equal combat: 'On, Myrmidons, and cry you all amain/ "Achilles hath the mighty Hector slain"' (5.8.13–14). In this scene the audience sees history being written; and it looks very much like a scam, fronted by the 'goodly armour' that conceals the cross-infected rottenness of the flesh within.

Shakespeare's play completes the process of conceptually disengaging armour from its bearer and investing it with a grotesque life of its own: a process that had been steadily at work over the preceding two centuries. There are other manifestations of this process, some contemporary with this one, which would be worth holding up as exemplary representations of the complex relationship between human flesh and the rigid social, cultural and moral carapaces we don in a vain attempt to contain and define it. The most notable of these is the armour of Quixote. The inadequacy of this ancestral iron shell (most notably the various home-made helmets with which he seeks to complete it) reflects the weakness of the bearer's ageing brain; but it also embodies his infectious delight in the imaginative glamour bestowed on the world by a romance sensibility, and his determination to invest the world with that glamour whatever the cost to his unguarded head. What is evident, however, is that armour that doesn't work deserves the same close attention Cooper gave to non-functional magic; and that it has enabled equally startling transformations, down the years, of the romance tradition. It is time to polish up the rusty mail.[23]

---

[23] My thanks to Matthew Woodcock for his comments on this essay. He asked me a number of excellent questions I have no space to answer here, among them 'Do you have a sense of when the "armour that doesn't work" anti-meme develops'? The fact that *Beowulf* is the first example I can think of (the episode in which the hero's specially forged iron shield fails him in his fight against the dragon, of course, but more interestingly the whole notion that Beowulf has never managed to fight with weapons because they have always failed him) suggests to me that it is as old as armour itself.

'Of his ffader spak he no thing'
Family Resemblance and Anxiety of Influence in Fifteenth-Century Prose Romance

⊰ MEGAN G. LEITCH ⊱

In recent decades, the traditionally disparaged medieval popular romances have received increased attention.¹ Studies of this previously marginalised genre have, however, tended to remain silent about texts at its own margins, such as the Middle English prose romances. The prose romances are even less frequently allowed into conversation with courtly romances, and if they figure anywhere, it is usually in discussions of Arthurian romance. Yet on the other hand, Malory's Arthuriad still tends to be considered as a genre unto itself, rather than as one among quite a few English prose romances written around the same time. According to Larry Benson, the other fifteenth-century English prose romances 'hardly established a tradition of English secular prose on which Malory could draw for his style', and if silence implies consent, more recent criticism has tended to agree.² This essay aims to explore the extent to which the English prose romances can be read together, as a sub-genre, and as a response to more conventional romances, a response in which the shift in form or medium may be as telling as the shift in content.

One auspicious exception to the relative neglect of the prose romances is Helen Cooper's 1997 essay 'Counter-Romance: Civil Strife and Father-Killing in the Prose Romances', which adumbrates a way in which Malory's *Morte*

---

¹ See *The Spirit of Medieval English Popular Romance*, ed. Ad Putter and Jane Gilbert (Harlow, 2000); *Pulp Fictions of Medieval England: Essays in Popular Romance*, ed. Nicola McDonald (Manchester, 2004); *A Companion to Medieval Popular Romance*, ed. Raluca L. Radulescu and Cory James Rushton (Cambridge, 2009); and the proceedings volumes of the biennial *Romance in Medieval Britain* conference, such as *Medieval Romance, Medieval Contexts*, ed. Rhiannon Purdie and Michael Cichon (Cambridge, 2011).

² Larry D. Benson, *Malory's 'Morte Darthur'* (Cambridge, MA, 1976), p. 21. The lesser known fifteenth-century English prose romances are elsewhere referred to less disparagingly but no less summarily: Derek Pearsall, 'The English Romance in the Fifteenth Century', *Essays and Studies* 29 (1976), 73; Douglas Gray, *Later Medieval English Literature* (Oxford, 2008), p. 180. Mark Lambert mentions a few of them, but only as foils for the *Morte*: see *Malory: Style and Vision in 'Le Morte Darthur'* (New Haven, CT, 1975).

Darthur can be understood as part of a larger insular genre.³ Cooper argues convincingly that these texts take a distinctly darker approach to individual success and chivalric cohesion than is found in earlier verse romances. Yet whereas Cooper focuses on the texts' concerns about family members betraying each other, this essay considers a wider range of familial anxieties: a range that sometimes includes, but goes beyond, betrayal within the family unit or affinity group. For instance, in the late prose romance *Huon of Burdeux* (c.1515), when Earl Amaury, the 'felon traytour', is glossed as 'son to on of the nevewse of the traytour Ganelon', the reader is invited to infer that Amaury is predisposed to be a traitor by blood.⁴ The idea of genetic 'treasonousness' is a recurring axiom in *Huon*; here, this is not a fear that a family will become fractured, but rather a fear that a family will show too much unity, but of the wrong sort. Other Middle English prose romances display a similar anxiety about inherited traits, such as the prose *Siege of Thebes* (c.1450), in which Pollymet, son of Oedipus, articulates his identity by saying 'þat he was of Thebes, son to Jocasta þe quene, but of his ffader spak he no thing'.⁵ Pollymet, it seems, worries about the influence of his father. While these romances worry that negative traits might be inherited, others – such as *Valentine and Orson* (c.1500) and *Melusine* (c.1490s) – worry that positive ones might *not* be. This essay addresses generational and genetic anxieties in these four prose romances and others such as the prose *Siege of Troy* (c.1450), Malory's *Morte Darthur* (1469) and Caxton's *The Foure Sonnes of Aymon* (1488). In so doing, it aims to give renewed attention to an understudied group of romances that testifies to continuities across the customary divide between medieval and Renaissance. Influenced by Cooper's pioneering scholarship on this sub-genre, I will argue that these fifteenth – and sixteenth-century rewritings of romance themselves betray an anxiety of influence that can illuminate matters of 'family resemblance': that is, family resemblance between romances, as well as between the relatives whose relationships they portray.

In Fair Unknown narratives such as *Libeaus Desconus*, *Perceval* and Malory's

---

³ In *The Long Fifteenth Century*, ed. Helen Cooper and Sally Mapstone (Oxford, 1997), pp. 141–62. More recently, see also William Kuskin, *Symbolic Caxton: Literary Culture and Print Capitalism* (Notre Dame, 2008), ch. 5; Joyce Boro, 'All for Love: Lord Berners and the Enduring, Evolving Romance', *Oxford Handbook of Tudor Literature, 1485–1603*, ed. Mike Pincombe and Cathy Shrank (Oxford, 2009), pp. 87–102; Megan G. Leitch, 'Thinking Twice about Treason in Caxton's Prose Romances: Proper Chivalric Conduct and the English Printing Press', *Medium Ævum* 81.1 (2012), 41–69; and Megan G. Leitch, *Romancing Treason: The Literature of the Wars of the Roses* (Oxford, 2015).
⁴ John Bourchier, *Duke Huon of Burdeux*, ed. S.L. Lee, EETS ES 40, 41, 43 and 50 (London, 1882–7), p. 5.4–8. Primary sources are cited first in full, and then by page and/or line number in the text.
⁵ Friedrich W.D. Brie, ed., 'Zwei mittelenglische Prosaromane: *The Sege of Thebes* und *The Sege of Troy*', *Archiv für das Studium der neueren Sprachen und Literaturen* 130 (1913), p. 50.

'The Tale of Sir Gareth of Orkney' and 'La Cote Male Tayle', the romance genre displays a conventional attitude towards familial inheritance. Whether or not these Fair Unknowns know of their parentage, and regardless of the fact that their family origins are, to begin with, concealed from those to whom they must prove themselves within their narrative world, these romance heroes convincingly demonstrate their worthy blood through their conduct. Here, noble progenitors produce noble protagonists, and it is customarily the latter's good manners and military prowess (and good looks) that confirm their elevated identity. Malory's Sir Tor, for instance, is proven to be the son not of the cowherd Aryes who has raised him, but rather of King Pellinor, because Tor is: 'passyngly well vysaged and well made'; rejects manual 'laboure' in favour of martial endeavour; and wants most of all 'to be made knyght'.[6] Merlin's subsequent revelation of the identity of Tor's true father serves only to further underwrite what the narrative treats as self-evident here: that Tor's physiognomy and behaviour are due to a genetic inheritance that differentiates him from the remainder of the cowherd's thirteen sons. The Fair Unknown meme demonstrates the successful passing on of positive traits from father to son even in extreme circumstances;[7] it shows how the romance genre often comfortably espouses the *opposite* of anxiety about inheritance.

Many of the late prose romances, by contrast, manifest a concern that positive traits may not be inherited, and/or that negative traits will be inherited. I would like to suggest that, in this ideological engagement, the prose romances may show an affinity with Chaucerian models of filial inheritance. In debates in *The Canterbury Tales* about whether one can inherit one's character from one's father, Chaucer often suggests that good qualities are not inheritable, or are, as A.C. Spearing observes, not 'naturally bequeathed'.[8] As the Loathly Lady in 'The Wife of Bath's Tale' puts it:

> For, God it woot, men may well often finde
> A lordes sone do shame and vileynye.
> And he that wole han pris of his gentrye
> For he was boren of a gentil hous
> And hadde his eldres noble and vertuous
> And nil himselven do no gentil dedis
> Ne folwen his gentil auncestre that deed is,

---

[6] Thomas Malory, *The Works of Sir Thomas Malory*, ed. Eugene Vinaver, 3rd edn., rev. P.J.C. Field, 3 vols. (Oxford, 1990), p. 100.5–14.
[7] Cooper, *Romance*, p. 3, employs the term 'meme', denoting a cultural gene, to describe the way in which romance motifs replicate and mutate.
[8] A.C. Spearing, 'Father Chaucer', *Writing After Chaucer: Essential Readings in Chaucer and the Fifteenth-Century*, ed. Daniel J. Pinti (New York, 1998), pp. 145–66.

> He nis not gentil, be he duc or erl,
> For vileyns synful dedes make a churl.⁹

Chaucer tends to write of 'gentillesse' and 'courtoisie' as virtues that are performed rather than inherited, that make themselves known in behaviour rather than in bloodlines. Chaucer's courteous Franklin can have a son who does not emulate his virtue, and the clerk in 'The Franklin's Tale' can act with gentility despite not being of gentle birth. From this perspective, gentility, as the Loathly Lady contends, is about living virtuously; it is about what one does, rather than who one is:

> Al were it that myne auncestres were rue,
> Yet may the hye God, and so hope I,
> Grante me grace to lyven vertuously.
> Thanne am I gentil, whan that I bigynne
> To lyven vertuously and weyve synne. (1172–6)

For Chaucer – as far as one can ever pin him down to a view – the new generation seems to be relatively independent, and those who *are* virtuous, like the low-born Griselde in 'The Clerk's Tale', have developed that virtue on their own, or at least have manifested it independently of their birth or class.

This 'Chaucerian' view is sometimes paralleled in the later prose romances, though not always optimistically. For instance, in *Valentine and Orson*, translated by Henry Watson and printed by de Worde in the first decade of the sixteenth century, the twin sons of the Emperor of Constantinople are separated from their parents – and from each other – in infancy, and grow into very different adults. Valentine is taken in as a fosterling by King Pepin of France, while Orson, as his name suggests, is raised by a bear. Pepin is Valentine's uncle, but neither of them know it; Valentine seems to prove that he must be of high birth by the combination of his battlefield prowess and his gentle behaviour. However, this romance does not replicate the Fair Unknown meme of inevitable nobility in a straightforward fashion, since Orson, although by birth indistinguishable from Valentine, shares only his brother's abilities as a warrior, and is otherwise as savage 'as a wylde beest' until his brother manages to partially domesticate him.¹⁰ Here, Valentine's twin brother effectively serves as a 'control group', demonstrating how little of Valentine's virtue is in fact due to inheritance. While the narrative perhaps displays a certain desire to present Valentine's virtue and nobility as innate, the example of Orson, who has received the same inputs as Valentine but has missed out on the civilising

---

⁹ Geoffrey Chaucer, 'The Wife of Bath's Tale', ll. 1150–8, *Riverside Chaucer*.
¹⁰ Henry Watson, *Valentine and Orson*, ed. Arthur Dickson, EETS OS 204 (London, 1937), p. 67.28. The late fifteenth-century French source was printed in 1489.

process,[11] suggests that it is the influence of the French court, rather than Valentine's blood, that underpins his virtue. Here, character is shown to be a product of nurture, rather than nature; aristocratic nature, when left to itself, produces the brutish Orson. Gentility, then, does not necessarily manifest itself where it should.

Valentine and Orson also has an intriguing instance of gentility appearing where it is *not* expected. A distinctly non-aristocratic merchant takes on the role of chivalric defender in this romance, not once but twice. When a squire has difficulty fighting off a wicked archbishop who – dressed 'in the habyte of a knyght' (26.13) – tries to force himself on the empress of Constantinople, 'a notable marchaunt' (30.9) comes to the rescue. The merchant:

> had grete pyte on her/ and sayd to the Archebysshop. Syr leve your enterpryse/ and touche not the lady/ for and the Emperoure knewe of this dede/ he wolde make you deye an evyll dethe before all the worlde. Also soone as the Archebisshoppe under stode the marchaunt speke/ he lefte the batayll quyckly and began for to fle thorughe the wodde. (30.18–24)

It is speech rather than combat that overcomes the archbishop here; yet, more significantly, it is the merchant's intervention, rather than the aristocratic squire's, that saves the empress. Moreover, later, the merchant further inhabits the chivalric role by undertaking a trial by battle to save the empress from the archbishop's false accusation of adultery. During an arduous judicial combat, the merchant falls off his horse and is dragged along the ground by it: 'the marchaunt was so trailed through the fielde that his horse foundred and fell down. And when the horse was down the marchaunt rose up that was valiaunt and hardy' (49.18–21). As this demonstrates, the merchant is not the most adept *chevalier*; however, despite this setback, he is eventually victorious. Clearly, his victory is due to the justice of his cause, and his bravery, rather than to his ability as a warrior. He is no Lancelot; he does not possess superlative martial prowess that could complicate perceptions of a just outcome to a trial by combat. But what this merchant lacks in the physical skills associated with chivalry, he makes up for in terms of the virtues: his behaviour is shaped by a firm sense of right and wrong. Thus, the merchant is effectively the opposite of a Fair Unknown such as Perceval, who has all the skill and ability of a knight but needs to learn the values according to which he should apply his skills. In the fourteenth-century Middle English *Perceval of Galles*, when the protagonist

---

[11] That Middle English literature contributes to what Norbert Elias has termed 'the civilising process' has been demonstrated by Ad Putter, in *Sir Gawain and the Green Knight and French Arthurian Romance* (Oxford, 1995), esp. p. 7; see also Norbert Elias, *The Civilising Process*, trans. Edmund Jephcott, 2 vols. (1939; Oxford, 1978).

first encounters three of Arthur's knights, he has to be disabused of the notion that they are deities:

> Than saide the fole one the filde,
> Was comen oute of the woddes wilde,
> To Gawayne that was meke and mylde
> And softe to ansuare,
> 'I sall sla yow all three
> Bot ye smertly now telle mee
> Whatkyns thynges that ye bee,
> Sen ye no goddes are.'[12]

Here, in contrast to the merchant, Perceval has the ability to fight but not (yet) to perceive right and wrong – or much else, for that matter – correctly. Furthermore, that in *Valentine and Orson* it is not a knight but rather a merchant who risks his life for what is right, for the sake of a wronged lady, suggests that chivalric behaviour can be learned or acquired by those of lower status.

In their implication that the virtues associated with chivalry are more important than the skills, perhaps these merchant-centred episodes in *Valentine and Orson* suggest a recentring of chivalry. This celebration of mercantile integrity (rather than avarice or cunning) seems especially relevant at a time when – as was the case in the late fifteenth and early sixteenth centuries – merchants were themselves increasingly reading romances, particularly as the advent of the printing press in England in the 1470s began to make copies more plentiful and affordable.[13] While Londoners' wills from 1300 to 1450 frequently bequeath religious books but rarely chivalric ones, by contrast, records from the later 1400s show that many copies of romances (such as Caxton's prose romances) were held by London merchants.[14] In addition, aldermen – as wealthy and influential merchants – were knighted in greater numbers during the reigns of Edward IV (1461–83) and Henry VII (1485–1509) than they had been beforehand.[15] Merchants, then, were increasingly given opportunities to aspire to, or to imagine themselves as, part of the knightly classes. It is perhaps all the more surprising that *Valentine and Orson*'s 'notable marchaunt', while rewarded with wealth and favour for his actions (47.30–48.2), is not made a knight afterward. Instead of a reductive incorporation of the best of the Other

---

[12] *Sir Perceval of Galles*, in *Sir Perceval of Galles and Ywain and Gawain*, ed. Mary Flowers Braswell (Kalamazoo, 1995), pp. 289–96.

[13] Yu-Chiao Wang, 'English Romance in Print from 1473 to 1535: Reception and the History of the Book' (unpublished doctoral thesis, University of Cambridge, 2008), p. 74.

[14] Caroline Barron, 'Chivalry, Pageantry and Merchant Culture in Medieval London', *Heraldry, Pageantry and Social Display in Medieval England*, ed. Peter Coss and Maurice Keen (Woodbridge, 2002), pp. 228–30.

[15] Barron, 'Chivalry, Pageantry and Merchant Culture', pp. 223–4 and 240.

(which romance offers when, for instance, virtuous and valiant Saracen knights such as Malory's Priamus and Palomydes become Christians and members of the Round Table), *Valentine and Orson* allows chivalric virtue to pertain to the non-knightly without retracting it afterward. The distinctiveness of this portrayal amongst romances is pointed up all the more by the partial parallel with the Middle English *Octavian*, which survives in two versions that differ in dialect, form and some details, but that both date from the early-to-mid fourteenth century. Like *Valentine and Orson*, *Octavian* features a calumniated queen and twin sons separated from their parents and each other at birth (and in this case both of them are raised by animals). The son who becomes the principal protagonist in this romance, Florent, is raised by the merchant Clement. Clement is rewarded for taking care of the emperor's son in both versions, but in the Northern *Octavian* he is mocked for his bourgeois values and mercantile attachment to money when 'At Clement loghe the knyghtes alle,/ So did the kynges in the haulle',[16] while in the Southern *Octavian* Clement is 'made kny3t/ For hys erdedes wys and wy3t'.[17] *Valentine and Orson* shows more ideological openness in neither mocking its merchant nor reclaiming him for the aristocracy through a knighthood afterward.

While a romance such as *Valentine and Orson* is unable to eradicate the idea that desirable traits might not be inherited, and even suggests that proper aristocratic inheritance might be less important than learned or performed virtue, other late prose romances dwell on the ways in which undesirable traits either are or might be inherited. In John Bourchier's *Huon of Burdeux*, treacherousness and cowardice are figured as inherited traits. The foremost traitor of the matter of France, Ganelon – whose betrayal of Charlemagne results in the death of Roland and defeat at the hands of Saracens – is connected with a traitor central to *Huon*'s narrative in a way that suggests that betrayal runs in the blood. As mentioned earlier, when Earl Amaury, an underhanded enemy of Huon, is described as a 'felon traytour' (5.4), the narrator further specifies that he is 'son to on of the neuewse of the traytour Ganelon' (5.7–8).[18] This idea of infelicitous familial propensities is given more explicit expression elsewhere in the text. For instance, the traitorous inclinations of the duke of Vienna, who wants to kill Huon and claim his wife Esclaramond for himself, are traced as follows: 'this duke Raoull was the untrewest traytoure that ever

---

[16] *Octavian*, in *Four Middle English Romances*, ed. Harriet Hudson (Kalamazoo, 2006), ll. 1253–4.

[17] *Octavian Imperator*, ed. Frances McSparran (Heidelberg, 1979), ll. 1807–8.

[18] John Bourchier, Lord Berners, had a French prose source written in the 1450s and printed by Michel le Noir at Paris in 1513 and 1516. A date of c.1515 is probable for the first English edition of *Huon*: see N.F. Blake, 'Lord Berners: A Survey', *Medievalia et Humanistica* 2 (1971), 119–32; updated by Joyce Boro, 'The Textual History of *Huon of Burdeux*: A Reassessment of the Facts', *NQ* 48.3 (2001), 233–7.

lyved: the which ylnes procedyd by ye duches his mother/ who was doughter to [...] the moost untrewest and falsest traytour' (315.21–5). Here, treacherous behaviour is explicitly figured as an 'ylnes', an explicitly inherited bad condition, or (though the sense of 'illness' as medical malady rather than as a moral disposition may not be otherwise attested until the seventeenth century) an ineradicable disease that is passed on in the genes.[19] Similarly, the actions of a certain Brohart, who acts with cowardice and treacherousness to drown the protector of Huon and Escaramond's daughter Clariet because he wants to marry her, are explained along genetic lines: 'the lyngnage and parentes issued of ye blode of Brohart, [...] always they have bene full of treason' (617.28–30). Reprehensible behaviour, then, is what demonstrates family resemblance in these cases. In this etiology of inheritance, even these nobly born figures cannot escape or rise above negative traits. This seems all the more pessimistic or disturbing when read in conjunction with *Valentine and Orson*'s suggestion that positive traits are not necessarily inherited. In these prose romances as in Chaucer's *Canterbury Tales*, negative traits are naturally bequeathed, while positive ones are not necessarily bequeathed – but are sometimes developed independently.

In another of the prose romances, disloyalty is again a family trait: here, not one that is reproduced across generations, but rather one that distinguishes one generation from another. In *The Foure Sonnes of Aymon*, translated and printed by William Caxton in 1488, Aymon's four sons rebel against their overlord Charlemagne, but their father does not join their rebellion. We are given a rationale for the father's choice to support Charlemagne instead of his sons when another of Charlemagne's supporters, Esmenfray, stresses to Aymon that 'a man of your age shoulde rather deye than he sholde doo ony treyson'.[20] Perhaps this figures treasonousness as a trait one is born with – as it is in *Huon*, except that here in *The Foure Sonnes* it is a disposition one ought to be able to control with maturity. Rachel Moss has discussed this intra-familial divide as a suggestion that Aymon may be a poor father, since the eldest son Renaud reproaches Aymon for siding against his sons by saying that to do so is to act not with 'love of a natureill fader, but [...] rigoure of a stepfader' (83.16–17).[21] Yet even though this aligns Aymon and his sons against each other in a civil war, it is not so much an instance of betrayal within a kin group as it is an instance of

---

[19] *OED*, s.v. 'illness', senses 1 and 3.
[20] William Caxton, *The Right Plesaunt and Goodly Historie of the Foure Sonnes of Aymon*, ed. Olivia Richardson, EETS ES 44–5 (London, 1885), p. 105.28–9.
[21] Rachel E. Moss, *Fatherhood and its Representations in Middle English Texts* (Cambridge, 2013), p. 161. Moss offers a productive analysis of fatherhood in Middle English popular romances alongside gentry letter collections, but, apart from brief mentions of *The Foure Sonnes of Aymon* and Malory's *Morte Darthur*, she does not consider the fifteenth-century prose romances.

treasonous behaviour being exhibited (towards Charlemagne) by the younger generation but not the older. What this distinction between the two demonstrates is that (perhaps unlike a *dis*loyal disposition) a loyal disposition, here, is shown to be *not* innate or inherited but rather performed, selected, or learned over time. Thus, in contrast to the fixed ontology of treacherousness in *Huon*, here in *The Foure Sonnes* the opposite of treacherousness is shown to be susceptible to change; these combine to express a similar pessimism, or perhaps a similar admonitory statement about an urgent need for self-regulation. As in *Valentine and Orson*, nurture is decidedly necessary.

In the prose *Siege of Thebes*, anxiety about negative inheritance is made more explicit – even, or especially, through silences. In the narrative tradition of the matter of Thebes, family relationships are famously problematised by the way in which Oedipus kills his father and marries his mother. However, the mid-fifteenth-century English prose version focuses primarily on the reprehensible behaviour of the next generation, Oedipus and Jocasta's incestuous sons, while making changes to its source's representation of Oedipus that emphasise that the sons inherit their tendencies from their father. In the poem upon which the prose *Siege of Thebes* is based, John Lydgate's c.1422 *Siege of Thebes*, Oedipus is depicted as killing his father when he joins in a 'tornement' at Pilotes, an unfamiliar castle at which he stops on his way to Thebes:[22]

> Edyppus put hymsilf in prees,
> As he that was ay redy to debat,
> Enforsyng hym to entren at the gate,
> Maugré all tho that hym wolde lette.
> And in the pres of aventure he mette
> Kyng Layus and cruelly hym slogh,
> Thow the story writ not the maner howh,
> Ne no wight can of alle the companye
> Be no signe verrely espye
> By whos hond that the kyng was slawe;
> For Edyppus in hast gan hym withdrawe
> And kept hym coy of entencioun. (576–87)

Oedipus does not at this point know that the man he kills is his father; moreover, although Lydgate mentions that Oedipus kills Layus 'cruelly', he does so in a melée, where violence and aggression are expected. The author of the prose version alters this episode in a way that emphasises Oedipus's intemperance, writing instead that:

---

[22] John Lydgate, *John Lydgate: The Siege of Thebes*, ed. Robert R. Edwards (Kalamazoo, 2001), p. 566.

at a Castel beside called Pilotes, lay þe king, making a turney, and a grete feste wheþer þis Edyppes toke his wey *in ful grete rage and oute of mesure* alight a downe, and tyed his horse at þe gate byndyng þe porter to open þe gate in hast; And for cause hit was not opened at þe first worde, with his swerde he smote þe porter, And slewe him. The king stonding in a windowe, seing this case, come sodenly rennyng to þe gate, rehercyng this Edippes, whi he didde þat offense within his Castell. – Edippes holding his swerde drawen in his honde, withoute eny more, *smote þe king his fader, and* þere *slowe him*. (48; emphasis mine)

Here, Layus is again holding a tournament, but, unlike in Lydgate's version, Layus is not himself taking part. In independently emphasising that Oedipus acts in a 'ful grete rage' and kills a relatively unoffending porter and a remonstrating king, the prose author foregrounds Oedipus's angry nature. Oedipus acts 'oute of mesure' – a phrase that Malory habitually applies to his own intemperate characters – at the moment when he 'smote þe king his fader': a rhetorical doubling that again parallels Malory's (later) *Morte Darthur*, since Malory employs an identical collocation when, in the final battle, Mordred 'smote his fadir, kynge Arthure' (1237.18–19). Highlighting Oedipus's trait of intemperance here means that while this episode, as a parricide, is about family betrayal, it also marks an inherited trait, connecting this encounter more strongly with another combat that the prose version relates soon after, in which one of Oedipus's sons also acts irascibly.

Like father, like sons: in the prose *Siege of Thebes*, intemperance is similarly a prominent trait of Oedipus's offspring, Pollymet and Etiocles, who quarrel over their father's throne until their lords convince them to divide the rule of Thebes on an annual basis. Pollymet accordingly leaves Thebes to await his turn elsewhere; when night comes, he shelters from the weather in a porch, and another man, Tydeus, requests to share his shelter. Even though the porch is 'large ynogh' for the two of them, and Tydeus speaks to Pollymet 'in ful gentil and sobre wise' (49), Pollymet gets so angry that he instigates an unnecessary duel with Tydeus. While this intemperate combat also takes place in Lydgate's version, the prose version gives it more weight, not least by choosing to reproduce it while eliding some episodes and most of the moralising glosses that characteristically augment Lydgate's much longer verse version.[23] Lacking the intervening moral exempla and without the divided parts of Lydgate's version, Pollymet's anger-induced combat reads in much closer juxtaposition to Oedipus's own combat, which the prose version *does* reconstrue to foreground intemperance.

When King Adrastus interrupts the duel and asks the pair 'of wens þei were,

---

[23] 'Introduction', in Lydgate, *Siege of Thebes*, ed. Edwards, p. 4; Derek Pearsall, *John Lydgate* (London, 1970), pp. 128–31, 138, 152 and 155.

and of what lynage twey come of', both answer in a way that reveals anxiety about family relationships:

> Tedeus answhering first and seid, þat he was son vnto king Calydon, And shuld be his eyre, And declared unto him þe cause of his exile, and of his metyng þere that tyme with Pollymet. Pollymet told þat he was of Thebes, son to Jocasta þe quene, but of his ffader spak he no thing. (50)

Tydeus mentions his lineage, and *Tydeus* speaks 'þe cause of his exile', but the *text* does not voice it: here, the narrator eschews any explicit reminder of the fact that Tydeus has been exiled for (accidental) fratricide, just as the text – and Pollymet – display unease about Pollymet's shameful parricidal and incestuous father: again, 'of his ffader spak he no thing', nor is there any mention of the fact that he is at odds with his own brother. As a late fifteenth-century reader puts it in an eight-line poem uniquely appended to Bodleian Rawlinson D 82, the one manuscript in which the prose *Siege of Thebes* is extant: 'Unneth a man now may truste his owne broþer.'[24] However, in the English prose romances, this lack of trust extends not only to family relationships, but also to family resemblance. The prose *Siege of Thebes*, that is, shows not only betrayal between those who are expected to be loyal to each other, but also betrayal of the expectation – whether genetic or generic, or both – that members of the same aristocratic family will have and/or inherit positive traits.

Pollymet's concerted silence about his father suggests a desire for his identity and reputation not to be tainted by his lineage. The text and Adrastus collude with this desire when Adrastus dwells upon Pollymet and Tydeus's 'berth, and blode riall', their 'noble and worthi blode' (50), when deciding that they are worthy mates for his two heiress daughters – as though the influence of Oedipus's engendering could be palimpsestually purged by being written over with a 'cleaner' version of their genetic inheritance. At the same time as the text seeks to write off the influence of the previous generation, Pollymet and Tydeus seek to rewrite their family ties: they each marry one of Adrastus's daughters, and 'thes two knightes by alliaunce, loved so truly togidre alwey during theire lyves, þat þere was never truer love founde bitwixt two breþeren' (50). Family, here, is fragile and flawed; text and characters seek to keep its influence at a distance both rhetorically and conceptually, while instead foregrounding acquired relationships that improve upon familial ones – or show what blood ties ought to be, but are not.

We can see this also in what is perhaps the prose romances' best known example of problematic inheritance: Malory's Mordred, who is, like Pollymet,

---

[24] The manuscript is c.1450, and the verse annotation and marginalia are late fifteenth-century: Oxford, Bodleian Library, MS Rawlinson D82, fol. 34r; 'Deceit, III', *Secular Lyrics of the XIVth and XVth Centuries*, ed. Rossell Hope Robbins (1952; Oxford, 1955), p. 101.

the incestuous son of a king. Here, legendary incest again seems to speak to wider anxieties about family inheritance; Mordred, 'the traytoure that all thys woo hath wrought' (1236.26–7), does not inherit his father's virtue, and like the prose *Thebes*, the *Morte Darthur* suggests that fellowship between brothers-in-arms, or *chosen* affinity groups such as the Round Table community, offers a potentially more reliable bond than family.[25] Thus, Malory's *Morte*, in its larger arc as opposed to in its self-contained Fair Unknown episodes, parallels other English prose romances in their attitude toward family inheritance. This distinction can be seen especially clearly in the different ways in which Malory's paragon Gareth relates to his family: on the one hand, in his role as a Fair Unknown in 'The Tale of Sir Gareth', and on the other hand, in his role when divisions instigate the downfall of Arthur and his realm. In his relatively self-contained Tale, Gareth begins with a positive relationship to his family: his stature, bearing, courtesy and military prowess demonstrate that he is 'com of men of worshyp' (294.19–20) en route to this Tale's happy ending with his marriage and the establishment of his chivalric identity. However, in his appearances in the *Morte* when the focus is the overarching Arthurian narrative, Gareth is keen to distinguish himself from his family, who are characterised by their collective ill-will and intemperance (and their treacherousness, like certain families in *Huon of Burdeux*). This attempt to keep negative family influence at a distance even inflects the otherwise happy solidarity of the end of 'The Tale of Sir Gareth', where Gareth chooses a different affinity:

> There was no knyght that sir Gareth loved so well as he dud sir Launcelot; and ever for the moste party he wolde ever be in sir Launcelottis company.
> For ever after sir Gareth had aspyed sir Gawaynes conducions, he wythdrewe hymself fro his brother sir Gawaynes felyshyp, for he was evir vengeable, and where he hated he wolde be avenged with murther: and that hated sir Gareth. (360.29–36)

This commentary, as Kate McClune observes, 'reveals the dark undercurrents of an ostensibly optimistic tale';[26] Gareth, then, seeks to distance himself from the negative traits of his family – like Pollymet in the prose *Siege of Thebes*, though more successfully. When Agravain's ill will prompts him to plot the betrayal of Launcelot and Guenevere and he seeks the support of his family, Gareth is one who responds that he 'woll nat be knowyn of your dedis'

---

[25] On the importance of non-familial relationships in Malory's *Morte Darthur*, see Elizabeth Archibald, 'Malory's Ideal of Fellowship', *RES* 43 (1992), 311–28.

[26] Kate McClune, '"the vengeaunce of my brethirne": Blood Ties in Malory's *Morte Darthur*', *Arthurian Literature* 28 (2011), 89–106; see also Barbara Nolan, 'The *Tale of Sir Gareth* and the *Tale of Sir Lancelot*', *A Companion to Malory*, ed. Elizabeth Archibald and A.S.G. Edwards (Cambridge, 1996), p. 169.

(1161.28–9).²⁷ Both Gareth and Mordred, in different ways, show how anxiety about influence informs the *Morte*'s trajectory.

In the prose *Melusine*, concerns about family inheritance are physical as well as performative. Whereas Melusine acquires her serpent's tail through a curse, Melusine and Raymond's own sons begin monstrous in shape, and, in some cases, monstrous in behaviour too. The first son, Urian, is 'moche fayre, and wel proporcyoned or shapen in alle hys membres/ except his vysage that was short and large/ one ey he had rede, and the other blew.'²⁸ The other sons are a similar combination of the expected aristocratic proportions and fairness with a deformity. For instance, the sixth son, Geffray, is born with:

> in hys mouthe a grete and long toth, that apyered without an ench long and more/ and therfore men added to his propre name Geffray with the grete toth. and he was moch grete and hye, and wel formed and strong, merveyllously hardy and cruel, In so moche that every man fered and dradde hym whan he was in age. (104.26–33)

Both Geffray's physical deformity and his cruelty deviate from hereditary expectations. In fact, he gets so angry when he hears that his brother Froymond has become a monk that he burns down the abbey, killing all the monks including his brother:

> he went out of the Chapter, and shetted the doores fast after hym, and closed thabbot and the monkes therynne/ and incontynent he made al the meyne of the place to bryng there wode and strawe ynoughe al about the Chapter, and fyred it/ and sware he shuld brenne them all therynne, and that none shuld escape. *Thenne came the ten knightes foorth tofore geffray, whiche blamed hym of þat horryble fayttel* sayeng: 'that Froymond, his broþer, was in good purpos, and that happly thrughe hys prayers and good dedes the sowles of his frendes and other myght be asswaged and holpen.' 'By the toeth of god,' sayd thenne geffray, 'nother he nor none monke in this place shal never syng masse nor say prayer, but they shal all be bruled and brent.' *Thenne departed the x knightes from hys presence/ sayeng that they wold not be coulpable of that merueyllous werke.* [...] Geffray anoon after that the ten knightes were departed fro hym, he toke fyre at a lampe within the chirche, and sette the fyre in the strawe all about the Chapter [...] What shuld I make long compte? Wel it is trouth, that all the monkes were brent/ and wel the half of the said Abbey or ever geffray departed thens. (309.1–32; emphasis mine)

---

²⁷ See also Christopher Cannon, 'Malory's Crime: Chivalric Identity and the Evil Will', *Medieval Literature and Historical Inquiry: Essays in Honour of Derek Pearsall*, ed. David Aers (Cambridge, 2000), pp. 159–83.
²⁸ *Melusine*, ed. A.K. Donald, EETS ES 68 (London, 1895), pp. 64.35–65.2.

Geffray does repent afterward, but his wicked intemperance in going through with such an unknightly action despite the censure and counsel of his knights underscores his moral deformity; he has not inherited his father's nature. This is also the case for the tenth son, the aptly named Horrible, who 'brought at hys birth thre eyen, one of the which was in the mydel of his forhed. he was so evyl and so cruel that at the fourth yere of his age he slew two of hys nourryces' (105.9–12). Horrible's murderous conduct partially aligns him with the protagonist of *Sir Gowther*, a text that is extant in two mid-to-late fifteenth-century manuscripts but was composed c.1400, and in which Gowther similarly kills (wet-)nurses in his infancy:

> He sowkyd hom so thei lost ther lyvys,
> Sone had he sleyne three!
> Tho chyld was yong and fast he wex –
> The Duke gard prycke aftur sex –
> Hende harkons yee:
> Be twelfe monethys was gon
> Nine norsus had he slon
> Of ladys feyr and fre.[29]

However, whereas Gowther has been fathered by a devil rather than by his mother's husband, *Melusine*'s monstrous progeny have been fathered by the admirable knight Raymond, and their mother, while a fairy, is aligned with good rather than evil. Thus, whereas the monstrosity of the child in *Sir Gowther* can be explained through his parentage, as a fitting inheritance from a fiend, the monstrous behaviour of the sons in the later prose *Melusine*, by contrast, is a deviation from their parents.

Despite the fact that Melusine and her family are the focus of this text's 'noble' origin narrative for the House of Lusignan, proper inheritance from a chivalric paragon is not at all guaranteed here. In fact, family inheritance is so perverted that the worst offshoot has to be destroyed. Although Melusine, when she is leaving the company of mortals due to the fulfilment of her mother's curse, instructs Raymond to keep Geffray with him because 'he shal preve a noble and valyaunt man' (318.5–6), she orders Horrible to be killed because, she says, 'wete it for certayn, yf he be lefte alyve/ never man dide, nor never shal doo, so grete dommage as he shall' (318.17–18). Raymond accordingly has Horrible trapped in a cave and suffocated in smoke. Thus, this family puts two of its own members to death by fire. Guyon killing Froymond and his fellow monks is an example of the deviant nature of Melusine and Raymond's offspring, while the execution of Horrible is a response to their sons' genetic

---

[29] *Sir Gowther*, in *The Middle English Breton Lays*, ed. Anne Laskaya and Eve Salisbury (Kalamazoo, 1995), ll. 113–20.

deviance; both, however, are markers of the same phenomenon of disastrous family inheritance.

Thus, in many of the English prose romances, positive inheritance is insecure, negative inheritance is all too likely, and both of these conditions are cause for concern. Moreover, in the prose romances, even when aristocratic progenitors do produce admirable offspring, this proper resemblance can be a liability instead of an insurance. While in the prose *Siege of Thebes*, Pollymet inherits his father's intemperance and engages in destructive behaviour until he and his brother Etiocles kill each other in battle, family inheritance initially seems more promising in the prose *Siege of Troy*, the other romance which is similarly solely extant in MS Rawlinson D 82. In the prose *Troy*, Jason's chivalric success in gaining the golden fleece and winning Medea as his bride seems secured by the birth of two strong and attractive sons. However, while Jason's sons inherit their father's physical appearance, this resemblance does not secure their future as it might in a Fair Unknown romance. Here, the sins of the father are visited upon the sons: Jason 'left hir in grete myschef, And toke anoþer lady; And he hadde by Medea ij sones, And by cause they were so like Jason, Medea slewe hem bothe' (276). Thus, whereas in Malory's stories of Gareth and Tor, being handsome and well-built (like their fathers) earns the characters respect and admiration and lends credence to their elevated origins, here the results of this aristocratic family resemblance are catastrophic rather than constructive, showing another way in which, in the prose romances, family anxieties are pervasive and multi-directional.

In considering the role of the anxiety of influence, my aim has been to think not only about representations of inheritance within the prose romances, but also about the texts' own literary inheritance. The romance genre has been productively understood through the theory of family resemblance. This theory recognises that any given characteristic may be absent without obscuring a text's nature as a romance[30] – even the happy ending commonly associated with romance but absent from texts such as the prose *Thebes*, *Melusine* and Malory's *Morte*.[31] These are all late romances: although prose became a medium for romances written in French from the thirteenth century onward, the first extant English prose romances survive from the mid-fifteenth century. I realise I might be accused of special pleading in singling out these romances, because they are not the only ones that fret about family inheritance in this

---

[30] Ad Putter, 'A Historical Introduction', *The Spirit of Medieval English Popular Romance*, p. 2; Cooper, *Romance*, pp. 8–9; Melissa Furrow, *Expectations of Romance: The Reception of a Genre in Medieval England* (Cambridge, 2009), p. 54. The concept is first articulated by Ludwig Wittgenstein, *Philosophical Investigations*, trans. G.E.M. Anscombe (Oxford, 1953), pp. 31–2, and applied to literary genres more generally in Alastair Fowler, *Kinds of Literature: An Introduction to the Theory of Genres and Modes* (Oxford, 1982), p. 41.

[31] Cooper, *Romance*, p. 9.

way; for one thing, the romances I have been discussing were translated from French romances or, in the case of the prose *Thebes* and *Troy*, reworked from earlier English verse romance. And on the other hand, one early sixteenth-century prose romance, *Robert the Devil*, is a version of the *Gowther* narrative, focusing on the son of a devil rather than problematised human inheritance. However, I have been suggesting that anxieties about inheritance are characteristic of many of these late English prose romances to an extent that may indicate something about them as a sub-generic movement. The fact that the translated prose romances manifest the same attitudes toward or anxieties about family inheritance as the prose romances that are altered from earlier English verse or – like Malory's *Morte Darthur* – partially independent from their French sources suggests the selectivity with which this literary culture sought out, reproduced and/or reworked narratives in order to reflect on these anxieties. This argument corroborates recent views of the fifteenth – and early sixteenth-century English prose romances as embodying a distinctive shift toward unhappy endings and censured betrayal.[32] Lack of inherited virtue, negative influence and intemperance are also recurring concerns here, and in moments such as that at which the prose *Siege of Thebes* alters its (English) source in order to highlight destructive intemperance as a worryingly inheritable trait – in ways that match other English prose romances written at this time – this sub-genre's concentration upon such concerns is especially clear.

The composition and survival of these earliest English prose romances coincides with and was informed by the Wars of the Roses and its aftermath.[33] Over the course of a few decades which were troubled by multiple viable claimants to the throne in the wars between Lancaster and York (1455–85) and by a new dynasty seeking to establish itself in the face of rebellions and fears of returned Yorkist claimants during the reign of the first Tudor king, Henry VII, families and neighbours were often divided against each other and old certainties were unsettled.[34] This seems relevant to how these romances – in their prose form, their darker take on family and their narrative arcs – make meaning in part through their tensional relationship to earlier English verse romances. Elsewhere I have argued that the particularly pervasive and admonitory concerns with treason in Malory's *Morte Darthur* and the other English prose romances written prior to c.1500 (including the prose *Siege of Thebes* and *Siege of Troy*, and Caxton's prose romances such as *The Foure Sonnes of Aymon*) distinguish them from those written further into the Tudor period (such as *Huon of Burdeux* and

---

[32] See Cooper, 'Counter-Romance'; Leitch, *Romancing Treason*.
[33] Cooper, 'Counter-Romance'; Leitch, *Romancing Treason*.
[34] Michael Hicks, *The Wars of the Roses* (New Haven, CT, 2010); Charles Ross, *The Wars of the Roses: A Concise History* (London, 1976); Anthony Goodman, *The Wars of the Roses: Military Activity and English Society, 1452–97* (London, 1981), esp. p. 8; S.B. Chrimes, *Henry VII* (London, 1977), pp. 68–94.

Valentine and Orson).³⁵ However, I would like to suggest that it is not contradictory to argue that the broader concerns with family that persist across all of these texts testify, on the other hand, to a different sort of continuity and shared preoccupation across this span. As Tudor governance became more centralised and stable, some concerns seem to have diminished while others remained the same; and new contributions to or incorporations into English romance offered a way of ruminating upon them.

Moreover, in offering a view of these English prose romances as a sub-generic movement, in dialogue with both popular romance and courtly romance, one of the aims of this essay has simply been to suggest that they would repay more critical attention, in form as well as content. Why, indeed, were they written in prose? Prose seems conducive to the registers of these romances through its associations with chronicles and didactic writing;³⁶ with authenticity, verifiability, realism and perhaps a certain 'grittiness'. Prose's claim to *verité*, to being a representation of the truth, perhaps underpins the more unsettling take on family relationships that these particular romances provide. Moreover, writing in prose facilitates expansion as well as elision, creating space for emphasising and recasting. As a medium, prose is flexible; it offers a way of responding to the literary tradition but at a distance. It is partly through the reader's sense of the norms of the romance tradition that the deviations here signify, without removing these prose texts from the romance family.

The prose romances distinguish themselves from the literary inheritance to which they are nonetheless indebted in part by how they represent problems with genetic inheritance. These romances often emphasise that the new generation is independent, as Chaucer does – but more pessimistically, or perhaps with more admonitory emphasis. This 'Chaucerian' resonance suggests a greater degree of sophistication or nuance in these understudied prose narratives than has usually been attributed to them; although their take on the lack of interdependence between rank and virtue is usually more conservative than Chaucer's (with the exception of *Valentine and Orson*'s portrayal of its merchant in shining armour), they nonetheless offer an ideological clear-sightedness here that we do not usually expect from popular verse romances, let alone the yet more disparaged prose ones. Moreover, if the new generation is prone to either inherit negative traits or fail to inherit positive ones, then there is all the more need for the romance genre's characteristic encouragement of young readers to emulate proper conduct. The prose romances, by

---

[35] Leitch, *Romancing Treason*.
[36] See Cooper, *Romance*, p. 363, and Ian A. Gordon, *The Movement of English Prose* (London, 1966), pp. 53 and 59. A similar argument is made with respect to medieval French literature in H.J. Chaytor, *From Script to Print: An Introduction to Medieval Vernacular Literature* (1945; London, 1966), and French chronicles in particular in Gabrielle M. Spiegel, 'History, Historicism, and the Social Logic of the Text in the Middle Ages', *Speculum* 65.1 (1990), pp. 80–2.

offering an ethical discourse that perhaps operates more through negative exempla than through the positive examples more customary of verse romance, participate in the didacticism of romance, but pursue a more forbidding mode of self-fashioning.[37]

Since the term 'the anxiety of influence' invokes the spectre of Harold Bloom, it might be worth acknowledging his background presence directly, despite the caveats concerning Bloom's model of literary influence and its anxieties. Bloom's idea of writers responding to other writers through a 'clinamen' or swerve is relevant here: this is a model in which influence is shown through difference.[38] Like some of the characters these prose romances portray, and a bit like Chaucer when he cites the made-up Lollius rather than Boccaccio as his source for *Troilus and Criseyde*, the writers of these prose romances seek to distance themselves from their verse-writing forebears. In both form and content, these texts present themselves partially independently, in a way that nonetheless emphasises, or makes meaning through, their relationship to the tradition from which they are descended. The disturbing murder of Jason's heirs and the execution of Raymond's son Horrible both emblematise the way in which the Middle English prose romances respond to the genre by killing the confidence in proper inheritance that infuses earlier popular romance, lingering instead on delinquents and disconcerting traits.

---

[37] On romance's didacticism, see Furrow, *Expectations of Romance*, and Phillipa Hardman, 'Popular Romances and Young Readers', *Companion to Medieval Popular Romance*, ed. Radulescu and Rushton, pp. 150–64. My use of the term 'self-fashioning' is, of course, indebted to Stephen Greenblatt, *Renaissance Self-Fashioning: From More to Shakespeare* (Chicago, 1980), though Greenblatt would perhaps not approve of the suggestion that an early modern mode might have inherited anything from the late medieval.

[38] Harold Bloom, *The Anxiety of Influence: A Theory of Poetry* (Oxford, 1973), p. 14; I refer to Bloom's model loosely, as I am not primarily concerned here either with poets or with named authors responding to other named authors in ways that are designed to ensure their own immortality; I am concerned, rather, with responses to or within a genre or tradition, in a more flexible, but nonetheless pointed, way. On another level, invoking the anxiety of influence while discussing filial relationships in a festschrift for one's former supervisor may seem a facetious gesture, but I hope it may serve as a token of my indebtedness to the generosity and rigour of Helen Cooper's supervision and scholarship – and especially to her essay on 'Counter-Romance', which inspired the 'swerve' of both this essay and my doctorate.

Writing Westwards
Medieval English Romances and their Early Modern Irish Audiences

⊰ AISLING BYRNE ⊱

In the early 1630s, the Irish historian Geoffrey Keating addressed the question of the historicity or lack thereof of the pantheon of Gaelic heroes known as the *Fian*. In terms that recall similar debates over Arthur and his knights, he cites oral tradition, ancient documents and surviving monuments as evidence for the reality of these ancient heroes. However, he notes that, even if the individuals involved existed, not everything written about them should be taken as historically accurate:

> Agus dá n-abradh aoinneach nach inchreidthe mórán dar scríobhadh ar an bh-Féin, is deimhin gurab fíor dó é, óir ní raibhe ríoghacht san bhith is nach scríobhthaidhe ré linn na Pagántachta sceoil da ngairthí *fabulae*. Féach *Ridire na Gréine*, *Bevis of Hamton*, *Huon of Burdex*, agus a samhail oile sin do scríobhadh lé linn an Chreidimh féin.

> (And should anyone say that much of what has been written about the *Fian* is not to be believed, he would certainly state the truth; for there was no kingdom in the world in which there were not written tales called *fabulae* in Pagan times, for example, the *Knight of the Sun*, *Bevis of Hamton*, *Huon of Burde[u]x*, and other such like, which were written even in the time of the Faith.)[1]

Keating's literary allusions here have generally been passed over by scholars, but they merit some examination. Of the three texts cited, we only have firm evidence for the circulation of one, *Sir Bevis of Hampton*, in Ireland before this point. Yet Keating, writing in Irish for an Irish audience, holds these texts up as examples of narratives with which he clearly expects his readers to be familiar. In the case of 'Huon of Burdex', the form in which the title is given suggests Keating is thinking of the romance as an English text, rather than a French one, probably in the version translated by Lord Berners around 1515 and which

---

[1] Geoffrey Keating, *Foras Feasa ar Éirinn: the History of Ireland*, ed. David Comyn and P.S. Dinneen, 4 vols. (Dublin, 1902–14), 4: 326–7.

went through numerous editions throughout the sixteenth century.[2] *Bevis of Hampton* was translated into Irish from Middle English at the end of the fifteenth century,[3] but once more the form that Keating gives for the title is so far removed from the form of the hero's name in that Irish translation – *Bibus o Hamtuir* – that it seems likely that he knew the romance in English. *Ridire na Gréine*, which translates as the 'Knight of the Sun', is a less easily identifiable text. Cecile O'Rahilly suggests that it is a reference to a late medieval Arthurian text apparently original to Ireland, *Eachtra an Mhadra Mhaoil* (The Adventure of the Cropped Dog), which first appears in a manuscript dated to 1517.[4] In *Eachtra an Mhadra Mhaoil* Arthur's knights are confronted by an enemy called *Ridire an Lóchrainn*, which might be translated as the 'Knight of Light' or the 'Knight of the Lantern' – a title very similar to the 'Knight of the Sun'. This theory gains in credibility when the evidence of a near contemporary lament by one Dáibhí Cúndún is taken into account. This poem, written in the 1640s or 1650s, includes a clear reference to *Eachtra an Mhadra Mhaoil* in which the poet uses the title 'Ridire na Gréine' when describing Arthur's nemesis.[5] However, the Irish text is never actually given that title in any of the surviving manuscripts or in allusions to it elsewhere and there is another possibility that should not be discounted: Keating may be referring to the *Espejo de principes y cavelleros* (Mirror of Princes and Knights) by Diego Ortuñez de Calahorra, which was also known as *El Cavellero del Febo* (The Knight of the Sun). The work was written in the middle of the sixteenth century and translated into English by Margaret Tyler in 1578 as the *Mirror of Princely Deeds and Knighthood*, though (as in Spain) it was also widely known as the *Knight of the Sun*.[6] Both the Spanish and English versions were highly popular. By 1615, the *Knight of the Sun* had attained sufficient popularity in England to be included in a short list of representative chivalric romances in Samuel Rowlands' satirical poem *The Melancholy Knight*.[7]

Keating, of course, had a wide range of reference points beyond the native tradition and his reading in chronicle, historical and pseudo-historical

---

[2] Cooper, *Romance*, p. 420.
[3] F.N. Robinson, ed. and trans., 'The Irish Lives of Guy of Warwick and Bevis of Hampton', *Zeitschrift für Celtische Philologie* 6 (1908), 9–180, 273–338, 556.
[4] R.A.S. Macalister, ed., *Two Irish Arthurian Romances: Eachtra an Mhadra Mhaoil, Eachtra Mhacaoimh-an-Iolair*, ITS 10 (London, 1908).
[5] Cecile O'Rahilly, ed. *Five Seventeenth-Century Political Poems* (Dublin, 1952), pp. 40, 123n.
[6] Margaret Tyler, *Mirror of Princely Deeds and Knighthood*, ed. Joyce Boro (London, 2014).
[7] 'I have red over (while youths glasse did run)/ Sir Lancelot of the Lake, the Knight of th' Sun,/ Sir Triamour, Sir Bevis, and sir Guy,/ Fowre sonnes of Amon, hors'd so gallantly': Samuel Rowlands, *The Complete Works of Samuel Rowlands*, ed. Edmund Gosse, 4 vols. (Glasgow, 1860), 2: 8 (texts are paginated individually).

material is well documented.⁸ One of his primary concerns is rebutting the various claims about Ireland made by Gerald of Wales, but he also displays acquaintanceship (direct or indirect) with the works of Bede, Nennius, Geoffrey of Monmouth, Ranulf Higden, John Speed, Raphael Holinshed, Edmund Spenser, Edmund Campion, William Camden, George Buchanan and Hector Boece. Although Keating trained as a priest in France and may have encountered some of this material there, many of the texts he cites were printed too late for him to have encountered them before he returned to his home country to serve as a priest in Tipperary.⁹ Clearly he was able to source a wide range of historical material in the apparently unpromising environment of rural Gaelic Ireland. It is clear that chapbook romances circulated in Ireland,¹⁰ but most of our evidence for this comes from urban areas and their Anglophone communities. Keating's passing allusion suggests a Gaelic-speaking world where non-native literary material of this sort was also known and read.

The purpose of this essay is to give an outline of some of the evidence for medieval romances from England circulating in Ireland between the fifteenth and seventeenth centuries. As Helen Cooper has demonstrated in the case of England, the romance genre was particularly successful in retaining its vitality and popularity across the transition from medieval to Renaissance. A similar tenacity can be observed in the Irish context, though the historical circumstances and the extent and nature of the surviving evidence are rather different. This literature appears to arrive in Ireland at the very end of what we think of as the Middle Ages. Irish translations of such texts do not tend to survive in manuscripts from earlier than the second half of the fifteenth century.¹¹ Indeed, the arrival of these medieval texts in Ireland seems, in some contexts, to be a result of social and historical currents elsewhere associated with the 'Renaissance'. Furthermore, a number of these texts only survive in seventeenth-century copies and the true impact of medieval foreign narratives on more local literary trends only becomes evident in that period. The Irish translations from foreign vernaculars that appear at the end of the fifteenth century are of texts that had already gained a wide readership in England:

---

⁸ Bernadette Cunningham, *The World of Geoffrey Keating: History, Myth and Religion in Seventeenth-Century Ireland* (Dublin, 2000), p. 83. See also Anne Cronin, 'The Sources of Keating's *Forus feasa ar Éirinn*', *Éigse* 4 (1945), 235–79.
⁹ Cunningham, *Geoffrey Keating*, p. 83.
¹⁰ Raymond Gillespie, 'Print Culture 1550–1700', *The Oxford History of the Irish Book, III: The Irish Book in English 1550–1800*, ed. Raymond Gillespie and Andrew Hadfield (Oxford, 2006), p. 26.
¹¹ On the translation of non-native material in medieval Ireland generally, see Nessa Ní Shéaghdha, 'Translations and Adaptations into Irish', *Celtica* 16 (1984), 107–24. There are also brief accounts of medieval translating activities in Robin Flower, 'Ireland and Medieval Europe', *Proceedings of the British Academy* 13 (1927), 271–303; and Michael Cronin, *Translating Ireland: Translation, Languages, Culture* (Cork, 1996).

for instance, Mandeville's *Travels*, *Guy of Warwick*, *Bevis of Hampton* and *Octavian*. The first book printed by William Caxton, *The Recuyell of the Histories of Troie*, was translated into Irish shortly after its initial appearance in print around 1474.[12] Irish readers do not exhibit significantly different tastes in this sort of reading than audiences from Britain and there is a strong case for a more thoroughly 'archipelagic' approach to the study of medieval English texts. Romance, broadly conceived, seems to have been a particularly popular genre among foreign literature read in Ireland and its tenacious hold on Irish audiences well into the early modern period mirrors its endurance in Britain.[13]

The story generally told about Irish literary culture in this period is one that ends with a whimper, rather than with a bang. Few literary or cultural historians would use the term 'Renaissance' when writing of Ireland.[14] The changes wrought by the upheavals of the sixteenth and early seventeenth centuries are usually expressed in terms of a distinction between 'medieval' and 'early modern'. In part, this is because 'early modern' is a label that can be voided of positive associations, particularly associations of cultural growth, in a way the term 'Renaissance' cannot. Furthermore, scholarship on Ireland in this period has often equated the term 'Renaissance' with something 'other', with foreignness, noting the easy meshing of 'Renaissance' values and imperialism in the work of a writer like Edmund Spenser. As Ann Dooley notes, when treating early modern Ireland it is easy to come to the conclusion that 'we are dealing here with [...] a classic example of conquistadorism, of a colonizing, European-Renaissance imperialism confronting in the other, in its Irish neighbours, its own archaic and barbarian face'.[15]

Be that as it may, there is significant overlap between the cultural currents that appear to have popularised foreign vernacular narrative in Ireland and those associated with 'Renaissance' trends elsewhere. Our most significant single witness to the circulation of foreign books in medieval Ireland is the Kildare Rental (London, British Library MS Harley 913), which includes two inventories of the library of the most powerful magnates in Ireland in that

---

[12] Gordon Quin, ed., *Stair Ercuil ocus a Bás: The Life and Death of Hercules*, ITS 38 (Dublin, 1939).

[13] For an overview of the diffusion of English romance in Ireland in the late Middle Ages, along with a checklist of medieval and early modern manuscripts of translations into Irish, see my essay 'The Circulation of English Romance in Medieval Ireland', *Medieval Romance and Material Culture*, ed. Nicholas Perkins (Cambridge, 2015), pp. 183–98.

[14] For recent work that debates the question of a 'Renaissance' in Ireland, see Thomas Herron and Michael Potterton, eds., *Ireland in the Renaissance, c.1540–1660* (Dublin, 2007); Jason Harris and Keith C. Sidwell, eds., *Making Ireland Roman: Irish Neo-Latin Writers and the Republic of Letters* (Cork, 2009); Michael Potterton and Thomas Herron, eds., *Dublin and the Pale in the Renaissance* (Dublin, 2011).

[15] Ann Dooley, 'Literature and Society in Early Seventeenth-Century Ireland: The Evaluation of Change', *Celtic Languages and Celtic Peoples*, ed. Cyril J. Byrne, Margaret Harry and Pádraig Ó Siadhail (Halifax NS, 1992), p. 516.

period, the Fitzgerald Earls of Kildare.[16] The first inventory dates from the late 1490s, probably between 1497 and 1500; the second is roughly twice as long and dated at 1531. The lists give a remarkable picture of a book collection in a state of considerable expansion over the course of three decades and between them the lists feature over 100 texts in Latin, French, English and Irish. The collection bears close comparison with the sorts of texts that were collected and read by educated nobility across Britain and north-west Europe in this period, and which ultimately reflected trends originating in the cultural efflorescence of the court of Burgundy, often termed the 'Burgundian Renaissance'. This sort of literature combined a valorisation of classical figures and texts with a deep reverence for the cult of chivalry and the idea of crusading. It was highly didactic, where 'ideas derived from Greek and Roman history merged with medieval precedents to form a corpus of writing concerned essentially with questions of individual reputation'.[17] The influence of these cultural currents is most evident in the number and titles of the books the Fitzgeralds owned that fell within the categories of history, romance, biography and manuals of conduct and chivalry. Some of these may have been purchased in, or imported from, France, and others may have been acquired in England. A work particularly characteristic of this fashionable literature is Raoul Lefèvre's *Le Recueil des Histoires de Troyes*. The work combines classical material with the attitudes of chivalric romance and the Earls seem to have acquired a copy some time after 1500.[18] Lefèvre was chaplain to Philip the Good of Burgundy and completed the book in 1464. The *Recueil* is characteristic of the sort of romance writing favoured by the Burgundians – lengthy, sober and edifying. It became the first work printed in English, when Caxton produced a translated edition in either Bruges or Ghent around 1474.[19]

The entry in the Kildare Rental is not the only evidence for the circulation of this particular work in Ireland. An Irish translation was made from Caxton's English version, probably before the 1490s. The ownership evidence in

---

[16] These two lists were transcribed in Gearóid Mac Niocaill, ed., *Crown Surveys of Lands, 1540–41, with the Kildare Rental Begun in 1518* (Dublin, 1992), pp. 312–14, 355f. My article 'The Earls of Kildare and their Books at the End of the Middle Ages', *The Library* 14 (2013), 129–53, explores the history and contents of the library at Maynooth in detail.

[17] Malcolm Vale, *War and Chivalry: Warfare and Aristocratic Culture in England, France and Burgundy at the End of the Middle Ages* (London, 1981), p. 15. For the Burgundian court as a model for Europe in general in this period, see Werner Paravicini, 'The Court of the Dukes of Burgundy: A Model for Europe?', *Princes, Patronage and the Nobility: The Court at the Beginning of the Modern Age*, ed. Ronald G. Asch and Adolf M. Birke (Oxford, 1991), pp. 69–102. For its impact on Elizabethan England, see Gordon Kipling, *The Triumph of Honour: Burgundian Origins of the Elizabethan Renaissance* (The Hague, 1977).

[18] Byrne, 'The Earls of Kildare', 147.

[19] On Caxton's ties to the Burgundian court and interest in Burgundian culture, see Diane Bornstein, 'William Caxton's Chivalric Romances and the Burgundian Renaissance in England', *English Studies* 57 (1976), 1–10.

the surviving manuscript of this translation gives some sense of the potential penetration of works of this sort through the various echelons of Irish society. Caxton's *Recuyell* survives alongside the Irish versions of *Guy of Warwick* and *Bevis of Hampton* in Dublin, Trinity College MS 1298, a late fifteenth-century manuscript.[20] All three romances are unique to this manuscript and all appear to be in the hand of their translator, Uilliam Mac an Leagha. Marginalia in this codex provides strong evidence that the works were produced for a minor branch of the Fitzgeralds, the Fitzgeralds of Allen.[21] The family was not a particularly prominent one and they have left little mark on the historical record. They owned a fair sized property at Kilmeage, Co. Kildare, but their level of prosperity was unremarkable by gentry standards. However, though the Fitzgeralds of Allen had many dealings with the Earls of Kildare in the period, there is no evidence that they drew on the rich and relatively nearby resources of the Earls' library when producing their own reading material. None of the three texts unique to this manuscript are mentioned in the Earls' library lists, and the *Recuyell* is, of course, translated from English, not from the French version owned by the Earls. The exemplars for the three Irish translations appear to have been sourced independently. The apparent ready availability of English literature to a relatively obscure family like the Fitzgeralds of Allen is another indicator that these texts may not have been difficult to come by. These texts reflect similar fashionable tastes to those in evidence in the Kildare inventories. *Guy of Warwick* and *Bevis of Hampton* are chivalric romances with a crusading emphasis and, in the case of *Guy of Warwick* in particular, a pronounced religious dimension. They are joined in this manuscript by the Irish translation of *Fierabras*, a text in a similar thematic vein and of a similar tone, which also survives in other copies.[22] The fact that reading material reflecting similar fashionable tastes was in the hands of both the Earls of Kildare and this relatively insignificant branch of the Fitzgeralds may give some hint as to the extent to which texts fashionable in England and in France and the Low Countries were popular and available in Ireland in this period.

The Irish *Fierabras* also provides us with the most extensive evidence for the popularity and survival of some of these translations into the early modern period. There are eight surviving medieval manuscripts of the text (the highest number of any translated romance), but the work also appears in several

---

[20] The Irish *Guy of Warwick* and *Bevis of Hampton* have been edited and translated in Robinson, 'Irish Lives', 9–180, 273–338, 556.

[21] For an analysis of the ownership evidence, see Aisling Byrne, 'Family, Locality and Nationality: Vernacular Adaptations of the *Expugnatio Hibernica* from Late Medieval Ireland', *Medium Ævum* 82 (2013), 112.

[22] The Irish *Fierabras* is edited and translated by Whitley Stokes as 'The Irish Version of Fierabras', *Revue Celtique* 19 (1898), 14–57, 118–67, 252–91, 364–93.

eighteenth-century manuscripts in somewhat adapted form.[23] The Irish *Fierabras* appears to have been translated twice in medieval Ireland, firstly into Latin from a version of the French *chanson de geste*, and thence into Irish. The sole surviving manuscript of the Latin version is Dublin, Trinity College, MS 667 – a miscellaneous manuscript from the 1450s that appears to have been compiled by Franciscans in the south-west midlands of Ireland.[24] A number of Latin works that feature in Trinity 667 also appear in Irish translation in the late fifteenth century. Among these are the *Pseudo-Turpin Chronicle* and *De Inventione Sanctae Crucis*, the translations of both of which are closely associated with the Irish *Fierabras* in the extant manuscripts.[25] Although it is several folios removed from the Latin *Fierabras* in Trinity 667, an Irish rendering of the *Inventio* functions as a prologue for *Fierabras* in manuscripts of the Irish translation. The Irish translation of the *Pseudo-Turpin Chronicle* follows directly after *Fierabras* in three of the eight surviving medieval manuscripts of the romance. The *Pseudo-Turpin Chronicle* occurs in a distinctive version in Trinity 667 and that bears closest comparison to the Middle English translation now preserved in the Huntington Library. It appears that the *Pseudo-Turpin Chronicle* in Trinity 667 reflects a distinctively insular tradition of the text that varied in small ways from the continental one.[26] The close association of this text with the *Inventio* and the *Fierabras* suggest that these texts might also have been brought to Ireland from England, rather than from continental Europe.

There is a strong crusading emphasis among the romance texts read and adapted into Irish in the second half of the fifteenth century. This is unsurprising. The upsurge in crusading fervour that attended the Fall of Constantinople in 1453 led to an increased interest in crusading texts in the second half of the fifteenth century.[27] A good deal of the widespread popularity of Charlemagne texts, like *Fierabras* and *Pseudo-Turpin*, throughout medieval Europe in earlier periods is owed to their close engagement with crusading ideology. Charlemagne's dealings with the pagan Saxons and, in particular, his campaigns in Islamic Spain, on which these two texts focus, were widely seen as precur-

[23] I am grateful to Emily Copeland (University of Edinburgh) for this information.
[24] The only edition of this Latin *Fierabras* text is an unpublished thesis: Michael Howard Davies, 'Fierabras in Ireland: The Transmission and Cultural Setting of a French Epic in the Medieval Irish Literary Tradition' (unpublished PhD thesis, Edinburgh University, 1995). The fullest description of the manuscript is in Marvin L. Colker, *Trinity College Library Dublin: Descriptive Catalogue of the Medieval and Renaissance Latin Manuscripts*, 2 vols. (Dublin 1991), 2: 1123–64.
[25] The Irish translation of *Pseudo-Turpin* has been edited as Douglas Hyde, ed., *Gabháltais Shearluis Mhóir: The Conquests of Charlemagne*, ITS 19 (London, 1917).
[26] The relationship of the Trinity 667 text to other versions of the *Chronicle* is discussed in Stephen H.A. Shepherd, 'The Middle English *Pseudo-Turpin Chronicle*', *Medium Ævum* 65 (1996), 19–34.
[27] Helen Cooper, 'Romance After 1400', *The Cambridge History of Medieval English Literature*, ed. David Wallace (Cambridge, 1999), pp. 698–9.

sors to the crusades. Accordingly, the late fifteenth century sees a renewed engagement with his legend across Europe. Indeed, the way in which the Charlemagne material is assembled in Trinity 667 also reflects wider trends and returns us to the wide-reaching influence of Burgundian court culture.[28] Michael Howard Davies has drawn attention to the apparently close relationship between the *Fierabras* translations and the *Pseudo-Turpin Chronicle* and suggests that the near contemporary work of David Aubert and Jean Bagynon might provide an instructive analogue to the treatment of these texts in the Irish tradition.[29] Aubert produced a two-volume Charlemagne cycle for Philip the Good in the years after the Fall of Constantinople by combining a range of source texts, both Latin and vernacular. To open his compilation he adapted the *chanson de geste* version of *Fierabras* into prose and translated the *Pseudo-Turpin Chronicle* into French to fill out the account of Charlemagne's activities in Spain. A similar linking of *Fierabras* and the *Pseudo-Turpin Chronicle* is visible in Jean Bagnyon's 1478 Charlemagne narrative, which draws on the latter text to create an epilogue for a prose version of the former.[30] The adaptation of *Fierabras* into Latin prose in Ireland creates a more obvious connection between it and the *Pseudo-Turpin Chronicle* and may have constituted the first step in transforming both into a composite text. The integration of the *Inventio* account into the *Fierabras* narrative evident in the Irish translations of these texts may also have formed part of such a programme. *Fierabras* and the *Pseudo-Turpin Chronicle* are never explicitly knit together in the Irish manuscript tradition, but their adjacent placement in several Irish manuscripts may also suggest that a composite Charlemagne text that synthesised this material was at one point envisaged.

Less programmatic interactions between translated texts of this period are also apparent. A translation of the insular version of the romance of *Octavian* shows clear influence from the text of the Irish *Fierabras*.[31] The Irish adaptor has enhanced the crusading theme of the work by reframing this romance within a Carolingian setting (no other version of the narrative makes any reference to Charlemagne at all), inserting brief episodes relating to Charlemagne and characters like Roland and Ogier le Danois. The tell-tale evidence that these interpolations derive from knowledge of a *Fierabras* text from the Irish tradition is the fact that the same distinctive, Latinised (and in some cases erroneous) renderings of the names of Charlemagne's vassals appear in the Irish

---

[28] Donald Bullough, 'Recycling Charlemagne in the Fifteenth Century, North and South', *Early Medieval Europe* 3 (2003), 389–97.
[29] Davies, '*Fierabras* in Ireland', 32–5.
[30] Davies, '*Fierabras* in Ireland', 35.
[31] The Irish *Octavian* was edited under the title *Sechrán Na Banimpire* (The Wanderings of the Empress) in Carl Marstrander, 'Sechrán Na Banimpire', *Ériu* 5 (1911), 161–99.

Fierabras, its Latin original and in the Irish *Octavian*.[32] This interpolation confirms what was already apparent from the number of surviving manuscripts: the circulation of the Irish *Fierabras* seems to have been particularly extensive.

With the Irish translation of *Octavian* we encounter a work that seems very likely to be late medieval, but which survives in a copy from the late seventeenth century. The sole copy of the Irish translation is preserved in an early modern manuscript, Dublin, Royal Irish Academy MS Stowe B iv 1 (also known as MS 236a).[33] From the evidence of the marginalia, this manuscript can be dated with relative certainty to between 1671 and 1674 and appears to have been chiefly written in the Shancoe district of Co. Sligo, in the north-west of Ireland.[34] The sole scribe signs himself 'David Duiginanus' at no fewer than twenty-nine points in the volume.[35] This is Dáibhí Ó Duibhgeannáin (David O'Duigenan, *fl.* 1651–96), a member of the learned family of Ó Duibhgeannáin who is also responsible for two other manuscripts now held in the Royal Irish Academy.[36] Ó Duibhgeannáin was a disciple of the seventeenth-century annalists known as the 'Four Masters' and his work reflects similar antiquarian interests – his manuscripts preserve much medieval material that would otherwise have been lost in the political and social tumult of early modern Ireland.[37] The material preserved alongside the Irish *Octavian* is largely medieval in origin and includes texts of *Cath Muighe Rath* (The Battle of Magh Rath), *Buile Shuibhne* (Sweeney's Frenzy), *Táin Bó Flidhais* (The Raid of Flidais's Cattle), *Leighes Coise Chéin* (The Healing of Cian's Leg) and *Tochmarc Becfhola* (The Wooing of Becfola). The Irish *Octavian* is preserved towards the end of the manuscript, over fols. 240r–248r. Placenames mentioned in Ó Duibhgeannáin's numerous scribal signatures demonstrate that the contents of the manuscript were compiled within a relatively confined area of Co. Sligo, but not at a single location. It seems likely that the book represents a compilation of material from exemplars, probably medieval, that were held by a network of families in that area and on which Ó Duibhgeannáin drew. What is less clear from Ó Duibhgeannáin's notes is the final purpose of the compilation. The evidence that can be gleaned from the manuscript itself suggests that

---

[32] Aisling Byrne, 'A Lost Insular Version of the Romance of *Octavian*', *Medium Ævum* 83 (2014), 286–301.
[33] Described in Mary E. Byrne et al., *Catalogue of Irish Manuscripts in the Royal Irish Academy*, 10 vols. (Dublin, 1926–70), 1: 586–93.
[34] Paul Walsh, 'David O Duigenan, Scribe', *Irish Men of Learning: Studies by Father Paul Walsh*, ed. Colm Ó Lochlainn (Dublin, 1947), p. 27.
[35] Byrne et al., *Catalogue of Irish Manuscripts*, p. 586.
[36] Paul Walsh, 'The Learned Family of O Duigenan', *Irish Men of Learning*, ed. Ó Lochlainn, p. 6. I would like to thank Dr Nollaig Ó Muraíle (National University of Ireland, Galway) for the generous information he supplied about this scribe.
[37] Alan Bruford, *Gaelic Folk-Tales and Mediaeval Romances: A Study of the Early Modern Irish 'Romantic Tales' and their Oral Derivatives* (Dublin, 1969), p. 47.

it remained in that region until the antiquarian Charles O'Conor (1710–91), also a local, acquired it. It then passed from him into the Stowe collection and thence to the Royal Irish Academy. One inscription in the manuscript, 'James Duignean his booke 1731', provides good evidence that the book stayed in the scribe's family after his death.[38] It may, of course, have been lent and consulted outside the family circle: on fol. 184 the name 'Philipus Roiley' occurs along with the date 1729; this seems likely to have been a member of the O'Reilly family, formerly lords of East Breffny in the same region.

Another Irish translation of a medieval romance that only survives in a seventeenth-century copy is *Eachtra Uilliam*, the Irish version of *William of Palerne*. A substantial fragment is preserved in a mid-seventeenth-century hand in Dublin, Royal Irish Academy MS Stowe A v 2.[39] The text occurs in a manuscript which appears to be made up of a range of originally separate material, bound together in a rather *ad hoc* manner.[40] The text is acephalous and imperfect and is the only text in the manuscript written in the hand of this particular scribe. In the absence of any earlier manuscripts, it is impossible to pin down a firm date of composition for this translation; however, the first half of the sixteenth century seems highly plausible.[41] Once more the exemplar for this work seems to have come from England and to have been written in English. The editor of the work, Cecile O'Rahilly, demonstrated a range of points at which the Irish text was closer to the English prose *William* (which is now only attested in two leaves of an early printed edition) than to any other extant version, including versions in French.[42] This prose version appears to be ultimately derived from the fourteenth-century English verse romance of the same name that now survives in a single manuscript (Cambridge, King's College MS 13). A notable feature of this text in Irish translation is the addition of twenty short poems throughout the text. Though interspersing poems is a feature of a good number of Irish medieval prose narratives, *Eachtra Uilliam* is the only translated romance in which this occurs. *Eachtra Uilliam* was clearly more popular than its survival in only a single manuscript suggests. One of the interpolated poems appears as a free-standing piece in three other manuscripts and Maura Carney has noted a clear reference to *Eachtra Uilliam* in an early modern poem, 'A bhean éaras imtheacht liom'.[43]

The fortunes of Arthurian material in Ireland between the fifteenth and

---

[38] Byrne et al., *Catalogue of Irish Manuscripts*, p. 236.
[39] Cecile O'Rahilly, ed., *Eachtra Uilliam* (Dublin, 1949).
[40] Byrne et al., *Catalogue of Irish Manuscripts*, pp. 2258–74.
[41] O'Rahilly, ed., *Eachtra*, p. xi.
[42] O'Rahilly, ed., *Eachtra*, pp. x–xvii. The printed fragment of the prose *William* seems to be from the press of Wynkyn de Worde and to date from around 1515. It is printed in G.H.V. Bunt, ed., '*William of Palerne*': *An Alliterative Romance* (Groningen, 1985).
[43] Maura Carney, 'Review of *Eachtra Uilliam*, ed. Cecile O'Rahilly', *Éigse* 6 (1948–52), 188.

seventeenth centuries are of particular interest and worth treating in their own right. Only one foreign Arthurian text was translated into Irish in the Middle Ages, yet a number of apparently native texts featuring Arthurian characters survive. References to the earliest of these native texts first appear around the same time as translated romances during the second half of the fifteenth century.[44] The surviving translation is of the *Queste del Saint Graal*, probably based on a French exemplar that may have originated in England.[45] The translation survives in incomplete form in three fifteenth-century manuscripts. Like *Fierabras* and the *Pseudo-Turpin Chronicle*, the earliest evidence for this text in Ireland connects it with a religious rather than secular milieu – a piece of marginalia in the earliest of the manuscripts (Dublin, Royal Irish Academy MS D 4 2) states that the scribe is working in the monastery of Kilcormack in Offaly. This was a Carmelite foundation and other pieces of marginalia indicate that the scribes were either clerics or clerical students at the monastery.[46] The Irish *Grail* translation also found a Hiberno-Norman secular audience: the copy that now forms part of Oxford, Bodleian Library MS Rawlinson B. 512 was in the hands of Sir John Plunkett, 3rd Baron Dunsany, who died around 1500.[47] The final and most fragmentary manuscript, University College Dublin MS A 10, includes only two folios from the text and, although it was certainly at the Irish Franciscan college at Louvain in the early seventeenth century, features no evidence of earlier readerships.[48] The Irish translation of the *Queste* seems to have been read long after the date at which the surviving manuscripts were produced. The late sixteenth-century poet Tadhg Dall Ó Huiginn makes passing reference in one of his works to a maiden who came to visit Arthur and his knights of the Round Table, an allusion that seems to reflect knowledge of the *Queste*.[49] The native romantic tale *Oidheadh Chloinne Tuireann* (The Death

---

[44] Joseph Falaky Nagy, 'Arthur and the Irish', *A Companion to Arthurian Literature*, ed. Helen Fulton (Malden, MA, 2009), p. 121. On the Arthurian romances: Bernadette Smelik, 'The Intended Audience of Irish Arthurian Romances', *Arthuriana* 17 (2007), 49–69.
[45] Sheila Falconer, ed., '*Lorgaireacht an tSoidigh Naomhtha*': *An Early Modern Irish Translation of the Quest of the Holy Grail* (Dublin, 1953). On the possible source of this text: Aisling Byrne, 'Malory's Sources for the *Tale of the Sankgreal*: Some Overlooked Evidence from *Lorgaireacht an tSoidhigh Naomhtha*', *Arthurian Literature* 30 (2013), 87–100.
[46] This location is mentioned in scribal marginalia on fols. 54v and 87v; Byrne et al., *Catalogue of Irish Manuscripts*, pp. 3297–307.
[47] The fullest account of this manuscript is Brian Ó Cuív, *Catalogue of Irish Language Manuscripts in the Bodleian Library Oxford and Oxford College Libraries* (Dublin, 2003), pp. 223–54.
[48] See Myles Dillon et al., *Catalogue of Irish Manuscripts in the Franciscan Library Killiney* (Dublin, 1969), pp. 21–2.
[49] Eleanor Knott, ed., *The Bardic Poems of Tadhg Dall Ó Huiginn*, 2 vols., ITS 22, 26 (London, 1922), 1: 268–71.

of the Children of Tuireann) also features a character called 'Ri Pisear', a clear translation of 'Fisher King'.⁵⁰

The translation of the *Queste* strikes a very different note from the other Arthurian texts produced in Ireland. The translation is long and literate and seems to have been produced for devotional ends. The other Irish Arthurian narratives are rather different. They are generally shorter and often comic, with none of the homiletic digressiveness of the *Queste*. They are most readily comparable to the more light-hearted, less politically and ideologically invested end of the spectrum of Middle English popular romance. As Bernadette Smelik observes, they differ from other Irish romantic tales in focusing on the adventures of the knightly class rather than on the sons of rulers.⁵¹ Their broad themes and structures are in alignment with Arthurian material from the French and English traditions. Five romances survive in all. *Céilidhe Iosgaide Léithe* (The Visit of Grey Thigh) treats the theme of the fairy mistress and invites comparisons with Arthurian lays such as *Lanval*. The remaining four, the Gawain romance *Eachtra an Mhadra Mhaoil* (The Adventure of the Cropped Dog), *Eachtra Mhacoimh-an-Iolair* (The Adventure of the Youth of the Eagle), *Eachtra an Amadáin Mhóir* (The Adventure of the Great Fool) and *Eachtra Mhelóra agus Orlando* (The Adventure of Melóra and Orlando), are quest stories. *Eachtra Mhacoimh-an-Iolair* is 'an identity-quest, which must lead to [the hero's] integration into society and his recognition by the members of Arthur's court'.⁵² *Eachtra Mhelóra agus Orlando* has less in common with other Arthurian material, but shows the influence of foreign material, notably *Orlando Furioso*, probably in its English translation.

The considerable discrepancies between the manuscript copies of several of these texts suggest the possibility of widespread oral transmission. By contrast, the surviving copies of the *Queste* are very similar. These other Arthurian narratives seem to be compositions that originate in Ireland, though there are obvious influences from foreign materials. Despite the paucity of direct translations, knowledge of key characters and common motifs from Arthurian material seems to have been widespread in Ireland. In exile in Louvain sometime in late 1618, the Irish poet Fearghal Óg Mac an Bhaird (c.1550–c.1633) wrote a poem which made reference to King Arthur:

> Cing Artúir, úaithne na talmhan
> trén ar an mbioth do bhí sé;
> teacht 'na dhal do dhligh gach duine,
> do thil clár na cruinne cé.

---

⁵⁰ Richard J. O' Duffy, ed., *Oidhe Chloinne Tuireann: The Fate of the Children of Tuireann* (Dublin, 1888).
⁵¹ Smelik, 'Intended Audience', 53.
⁵² Smelik. 'Intended Audience', 54.

Bíadh ná curim ní chaitheadh Artúr
gan iongnadh núa, núaidhe in barr,
go hég íar rúachtain san ríghe,
gég úachtair na tíre thall.

(King Arthur, the prop of the world, was mighty upon earth; every man was bound to pay court to him, he ruled the plain of this world.

Arthur never took food nor drink without some new marvel – strange was the addition – until his death, when he had attained sovranty, he the topmost branch of yonder land.)[53]

The reference to Arthur refusing to eat is a familiar one and occurs in a number of romances across several languages. Mac an Bhaird appears to be utilising a motif that had attained something like a proverbial quality in the culture in which he moved. As with Keating's references to *Huon*, *Bevis* and the *Knight of the Sun*, the offhand nature of the allusion suggests that the author assumes some knowledge of the literature in question on the part of his audience.

Of the five Arthurian narratives original to the Irish context, only two can be securely dated to before 1600. All but one survive in early modern rather than in medieval manuscripts, though British Library, MS Egerton 1781, a manuscript from the 1480s, appears to have contained a, now lost, copy of *Céilidhe Iosgaide Léithe* at one point.[54] Their survival rates are rather varied, though one work mentioned above, *Eachtra an Mhadra Mhaoil* (The Adventure of the Cropped Dog), survives in around thirty-six manuscripts.[55] The plot of *Eachtra an Mhadra Mhaoil* gives a sense of the tone of these works. It begins with Arthur and his party out hunting on the 'Plain on Wonders'; there they encounter the Knight of the Lantern who binds them all, with the exception of Gawain, using his magical powers. Gawain sets off to help the enchanted king and his court. At the fountain of virtues he meets a dog with no ears or tail who turns out to be the Knight of the Lantern's half-brother and the enchanted son of the King of India. The dog accompanies him on a series of marvellous and loosely connected adventures in pursuit of the Knight of the Lantern through locations both mythical (such as the Island of the Amazons) and real (such as Egypt). At the end of the story, the dog is returned to his human form. The plot, with its episodic construction, its stress of the supernatural and its wide geographic scope, could fairly be described as romance. The central figure of

---

[53] Pádraig A. Breatnach, 'The Aesthetics of Irish Bardic Composition: An Analysis of *Fuaras iongnadh, a fhir chumainn* by Fearghal Óg Mac an Bhaird', *Cambrian Medieval Celtic Studies* 42 (Winter 2001), 51–72.

[54] Joseph Falaky Nagy, 'Arthur and the Irish', *A Companion to Arthurian Literature*, ed. Helen Fulton (Malden, MA, 2009), p. 121.

[55] Nagy, 'Arthur and the Irish', p. 117.

the dog-man may owe something to the werewolf romance *William of Palerne*, perhaps in its Irish translation. The aid the cropped dog gives Gawain in his adventures recalls similar help offered by shape-shifting figures like the Turk, in the Middle English *The Turk and Sir Gawaine*. Affinities with foreign texts are also visible in another Irish Arthurian romance, *Eachtra an Amadáin Mhóir*, which, it has long been recognised, bears interesting comparison to the *Perceval* story.[56] However, in some ways it is particularly readily comparible with the fourteenth-century English adaptation of *Perceval*, *Percyvell of Galles*, rather than with Chretien's text. Both tales share a comedic spirit even more pronounced than Chretien's, (though the Irish tale is, in many respects, rather more absurd than its English counterpart) and both eliminate the Grail material from the narrative, presumably as part of that more light-hearted reshaping.

Although the Irish Arthurian tales do not have any clear non-native exemplars and feature many elements that draw on distinctively Irish literary traditions, it would be rash to classify these as 'native' in the strict sense. The source material for these tales has always been a matter of mystery. The most extensive evidence for the origins of any of them comes in the form of a colophon to *Eachtra Mhacaoimh an Iolair*, which suggests that the story was originally a French one.[57] Yet nothing resembling the narrative survives in that language and such an attribution ought to be treated with caution; after all, the Irish translator of John Mandeville's *Travels* states his work is translated from Latin and Hebrew, when plainly he worked from a Middle English text.[58] What colophons like this may gesture towards is a supposed ultimate source (real or imagined), rather than an immediate exemplar. Indeed, Caoimhín Breathnach has suggested that certain linguistic features of *Eachtra Mhacaoimh an Iolair* suggest that the text was, at least in part, derived from an English-language source, though no English-language text survives that resembles it.[59]

The Irish Arthurian narratives bring us to the wider context of the *scéalta rómánsaíochta* (romantic tales) amongst which they can readily be classified. It is in this vast, but very understudied, group of stories recited, written and read more or less continuously across the upheavals of the Irish transition from the medieval to early modern periods that the greatest impact of non-native

---

[56] T. Ó Rabhartaigh and Douglas Hyde, 'An t-Amadán Mór', *Lia Fáil* 2 (1927), 191–228. For an analysis of the relationship of this text and Chretien's *Perceval*, see Linda Gowans, 'The *Eachtra an Amadáin Mhóir* as a Response to the *Perceval* of Chrétien de Troyes', *Arthurian Literature 19: Comedy in Arthurian Literature* (2003), 199–230.

[57] Nagy, 'Arthur and the Irish', p. 123.

[58] Whitley Stokes, 'The Gaelic Maundeville', *Zeitschrift für Celtische Philologie* 2 (1899), 1–6, 226–300.

[59] Caoimhín Breathnach, 'Brian Ó Corcráin and *Eachtra Mhacaoimh an Iolair*', *Éigse* 34 (2004), 44–8.

vernacular writing may be discerned, albeit through a glass darkly. The earliest of these tales appear to originate in the fifteenth century, around the same time that Irish translations of foreign romance appear, and manuscript copies survive more or less continuously from that point, though a large number are preserved in manuscripts written from the seventeenth century onwards.[60] Like British and continental romances, they are often characterised by their vast geographic scope and highly episodic nature. Joseph Falaky Nagy describes them as 'narratives featuring virtually interchangeable heroes and their exploits, adventures, and encounters with the marvelous [...] they are thought to have been literary creations modeled upon or inspired by the romances in English and French available to early modern Irish *literati*'.[61]

A particularly neat example of this sort of inspiration is found in a narrative preserved in Trinity 1298. *Stair Nuadat Find Femin* (The History of Nuadu Find Femin) centres on the adventures of a legendary Irish hero and exhibits numerous characteristics of European romance.[62] It survives uniquely in the same manuscript and in the same scribal hand as the translations of *Guy*, *Bevis* and the *Recuyell*. It seems plausible on stylistic grounds that the translator of those texts was also the author of this one.[63] Certain features of *Bevis* and *Guy* may also have informed the plot of *Stair Nuadat*. Erich Poppe has suggested that various qualities of this narrative, such as its highly episodic structure and the essential passivity of its hero, affiliate the work very strongly with contemporary romance.[64] Alan Bruford has also grouped *Stair Nuadat* with a small number of (mostly later) Irish texts that, in his eyes, exhibit particularly loose narrative 'patterns such as are often found in continental romance'.[65] To summarise the plot: Nuada is son to the King of Ireland. When Nuada's mother dies, the king marries a young and beautiful wife who attempts to seduce Nuada. Nuada rebuffs her and she responds by accusing him of rape. The furious king sets his men on his son who flees to an island off the coast of Donegal. There he encounters a company of Norsemen whom he thoroughly decimates in a series of elaborate set-piece battles. He then defeats their prince in single combat. His father's men arrive on the island and mistake one of the corpses for Nuada and mourn him. Meanwhile, Nuada has left and travels all

---

[60] Bruford, *Gaelic Folk-Tales and Mediaeval Romances*, p. 47.
[61] Joseph Falaky Nagy, *A New Introduction to Two Irish Arthurian Romances*, ITS Subsidiary Series 7 (London, 1998), p. 1. See also Joseph Falaky Nagy, 'In Defense of *Rómánsaíocht*', *Ériu* 38 (1987), 3–19; and Gerard Murphy, *The Ossianic Lore and Romantic Tales of Medieval Ireland* (Dublin, 1961), pp. 37–55.
[62] *Stair Nuadat* has been edited with a German translation by Käte Müller-Lisowski, 'Stair Nuadat Find Femin', *Zeitschrift für Celtische Philologie* 13 (1921), 195–250.
[63] Quin, ed. *Stair Ercuil*, pp. xxxix–xl.
[64] Erich Poppe, 'Stair Nuadat Find Femin: Eine irische Romanze?', *Zeitschrift für Celtische Philologie* 49–50 (1997), 749–59.
[65] Bruford, *Gaelic Folk-Tales and Mediaeval Romances*, p. 9.

over Europe performing great deeds. He marries the daughter of the King of Denmark before returning to Ireland, revealing his identity and claiming his patrimony.

Various motifs in this text parallel those that crop up in *Guy* and *Bevis*. The story has the 'exile and return' structure common to the two English romances and the Norse threat is common to both *Guy* and *Stair Nuadat*. Nuada's cross-cultural marriage with the daughter of the King of Denmark is reminiscent of Bevis's union with Josian, the daughter of the Saracen king. If, indeed, *Stair Nuadat* is Mac an Leagha's work, then it seems to be a work very much inspired by romance, most particularly the company it keeps in this manuscript.

However, the tendency of modern scholars to call works like *Stair Nuadat* 'romantic tales' rather than 'romances' betrays unease with aligning them too closely with the European mainstream. The general reluctance to categorise these works as 'romance' may in part have contributed to the relative neglect of the romantic tales by Irish literary scholars. One sticking point appears to be the degree to which these Irish tales draw on the native pantheon of legendary figures rather than the stock heroes of European romance, Charlemagne, Arthur and so forth. Yet, as a text like *Stair Nuadat* demonstrates, echoes of the mainstream romance tradition are readily observable in the motifs and narrative structures deployed. Considered in terms of a shared lexicon of recurring motifs, rather than in terms of key characters, these texts generally fit quite neatly into the broad category of 'romance'. Motif-based approaches to romance, of the sort developed by Helen Cooper in *The English Romance in Time*, could provide a framework within which the Irish romantic tales might be studied alongside European romance.[66]

The story of romance in Ireland begins rather late and features numerous lacunae. The persistence of the popularity of romance well into the early modern period in England can partly be attributed to the long history and consequent deep entrenchment of the genre in that country.[67] In Ireland there was no such background, but the genre proved tenacious nonetheless. Low manuscript survival rates from the Middle Ages do not make it easy to assess the extent of the popularity of the translated romances. Yet, evidence such as allusions to these works in other texts seems to point to a reasonably wide dissemination, as does the fact that so many seem to have been read into the seventeenth century and beyond. Perhaps the most interesting and least explored dimension of the story is the parallel development of the romantic tales in Ireland, a development that seems very likely to have been stimulated by the widespread circulation of foreign romances in the country. The rise of the romantic tales suggests an even wider diffusion and a greater social impact for

---

[66] Cooper, *Romance*, p. 8.
[67] Cooper, *Romance*, p. 6.

foreign romance than any of the other evidence. The romantic tales developed rapidly and became one of the most widely diffused genres of Irish writing in the early modern period and beyond. The true impact of foreign medieval romance in Ireland may be greater than is traditionally assumed, but we need to shift our vantage point somewhat in order to see it. In many respects the influence of foreign romance becomes most evident when viewed from a cross-period perspective and most pronounced where it might appear to initially be least obvious, in the native narrative tradition itself.

Penitential Romance after the Reformation

JAMES WADE

An intellectual history of the English Middle Ages might begin in 1570, when John Foxe first brackets off a 'middle age' between the earliest and purest 'primitive tyme' of the church and Foxe's own time, an era reformed on those primitive – or first – principles.[1] So far as we know, the plural, 'middle ages', was not used until 1605, when John Donne similarly uses the term to represent a chronology of Catholic practice. For both writers, periodisation tracks 'the Ecclesiasticall Story'; here, the steady pace of human time is punctuated by the shifting progress and regress of the church, not by advances in technology or industry, such as the advent of the printing press, nor by dynastic or political transitions, such as the rise of the Tudors following the death of Richard III in 1485. Another narrative embedded in a history of ideas, running parallel to the fortunes of the English church, is that of humanism and the rebirth of classical literature. Humanism in England stretches back to the 1430s, and indeed back to Petrarch and his followers on the continent, but in 1605, the same year that Donne references the 'middle ages' in a theological context, the historian William Camden refers to this same 'middle age' in a way that accords with the familiar Renaissance story.[2] It is, he says, an age overcast with 'thicke fogges of ignorance' and a period whose poetic remains are not to be taken too seriously. If you want literature of real substance and style, look to writings produced in the 'more ancient and better times' of the classical era.[3]

---

[1] John Foxe, *Actes and Monuments* (London, 1570), p. 202.
[2] William Camden, *Remaines of a greater worke, concerning Britaine* (London, 1605), p. 2; Helen Cooper, 'Introduction', *Medieval Shakespeare: Pasts and Presents*, ed. Cooper, Ruth Morse and Peter Holland (Cambridge, 2013), pp. 1–2. For work on early humanism, see Daniel Wakelin, *Humanism, Reading, and English Literature 1430–1530* (Cambridge, 2007); and David Rundle, ed., *Humanism in Fifteenth-Century Europe*, (Oxford, 2012).
[3] On issues of periodisation, see David Matthews, 'Periodization', *A Handbook of Middle English Studies*, ed. Marion Turner (Chichester, 2013), pp. 253–66; Greg Walker, 'When did "The Medieval" End? Retrospection, Foresight, and the End(s) of the English Middle Ages', *The Oxford Handbook of Medieval Literature in English*, ed. Elaine Treharne and Greg Walker (Oxford, 2010), pp. 725–38; Margreta De Grazia, 'The Modern Divide: From Either Side', *JMEMS* 37 (2007), 453–67; Debora K. Shuger, *Habits of Thought in the English Renaissance* (Berkeley, 1990). See also the introduction to this volume.

Middle English romance, especially of the more popular variety, may seem to be largely tangential to these broader issues of periodisation, religious reform and intellectual history. It turns out, however, that all press is good press from an antiquarian point of view, as it was precisely their distance from Protestant and humanist values that prompted their inclusion in these larger discourses – as common targets of abuse. C.S. Lewis memorably captures the state of affairs in a comment on Roger Ascham:

> Ascham's attack on the Arthurian stories is sometimes called a puritan attack; but Ascham the humanist would have made it whether he were a puritan or not. The only difference in this matter between a Roman and a Protestant humanist was that the former had to be content with calling the romances barbarous and silly while the latter could add 'And popish too'. Both beat the same dog, but the Protestant had an extra stick.[4]

This portrait of Ascham prompts a warning against the habit of identifying Protestantism and humanism as largely distinct intellectual traditions in the sixteenth century. Humanists such as Ascham might scoff at romances for being ridiculous and old-fashioned, but in fact the bulk of their invective was directed at romance's moral and theological dangerousness, a form of criticism more often aligned with religious reformers such as William Tyndale.[5] Lewis also noted that the eagerness to sniff out and condemn traces of barbarism in one's neighbour's Latin had much in common with an eagerness to sniff out and condemn traces of Catholicism in the church, but for the humanists the old romances tended to provoke rebuke almost entirely in terms of theological error rather than silliness of content or ineptitude of style.[6] Those faults, presumably, were taken as given.

While 1570 saw the printing of the second edition of the *Actes and Monuments*, which adds Foxe's discussion of the tripartite chronology of the church, it also brought in the posthumous publication of Ascham's *The Scholemaster*, a guide to teaching Latin that turns out to be as much about manners as about

---

[4] C.S. Lewis, *English Literature in the Sixteenth Century Excluding Drama* (Oxford, 1954), p. 29.
[5] In *The Obedience of A Christen Man* (London, 1528), sig. C4r, Tyndale indulges in the commonplace argument that supporters of the Reformation would put bibles in the hands of lay people, where otherwise they would only have books of popular tales such as Robin Hood and *Bevis of Hampton*, all of which are full of ribaldry 'as filthy as herte can thinke'.
[6] Thomas Nashe's scorn for *Bevis of Hampton*'s bad poetry in *The Anatomie of Absurditie* (London, 1589), sig. C1r, is certainly an outlier: 'Who is it, that reading Bevis of Hampton, can forbeare laughing, if he marke what scambling shyft he makes to end his verses a like?' For more on sixteenth - and seventeenth-century condemnations of romance: Alex Davis, *Chivalry and Romance in the English Renaissance* (Cambridge, 2003), pp. 6–17. On the Renaissance reception of medieval romance: Ronald S. Crane, *The Vogue of Medieval Chivalric Romance during the English Renaissance* (1919; rpt. Norwood, PA, 1977); Arthur Ferguson, *The Indian Summer of English Chivalry* (Durham, NC, 1960); Cooper, *Romance*, esp. pp. 36–9.

grammar. It first takes a high-humanist swipe at writings in the vernacular languages and even in Latin (excepting Cicero), these being 'patched cloutes and ragges' compared with the 'faire woven broade clothes' of the literature that came out of Athens.[7] Then Ascham turns to romance, both to recent translations of Italian productions and to the great English romance of the previous century: Malory's *Morte Darthur*. When 'Papistrie, as a standyng poole, covered and overflowed all England', Ascham says,

> fewe bookes were read in our tong, savyng certaine bookes of Chevalrie, as they sayd, for pastime and pleasure, which, as some say, were made in Monasteries, by idle Monkes, or wanton Chanons: as one for example, *Morte Arthure*.[8]

This is an oft-quoted passage in romance criticism, though it is nearly always used to illustrate a view of romance's moral vulgarity, as books that trade in 'open mans slaughter, and bold bawdrye'.[9] But while Ascham notes that romances such as these exemplify and provoke bad behaviour, the thrust of his argument is aimed at theology, not morality.[10] Romances inflame vanities, he says, but the real danger is that such vain living breeds false judgements of doctrine. In other words: 'sinne and fleshlines bring forth sectes and heresies'. Foxe makes much the same point in his second edition of the *Actes and Monuments*, tying monastic practices of the 'middle tyme' to luxury, and eventually to doctrinal error. Just as, for Ascham, romances were products of the monasteries, penned by idle monks, for Foxe the proliferation of Catholic infrastructure ('monasteryes and nunneryes') led not only to an idleness borne of wealth and riches, but also to the errors of ignorance, hypocrisy and empty ritual. Evoking the image of a cesspool, also stirred up in Ascham's description of Catholic England, Foxe argues that monks 'did swymme in superstition' as a consequence of their luxurious cloistered lifestyles.[11]

There are strong links in the sixteenth century between superstition, the old religion and popular romance. Tyndale was only one in a long line of reformers to rail against Catholicism's exploitation of the simple-minded, even

---

[7] Roger Ascham, *The Scholemaster* (London, 1570), sig. C1v.
[8] Ascham, *Scholemaster*, sig. I3r.
[9] Ascham, *Scholemaster*, sig. I3r.
[10] Ascham then says: 'What toyes, the dayly readyng of such a booke [as the *Morte Darthur*], may work in the will of a yong jentleman, or a yong mayde, that liveth welthelie and idlelie, wise men can judge, and honest men do pitie'; see *Scholemaster*, sig. I3r. For Ascham and his early readers, 'toyes' here carry connotations not only of fantastic or frivolous conceits (*OED*, s.v. 'toy', n. 3a, 4a), but also of amorous dalliance (*OED*, s.v. 'toy', n. 1). In 1577 Meredith Hanmer also uses 'toyes' perjoratively: 'Many nowe adayes had rather reade' the tales of 'Kinge Arthur', 'Bevis of Hampton' and 'many other infortunate treatises and amorous toies'. As for 'bookes of divinitie, to edifie the soule, and instructe the inwarde man', however, 'it is the least part of their care'; see *The Auncient Ecclesiasticall Histories of the First Six Hundred Yeares after Christ* (London, 1577), sig. A2v.
[11] Foxe, *Actes*, p. 202.

going so far as to compare the pope to Robin Goodfellow.[12] The position might be illustrated by the work of astronomer and physician John Harvey, who in 1588 published *A Discoursive Probleme Concerninge Prophesies*. How easy is it, Harvey asks disdainfully, 'to set countenance upon some stale poeticall fragment, or other antique record?', and is there anything simpler, he asks again, than 'to revive some forlorne *Merlin*, or *Pierce Plowman*, or *Nostradame*, or the like supposed prophet? Alas, is this wise world so simple, to beleeve so foolish toyes, devised to mocke apes, and delude children?'[13] Later, Harvey turns to discuss the origins of these prophecies and the romances that carried them, such as the *Morte Darthur, Bevis of Hampton, Launcelot du Lake, Sir Tristram* and *Guy of Warwick*. They are all the products, we are told, of 'idle Cloistermen, mad merry Friers, and lustie Abbey-lubbers', who use both the prophecies and the romances as distractions to keep the masses from attending to important matters of politics or church governance. After all, it was the 'graund pollicie of that age, wherein those counterfet prophesiers chéefly flourished, to occupie and carry away the commons with od rumors, by flimflams, wily cranks, and sleightie knacks of the maker'. Once again, Middle English romances are tied to the corruption of the medieval monasteries, and to the superstitions of 'that age', though for Harvey this was part of an outright conspiracy. Some 'trim worke', he called it, to keep the monks in power and their bellies full.[14]

However, the polemicists bent on connecting old romances with corrupt Catholicism, and blaming lazy monks for the production of these texts, seem to have had little effect on romance's popularity in the second half of the sixteenth century. The claim of a 1539 tract, that the Light of God had utterly abolished the 'impure filth' of romances such as *Guy of Warwick* and *Bevis of Hampton* turns out to have been little more than prudish wishful-thinking.[15] Even warnings such as Ascham's, that reading romance could lead to immorality and even recusancy, did not stop a flourishing of romance from the 1550s

---

[12] Tyndale, *Obedience*, sig. C4r.
[13] John Harvey, *A Discoursive Probleme Concerninge Prophesies* (London, 1588), p. 2. On the link between prophecy and romance: Howard Dobin, *Merlin's Disciples: Prophecy, Poetry, and Power in Renaissance England* (Stanford, 1990); Helen Cooper, 'Thomas of Erceldoune: Romance as Prophecy', *Cultural Encounters in the Romance of Medieval England*, ed. Corinne Saunders (Cambridge, 2005), pp. 171–87; Cooper, *Romance*, esp. pp. 187–97.
[14] Harvey, *Discoursive*, pp. 68–9. Nashe, a contemporary of Harvey's at Cambridge, makes much the same point in his *Anatomie of Absurditie*, sig. A2r. Indeed, while 'abbey-lubber' was a common term of derision in Protestant England, Nashe's use of the phrase suggests he had Harvey's work in mind. He refers to those 'Abbie-lubbers, from whose idle pens, proceeded those worne out impressions of the feyned no-where acts of Arthur of the rounde table, Arthur of litle Brittaine, sir Tristram, Hewon of Burdeaux, the Squire of low degree, the foure sons of Amon, with infinite others'.
[15] From 'A Declaration of the Faith, and a Justification of the Proceedings of King Henry the Eighth in Matters of Religion', Jeremy Collier, *Ecclesiastical History of Great Britain*, 2 vols. (London, 1708–14), 2: 'Collection of Records', no. 47.

through to the end of the century. The Middle English romances served as cheap material for the printing presses, as sources for popularising and modernising balladeers, and as inspiration for poets of the court. Nearer the end of the century, they also served as a consistent source of material for artists working in the emerging form of popular entertainment: the public theatre. If Thomas Nashe betrays a suspicious familiarity with popular Middle English romances such as *Bevis of Hampton*, so does Shakespeare.

Even more surprising, however, is the popularity of penitential romance in this period. Penitential romances, as they have been termed, are chivalric narratives whose actions take a penitential arc, or whose adventures take the form of a quest for absolution, and as far as the surviving evidence suggests, they were at least as popular after the Reformation as before.[16] William Copeland, for instance, printed *Guy of Warwick* in 1553, and then again in 1565; *Sir Isumbras*, a bestseller, survives in eight manuscripts from c.1350 to the start of the sixteenth century, but also in five print editions from c.1530 to c.1565; and *Robert the Devil* (its Middle English version known as *Sir Gowther*) saw prints of both a metrical and a prose version in the early sixteenth century, and a rewriting by Thomas Lodge in 1591. The adaptation by Lodge, along with the surviving manuscripts of recusant Edward Banyster, suggest that these romances were favourites amongst those with strong Catholic sympathies, but they also seem to have had a much broader appeal across the span of a long sixteenth century, even over and above the less theologically dangerous romances and tales of adventure.[17] One question in the history of this literature, therefore, has to do with surprising continuities, with why those romances with the strongest ties to the old religion not only survived but thrived in the decades following the Reformation. A second question, however, deals with change, with an explicit and profound break with the past. It asks what happened to penitential romance in the course of the sixteenth century, and how these writers dealt with the knowledge that they were living in a new age, a period after the long 'middle tyme' of the church.

Penance as a theme or trope – as opposed to a narrative architecture – has a long history in English romance. *Sir Gawain and the Green Knight*, *The Erle of Tolous* and *Valentine and Orson*, among other romances, all take up the

---

[16] A defining study is Andrea Hopkins, *The Sinful Knights: A Study of Middle English Penitential Romance* (Oxford, 1990). Hopkins focuses on four romances – *Guy of Warwick*, *Sir Isumbras*, *Sir Gowther* and *Roberd of Cisyle* – though Appendix A contains a brief discussion of other English romances containing penitential episodes.

[17] Banyster copied two manuscripts for personal use. Oxford, Bodleian Library, MS Douce 261 contains *Sir Isumbras* and *Sir Eglamour of Artois* (another romance with penitential themes); BL, MS Egerton 3132A preserves a metrical version of *Robert the Devil*. See Maldwyn Mills, 'EB and his Two Books: Visual Impact and the Power of Meaningful Suggestion. "Reading" the Illustrations in MSS Douce 261 and Egerton 3132A', *Imagining the Book*, ed. S. Kelly and J.J. Thompson (Turnhout, 2005), pp. 173–91.

subject. As Andrew King notes, heroic exploits track well with Catholic spirituality, in which individual works can be efficacious in attaining salvation.[18] Malory's *Morte Darthur*, first printed by Caxton three weeks before the events at Bosworth Field, also ends with a penitential shape – with the Grail Quest leading onto the final penitential trajectories of Lancelot and Guinevere. It was printed again in 1498 by Wynkyn de Worde, but as the quotations above suggest, it was well known throughout the sixteenth century, its circulation being refreshed by new editions of 1529, 1557 and 1582. The long survival of Malory's Middle Ages, however, is part of another story in literary history: the refashioning of chivalric romance during the Elizabethan literary revival. A vogue for the new prose romance emerged as early as the 1560s, along with translations of romances from Latin and Greek, such as Apuleius's *Golden Asse* (1566).[19] By the 1590s new romances such as Sidney's *Arcadia* reflected a more secularised chivalry, leaning heavily on conventions of pastoral and the novella, while Spenser's *Faerie Queene* (1590 and 1596) pushed the classical and biblical roots of romance while shaping the genre for both Protestant and Nationalist ends. As is well known, however, the *Faerie Queene* is also highly reliant upon a number of Middle English romances, including the penitential *Guy of Warwick* and Malory's *Morte Darthur*.[20] Reading habits, even amongst the most learned of the age, do not seem to follow any tidy narrative of artistic progress or suggest a clear break with the old, nor do they seem to fit into convenient categories of courtly literature versus popular fiction.

Spenser, drawing on romances such as the *Morte Darthur*, has Redcrosse work through a full penitential arc in Cantos ix and x of Book I.[21] Here the knight moves from the near-fatal cave of Despair, through 'godly sorowe' and repentance, to a fresh state of spiritual cleanness. In doing so he uses a full set of Catholic penitential accoutrement, including ashes, sackcloth, fasting, scourging and floods of cleansing tears, but the allegory keeps Catholic institutionalism at arm's length. His doctor is Patience, not a parish priest, and there is no hint of the kind of legalism inherent in a pre-set penitential programme. Spenser's theology, too, makes an unequivocal break from the romances of the 'middle tyme', as Redcrosse's path to absolution is emphatically not a knightly quest, and his suffering is not heroic in any chivalric sense. Canto x begins

---

[18] Andrew King, *The Faerie Queene and Middle English Romance: The Matter of Just Memory* (Oxford, 2000), p. 126.

[19] See Steve Mentz, *Romance for Sale in Early Modern England: The Rise of Prose Fiction* (Aldershot, 2006).

[20] See King, *Faerie Queene*. pp. 105–25; King, '*Guy of Warwick* and the *Faerie Queene*, Book II: Chivalry Through the Ages', *Guy of Warwick: Icon and Ancestor*, ed. Alison Wiggins and Rosalind Field (Cambridge, 2007), pp. 167–84; Paul Rovang, *Refashioning 'Knights and Ladies Gentle Deeds': The Intertextuality of Spenser's Faerie Queene and Malory's Morte Darthur* (Madison, NJ, 1996).

[21] Spenser, *Faerie Queene*, I.x.1.

with a stanza that makes Spenser's Protestantism absolutely clear: grace, not human endeavour, is the cause of salvation.[22]

Redcrosse's spiritual healing in the House of Holiness offers a key to understanding attitudes toward penance in the early reformed church. Before the Reformation, for comparison, the sacrament of penance constituted a sequential performance of contrition, confession and atonement conducted under the aegis of a priest. The *Lay Folks' Catechism* sums it up well:

> The third sacrament is cald penaunce,
> That is sothefast forthinking we have of our syn
> Withouten will or thoght to turne ogayne to it.
> And this behoves have thre thinges if it be stedefast:
> Ane is sorow of our hert that we have synned;
> Anothir is open shrift of our mouth how we haf synned,
> And the third is rightwise amendes makyng for that we haf synned.
> This thre, with gode will to forsake our syn,
> Clenses us and wasshes us of alkyn synnes. (307–15)[23]

Despite the rigour of its structure, guidebooks such as the *Lay Folks' Catechism* stress that penance is not a strictly ritualistic or mechanical exercise. First there must be genuine sorrow for one's sins, and the final two stages of verbal confession and the making of satisfaction must be undertaken with every good intention not to commit the sin again. The reformers' challenge to this sacrament, however, did not simply involve a critique of its legalism or its insistence upon institutional intercession. The Protestants objected, more fundamentally, to the concept of 'amendes makyng' – that absolution could be won off the back of human works. In a sermon published in 1570, Foxe ties this question of penitential works to nothing less than an understanding of the Crucifixion, in which Christ's sacrifice becomes 'a perfect deliverance of all his people from the beginning to the end of the world', and a 'full satisfaction once and ever for all our sinnes, and absolute discharge and acquittance for all our debtes'. Of course, as Foxe continues, Catholics do not see it this way, 'as may sensibly appeare by their doctrine and institutes, by their auricular confession and satisfaction for sinnes, by their dayly sacrifices, propitiatory Masses, trentals, and Purgatory, by merites of supererogation, invocation of Saintes, the popes pardon, and dispensations'.[24]

---

[22] The classic study is Rosemond Tuve, 'The Red Crosse Knight and Medieval Demon Stories', *Essays by Rosemond Tuve: Spenser, Herbert, Milton*, ed. Thomas P. Roche (Princeton, 1970), pp. 39–48.

[23] *The Lay Folks' Catechism*, ed. Thomas Frederick Simmons and Henry Edward Nolloth, EETS OS 118 (London, 1901), pp. 64–6.

[24] John Foxe, *A Sermon of Christ Crucified* (London, 1570), sig. A4r. Henry Smith, perhaps the most popular puritan preacher of Elizabethan London, argued that penance detracts from

While 'satisfaction for sinnes' became a hallmark of the mechanistic logic of Catholicism, the reformed church in no way abandoned penance. The Ten Articles of the Henrician Church, from 1536, maintained that penance was 'instituted by God in the New Testament, as a thing so necessary for man's salvation' that no one can be saved without it. Although 'Christ and his death be the sufficient oblation, sacrifice, satisfaction and recompense [...] yet all men truly penitent, contrite and confessed, must need also bring forth the fruits of penance.'[25] When it came to penance, therefore, the fundamental difference between Catholics and Protestants was aetiological: in the former, penance was the cause of salvation; in the latter, penance was its effect. This is a fine distinction in practice, and what the reformers latched onto, therefore, was predominantly the notion of ledger-balancing: that there could be a routine calculation, institutionally administered, of precise equivalencies between acts of sin and acts of penitential restitution. Perhaps the nuances in this shift account for the fact that penance was one of the last sacraments of the old religion to be rejected by the Church of England, in 1553, outliving sacraments of holy orders, marriage, confirmation and extreme unction. Its eventual rejection, however, was made on the grounds that as an institutional construct it insisted on confession to a priest, that with its basis in physical mortification it had links to the concept of purgatory, and that with its weights-and-measures logic it turned salvation into a debt-economy of human works.

From this context, it is fairly easy to see how the penitential experience of Spenser's Redcrosse would not have given sixteenth-century reformers much to worry about. In this respect, though, much the same is true for the Middle English romances Spenser would have known. Even the penitential romances, while certainly predicated on salvific works, never model the sacrament as institutionally administered, at least not in any ordinary way. Adventure, even for the pious romances, remains the overriding impetus of the genre, an aesthetic that leaves little room for the mundane sequence outlined in the *Lay Folks' Catechism*. Sir Gowther, for instance, will confess his monumentally grotesque sins only to the pope himself, and his journey to absolution becomes bound up in his journey to Rome. This is confession as quest, or confession reshaped by a romance ethos and for an audience anticipating larger-than-life

---

Christ's sacrifice: 'the Prince himself, which should have crucified us, came to be crucified of us, for us that we might say with stedfast faith, I beleeve the remission of sinnes, not the satisfaction of sinnes, but the remission of sinnes. Marke this distinction against popish merites or werkes, or penance, Christ hath satisfied and not we; we are remitted and not Christ'. He goes on to say, 'If there be a satisfaction for our sinnes by our workes, or by our Pilgrimages, or by our masses, or by our penance, let Christ never be called a forgiver, but an exchanger like the pope'; see Henry Smith, *A Treatise of the Lord's Supper* (London, 1591), sig. E4r.

[25] Quoted from *Documents of the English Reformation: 1526–1701*, ed. Gerald Bray (Cambridge, 2004), p. 168.

romance expectations. Andrea Hopkins makes the point that readers would have easily recognised the grandiose romancing of Catholic procedures in romances such as *Sir Gowther*. Catholics would have been drilled in orthodox penitential procedures, either through their parish priest, or though widely known instructional treatises such as the *Prick of Conscience* or *Handlyng Synne*, or both.[26] While sixteenth-century audiences would have known that, within a Catholic paradigm, contrite confession to one's parish priest and the appropriate performance of penance is essential for the forgiveness of sin, in *Sir Isumbras* the hero is alone in a forest when he is given his penance by a spiritual messenger in the shape of a bird – hardly an ordinary or orthodox confessional encounter. Similarly, Catholic penitents would work hard to rigorously remember all the details of their lives so as to make them available for examination in the confessional, but in *Guy of Warwick* the hero does not even attend confession with a priest before he imposes his own penance. Guy's new bride, quite understandably, suggests that the foundation of a religious house might be a more suitable penance, but common sense of this sort has little place in romance. As Sir Gowther and Robert of *Robert of Cisyle* become debased court fools to pay for their sins, Guy takes flamboyant penance a step further. He gives up his newly won wife in favour of a lifetime of extraordinary hardship in the service of God. If *Sir Gowther* scripts confession as quest, *Guy of Warwick* turns pilgrimage into quest and thus quest into penance, without bothering with the details of confession first.

While the lax proceduralism and the casual mixing of sacraments with sensation and marvel may have helped keep these romances out of the reformers' bonfires, it is likely that such qualities also made them extremely popular. Aside from their successes in manuscript and print, several penitential romances, or romances with penitential episodes or themes, made the translation to the stage: *Robert of Cisyle* (1447–53, 1529, 1623), *Eglamour of Artois* (1444), *Valentine and Orson* (1549, 1595, 1598) and *Guy of Warwick* (?1593, 1618, 1620).[27] Of the three *Guy* dramatisations only the earliest survives, from an edition of 1661. The print gives the title *The Tragical History, Admirable Atchievments and various events of Guy Earl of Warwick*, though its sixteenth-century audiences would have likely understood it not as a tragedy but as a romance. Plays that end with the hero dying on stage may have become a hallmark of Renaissance tragedy by 1661, but audiences steeped in the expectations of penitential romance, and of the *Guy* legend in particular, understood that the promised end could happen off stage because what is promised after so much suffering

---

[26] Hopkins, *Sinful Knights*, pp. 196–7.
[27] See Cooper, *Romance*, Appendix.

is found in the world beyond.[28] There is a possibility that a young Shakespeare may have had a hand in it, perhaps even playing the role of the clown, a 'high mounting lofty minded' character named Sparrow, who was born 'at Stratford upon Avon in Warwickshire'.[29] The geographic connection makes the possibility enticing, as Guy was Shakespeare's local hero. Relics of his marvellous adventures were scattered across the county, from the monstrous boar's shoulder-bone hung on Coventry's Great Gate, to a rib from the giant Dun Cow on display at Warwick castle. The play ends with King Athelstan ordering the instalment of these monuments, along with a 'Hermitage' at Guy's Cliffe, on the River Avon.

The final – and perhaps unnecessary – reference to a hermitage at the end of the play shows a willingness to represent Catholic practices and ideals on stage, without criticism or comment. As in previous versions of the romance, Guy commits to undertake his pilgrimage to the Holy Land without any sacramental procedure, and he does so principally for 'holy zeal to see my Saviours Tomb', rather than any piercing contrition. But after fighting Saracens he commits the residue of his life to 'zealous Prayers and repentant Tears' for his sinful youth, and in a moment of introspection he articulates an analogy between chivalric prowess and penitential quest that shows 'amendes makyng' to be at the heart of his adventure:

> *Guy*: Thou Fight with Monsters, Fight thou with thy Grave,
>   And for thy sins humble forgivenesse crave.

This understanding of forgiveness as an outcome of penitential sweat and tears is given divine endorsement near the play's end, when an angel appears before Guy in his cave:

> *Angel*: Now Guy of Warwick is accomplished,
>   The full effect of all thy Pilgrimage.
>   Then rise and pray, thy sins may be forgiven,
>   For Angels wait to bear thy soul to Heaven.

As much as the romance takes the old religion's view of penance seriously, it is not so sober-minded when it comes to its own form. In Act II Guy finds

---

[28] The other Middle English penitential romances give their heroes the best of both worlds – prosperity in later life and heaven after – but the lack of a bonus earthly reward for Guy would not have tipped the genre from romance to tragedy.

[29] *The Tragical History, Admirable Atchievments and various events of Guy Earl of Warwick* (London, 1661), sigs. E2v, E3r. Helen Cooper points out that Sparrow also self-identifies as a 'bird of Venus', perhaps an allusion to the poet of *Venus and Adonis*. The name Sparrow may also be a response to Greene's 1592 attack on Shakespeare as an 'upstart crow'; see 'Guy of Warwick, Upstart Crows and Mounting Sparrows', *Shakespeare, Marlowe, Jonson: New Directions in Biography*, ed. Takashi Kozuka and J.R. Mulryne (Aldershot, 2006), pp. 119–38.

himself frozen by an enchanter's spell, and he is only saved when the Fairy King Oberon shows up in the nick of time, with the hero of another medieval romance, Huon of Bordeaux. But the fairy intrusion leads only to further calamities. After a bout of fairy music and dancing, Sparrow is tackled by the fairies and pinched on the bottom. The silliness of this Act only ends when the narrator Time shows up to whisk all of us to the Holy Land, a place populated with caricatured Saracens, including a Sultan and his side-kick sorcerer Zorastes, who fly (rather than charge) into battle against the Christians. This is mature romance at its most ripe, in which writers with nearly four hundred years of generic expectations at their back can play with the well-worn conventions of superstition and old magic, precisely the 'foolish toyes' that the Protestants railed against and the humanists found quaint.[30]

While the last decade of the sixteenth century saw penitential romances adapted for the popular stage, it also saw them reworked by the so-called University Wits. Thomas Lodge's romance, *The famous, true and historicall life of Robert second Duke of Normandy, surnamed for his monstrous birth and behaviour, Robin the Divell* (1591), is a work of euphuistic prose steeped in the conventions of the novella and the pastoral. But while it taps into the Elizabethan vogue for contemporary continental romances, it is also a work of antiquarianism that shows Lodge's fascination with the Middle Ages and with Catholicism, a fascination that would eventually lead to his conversion. The earliest surviving version of the Robert the Devil story in English, *Sir Gowther* (c.1400), contains those elements of folk-belief and superstition that, like Oberon and the fairies, reformers considered to be characteristic of an age that 'did swymme in superstition'. When Gowther's mother prays to the Virgin to give her a child by any means necessary ('On what maner scho ne roghth', line 66), a shapeshifting incubus demon appears to impregnate her, first in the form of her husband and then, once the deed is done, as a 'felturd fende' (shaggy fiend, line 74) who happens to be Merlin's father as well.[31] Gowther's gratuitous sins, from nun-raping to abbey-burning, are thus a product of the fact that he is literally half demon, but this makes his penitential arc all the more astounding because it is all the more steep – from devil to saint.[32]

---

[30] The surviving print of *Guy* preserves a note at the foot of the final page: 'This piece might serve for a Bartholomew fair Droll' (sig. F4r). It is dated 1793, but the sentiment may not have been out of place amongst certain audiences in 1593 (nor indeed amongst modern-day audiences).

[31] *Sir Gowther*, in *The Middle English Breton Lays*, ed. Anne Laskaya and Eve Salisbury (Kalamazoo, 2001), p. 267.

[32] The modern title *Sir Gowther*, which in itself creates expectations of romance, comes from 'Explicit Syr Gother' following the text in one of the two manuscripts that preserve it: Edinburgh, National Library of Scotland, MS Advocates' 19.3.1. The other surviving manuscript to preserve the text (BL, Royal MS 17.B.43) ends the text with 'explicit vita sancti'. The veer towards hagiography is reinforced in the Royal text with additional lines near the end of the

In both the metrical and prose versions of the early sixteenth century, Robert is not actually the son of a devil; rather, his mother makes the rash promise of giving him to the devil at his conception.[33] Lodge's version offers no hint of the diabolical whatsoever, though Lodge notes that some 'historiographers' – his sources – thought Robert was enchanted, since rather than drawing nourishment from his wet-nurse he bites off her nipples. Ascribing the marvellous or the strange to reports of other historians is typical of the way Lodge positions himself in relation to his subject's Catholic past. He locates Robert in a plausible (if inaccurate) lineage and he sets the romance in real time: 'about the yeare of our Lord 750'.[34] It is a tale 'drawne out of the old and ancient antiquaries' (sig. A2v), in which the antique is the Middle Ages, not the classical past, and it is an age that, in the epistle to the reader, he sets apart as being distinct from his own. Lodge also consistently embraces, in the particularities of detail, the Catholic landscape of his romance. A common objective in the writing of history is to use the distant past as a means of commenting on the present, and one wonders how readers in the 1590s, some perhaps with living memory of the dissolution, would have reacted to passages such as this:

> Oh the horror and confusion of those times, where iniquitie was held for equitie, and divelishnes accompted desert. In religious houses this Devill of a man, and divelish man, in stead of reverencing the learned, rid them of their lives; for at *Ambois* he entered a Monastery of Minorites, and cutting off the fattest Friers heads, he pitched them upon powles, causing the veriest knave to carrie the crosse, and the rest apparelled in Coapes, to tune a divelish Dirge of impietie. (sig. E4v)

Certainly, every version of the Robert story revels in the gratuity of the hero's pre-penance antics, but where Lodge's text shows its historical situation, its distance from the 'middle tyme' of its own setting, is in the treatment of Robert's conversion, which may be considered in relation to the pre-Reformation versions.

In *Sir Gowther*, the hero is suddenly roused to consciousness of his spiritual state when, almost in passing, someone mentions that he is probably 'full syb

---

text: 'There he lyeth in a shrine of gold/ And doth maracles, as it is told,/ And hatt Seynt Gotlake'. Guthlac (c.673–714) was a Mercian warrior who took up a hermetic life at Crowland. He was seen as one of the most important saints of pre-conquest England.

[33] The early sixteenth-century prose version, printed by Wynkyn de Worde in 1500 and 1517, is a translation of the French prose romance *Vie du terrible Robert le Diable*. The English metrical version of 1510, which survives in its entirety only in a Banyster manuscript (MS Egerton 3132A), is based on the English prose version. The Middle English *Sir Gowther* is based on the twelfth-century French romance *Robert le Diable*.

[34] Thomas Lodge, *The famous, true and historicall life of Robert second Duke of Normandy, surnamed for his monstrous birth and behaviour, Robin the Divell* (London, 1591), sig. B1r.

tho deyll' (212). Given his history of mayhem, something twigs, and he rides to his mother's castle to learn the truth:

> He seyd, 'Dame, tell me in hye,
> Who was my fadur, withowt lye,
>   Or this schall thoro the glyde';
> He sette his fachon to hur hart:
> 'Have done, yf thu lufe thi qwart!'
>   Ho onswarde hym that tyde –
> 'My lord', scho seyd, 'that dyed last'.
> 'Y hope', he seyd, 'thou lyus full fast';
>   Tho teyrus he lett don glyde.
>
> 'Son, sython y schall tho sothe say:
> In owre orcharde apon a day
>   A fende gat the thare,
> As lyke my lorde as he myght be,
> Undurneyth a cheston tre';
>   Then weppyd thei bothe full sare.
> 'Go schryfe the, modur, and do tho best,
> For y wyll to Rome or that y rest
>   To lerne anodur lare'. (220–37)

The passage begins with an analogical foreshadowing. Just as Gowther's solid blade is poised to 'glyde' through his mother's soft heart, so too, by the end of the stanza, do Gowther's tears 'glyde' down, a physiological manifestation of the inner softening of his own heart. The weeping continues after the story of his diabolic progeny is verified, the tears being a standard confirmation of contrition, but only his mother is to undertake an ordinary procedure of confession. Gowther, as he repeats a few lines later, opts for something more extravagant: 'Y wyll to Rome to tho apostyll,/ That he mey schryfe me and asoyll' (250–1). The reference to the pope as 'the apostle' did not, of course, survive the Reformation, but neither did the quest to Rome for absolution. In the prose version of 1500 Robert swears to 'leve my synnes and do penaunce therfore', but first he vows to 'take the waye to Rome to be assoiled of my synnes', a journey he likewise undertakes in the metrical version of 1510.

By 1591, Robert's extravagant insistence on confessing only to the pope himself is replaced by the lengthy doctoring of an old hermit. Gone, too, is any mechanistic correlation between penance and absolution. The hermit encourages him 'for pennance to goe barefoote to Rome on Pilgrimage, wearing at his back a cloth of haire' (sigs. E3v–E4r), but this is only after the hermit 'reconciled him to a stayed and holie course of life' (sig. E3v). The major spiritual battle in this 1591 version has nothing to do with the austerity of Robert's pilgrimage to

Rome, nor with any adversity he may face there, as a fool in court or as a knight in battle against the Saracens. Instead, the principal adversary is 'despair', or as Lodge also puts it, 'cursed melancholie' (sig. E2v). Just as Redcrosse begins his penitential trajectory in the cave of Despair, so is Robert nursed back to health with a homily that begins with the precept that God is 'mercifull to forgive beyond our conceit' (sig. E3r). The idea that God is omnipotent and, despite the severity of our sins, capable of extraordinary mercy, is commonplace in the religious literature of the Middle Ages. Indeed, it is at the heart of many surviving sermons and sermon exempla in Middle English. *Sir Gowther* ends on much the same point. Just as God makes the blind see, the dumb speak, the crooked straight and the mad sane, so too does he have the miraculous capacity to forgive, despite everything (lines 733–44). Of course, this belief is shared by Catholics and Protestants alike; the difference lies in the path to forgiveness, forged either by divine grace or by the sweat and tears of making amends.

As the several *Robert the Devil* texts make clear, the idea of self-knowledge is central to the penitential process. The hermit says to Robert: 'the knowledge of thy sinne is a mighty step to thy repentance', a sentiment captured in the metaphor that 'deawes of teares', central to the previous *Robert* texts as well, can become 'sinewes and strings to drawe thee to heaven' (sigs. E2v–E3r). The image is nearly the exact opposite of what we find in another penitential narrative from a few years later:

> *Lear.* You do me wrong to take me out o' the grave:
> Thou art a soul in bliss; but I am bound
> Upon a wheel of fire, that mine own tears
> Do scald like moulten lead. (Folio text, IV.vi.38–41)[35]

It is a conceit that would have been entirely recognisable to audiences familiar with popular afterlife visions, including readers of the two late fifteenth-century manuscripts preserving *Sir Gowther*: the Advocates' MS, which also contains the *Vision of Tundale*, and the Royal MS, which contains a copy of *St Patrick's Purgatory* as well as the *Vision of Tundale*. The flipped logic of Lear's weeping, that what redeems in life becomes that which torments in hell, is a standard technique of psychological torture in visions of purgatory and hell. Lear's imagining that he has been dragged out of the grave, and given a painfully momentary glimpse at bliss, might have also recalled the engraved title page to Foxe's *Actes and Monuments*, which shows heaven on one side and demons dragging souls into a fiery hell on the other. The play also represents Lear as bound to another device, a rack, evoked by Kent to suggest the maliciousness of Lear's fate: 'O, let him pass. He hates him/ That would upon the

---

[35] All references from the play are from *The Oxford Shakespeare: The Complete Works*, ed. Stanley Wells et al., 2nd edn. (Oxford, 2005).

rack of this tough world/ Stretch him out longer' (Folio text, V.iii.289–91). In Act II, when there is still time to make amends, Lear's Fool warns against the downward spin of the Wheel of Fortune (II.ii.245–6), but by Act IV, the wheel becomes another tool of torture, and it does not matter whether one is at the top or the bottom as the whole of it is engulfed in flames.

It has been argued before that Shakespeare drew from the penitential romances in writing *Lear*. In particular Lodge's 1591 *Robert* is credited as a source, along with some version of *Robert of Cisyle*, since in both works penance takes the form of the hero (in the case of *Robert of Cisyle*, a king) humbling himself to the position of a court fool.[36] The play's investments in penitential fiction, however, are much more ingrained than a borrowing of motifs or plot devices.[37] Regan says that her father is a man who 'hath ever but slenderly known himself' (Folio text, I.i.292–3), and as is clear from the penitential manuals of the Middle Ages as much as from the several *Robert the Devil* romances, introspection and self-knowledge are fundamental to contrition and repentance. It is, moreover, a necessary first step in the process of making amends. From the play's very first inquisition, in which Cordelia, unlike her sisters, is only able to be honest, Shakespeare utilises several strategies for addressing the problem of how to make inner-selves – and hidden truths – openly known. There is Kent's disguise, and his shifty response to Lear that evokes contemporary anxieties of religious identification: 'I do profess to be no less than I seem […] and to eat no fish' (Folio text, I.iv.14, 18). Then the Gloucester subplot takes up the feigning of Edmund and the disguise of Edgar, and resolves the problem of hidden truth using the standard method of medieval romance: trial by combat. Even all those colourful insults are attempts to characterise disguised identity and interiority. 'What dost thou know me for?' is the question Oswald asks that sets off Kent's torrent of abuse: 'whoreson, glass-gazing, superserviceable, finical rogue', etc (Folio text, II.ii.12, 16–17). Of course Kent knows more than Oswald's exterior betrays.

Perhaps the play's most penitential moment, however, comes in the midst of the storm:

> *Lear.* Let the great gods,
>   That keep this dreadful pother o'er our heads,
>   Find out their enemies now. Tremble, thou wretch
>   That hast within thee undivulged crimes

---

[36] *Robert of Cisyle* was extremely popular. It survives in ten manuscripts, but it was also a known folk-type, and from what sources indicate, it was popular on the stage; see Donna B. Hamilton, 'Some Romance Sources for *King Lear: Robert of Sicily* and *Robert the Devil*', SP 71 (1974), 173–91.

[37] On *Lear*'s ties to the Middle Ages, see Helen Cooper, *Shakespeare and the Medieval World* (London, 2010), pp. 164–9.

> Unwhipped of justice; hide thee, thou bloody hand,
> Thou perjured and thou simular man of virtue
> That art incestuous; caitiff, to pieces shake,
> That under covert and convenient seeming
> Hast practised on man's life; close pent-up guilts,
> Rive your concealing continents, and cry
> These dreadful summoners grace. I am a man
> More sinned against than sinning. (Folio text, III.ii.49–60)

This is language deeply indebted to discourses of confession, and with the 'undivulged crimes/ Unwhipped of justice', an 'amendes makyng' logic of penance. Articulating the various wrongdoings as 'sin' is only the final steer to a Christian moral paradigm, or at least one that Lear cannot know in particular but can wish for in principle. 'Rive your concealing continents, and cry/ These dreadful summoners grace' is, in essence, just a more poetic way of instructing sinners in 'open shrift of our mouth how we haf synned', from the *Lay Folks' Catechism*. The Quarto text of *Lear* gives 'concealed centres' instead of 'concealing continents', which puts more weight on the connection between interiority and identity, while 'continents' puts more emphasis on the idea of exposure, of 'open shrift'. However, just as the great gods will not hear a confession, so too, in Shakespeare's strict maintenance of a pre-Christian cosmology (despite Lear's yearnings), is there no hope of penance leading to a happy ending. The 'Ecclesiasticall Story', with its tripartite chronology of the primitive church, the 'middle tyme' and the present reformed church, does not have room for Lear and his pagan world. If Guy of Warwick can die on stage as a romance hero, it is because his reward in bliss is assured. But it is only when Lear dies on stage, with Cordelia in his arms, that the audience realises that the whole of his penitential process counted for nothing. There is no one checking the 'amendes makyng' ledger-balance, and there is no grace. Lear's promised end is indeed a wheel of fire.

The English Laureate in Time
John Skelton's *Garland of Laurel**

⁋ MARY C. FLANNERY ⁋

> Skelton was writing on the cusp between the Middle Ages and the Renaissance, and almost all criticism of him grounds itself on a recognition of that transitional or ambiguous quality in him.
>
> Helen Cooper, 'Skeltonics'[1]

The poetry of John Skelton occupies an uneasy position in time. Unclaimed either by medievalists or by early modernists (or at least fervently claimed by neither), his canon has been relegated by contemporary periodisation to the no man's land between the late medieval and early modern periods. While aspects of his style and choices of genre recall medieval trends, his politically themed verse reflects the controversies of his own time, controversies in which he was sometimes personally embroiled.[2] He claims to work in the mould of the great English poets of the medieval period – Chaucer, Gower, and Lydgate – while anticipating developments such as the fascination with fame and immortality that are often deemed characteristic of Renaissance verse.[3] Consequently, he has come to be viewed, in the words of one critic, 'as a transitional figure within modern accounts of literary history and periodization'.[4]

Skelton's marginal position in time mirrors the shifting temporality that

---

* My thanks to Ellen Muehlberger and Stephanie Downes for their help in accessing crucial secondary material for this essay. I am very grateful to the editors of this volume, and to James Wade, for their comments on earlier drafts.
[1] Helen Cooper, 'Skeltonics', *LRB* 28, 14 December 2006, p. 32.
[2] On Skelton and Tudor politics, see Greg Walker, *John Skelton and the Politics of the 1520s* (New York, 1988). For an account of Skelton's life and work, see John Scattergood, 'John Skelton', *ODNB*, as well as Scattergood's more recent *John Skelton: The Career of an Early Tudor Poet* (Dublin, 2014). On Skelton's posthumous reputation, see A.S.G. Edwards, ed., *John Skelton: The Critical Heritage* (London, 1981), esp. pp. 7–12.
[3] For the argument that this fascination with fame derived from Burgundian fashions, see Gordon Kipling, *The Triumph of Honour: Burgundian Origins of the Elizabethan Renaissance* (Hague, 1977). On the preoccupation with fame as one of the hallmarks of Renaissance culture, see also Jacob Burckhardt, *The Civilization of the Renaissance in Italy* (London, 1990). As I have argued, however, this preoccupation with fame is also a distinguishing feature of Lydgate's verse: *John Lydgate and the Poetics of Fame* (Cambridge, 2012).
[4] Maura Tarnoff, 'Sewing Authorship in John Skelton's *Garlande or Chapelet of Laurell*', *ELH* 75 (2008), 415.

accompanies his preoccupation with his laureate status. In the prologue to his *Eneydos* (published in or around 1490), William Caxton describes 'mayster John Skelton' as 'late created poete laureate in the unyversite of oxenforde', a title he seems also to have received from the University of Louvain by 1492, and from the University of Cambridge in 1493.[5] As Skelton's modern biographers have noted, these titles reflected an academic achievement in rhetoric rather than what early humanists or modern readers would understand by either 'poet' or 'laureate'.[6] Nevertheless, Skelton's oft-remarked reiteration of these titles throughout his corpus is indicative of his investment in them, an investment that Seth Lerer, among others, has argued borders on obsession.[7] Moreover, as Skelton's most thoroughly laureate poem, *The Garland of Laurel*, demonstrates, his ambition seems to have been to imbue the purely academic title with all the classicised lustre associated with the title awarded to Francis Petrarch (1304–74), which – as Petrarch's own coronation address noted – linked laureate poets to the performance of a specific task: 'the memorialization of the glory of those whom they serve'.[8] Thus, in the *Garland*, Skelton

---

[5] Caxton quotation taken from Edwards, ed., *Skelton: The Critical Heritage*, p. 43. See Scattergood, 'Skelton', *ODNB*; Edwards, ed., *Skelton: The Critical Heritage*, pp. 49–53; and Walker, *John Skelton*, pp. 35–40.

[6] See A.W. Barnes, 'Constructing the Sexual Subject of John Skelton', *ELH* 71 (2004), 48n1; H.L.R. Edwards, *Skelton: The Life and Times of an Early Tudor Poet* (London, 1949), p. 35; and Maurice Pollet, *John Skelton: Poet of Tudor England*, trans. John Warrington (London, 1971), p. 11. John Dryden was the first poet to be appointed England's official poet laureate, in 1668. The first English poet to lay claim to the title, however, was John Kay, in the English prose translation of *The Siege of Rhodes* he produced for Edward IV (c.1482); see also Robert Meyer-Lee, *Poets and Power from Chaucer to Wyatt* (Cambridge, 2007), pp. 15, 273n58). Jane Griffiths notes that 'the fourteenth-century Italian reinvention of a supposed classical tradition of the laureation of poets' coincides with a conflation of the more academic understanding of the laureate's achievements in rhetoric and grammar and the notion of 'independent poetic production'; see *John Skelton and Poetic Authority: Defining the Liberty to Speak* (Oxford, 2006), p. 26.

[7] 'It is the fascination with the name, with the investment of authority in the sign of the writer, that John Skelton raises almost to an obsession. Skelton's poetry is in large degree about self-naming and self-titling'; see Seth Lerer, *Chaucer and His Readers: Imagining the Author in Late-Medieval England* (Princeton, 1996), p. 193. In her study of the transmission of Skelton's laureate title in manuscript and print, Griffiths also refers to 'the almost obsessive emphasis on the title of laureate in later Tudor editions of Skelton's works', but argues that this obsessiveness 'is less the result of conscious choice than of a conspicuous lack of interest on the part of his printers'. However, she also argues that references to Skelton's laureate title in printed editions of his texts produced during his lifetime suggest that, in these instances, 'the obsession with the author's status may be construed as the poet's own'; see Jane Griffiths, 'What's in a Name? The Transmission of "John Skelton, Laureate" in Manuscript and Print', *HLQ* 67 (2004), 217.

[8] Meyer-Lee, *Poets and Power*, p. 20. For Petrarch's coronation address, see *Scritti Inediti di Francesco Petrarca*, ed. Attilio Hortis (Trieste, 1874), pp. 311–28; for the English translation, see Ernest H. Wilkins, *Studies in the Life and Works of Petrarch* (Cambridge, MA, 1955), pp. 300–13. Griffiths goes so far as to argue that '[t]he very multiplicity of stances on which [Skelton] draws and the way in which he repeatedly names himself as poet, *vates*, and *poet laureate*

depicts his own quest for the laurel crown as one that must be accomplished through the memorialisation of a series of female patrons, to whom he is bound as their 'remembrauncer' (864).⁹ But as I will show, Skelton's emphasis on memorialisation situates the laureate poet between temporalities, forever looking to the past for models to emulate, memorialising past and present, and yet always bearing the future in mind while combatting the threat of future obscurity.

This essay explores Skelton's understanding of the laureate poet's position in time by means of the poem that enacts Skelton's fictional crowning as poet laureate. As I will show, *The Garland of Laurel* repeatedly insists that the laureate's position in time is both inherently and necessarily retrospective, but also anticipatory. Skelton's poem suggests that the laureate mindset must continually look to the past, but also to perpetuity, to the literary afterlife. I begin by considering the *Garland*'s account of the origin myth of the laurel and laureation, which initiates what I show to be the poem's relentless preoccupation with the passing of time. I then consider how the dream vision's opening debate between Pallas and the Queen of Fame, together with the *Garland*'s series of concluding envoys and poems, formalises the simultaneous looking-back and looking-forward in time that characterises Skelton's understanding of the laureate enterprise. In my conclusion, I suggest that we might use Skelton's depiction of the laureate in time to reflect on his status as a temporally marginalised figure in the English literary canon.

Delayed Gratification and Laureate Desire

Richard Faukes's 1523 print edition of *The Garland of Laurel* introduces the poem as '[a] ryght delectable treatyse upon a goodly Garlande or Chapelet of laurell by mayster Skelton Poete laureat'.[10] Although the printed text's colophon gives its date of publication as 1523, it is likely that Skelton composed the poem as early as the 1490s, and that the later print edition was an 'updated version'.[11]

---

suggests that none of the sources of authority that he is able to name is quite sufficient for him'; see *John Skelton and Poetic Authority*, p. 5. I am suggesting instead that he aims to ascribe greater weightiness to the laureate titles he already possesses.

[9] John Skelton, *Garlande or Chapelet of Laurell*, *John Skelton: The Complete English Poems*, ed. John Scattergood (London, 1983), pp. 312–58. All citations from the poem will be taken from this edition and cited above by line number. This notion of the poet as 'remembrauncer' recalls Chaucer's Prologue to the *Legend of Good Women*, which describes 'olde bokes' as 'of remembraunce the keye' (cited from the F version of the Prologue in *Riverside Chaucer*, lines 25–6). On this theme, see also Robert O. Payne, *The Key of Remembrance: A Study of Chaucer's Poetics* (New Haven, CT, 1963).

[10] *A ryght delectable traytyse upon a goodly Garlande or Chapelet of Laurell by mayster Skelton Poete laureat* (London, 1523), sig. A1r.

[11] Meyer-Lee has argued that Skelton composed the *Garland* in three stages, beginning in 1492: *Poets and Power*, p. 215; and, for a detailed account, Appendix 1 in *The Latin Writings of John*

The poem's introduction establishes a grand, authoritative tone that persists throughout the text, which Skelton explicitly frames as a laureate product, a laurel garland in verse.

Laureation has been described as 'very much a product of the later Middle Ages', a concept that 'straddles the divide between the medieval and the early modern'.[12] At the same time, as a concept that derives etymologically and thematically from the association of Phoebus, god of poetry, with the laurel crown, laureation looks back to classical concepts regarding poetry and its ability not only to confer undying fame on its subject, but also to secure it for its author.[13] For late medieval authors, the consummate example of the poet laureate was Petrarch, whose laureation took place in Rome in 1341. Indeed, the English word *laureate* ('[c]rowned with laurel as a mark of poetic excellence'; 'distinguished, honored') first appears in reference to Petrarch, when Chaucer's Clerk describes 'Frauncesys Petrak, the lauriat poete' as the man 'whos rethorike sweete/ Enlumyned al Ytaille of poetrie'.[14] Although the post of England's poet laureate did not exist before the seventeenth century, English poets writing as early as the fifteenth century drew on Petrarchan models of laureate poetics in their work, stressing the ability of laureate poetry to immortalise the past for the future.[15] Thus, as I have argued elsewhere, if laureate discourse is 'a poetics of loss', perpetually 'recalling the lost customs of antiquity', it is also a poetics of remembrance, enacting and enabling memorialisation of a wide range of entities and subjects, from the classical past to the poet and his works.[16] Whereas Lerer has suggested that 'reading like a laureate' involves 'not just reading for the past but writing for the present', I would suggest that the Petrarchan model of writing like a laureate involves continually looking to the past, seeing the past as present, and writing for the future.[17] In other words, writing laureate poetry involves a continuous making-present of the past, but for future readers – those for whom the current present will be the past – whether in the distant or immediate future.

Skelton, ed. David R. Carlson, *SP* 88 (1991), 102–9. See also Melvin J. Tucker, 'The Ladies in Skelton's "Garland of Laurel"', *Renaissance Quarterly* 22 (1969), 344, and 'Skelton and Sheriff Hutton', *English Language Notes* 4 (1967), 245–59; and Owen Gingerich and Melvin J. Tucker, 'The Astronomical Dating of Skelton's *Garland of Laurel*', *HLQ* 32 (1969), 207–20.

[12] Larry Scanlon, 'Lydgate's Poetics: Laureation and Domesticity in the *Temple of Glass*', *John Lydgate: Poetry, Culture, and Lancastrian England*, ed. Larry Scanlon and James Simpson (Notre Dame, 2006), p. 63.

[13] On the unlikelihood that laureation ceremonies took place in antiquity, see J.B. Trapp, 'The Owl's Ivy and the Poet's Bays: An Enquiry into Poetic Garlands', *Journal of the Warburg and Courtauld Institutes* 21 (1958), 235.

[14] 'The Clerk's Prologue' (lines 31–3), *Riverside Chaucer*. See also *MED*, s.v. 'laureate'.

[15] Meyer-Lee, *Poets and Power*.

[16] On what I have termed 'laureate memorialisation', see *John Lydgate and the Poetics of Fame*, pp. 106–14. On the laureate 'poetics of loss', see Scanlon, 'Lydgate's Poetics', p. 69.

[17] Lerer, *Chaucer and His Readers*, p. 174.

Although it is introduced as the product of 'mayster Skelton Poete laureat', the entire premise of *The Garland of Laurel* centres on the question of whether or not Skelton has 'made sum memoryall,/ Wherby he myght have a name inmortall' and 'avaunce/ Unto the rowme of laureat promotyve' (115–19). The poem depicts Skelton's quest to prove his worthiness for the laurel crown and his fictional crowning as a laureate in a dream vision.[18] The *Garland* opens with the narrator's reflections on '[h]ow all thynge passyth as doth the somer flower' and '[h]ow oftyn fortune varyeth in an howre', which weary him so much that he leans against the stump of an oak to rest, and eventually falls asleep (8–14). He dreams that he stands before a richly decorated pavilion, within which Dame Pallas and the Queen of Fame are debating whether or not Skelton deserves a place in the Queen's court. Skelton is conveyed to the pavilion by Gower, Chaucer and Lydgate, where Pallas commands that he be brought to the palace of the Queen of Fame. After bringing him to the palace, the three English poets leave him in the care of Fame's registrar, Dame Occupation. Occupation guides the dreamer-Skelton through a series of alternately troubling and paradisiacal scenes, until he arrives at a room occupied by noble female figures from Skelton's own life. Led by Skelton's patroness, the Countess of Surrey, these women are engaged in making a 'cronell of lawrell' for Skelton (776); as the Countess argues,

> For of all ladyes he hath the library,
> Ther names recountyng in the court of Fame;
> Of all gentylwomen he hath the scruteny,
> In Fames court reportyng the same;
> For yet of women he never sayd shame,
> But if they were counterfettes that women them call,
> That list of there lewdnesse with hym for to brall. (780–6)

In gratitude to his patroness and her companions, 'Poeta Skelton' proceeds to compose a series of lyrics in their honour, which prompts Occupation to lead Skelton back to the Queen of Fame so that his works may stand as evidence of his merit. While the rest of the court admire his laurel, Occupation reads an account of Skelton's work from a marvellously illuminated book, which, when she reaches her account of Skelton's laurel, causes '[a]ll orators and poetis, with other grete and smale' to shout '*Triumpha, triumpha!*' (1504–6). The Queen of Fame commands Occupation to shut the book, and the dreamer awakens to behold Janus in the heavens. The *Garland* concludes with a series of envoys and short verses anticipating the poem's reception.

The *Garland*'s dream vision constitutes a fictional account of the task by

---

[18] On the *Garland*'s relationship to the medieval tradition of dream poetry, see A.C. Spearing, *Medieval Dream-Poetry* (Cambridge, 1976), pp. 211–18.

which poets become laureate ('the memorialization of the glory of those whom they serve'), as well as a fictional account of the award awaiting the poet who performs that task.[19] Indeed, as A.C. Spearing has put it, by the end of the poem, 'one begins to suspect that "the laurel" has come to refer not just to the garland Skelton as dreamer is wearing but also the poem called after it which Skelton as poet is writing'.[20] The *Garland* is thus a self-fulfilling artefact, one that is presented as cause, means, and effect of Skelton's laureate status. At the same time, however, the poem's dream-vision framework and the dreamer's rude awakening at precisely his moment of triumph within the dream function as reminders that this particular story of laureation 'could only happen in a dream'.[21] Thus the very poem that enacts Skelton's fictional laureate crowning, and which embodies the crown with which he envisions himself being rewarded, also stands as evidence of something missing, or something not-yet-achieved.

That *The Garland of Laurel* might simultaneously dub Skelton 'Poete laureat' and conclude with Poeta Skelton waking to no crown at all is not altogether surprising. By depicting his dream-laureation and his non-laureate state on waking, the *Garland* might easily be read as a bid for further recognition. I would argue, however, that the poem's simultaneous depiction of the fulfilment and non-fulfilment of Skelton's laureate status reflects the nature of laureation itself, which in turn may be read as springing from the origin story of laureation and of the tree from which it derives its name. This origin story is, in fact, depicted very early on in the *Garland*, when the Queen of Fame commands Aeolus to blow his trumpet and summon '[w]hat poetis we have at our retenewe' '[t]o se if Skelton wyll put hymselfe in prease/ Amonge the thickeste of all the hole rowte' (238–40). When the crowd of famed poets appears, Skelton notes that it is led by the god of poetry himself:

> I sawe come after, I wote, full lytell lake
> Of a thousande poetes assembled togeder.
> But Phebus was formest of all that cam theder;
>
> Of laurell levis a cronell on his hede,
> With heris encrisped yalowe as the golde,
> Lamentyng Daphnes, whome with the darte of lede
> Cupyde hath stryken so that she ne wolde
> Concente to Phebus to have his herte in holde,

---

[19] Meyer-Lee, *Poets and Power*, p. 20.
[20] Spearing, *Medieval Dream-Poetry*, p. 217.
[21] Ibid., p. 218. Spearing suggests 'Skelton is here once more making fun of himself: his vanity is as much a literary device as Chaucer's modesty, though no doubt both grew out of the actual life-styles of the poets as men'. As I argue below, however, this mock-vanity also seems to resonate with the poem's interest in laureation and time.

> But, for to preserve her maidenhode clene,
> Transformyd was she into the laurell grene.
>
> Meddelyd with murnynge the moost parte of his muse,
> 'O thoughtfull herte,' was evermore his songe!
> 'Daphnes, my derlynge, why do you me refuse?
> Yet loke on me, that lovyd you have so longe,
> Yet have compassyon upon my paynes stronge.'
> He sange also how, the tre as he did take
> Betwene his armes, he felt her body quake. (285–301)

The first thing that the dreamer notes about Phoebus's appearance is his laurel crown. The syntax of these lines makes it difficult to be sure of whether it is Phoebus or his laurel crown – or both – that is '[l]amentyng Daphnes', the nymph who, struck by Cupid's leaden arrow, spurned the lovestruck Phoebus (whose heart Cupid had spitefully pierced with a golden arrow to incite a love he knew the nymph would never return). Daphne's prayers to evade the pursuing Phoebus were answered by her transformation into the laurel tree, which Phoebus then adopted as his personal emblem.[22] Thus, while it is symbolic of the god of poetry and of immortality, the laurel is also a symbol of Phoebus's frustrated desire, a desire that will never be fulfilled. In linking such a symbol to poetic achievement, laureation inscribes itself within an origin myth in which gratification is perpetually delayed and impossible to achieve. Notably, Skelton depicts Phoebus as *still* lamenting, in the present tense: 'Daphnes, my derlynge, why do you me refuse?/ Yet loke on me, that lovyd you have so longe,/ Yet have compassyon upon my paynes stronge.' The god's repeated use of 'yet' (which in Middle English can mean both 'contrary or in contrast to the foregoing' and 'even now') denotes the continued frustration of his desire.[23] But this is not simply a straightforward retelling of the origin myth in real time; rather, Phoebus performs his identity as chief laureate poet (based on his past adoption of the laurel tree) while heading the procession of famous poets passing before the dreamer's eyes. Phoebus's unceasing lament suggests that he is somehow frozen in time, forever caught in the moment of desiring Daphne and not attaining her.

This same impossibility of attainment is precisely what inspires Phoebus to link the laurel tree to the art of poetry:

> O fatall Fortune, what I have I offendid?
> Odious Disdayne, why raist thou me on this facyon?
> But sith I have lost now that I entended,

---

[22] The story is recounted in Ovid's *Metamorphoses*; see *Metamorphoses I*, trans. Frank Justus Miller, rev. G.P. Goold, 3rd edn., 2 vols. (Cambridge, MA, 1977), 1: 438–567.
[23] *MED*, s.v. 'yet'.

And may not atteyne it by no medyacyon,
Yet, in remembraunce of Daphnes transformacyon,
All famous poetis ensuynge after me
Shall were a garlande of the laurell tre. (316–22)

The fact that Phoebus 'may not atteyne' what he desires triggers his act of remembrance, a gesture that will in turn be remembered by its embeddedness in laureate identity: 'All famous poetis ensuynge after me/ Shall were a garlande of the laurell tre.' Just as the laurel crown memorialises the divine remembrancer for his act of remembrance, so does the laureate poet's crown memorialise *him* for his memorialising poetry. The laureate's crown symbolises a moment when the attainment of a god's desire was made impossible, and entangles laureate poets in the same cycle of desire, frustration, and remembrance. As if to seal the connection between the myth and the poetic practice, no sooner has Phoebus made his decree than he is followed by 'a great nowmber ... [o]f poetis laureat of many dyverse nacyons' (323–4).[24]

The myth of Phoebus and Daphne is at heart a narrative of indefinitely delayed gratification that results in a symbol both of eternity and of what can never be achieved: the garland of laurel and everything it signifies. By beginning his dream vision with this reference to the origin story of the laurel tree, Skelton points to the way that the myth positions the laureate poet in time. Like Phoebus, the laureate poet is forever looking to the past as well as to the future. Although they work to memorialise their subject matter, laureate poets can never be sure of achieving the immortality for which they strive. This perspective sheds new light on what has long been one of the most oft-cited moments in *The Garland of Laurel*: the moment when the dreamer Skelton is confronted with the triumvirate of medieval England's greatest poets. Among the parade of famous poets in Phoebus's retinue, the dreamer sees

Gower, that first garnisshed our Englysshe rude,
And maister Chaucer, that nobly enterprysyd
How that our Englysshe myght fresshely be ennewed;
The monke of Bury then after them ensuyd,

---

[24] In a compelling article on the relationship between Skelton's laureate status and the 'laurel' embroidered for him by the ladies in *The Garland of Laurel*, Tarnoff remarks that, 'In the laureation scene [where the women embroider his laureate cap], Skelton deflects the erotic charge of a sexual encounter that never takes place onto a world of objects – the tokens of public ritual and textual transmission, the garment and the latter' ('Sewing Authorship', 416–17). Remarkably, however, she almost entirely overlooks the most important 'sexual encounter that never takes place' in the laureate tradition: that between Phoebus and Daphne, the origin myth of the laurel itself. (She only notes in passing that the poem interweaves 'Daphne's transformation into a laurel tree with the practice of needlework by aristocratic women' (418).)

Dane Johnn Lydgate. Theis Englysshe poetis thre,
As I ymagenyd, repayrid unto me,

Togeder in armes, as brethern, enbrasid;
There apparell farre passynge beyonde that I can tell;
With diamauntis and rubis there tabers were trasid,
None so ryche stones in Turkey to sell;
They wantid nothynge but the laurell[.] (387–97)

The last enigmatic line of this extract has attracted varied commentary. While acknowledging its ambiguity, Lerer argues that it 'denies the laureation to the older English poets', placing them 'outside the catalogue of laureates'.[25] Conversely, John Scattergood has suggested that the implication of this line might be that 'because of the nature and importance of their achievements in poetry these English poets ought to have been awarded the laurel, but had not been'.[26] Spearing opines that 'Skelton remarks patronizingly that "Thei wantid nothynge but the laurel" … for they, unlike Skelton himself in real life, had not received this academic distinction'.[27] I would argue, however, that regardless of – or perhaps even because of – the many laureate titles Skelton possessed at the time of his writing the *Garland*, his poem depicts him in a similarly 'wanting' position to that occupied by his three eminent predecessors. Skelton's remark concerning his predecessors resonates with laureation's own emphasis on lack and loss, on that which is wanting and perhaps can never be achieved. Following so closely on the heels of the laurel's origin myth, the remark chimes poignantly with Phoebus's story of unfulfilled desire. Even if Skelton presents himself as the culmination of English poetic achievement, he himself has not yet attained the laurel crown within the *Garland*'s dreamworld, and the very prize he hopes to secure is not a terminus, but instead a symbol of what laureates must continually strive for but can never be sure of attaining.

Janus-faced Laureates

The opening dream-scenes of Skelton's *Garland of Laurel* represent the laureate's peculiar position in time: as a poet who constantly remembers and memorialises but who always does so with posterity in mind. Even as the laureate poet labours in the service of future fame, the future moves away from him like Daphne eluding Phoebus, never to be caught. As I will show, Skelton's

---

[25] Lerer, *Chaucer and His Readers*, p. 207.
[26] John Scattergood, 'Skelton's *Garlande of Laurell* and the Chaucerian Tradition', *Chaucer Traditions: Studies in Honour of Derek Brewer*, ed. Ruth Morse and Barry Windeatt (Cambridge, 1990), p. 126.
[27] Spearing, *Medieval Dream-Poetry*, p. 214.

positioning of the laureate in time resonates with the structure of *The Garland of Laurel*, and with its preoccupation with the passage of time.

The early part of the *Garland* makes clear that the dreamer Skelton's attainment of the laurel crown depends on how he uses his time in the *Garland*'s dreamworld. Indeed, the main point of debate between Pallas and the Queen of Fame at the beginning of the dream concerns how Skelton has used his time up to the present. Although the Queen notes that Pallas has commanded that 'in my courte Skelton shulde have a place,/ Bycause that he his tyme studyously hath spent/ In your servyce', she argues that in fact 'Skelton is wonder slake,/ And, as we dare, we fynde in hym grete lake' (57–70). The Queen contends that Skelton should have spent more of his time attempting to 'purchase/ The favour of ladys with wordis electe' (75–6), and Pallas counters that, had he done so, he would have been vilified as a flatterer. After arguing for some time, the Queen agrees that if Skelton can present her with some evidence that he has written worthily and sufficiently, she will consider his candidacy, since in her opinion he is one who 'aquentyth hym with ydilnes' (228). To this end, Skelton's three companions in Fame's palace – Gower, Chaucer and Lydgate – introduce him to the guide who will accompany him during the rest of his journey:

> Lo, hither commyth a goodly maystres,
> Occupacyon, Famys regestary,
> Whiche shall be to you a sufferayne accessary,
> With syngular pleasurs to dryve away the tyme,
> And we shall se you ageyne or it be pryme. (521–5)

Medieval England's poetic triumvirate stresses both the fact that time is passing in the dreamworld (they will reconvene with Skelton 'or it be pryme') and that what matters is how Skelton the dreamer makes use of it. The figure of Occupation will not only help 'to dryve away the tyme', but will also record how Skelton spends it in order to provide evidence of his authorial industry at the end of the poem. Occupation's own words to Poeta Skelton establish the itinerary for the rest of the dream, an itinerary that is vague, but by no means aimless:

> And then she sayd, 'Whylis we have tyme and space
> To walke where we lyst, let us somwhat fynde
> To pas the tyme with, but let us wast no wynde,
> For ydle jangelers have but lytill braine;
> Wordes be swordes, and hard to call ageine.' (563–7)

Occupation's words ('Whylis we have tyme and space') make clear that Skelton has a finite amount of time in which to prove his worthiness. They may walk 'where we lyst', but this is not time to be wasted idly; indeed, her warning that they should 'wast no wynde' briskly forecloses the possibility of idle speech, or 'jangling'.[28] At the same time, her concluding remark concerning the damage that words can do suggests that the dreamer must also use his words with discretion, speaking neither idly nor without regard for the consequences.

The debate between Pallas and the Queen of Fame, the remarks of England's greatest poets, and Occupation's warnings combine to create a sense that time is hurrying by in the *Garland*. Time is a key factor for would-be laureates: they cannot sit – or write – idly, but instead must remain constantly aware of time and of their position in it. This sense of movement through time – or, more precisely, of one's position in relation to time that is moving – recalls the narrator's introductory reflections on mutability and the passage of time:

> In place alone then musynge in my thought
> How all thynge passyth as doth the somer flower,
> On every halfe my reasons forthe I sought,
> How oftyn fortune varyeth in an howre,
> Now clere wether, forthwith a stormy showre;
> All thynge compassyd, no perpetuyte,
> But now in welthe, now in adversyte. (8–14)

These musings frame the poem's laureate contents within an awareness that time is flying, and that there is 'no perpetuyte'. Yet perpetuity is precisely the aim of laureate memorialisation, and precisely what the evergreen laurel garland is itself meant to signify. And ironically enough, these reflections on mutability initiate an overarching structure that is spatially and temporally circular, as well as symbolic of the laurel garland's circularity. At the beginning of the poem, the dreamer's musings on mutability weary him and cause him to dream of the debate concerning whether or not he should be awarded the laurel crown, which in turn leads him to arrive at Fame's palace. At the conclusion of the dream vision, he returns to Fame's palace, having won the laurel, and the proof of his worthiness is recited by Occupation to an admiring crowd before he wakes to the same musings with which the poem began, musings that find their counterpoint in the first thing he sees before his eyes:

> My mynde of the grete din was somdele amasid.
> I wypid myne eyne for to make them clere.
> Then to the hevyn sperycall upwarde I gasid,
> Where I saw Janus, with his double chere,
> Makynge his almanak for the new yere;
> He turnyd his tirikkis, his volvell ran fast,
> Good luk this new yere, the olde yere is past.

---

[28] See *MED*, s.v. 'janglen': 'to chatter, talk idly, gossip'.

Mens tibi sit consulta, petis? Sic consule menti;
Emula sit Jani, retro speculetur et ante. (1512–20)

[Do you wish your mind to be skilful? In that case, pay attention to your mind; let it be like that of Janus which looks back and forward.]²⁹

Janus, the ancient Roman god of beginnings, endings, and gateways, here appears with his 'double chere': his two faces, one of which looks forward and the other of which looks backward.³⁰ Looking both to the new year and to the year that is past, Janus's position is emblematic of the position of the laureate poet, who is similarly Janus-faced, forever looking to the past, to what must be memorialised, but also looking ahead to the time to come, for which memorialisation is effected. The reference to Janus also serves to link the classical elements of the *Garland*'s dreamworld to Skelton's present in the waking world. Appearing in the very last lines of the main body of the poem, Janus brings the *Garland* full circle, returning the dreamer to his not-yet-mythically-laureate state. This circular structure in itself also mirrors the circularity of writing like a laureate, which involves the creation of new works of poetry that in turn are deemed worthy of the laurel when they appropriately memorialise their subject matter. It is unclear to whom the Latin quotation at the conclusion is being addressed, but one might imagine it addressed to fellow aspirants to the laureate crown: those who would earn that crown in the future must look to the past for their models and for their subject matter.

Both thematically and structurally, time and the urgency of its unceasing movement are key features in *The Garland of Laurel*. But I would argue that their importance does not derive solely from their prominence within the poem, but from the way that Skelton interweaves them with laureate concerns. The *Garland*'s preoccupation with the passing of time both reflects and embodies the laureate mindset, hyperconscious of its own position in relation to time that will continue to pass by. The poet laureate is writing against the clock, continually trying to suspend the possibility of obscurity and to secure immortality through his verse. Yet neither of these objectives can ever fully be achieved: even when posterity has passed judgement, it will turn into another present, and then another past.

---

[29] Scattergood's translation, Skelton, *Garlande*, p. 512.
[30] As V.A. Kolve notes, the name 'Janus' 'gives us (or is derived from) the common Latin name for a domestic door or gate (*janua*), as well as the name for a covered passage, an arcade, or a civic arch (*janus*) erected over a major thoroughfare'; see *Telling Images: Chaucer and the Imagery of Narrative II* (Stanford, 2009), p. 289n13. It is unclear what Skelton is meant to be seeing when he looks up to the 'hevyn sperycall', although Kolve suggests that, '[b]ecause the sun had been worshiped in his name in early Rome, some think his two faces originally symbolized the alternation of day and night' (p. 97).

Conclusion: 'Go, litill quaire ...'

When the dream vision draws to an end in *The Garland of Laurel*, the poem itself is far from over. Indeed, the dream vision is succeeded by one of the aspects of the *Garland* that has attracted the most critical commentary: a series of envoys addressed to Henry VIII and, more remarkably, Cardinal Wolsey, a long-time subject of Skelton's satirical verse. These envoys evidence what Stanley Fish has described as Skelton's 'disconcerting habit of attaching afterthoughts to his poems', and have led Lerer to remark that 'the *Garlande of Laurell* is itself a poem that refuses to end: a poem that continues to emend itself in different languages, meters, and styles'.[31] By way of a conclusion, I would like to argue that the unending quality of the *Garland*'s series of envoys reflects what Skelton presents as the laureate's unfinished, and perhaps unfinishable task: his effort to achieve immortality for himself and his subject matter.

The two early print editions of *The Garland of Laurel* boast a variety of envoys and short verses at the poem's conclusion. The 1523 edition includes two envoys that directly address the poem itself. The first, in Latin, instructs the poem,

> Ite, Britannorum lux O radiosa, Britannum
> Carmina nostra pium vestrum celebrate Catullum!
> Dicite, Skeltonis vester Adonis erat;
> Dicite, Skeltonis vester Homerus erat. (1521–4)

> [Go, shining light of the Britons, and celebrate, our songs, your worthy British Catullus! Say, Skelton was your Adonis; say, Skelton was your Homer.][32]

Skelton reassures his text that though it is 'barbarous' ('[b]arbara' (1525)), it is capable of rivalling the Latin verse of his classical predecessors. The Latin envoy is succeeded by an English envoy that also begins with Skelton addressing his poem. In Chaucerian fashion, he instructs his poem to 'Go, litill quaire,/ Demene you faire' (1533–4) before its readers, and simultaneously expresses hope that it will find a positive reception and fear that it may meet with hostility. This pair of envoys is then followed by a Latin poem on the laurel tree, and by a brief poem translated into French, Latin, and English that laments the death of Justice, the slumbering of Truth, and the departure of Right and Reason:

> No man wyll undertake
> The first twayne to wake;

---

[31] Stanley Fish, *John Skelton's Poetry* (New Haven, CT, 1965), p. 98; Lerer, *Chaucer and His Readers*, p. 201.
[32] Scattergood's translation, Skelton, *Garlande*, p. 512.

And the twayne last
Be withholde so fast
With mony, as men sayne,
They can not come agayne.[33]

Printed several decades after the poet's death, John Stow's 1568 edition of Skelton's works includes both Skelton's Latin and English envoys to his 'quaire', as well as an extra envoy (in Latin and English) addressed to Henry VIII and Cardinal Wolsey.[34] It omits the short poem on the laurel, as well as the translations of his poem on Justice, Truth, Right, and Reason.

All told, Skelton seems to have composed a total of three short envoys to follow *The Garland of Laurel*, as well as a number of short verses. Although all three envoys were not included in the same early print editions of the poem, they suggest the extent to which Skelton took pains not only to revise, but also to re-present his work to potential readers between the likely date of the poem's initial composition in the 1490s through to the end of his life in 1529. The three envoys – two addressed to the poem itself, the third addressed to current or potential patrons – function as letters to the future, and freeze the *Garland* in an act of appealing to posterity.[35] As the added envoy in the 1568 edition of the *Garland* demonstrates, even after his death Skelton's poem continued to look ahead to anticipated future readers, even though the two future readers being directly addressed were, like the author himself, long dead.

It is certainly possible to read these envoys as further evidence of Skelton's obsessive self-referentiality, or of his habits of repeated revision, but they also reflect Skelton's understanding of the nature of the laureate enterprise. Like Phoebus's fruitless pursuit of Daphne, and like the laureate's efforts to stave off obscurity, *The Garland of Laurel* is frozen in time, looking forward to a future that it has not yet reached. The *Garland*'s envoys echo its thematic and structural circularity, and Skelton's penchant for revising his works reveals him to be truly a laureate in the way that he keeps an eye on his past works, not only as they are at the moment of publication, but as they may be received in the future. Such a reading of the envoys is also consistent with the kind of poem the *Garland* is: a laureate poet's fictionalised wish-fulfilment, in which

---

[33] Skelton, 'Owt of Latyne into Englysshe', the final envoy after the *Garland*, Skelton, ed., Scattergood, p. 358 (lines 10–15).

[34] *Pithy plesaunt and profitable workes of maister Skelton, Poete Laureate* (London, 1568).

[35] While some have argued that Skelton's envoy to Wolsey is meant to be conciliatory, Griffiths has suggested that Skelton might have viewed such an envoy 'as an occasion to remind Wolsey of his promised patronage'; see *John Skelton and Poetic Authority*, p. 30; and 'Text and Authority: John Stow's 1568 Edition of Skelton's Works', *John Stow: Author, Editor and Reader*, ed. Ian Gadd and Alexandra Gillespie (London, 2004), pp. 127–34. On the 'epistolary tone' of envoys and other direct poetic addresses to patrons and readers, see Russell Rutter, 'William Caxton and Literary Patronage', *SP* 84 (1987), 449–53.

his laureate status is awarded in the most highly symbolic manner, a manner only possible in the context of a dream vision.

Skelton's own perspective regarding the laureate poet's position in time contrasts strangely with modern scholarly efforts to freeze time into concrete periods, and to immobilise our authors within those periods. And yet it is precisely because of this contrast that his perspective may go some way towards enabling us to rethink the relationship between time and literary studies. *The Garland of Laurel* shows Skelton to be the quintessential poet-in-progress. He is acutely aware of his peculiar position in time, and of how the future is always moving away from him – the *Garland*'s opening reflections on mutability, and its vision of the origin myth of laureate poetry, and of the laureate enterprise itself, make that abundantly clear. Although *The Garland of Laurel* is not a poem about periodisation, it *is* a poem about poetry and poets in time, and about laureate poetry's efforts to counteract time's constant forward motion. Through the *Garland*'s depiction of the fourteenth-century Petrarchan model of laureation and fifteenth-century Chaucerian sensibilities slipping into what we now call the early modern period, Skelton presents laureate literary activity as a continuous and evolving process, a process that in turn challenges the rigidity of contemporary periodisation.

Thomas Churchyard and the Medieval Complaint Tradition

MATTHEW WOODCOCK

Throughout his long literary career, the writer and soldier Thomas Churchyard (c.1529–1604) composed works that display an evident debt to generic traditions commonly found in fourteenth – and fifteenth-century literature (including dream vision, fabliaux, beast fable and estates satire), and that signal the influence of the style, form and concerns of writers such as Chaucer, Langland, Lydgate and Skelton. Churchyard's use of such traditions and authors is rarely viewed in a positive light, however, and he is frequently criticised or dismissed by modern critics as being backward-looking, conservative and an emblematic representative of what C.S. Lewis infamously termed the Drab Age of Renaissance verse.[1] When briefly considering Churchyard's earliest work – the subject of the present essay – Lewis identified the presence of what he called a 'pre-Drab', late medieval structure and drew unfavourable comparisons between Churchyard's workmanlike metrical regularity and that of the contemporary poet and printer Robert Crowley.[2] Although, as we shall see, these observations are fundamentally correct, the tenor of such comments and the apparently negative connotations and implications these have within Lewis's progressivist literary history need to be called into question. It should be stressed that my essay is not intended as an exercise in Lewis-bashing, which would be uncharitable in a volume dedicated to a recent incumbent of Lewis's chair in medieval and Renaissance English at Cambridge. This essay will, nevertheless, take issue with Lewis's implied resistance to appreciating nuances of continuity between medieval and Renaissance literature. I have also found myself guided here by the example of Helen Cooper's treatment of forms, genres and cultural practices that span the medieval and Renaissance periods, and the characteristically positive and receptive manner in which she handles continuities between these periods. This essay argues that Churchyard's use of medieval literary genres – focusing here on satirical complaint – is not as staid, straightforward or retrograde as has been commonly

---

[1] C.S. Lewis, *English Literature in the Sixteenth Century, Excluding Drama* (Oxford, 1954), pp. 264–5.
[2] Lewis, *English Literature*, p. 264.

perceived. In the hands of writers such as Chaucer, Gower and Langland, the medieval complaint tradition variously attempted to expose, criticise and, ideally, reform contemporary abuses through lamenting of the state of society or the world at large, and anatomising the shortcomings of individual estates, groups, or institutions. After considering how we can identify the essential continuity of this tradition into the mid-sixteenth century, attention turns to two examples of Churchyard's use of satirical complaint, both from the 1550s. We shall see how Churchyard refashions the medieval *de contemptu mundi* commonplaces for an Edwardian audience and adapts the complaint tradition so as to explore conceptions of authorial identity and the function of poetry in the mid-Tudor period.

Like many genres, complaint poetry is perhaps easier to recognise than to define and encompasses a wide-ranging, what John Kerrigan calls 'generically complicated', tradition centred on articulation of distress and lament.[3] At around the same time that Lewis was assembling his well-known survey of sixteenth-century literature, John Peter attempted to distinguish complaint from satire, seeing the former as corrective and impersonal (typified by *Piers Plowman*) and the latter as engaged with the more self-conscious personal observation found in Latinate traditions (as seen, so Peter says, in Chaucer's poetry).[4] Peter's taxonomy is ultimately inconsistent and unhelpful, and satire and complaint – or indeed, satirical complaint – are perhaps more useful when thought of as largely synonymous terms for a literary mode, a stance that writers of any genre might assume when it suited their purpose.[5] This is certainly the case with Churchyard's writings, where complaint is something voiced through a range of forms and genres including love lyrics, elegies, anti-curial satires, *Mirror for Magistrates* tragedies, and in the many remonstrances against worldly misfortune included in his verse miscellanies.

A significant distinction can be drawn between complaints that condemn the woes of the world but which counsel little more than passive acceptance and patient endurance (such as Innocent III's *De Contemptu Mundi* and Gower's *Mirour de l'Omme*), and those that speak in more specific terms about the world's failings and call for social and political remedies rather than otherworldly aid, identifying remediable faults and potential agents of change.[6]

---

[3] John Kerrigan, *Motives of Woe: Shakespeare and 'Female Complaint'* (Oxford, 1991), p. 1. Helen Cooper, *Oxford Guides to Chaucer: The Canterbury Tales*, 2nd edn. (Oxford, 1996), p. 63, makes a similar point with reference to defining medieval romance.

[4] John Peter, *Complaint and Satire in Early English Literature* (Oxford, 1956).

[5] Ignoring such taxonomic complications, Charles A. Knight, *The Literature of Satire* (Cambridge, 2008), p. 4, proposes that satire is 'pre-generic' and that it might best be thought of as a 'mental position that needs to adopt a genre in order to express its ideas as representation'.

[6] In 1576 Henry Kirton produced a translation of *De Contemptu Mundi*, entitled *The Mirror of Mans Lyfe*. George Gascoigne included his own translation of the text in *The Droomme of doomesday*, which appeared the same year.

The former kind of complaint is essentially private and enclosed in conception, and rarely directed towards a particular individual with the intention of ending the lamented circumstances; it is expressive and didactic rather than directly instrumental. Chaucer's 'Lak of Stedfastnesse' is a good example of the latter form of complaint. It bewails the variable, unstable nature of the world but then its 'Lenvoy' to Richard II at the end looks directly to the means by which the king can restore truth and steadfastness.[7] Thomas Hoccleve in the prologue to *The Regiment of Princes* similarly looks to royalty – Prince Henry, son of Henry IV – as the identifiable source of present and future stability in a 'troubly world'.[8] There is clearly a gestural, transitive nature to such pointedly directed complaints. Wendy Scase has examined how the more purposive forms of medieval complaint had roots in legal pleading, specifically the introduction during the thirteenth century of written complaints for instigating a legal action.[9] Judicial process came to provide a new structure and vocabulary for articulating grievance and seeking redress that was adopted in literary texts, and evinced in works presented as 'bills', 'petitions', 'supplications' (such as Chaucer's 'Complaint Unto Pity'). The judicial provenance may help to account for the kind of narrative voice commonly found in literary complaints, the first-person, monologic voice of one pleading or crying, and this vocal emphasis is an important, constitutive characteristic of the complaint tradition. As Peter and others have found, Langland's *Piers Plowman* consistently resists and frustrates most critical attempts to assign it a genre, though it certainly engages with the concerns and methods of articulation of contemporary complaints, and initiates a tradition of its own stretching from the fourteenth century through to the late sixteenth century. It would be an oversimplification to suggest there is a continuous, acknowledged tradition of complaint to which medieval and early modern writers made conscious recourse, but writers of complaints in both periods drew upon a shared stock of topoi and commonplaces when it came to identifying the objects of their critique and their individual vices or abuses. As John Yunck observes, even by Langland's day, who could really identify the point at which writers first attacked corruption of the Church, cheating craftsmen, venal judges, avaricious lawyers, or the pernicious, degenerate effect of money on fallible, fallen mankind?[10] Objects of scorn in medieval sources are also frequently already

---

[7] *Riverside Chaucer*, p. 654.
[8] Thomas Hoccleve, *The Regiment of Princes*, ed. Charles R. Blyth (Kalamazoo, 1999), p. 39.
[9] Wendy Scase, *Literature and Complaint in England, 1272–1553* (Oxford, 2007). On complaint in late medieval culture, see John Burrow, 'The Poet as Petitioner', *Studies in the Age of Chaucer* 3 (1981), 61–75; Nicholas Perkins, *Hoccleve's Regiment of Princes: Counsel and Constraint* (Cambridge, 2001), pp. 34–8.
[10] John A. Yunck, 'Satire', *A Companion to Piers Plowman*, ed. John A. Alford (Berkeley, 1988), p. 137.

the topic of classical satire.[11] The aim of my essay is therefore not to track down the sources of Churchyard's satirical works but to consider what he does with the long-established tradition of seemingly perennial complaints. To this end I want to look in more detail at one of Churchyard's earliest works, *Davy Dycars Dreame* (1551), and to a lesser extent at his *A Myrrour for Man wherein he shall see the myserable state of thys worlde* (1551–52).

Davy Dycars Dreame is typically only discussed in relation to the literary contention it initiates between Churchyard and a hitherto unpublished Norfolk-based contemporary called Thomas Camell, who read the poem as an attack on the government of Edward VI.[12] The contention occasioned fifteen individual responses in print during 1551 and helped to make Churchyard's name as a published author.[13] It is important to distinguish between reading the poem as a single, stand-alone work that uses the commonplaces of the mid-Tudor commonwealth tradition (discussed in a moment) – which then in turn contributes to this body of writings – and viewing the *Dreame* through the lens of historical and critical hindsight as the opening move in a literary contention. Churchyard enters the world of mid-century print culture not as a controversialist but as a satirist and social commentator; he is guilty of querulousness rather than quarrelling.

There was much for Churchyard to complain about in 1551. Edwardian England, governed by Lord Protector Edward Seymour, Duke of Somerset, was beset by a host of social and economic problems, many of which were inherited from Henry VIII's reign. War with France and Scotland had drained royal funds and led to successive debasements of the coinage between 1547 and 1551. At the same time – largely as a consequence of debasement – landlords and landowners safeguarded themselves against inflation through rent-raising and increased enclosure of common arable lands for the more cost-effective pasturing of sheep and cattle. Wages fell in town and country, but prices of commodities, foodstuffs and land rose. Growers and middle-men were frequently assailed in both royal proclamations and contemporary sermons for hoarding food and other commodities to inflate prices and profits. Hugh Latimer attempted to bring this to the king's attention in a sermon on covetousness

---

[11] Juvenal's tenth satire, for example, concerning the transience of temporal glory and riches and the futility of looking to fortune for reward, anticipates many of the commonplaces taken up in medieval *de contemptu mundi* complaints; see Juvenal and Persius, *Satires*, trans. S.M. Braund (Cambridge, MA, 2004), pp. 366–97.

[12] Scott Lucas, 'Diggon Davie and Davy Dicar: Edmund Spenser, Thomas Churchyard, and the Poetics of Public Protest', *Spenser Studies* 16 (2002), 151–65; Wendy Scase, '*Dauy Dycars Dreame* and Robert Crowley's Prints of *Piers Plowman*', *YLS* 21 (2007), 171–98; Cathy Shrank, 'Trollers and Dreamers: Defining the Citizen-Subject in Sixteenth-Century Cheap Print', *Yearbook of English Studies* 38 (2008), 102–18; Eric Nebeker, 'The Broadside Ballad and Textual Publics', *SEL* 51 (2011), 1–19.

[13] See Matthew Woodcock, *Thomas Churchyard: Pen, Sword, and Ego* (Oxford, forthcoming).

preached to the court during Lent 1550.[14] Such gestures were to little avail, however, and the middle years of the century saw widespread dearth, poverty, hunger and discontent. Further tensions for Somerset's protectorate were generated by the introduction of the new Prayer Book in 1549, which sparked full-scale rebellion in Devon and Cornwall. The western rebels' economic grievances were coupled with demands for the abolition of the Bible and Prayer Book in English and the reinstitution of the Henrician (effectively pre-Reformation) Six Articles of 1539.[15] Somerset eventually put down the western rebellion but not before entertaining the rebels' demands and offering limited concessions on local taxes. A similar willingness to respond to local sources of social tension was seen in his appointment of commissions in 1548–49 aimed at enforcing legislation against enclosures, and his general inclination to listen to the complaints of the 'poor commons' directed at repressive landlords and failing magistrates. Somerset's apparent receptiveness to popular grievances raised the expectations of groups that rose in revolt across England in 1549, including most notably that led by Robert Kett in Norfolk during July and August. Kett's rebellion came to a bloody end in a pitched battle fought outside Norwich on 27 August. Economic misery and popular unrest continued into the early 1550s and in the summer of 1551, at around the same time as Churchyard wrote the *Dreame*, additional misery was visited upon the kingdom in the form of a virulent outbreak of the sweating sickness that killed many hundreds.

While government representatives like Sir Thomas Smith analysed economic causes of the mid-century dearth in *The Discourse of the Common Weal* (written 1549, published 1581), popular dissatisfaction articulated through protest and print was directed towards the corruption of local nobility, landowners and administrators of justice.[16] One repeatedly encounters the complaint that concern for common wealth, and *the* commonwealth, had been supplanted by self-interest and a preoccupation with private wealth. Dearth and hunger were viewed as the result of moral shortcomings and the failure of charity. It is in this period that one witnesses the maturation of a broadly conceived tradition of commonwealth writing that combined social critique with a mixture of economics, religion and morality, and urged (as Scott Lucas puts it) 'the shaping of England into a polity based on fraternal love and mutual devotion among all classes'.[17] The existence of a coherent Edwardian

---

[14] Hugh Latimer, *Sermons*, ed. George Elwes (Cambridge, 1844), p. 279.
[15] Anthony Fletcher and Diarmaid MacCulloch, *Tudor Rebellions*, 5th edn. (Harlow, 2004), pp. 151–3.
[16] [Thomas Smith], *A Discourse of the Common Weal of this Realm of England*, ed. Elizabeth Lamond (Cambridge, 1954).
[17] Andy Wood, *The 1549 Rebellions and the Making of Early Modern England* (Cambridge, 2007), p. 101; Scott Lucas, *A Mirror for Magistrates and the Politics of the English Reformation* (Amherst, 2009), p. 27.

commonwealth 'party' committed collectively to social reform has been much contested, though one can nevertheless identify a shared tradition of language and preoccupations that brings together individuals, who otherwise worked independently, into a nominal textual community.[18] Commonwealth writing took many different forms. John Hales, one of the leading figures on the enclosure commissions, attempted to address rural hardship through bills to parliament that confronted the immoral roots of agrarian malpractices. Hales claimed in his 1548 'Bill on the decay of tillage' that the body politic was now decayed 'by reason of disordre, self love and pryvat profytt'.[19] Preachers such as Latimer, Thomas Lever, Bernard Gilpin and Thomas Becon similarly identified greed and covetousness as the cause of their present woes.

Works concerned with the state of the commonwealth feature heavily in mid-century popular print culture. From the outset of the protectorate, Somerset was an active literary patron who remained committed to propagating popular debate about religious and social reform through print.[20] The first few years of the protectorate saw a massive increase in the output of printed books, in part as a result of the Council's removal of the restrictive Henrician censorship and licensing regulations. Censorship laws were reimposed in August 1549 following outbreaks of rebellion, and further proclamations in April and May 1551 reaffirmed the Council's sensitivity towards the dissemination of sedition through print. Churchyard himself may have fallen foul of these new strictures after the *Dreame* first appeared, which necessitated Somerset to intervene with the Privy Council on his behalf.[21] Nevertheless, despite the shifting censorship measures, alongside the many radical Protestant works produced at this time that engaged in anti-papal critique and doctrinal controversy there was a rich tradition of texts that urgently maintained that the remedy to the commonwealth's social and economic ills lay in individual and collective moral reform.[22] Using a common stock of critical topoi and objects of complaint, pamphlets such as the *Prayse and Commendacion of Suche as Sought Comen*

---

[18] On attempts to identify a commonwealth tradition and discourse, rather than an actual 'party', see G.R. Elton, 'Reform and the "Commonwealth-Men" of Edward VI's Reign', *The English Commonwealth, 1547–1640*, ed. Peter Clark, et al. (Leicester, 1979), pp. 23–38; Chris Skidmore, *Edward VI: The Lost King of England* (London, 2008), pp. 92–3; Mike Rodman Jones, *Radical Pastoral, 1381–1594: Appropriation and the Writing of Religious Controversy* (Farnham, 2011), pp. 11–47.

[19] [Smith], *Discourse*, p. xlvi.

[20] On Somerset's patronage and support of popular print, see John N. King, *English Reformation Literature: The Tudor Origins of the Protestant Tradition* (Princeton, 1982), pp. 27, 47, 106–21.

[21] Thomas Churchyard, *The Fortunate Farewel to the most forward and noble Earle of Essex* (London, 1599), sig. A1v.

[22] Helen C. White and John N. King have mapped out the full extent of mid-century commonwealth complaint literature and demonstrated the role that print played in increasing public sensitivity towards poverty and its causes: Helen C. White, *Social Criticism in Popular Religious Literature of the Sixteenth Century* (New York, 1965); King, *English Reformation*

Welthes (1548), *A Ruful complaynt of the publyke weale to Englande* (1550) and William Conway's *Exortacion to Charite* (1551) offered anatomies of a dysfunctional society characterised by self-interest, greed and a lack of neighbourliness.[23] The *Ruful complaynt*, for example, takes the form of a simple verse dialogue in which England itself, replying to the voice of 'Publyke weale', attempts to account for its parlous state and lays blame squarely at the door of the ever-acquisitive rich and their enclosure of land. The figure of 'Publyke weale' also appeals to parties outside the text and calls for 'Some good man for the commons speake/ Thats ryche men marre not all', a plea that looks to other writers more qualified or better placed to speak out for the poor as well as to those (like Somerset) capable of exerting political pressure directly.[24] Again, it should be stressed that this might not have been entirely naive thinking on the author's part since there are similarities between the complaints articulated in the commonwealth tradition and the aims of Somerset's social policies.

Crowley's works exhibit a sustained commitment to both speaking up for the urban and rural poor and attacking the malpractices of the greedy gentry. Crowley's first published statement on this theme, *An Informacion and Peticion Agaynst the Oppressours of the Poore Commons* (1548), was directed towards parliament and advocated legislative intervention to restore the Christian body politic in which everyone worked together for common profit. Crowley experimented with a variety of genres to deliver a series of blistering attacks on contemporary abuses and shortcomings: *The Voyce of the Last Trumpet* (1549) adapts traditional estates satire to criticize rent-raising, hoarding and general avarice; *One and Thyrtye Epigrammes* (1550) targeted individual causes of social unrest (merchants, commotioners, usurers); and his most original work, *Philargyrie of Great Britayne* (1551), depicted the incursion and expulsion of greed and self-love from the kingdom through a satirical, allegorical fable. Perhaps the best example of how Crowley speaks up for the oppressed and disaffected is his prose tract *The Way to Wealth* (1550), in which at one point he professes to know what a poor man would say were he asked the causes of the previous year's seditions and unrest:

> He woulde tel me that the great fermares, the grasiers, the riche buchares, the men of lawe, the marchauntes, the gentlemen, the knightes, the lordes, and I can not tel who, Men that have no name because they are doares in al thinges that

---

Literature. See also Whitney R.D. Jones, *The Mid-Tudor Crisis 1539–63* (London, 1973), p. 135; Tessa Watt, *Cheap Print and Popular Piety, 1550–1640* (Cambridge, 1991), pp. 96–9.

[23] The *Prayse and Commendacion* appears to have been written earlier in the 1530s and demonstrates the degree of continuity between the commonplaces of Henrician and Edwardian social complaint. See also Henry Brinkelow, *The Complaynt of Roderyck Mors* (c.1542), and the anonymous *Supplication to the Poore Commons* (1546); Jones, *Radical Pastoral*, pp. 102–16.

[24] *A Ruful complaynt of the publyke weale to Englande* (London, 1550), sig. A4v.

ani gaine hangeth upon. Men without conscience. Men utterly voide of goddes feare. Yea men that live as thoughe there were no God at all! Men that would have all in their owne handes; men that would leave nothyng for others; men that would be alone on the earth, men that bee never satisfied. Cormerauntes, gredye gulles, yea, men that would eate up menne, women and chyldren: are the causes of Sedition! They take our houses over our headdes, they bye our growndes out of our handes, they reyse our rentes, they leavie great (yea unreasonable) fines, they enclose oure commens![25]

Notice how by the end of this passage Crowley has momentarily taken on the first-person voice of the poor man. One of the issues contemplated in the Davy Dycar contention is whether commonwealth discourse is as much about who has the right and duty to articulate complaint as it is the causes of such complaints themselves.

Crowley's interest in appropriating the voice of the plain-speaking countryman, or more generally that of the poor commons, to criticise the inequities of the commonwealth intersects with the popular tradition that continued to develop during the mid-sixteenth century of using the ploughman figure as the spokesman and emblem of social and religious complaint.[26] Crowley both capitalised upon and reinvigorated this tradition through his 1550 edition of *Piers Plowman*.[27] The period of Edward's minority invited comparison with the circumstances in which *Piers* was first written during the earlier part of Richard II's reign.[28] The full extent of the Tudor ploughman tradition, and the afterlife of Langland's poem within Protestant discourse, has already been widely discussed.[29] Recent scholarship has been inclined to associate Crowley's edition, and sixteenth-century uses of the ploughman figure, with social

---

[25] Robert Crowley, *Select Works*, ed. J.M. Cowper, EETS ES 15 (London, 1872), pp. 132–3.
[26] See the anonymous *I playne Piers which cannot flatter*, *A godly dyaloge and dysputacyon betwene Pyers plowman and a popysh preest*, and *Pyers plowmans exhortation unto the lordes, knightes and burgoysses of the parlyamenthouse*. ESTC dates these to 1550 though Sarah A. Kelen argues that they may pre-date Crowley's edition; see *Langland's Early Modern Identities* (Basingstoke, 2007), p. 47. The period also saw the publication of several medieval texts in which Langland's criticism of abuses in the Church would be recast retrospectively as proto-Protestant: *The Praier and Complaynte of the Ploweman unto Christ* (1531), *The Plowman's Tale* (1548) and *Pierce the Ploughmans Crede* (1553).
[27] William Langland, *The Vision of Pierce Plowman* (London, 1550).
[28] Crowley cautiously acknowledged the similarities between the minorities of Richard II and Edward VI when annotating the belling of the cat episode from the prologue to *Piers*; see John N. King, 'Robert Crowley's Editions of *Piers Plowman*: A Tudor Apocalypse', *MP* 73 (1976), 350.
[29] White, *Social Criticism*, pp. 28–34; King, *English Reformation Literature*; Anne Hudson, 'Epilogue: The Legacy of *Piers Plowman*', *Companion*, ed. Alford, pp. 251–66; Charlotte Brewer, *Editing Piers Plowman: The Evolution of the Text* (Cambridge, 1996), pp. 7–19; Kelen, *Langland's Early Modern*, pp. 31–76; Jones, *Radical Pastoral*; Katherine C. Little, *Transforming Work: Early Modern Pastoral and Late Medieval Poetry* (Notre Dame, 2013), pp. 111–41.

commentary and reform rather than with more narrowly conceived religious and doctrinal controversy.[30] As Lawrence Manley writes, 'the fundamental appeal of the ploughman persona was its power to accommodate the ideals of honest labor and obedience to a model of ordered society, a model epitomized in Langland's sixth passus, where Piers ploughs his half-acre and all work together, each in his own way'.[31] Reference to Piers's attempts to establish order in his half-acre brings us to the point at which Churchyard intervenes in the imaginative space of Langland's poem. Churchyard takes the name of his titular dreamer directly from *Piers*, in which Davy Dykere is a ditcher, or perhaps more generally a labourer, first encountered among Gluttony's drinking companions.[32] Davy later appears in passus six at the end of a cryptic prophecy in which 'werkmen' are urged to produce food while they can in advance of an impending period of famine and death that will see 'Dawe the Dykere deye for hunger/ But if God of his goodnesse graunte us a trewe'.[33] Churchyard thus contrives the complaint of one who might otherwise simply have expired in silence and, like Crowley, gives voice to the figure of the suffering poor man.

Davy Dycars Dreame is deeply enmeshed with the language, ideas and conventions of the mid-Tudor commonwealth tradition. Whether or not he was prompted by social conscience and a genuine desire to engage in a popular discourse on social reform, Churchyard evidently recognised that there was a burgeoning market in the mid-sixteenth century for works urging others to act, repent, or otherwise participate in said discourse, and he appears to have responded to this opportunity when making his debut appearance in print. Furthermore, as noted above, his decision to publish may have been made with an awareness that there was an audience for printed contributions to commonwealth discourse not only among the book-buying public but (at a more elevated level) in the form of the receptive stance of Somerset himself towards popular articulation of social criticism. The *Dreame* is a metrical list of the reforms that need to be made to the values, conduct and practices of society and its rulers, each of which is lamented in its absence through a syntactic formula that looks forward to 'when' each change will come about. Thirteen couplets of 'when' clauses are concluded by a restorative prophetic promise of collective harmony and contentment. Churchyard's appropriation

---

[30] Larry Scanlon, 'Langland, Apocalypse, and the Early Modern Editor', *Reading the Medieval in Early Modern England*, ed. Gordon McMullan and David Matthews (Cambridge, 2007), pp. 51–73; Lawrence Warner, 'An Overlooked *Piers Plowman* Excerpt and the Oral Circulation of Non-Reformist Prophecy, c.1520–55', *YLS* 21 (2007), 135–40. Crowley was, nevertheless, deeply involved in Protestant polemic in many of his other works; see J.W. Martin, 'The Publishing Career of Robert Crowley: A Sidelight on the Tudor Book Trade', *Publishing History* 14 (1983), 85–98.

[31] Lawrence Manley, *Literature and Culture in Early Modern London* (Cambridge, 1995), p. 101.

[32] William Langland, *Piers Plowman*, ed. A.V.C. Schmidt (London, 1995), 5: 78.

[33] Langland, *Piers*, 6: 328–9.

of the Davy Dykere figure brought with it both thematic allusions to hunger and dearth, which had particular resonance for his immediate readership, and a formal tradition (prophetic dream-vision) that could be used to anatomise the degenerative conditions producing contemporary discontent. The poem deviates from conventions of the dream-vision genre almost immediately in that all twenty-eight lines relate to the dream itself and, albeit obliquely, its projected outcome. That is to say, unlike in dream-visions by Chaucer or Langland, there is no representation of a waking state that frames the entrance to, and exit from, the dream itself.

Churchyard exploits several rhetorical traditions found in medieval complaint poetry that offer varying visions of the current state of the world turned upside down in order to project a vision of how it should be. We are shown what is desired by the implied comparison between the real world and that evoked by the poet, as in the following excerpt from a fifteenth-century poem:

> Religious pepille levyn in holynesse,
> Serviabli with-owte transmutacion.
> Envy exilid is fro gentylnesse;
> And for ypocrosye ys set devocion.
> In lawe trouthe hathe his dominacion;
> All dowblenesse venquesschid bi right at þe desire;
> Stablenesse foundon, and spesialli in a-tire.[34]

In the final stanza, however, all of these ideals are reversed since 'All these lightli shold tornyn up so doune,/ Ne were of wommen þe perfight stablenesse'. Everything listed above should be inverted unless women prove to be models of constancy. John Scattergood identifies several fourteenth – and fifteenth-century complaint poems that similarly construct an ideal state of things contingent on the occurrence of something seemingly impossible: when pigs fly, or as Lydgate puts it in a variant on this theme, 'so as þe crabbe goþe forward' (i.e. when the traditionally side-scuttling crab walks forwards).[35] As Ernst Curtius has shown, the tradition of writing poetry constructed of impossibilities deploying the rhetorical figure *adynaton* dates back as far as the seventh century BC and the work of the Greek satirist Archilochus.[36] Projections of a better world that seemingly cannot exist also bring to mind those found in medieval and early modern Utopian texts, such as the fantastic, bawdy landscape of the mythical Cokaygne or the more austere feigned commonwealth of Thomas More's *Utopia*, the first English translation of which appeared the

---

[34] Rossell Hope Robbins, ed., *Historical Poems of the XIVth and XVth Centuries* (New York, 1959), p. 150.
[35] V.J. Scattergood, *Politics and Poetry in the Fifteenth Century* (London, 1971), pp. 302–3.
[36] Ernst Robert Curtius, *European Literature and the Latin Middle Ages*, trans. W.R. Trask (London, 1979), p. 95.

same year as the *Dreame*.³⁷ In a later pamphlet of the Davy Dycar contention, an imagined reader of the *Dreame* makes a similar observation through comparing Churchyard's poem to Plato's *Republic*.³⁸ The *Dreame* also evinces the influence of Churchyard's greatest acknowledged literary forebear, John Skelton, as it revisits the social ills enumerated in *Collyn Clout* (1522) and recasts the older poet's complaints about Cardinal Wolsey's abrogation of royal power during the 1520s (and how he 'ruleth the roste') in terms relevant to mid-Tudor politics.³⁹

The 'when' formula that Churchyard employs clearly evokes the same proleptic structure commonly found in medieval vatic poetry such as the prophecy ascribed to Merlin – and in some sources Chaucer – that predicts the confusion that shall afflict 'the londe of Albeon'

> When feythe fayleth in prestys sawys,
> And lordys wyll be londe lawys,
> And lechery is prevy solas,
> And robbery ys goode purchas.⁴⁰

The formula also informs the passage of prophecy at the end of passus six of *Piers* in which Langland's Davy Dykere is mentioned:

> Ac I warne yow werkmen – wynneth whil ye mowe,
> For Hunger hiderward hasteth hym faste!
> He shal awake thorugh water, wastours to chaste,
> Er fyve yer be fulfilled swich famyn shal aryse:
> Thorugh flodes and thorugh foule wedres, fruytes shul faille –
> And so seith Saturne and sent yow to warne:
> Whan ye merke the sonne amys and two monkes heddes,
> And a mayde have the maistrie, and multiplied by eighte,
> Thanne shal deeth withdrawe and derth be justice,

---

³⁷ Robbins, *Historical Poems*, pp. 121–7.
³⁸ [William Baldwin], *Westerne Wyll upon the debate betweene Churchyarde and Camell* (London, [1551]), sig. A3v.
³⁹ John Skelton, *Complete English Poems*, ed. John Scattergood (Harmondsworth, 1983), p. 272. Churchyard described Skelton as 'The tree wheron in deed, My branchis all might groe' in the preface to John Stow's *Pithy pleasaunt and profitable workes of maister Skelton* (London, 1568), unpaginated first gathering. See also John Scattergood, *John Skelton: The Career of an Early Tudor Poet* (Dublin, 2014), ch. 17.
⁴⁰ James M. Dean, ed., *Medieval English Political Writings* (Kalamazoo, 1996), p. 10. This is the version from Cambridge, Magdalene College MS 1236, fol. 91r, produced c.1460. See also Siegfried Wenzel, *Preachers, Poets, and the Early English Lyric* (Princeton, 1986), pp. 193–203; Cooper, *Romance*, pp. 189–90. The same formula is taken up in the Fool's prophecy in Shakespeare's *King Lear*, 3.2.80–94.

> And Dawe the Dykere deye for hunger –
> But if God of his goodnesse graunte us a trewe.[41]

Passages from *Piers* presenting forms of prophecy were often extracted from the poem and circulated separately until well into the sixteenth century, both within an oral tradition and in manuscript collections of political prophecies.[42] Of particular relevance here is a manuscript discussed by Wendy Scase and Lawrence Warner – British Library, MS Sloane 2578 – in which the 'hunger' prophecy from passus six is conjoined with a version of the so-called 'Abbot of Abingdon' prophecy from passus ten that alludes to the corrective intervention of a king:

> For þer shall
> com a kinge and correcte you religious, and beate you
> as þe byble telles, For breakinge of your rule and
> nunnes, munkes and chanons, and putt þem to þer
> penance ad pristinum statum [ire] [to return to their first state].[43]

These same two Langland passages underpin Churchyard's poem and are extracted and collocated again in an earlier manuscript collection, Cambridge University Library, MS Gg.4.31; they are also the only excerpts from the poem that Crowley quotes in the preface to his edition of *Piers*.[44] Crowley refers to these passages when attempting to pre-empt any accusation that his chosen text overtly engages in potentially controversial political prophecy by suggesting that they 'lyke to be a thinge added of some other man than the fyrste author.'[45] Churchyard very likely came to *Piers* with an awareness of the thematic resources of the Tudor ploughman tradition, and of the rhetorical stance of the plaintive ploughman. But he also surely identified – perhaps with direction from Crowley's specific, though deflective prefatorial references to the passages most apposite for the prophetic register – that the poem had the capacity to provide a particular mode of voice for his titular dreamer, which carried with it a carefully positioned allusive authority. The prophetic

---

[41] Langland, *Piers*, 6: 319–29.
[42] Scase, '*Dauy Dycars Dreame*', 183–5; Warner, 'Overlooked'; Kelen, *Langland's Early Modern*, pp. 34–8. John Bale, for example, wrote of *Piers*: 'In this erudite work, on account of various and happy similitudes, he prophetically foresaw many things which we have seen come to pass in our own days'; quoted in James Simpson, *Reform and Cultural Revolution* (Oxford, 2002), p. 27.
[43] Warner, 'Overlooked', 134; this is a variant of *Piers*, 10: 316–19. See also Sharon Jansen [Jaech], 'British Library MS Sloane 2578 and Popular Unrest in England, 1554–56', *Manuscripta* 29 (1985), 30–41; and 'Politics, Protest, and a New *Piers Plowman* Fragment: The Voice of the Past in Tudor England', *RES* 40 (1989), 93–9.
[44] Scase, '*Dauy Dycars Dreame*', 184.
[45] Scase, '*Dauy Dycars Dreame*', 192–3.

formula Churchyard employs could thus imply with certainty that the propitious conclusion promised in the 'then' clause was the inevitable consequence of achieving the conditions listed in the 'when' clauses, but at the same time remained elusive as to how or when exactly these conditions might be realised. It was this allusive elusiveness that caused controversy for Churchyard, and prolonged the interpretative interactions with the *Dreame* following its initial appearance.

Churchyard makes no direct mention of Langland's ploughman but we are never very far in the *Dreame* from the language and concerns of Piers's half-acre. The first half of the poem identifies what needs to be in place in order to achieve social justice and harmony (honesty, mutual dependence, industriousness) and the impediments that need to be removed (self-interest and greed, duplicity, 'lewterers' and 'wyly workers').[46] 'Gropers after gayne' should 'carpe' – that is, speak up for – 'comen welth'. The personified figure representing wealth and payment in *Piers*, Lady Mede, is evoked in the reference to 'law' looking not to 'meede'. Later in the *Dreame* the image of 'truth' treading the streets embodies another of Langland's complex and enigmatic allegorical concepts, and indeed it is the pilgrimage to Truth that occupies Piers's followers on the half-acre. Churchyard moves on to address specific, tangible objects of abuse, and his professed desire that 'covetous creepes not into Courte', together with an allusion to courtly debtors, are his first articulations of what became a lifelong preoccupation with anti-curial complaint. Familiar grievances from the commonwealth tradition also appear. The lack of financial support from patrons for the learned to fund their education echoes Latimer's complaint of the same in his 1548 sermon of the plough.[47] Churchyard's exhortation that 'lords shal sell no sheepe' clearly targets enclosures, while the subsequent line looks to the cessation of hoarding: 'When lucre lasts not long, and hurd great heaps doth hate'. The penultimate 'when' clause falls back on a principle widely found in the commonwealth tradition that stability will be achieved when 'every wight is well content, to walke in his estate': when everyone knows their place in society and does not attempt to advance beyond their station. The notion that one should acknowledge and retain one's place in a divinely ordained social structure is found in Langland, Gower and Lydgate, and was echoed during the mid-sixteenth century in the 1547 Book of Homilies, in printed responses to the 1549 rebellions by Crowley and John Cheke, and to a degree in the demands of the Norfolk rebels themselves. Conjoining such sources is the shared belief in a conservative social vision of a static polity of order, obedience and obligation to one's estate. But in the complaints of the

---

[46] Thomas Churchyard, *Davy Dycars Dreame* (London, [1551]). All subsequent citations in the text are from this edition.
[47] Latimer, *Sermons*, pp. 64–5.

commonwealth tradition this is often accompanied simultaneously by a seemingly contradictory, potentially radical call for reform to achieve a return to such a model of the conservative status quo.[48] Churchyard's *Dreame* is a good example of this apparently contradictory position since it looks ahead to a moment of social change conceived as the restoration rather than the toppling of order. Obligation to the discrete duties of one's occupation or estate informs the exhortation that the nobility and gentry, who are referred to metonymically as 'might', do not associate or have dealings with mercantile enterprise. Similar sentiments on the blurring of social boundaries are expressed in the *Ruful complaynt*:

> Marchauntes they become lordes
> and Lordes useth marchaundyse
> A lorde a sheppard nothyng accordes
> Or a grayser that is new gyse.[49]

Skelton had already explored figurative associations between merchants and courtiers in *The Bowge of Court* (1498). Churchyard's poem also endorses what amounts to a form of sumptuary restriction in proposing that 'javels' ('rascals or poor fellows' (*OED*)) 'weare no velvet weeds'.[50]

The *Dreame*'s most contentious line is in the final 'when' clause, the reference to the point at which 'Rex doth raigne and rule the rost, and weeds out wicked men'. Its position just before the restorative closing couplet of the 'then' clause strongly implies that this is to be the decisive condition, the *sine qua non* that underpins and brings about all of the other looked-for objects of Davy's dream. It is also the most concrete and potentially realisable item in a list of otherwise largely abstract desiderata because it calls for an identifiable individual to perform what should be an automatic, uncontroversial action. Specifically, the call for 'Rex' to rule speaks to the circumstances of Edward's minority, the rule of the kingdom (in his name) by the Privy Council headed in 1551 by John Dudley, earl of Warwick (following Somerset's deposition in 1549), and the growing suggestions made the same year that the king would indeed shortly achieve his majority and assume rule in his own name.[51] The distinction that Churchyard draws between 'Rex' reigning and ruling addresses the particular constitutional circumstances of Edward's minority, and

---

[48] Wood, *1549 Rebellions*, pp. 33–4; John Cheke, *The Hurt of Sedition* (London, 1549), sigs. A3v–A4r. See also Jones, *Radical Pastoral*, pp. 5–6.
[49] *Ruful complaynt*, sigs. A3r–A3v.
[50] King Edward himself proposed a bill of sumptuary laws at this time restricting the wearing of blue or crimson velvet to Knights of the Garter; see Skidmore, *Edward VI*, pp. 324–5n7.
[51] Edward did not really exhibit an active involvement in government until 1552; see Diarmaid MacCulloch, *Tudor Church Militant: Edward VI and the Protestant Reformation* (Harmondsworth, 1999), pp. 35–9; Skidmore, *Edward VI*, pp. 230–4.

looks with great expectation at the moment when the king would finally rule in person, rather than through the Council. Edward's assumption of personal political power was thus cast by Churchyard as the most obvious, most desirable transformative action that would end England's current 'dreedfull daies'. A similar form of redemptive royal intervention is imagined at the end of Crowley's *Philargyrie*, where the calamities caused to the realm by the eponymous giant are redressed immediately by the appearance of the hitherto absent king.[52] These kinds of representation of the king also aligned with how Edward was viewed by contemporary reformers in millenarian terms as the ruler who would come to restore the true church to his people, as had the Old Testament boy-king Josiah.[53] Just as in contemporary texts in the *Piers Plowman* tradition, the appeal in the *Dreame* and *Philargyrie* is to higher, secular powers rather than the commonwealth as a whole, and it models a top-down means of achieving reform through the initiative of the king and his government.[54]

The 'wicked men' that would be weeded out once the king takes up personal rule could easily be interpreted as the nameless exploitative landlords and corrupt officers that exercised the commonwealth writers and commotioners. The action of weeding again evokes the language of the half-acre as it is one of the tasks with which Piers's followers are occupied.[55] The weeding out of 'wicked men' could also be construed as a veiled attack on Warwick, who attracted criticism in 1551 due to his identification with the country's continuing economic crisis and through popular perceptions that he abused his position for personal gain. Viewed in this light, the *Dreame* can be read as a public intervention in factional struggles between Warwick and Somerset that leans heavily towards the interest of the latter (following the earl's instrumental role in Somerset's deposition) and intimates that Edward's assumption of rule would precipitate Warwick's removal. This may further explain why Churchyard received support from Somerset when his poem led him into difficulties with the Council.

Given the potentially contentious sentiments articulated in the *Dreame* it is important to consider the nature of the narrative voice employed therein since it informs our perception of exactly who is speaking in the poem and of what kind of agency and responsibility is being claimed for these words. Who is the 'I' in the final line whose promise underwrites the prophesied end to England's 'dreedfull daies'? The title suggests that the whole of the poem is rehearsed by Davy Dycar who, like similar figures in contemporary ploughman texts, petitions those in a position of power. On the other hand, unlike the authors of many commonwealth complaints, Churchyard clearly puts his name to the

---

[52] Robert Crowley, *Philargyrie of Great Britayne* (London, 1551), sigs. D8r–D8v.
[53] Diarmaid MacCulloch, *Thomas Cranmer: A Life* (New Haven, CT, 1996), pp. 364–5.
[54] Simpson, *Reform*, p. 368.
[55] Langland, *Piers*, 6: 110–11.

poem. The question of who is speaking in the poem is a central concern in the contention that unfolds. Churchyard *is* clearly the author: it is his work, formed of his words, to which he has openly put his name. Indeed, there is a proudly declamatory tone to the poem engendered by the bold claims of what is promised. In the defence of Churchyard's poem that develops in subsequent publications, the precise issue of agency, authority and ownership of potentially contentious words is hotly discussed, as is the question of the degree to which one can attempt to recover an author's intention in a text. Where one hears and locates Churchyard in the poem is thus of great significance, and the lines of questioning that are collectively pursued in the contention continually seek to establish where we can identify the presence and voice of the author in his work.

There is not the space here to work through the next fifteen pamphlets of the contention. However, as Churchyard switches from social commentator to literary polemicist, the contention furnishes him with a great opportunity to comment upon and defend the good intentions of his initial poem, and at the same time advance his own name and reputation. The central concern of all the contention's contributors is the reading and interpretation of Churchyard's first text, and much of his and Camell's energies are spent attempting, respectively, to either encourage or forestall a closer textual exposition of exactly what makes the *Dreame* so controversial. At one point in the contention Camell's shortcomings as a reader are characterised using a Langlandian referent. Churchyard accuses his opponent of reading like the nun to whom Conscience compares Lady Mede (in passus three of *Piers*) who interprets scripture selectively for her own ends and only chooses to read half of the line that she cites.[56] At the heart of the Davy Dycar contention there is still a poem of complaint, but it is surrounded by an extended exploration of who is making and voicing such complaint. The contention concludes with Churchyard's self-conscious defence of his role as social commentator in *A Playn and Fynall Confutacion: Of cammells corlyke oblatracion* (1551):

> What thinkes this man he hathe more witte, and learning in his head:
> Than hathe fyve thousand other men, that Dycarres dreame hath read.
> Or thinkes he that I am so rashe, to run so far from square:
> Or that I make suche obscure thinges, that I dare not declare.
> Than is he blynde and very fond [foolish], and scarce him selfe doeth know:
> Let him loke on his booke agayne, his rule is nothinge so.[57]

The claim he makes here that 5,000 people have already read the *Dreame* is obviously an optimistic exaggeration but it acknowledges, nevertheless, the

---

[56] Langland, *Piers*, 3: 338. Thomas Churchyard, *A Playn and Fynall Confutacion: Of cammells corlyke oblatracion* (London, [1551]), sig. *2r.
[57] Churchyard, *Playn and Fynall Confutacion*, sig. *1r.

open, public nature of his contention with Camell and gestures towards an overwhelmingly sympathetic imagined audience. The printer Owen Rogers evidently judged that reprinting a collected edition of these pamphlets in 1560, nearly a decade after they first appeared, made profitable business sense, and he capitalised further upon the contention's popularity and Langlandian texture when he reprinted a third edition of Crowley's *Piers Plowman* in 1561.

Churchyard exhibits a similar form of self-consciousness towards his role as complainant in his poem *A Myrrour for Man*. Elements of the *Myrrour* cover well-trodden ground of the *contemptu mundi* tradition seen nearly two centuries earlier in Gower's poem of a similar name. However, once Churchyard starts to turn to specific abuses needing redress, the *Myrrour* again adopts the language and commonplaces of the mid-Tudor commonwealth tradition, and criticises rent-raisers, enclosures and the avarice rife at every social level. There is again an interest in the voices used to articulate complaint, and as in Gower's *Vox Clamantis*, Crowley's *Way to Wealth* and Churchyard's own *Dreame*, the author adopts the pose that he is passing on the words of another. Nearly half of the text takes the form of an embedded, unmediated rehearsal of the *vox populi*:

> Soch woful morninge, as is in Englande
> Was never before, I dare take in hande
> In every place, where as I do walcke
> I heare men complayne, and thys is theyr talcke.[58]

Churchyard goes further than earlier examples of complaints in that he appears to be concerned as much with the means by which the poor might have their plight articulated and made known as he is with the causes and effects of the kingdom's misery. His plaintive embedded speaker states that

> The riche that fares well, and hath nothing skant
> Doth never conceave, what the poore doeth want
> But yf that some men, on them take no rueth
> They are all undone, this is the playne trueth
> I wold this were knowen, among the best sorte
> Than shuld the poore men, soone have some comforte.[59]

Through its attention to the complainant as much as their subject-matter, the *Myrrour* reveals again the influence of Skelton's *Collyn Clout* upon Churchyard's early poetry. Rather than simply lamenting the state of the world and passing on what he professes to have seen and heard first-hand, as is commonplace

---

[58] Thomas Churchyard, *A Myrrour for Man wherein he shall see the myserable state of thys worlde* (London, [1551–52]), sig. A1v.
[59] Churchyard, *Myrrour*, sig. A1v.

in medieval and Renaissance complaints, the author dwells upon his role as a guide for his readers who should themselves serve as agents of repentance and reform. The *Myrrour* is far closer to the *contemptu mundi* type of complaint than the *Dreame* in looking to God for redress, but it stands out from other earlier examples of the form through its insistent advertisement of the vital role played by the complainant himself:

> Here have I set forth, after a playne sorte
> The state of thys worlde, in terms ryght shorte
> For the thou blynde man, that goeth astraye
> I lyghten thys lampe, to learne thee the waye [...]
>
> I wold that my wordes, were graven in stone
> That al the whole worlde, myght like them uppon [...]
>
> If I could thonder, in every mans eares
> I wold them exhort, wyth wepynge and teares.[60]

The poem closes with an exasperated expression of the frustrated lot of the social and moral commentator. The complainant whose words go unheeded is an accepted commonplace of the tradition, and in the dream-vision complaints of Chaucer, Langland, Gower and Hoccleve we are used to seeing various projected versions of the author-as-dreamer. But with Churchyard the emphasis is not just on the author's contrivance of a personal experience that occasions complaint (a dream, an early morning walk, etc.), but on the author recording such complaints and transmitting them to a wider, ideally receptive audience.

Previous generations of criticism, following Alvin Kernan's 1959 study, *The Cankered Muse*, were keen to avoid any projection of biographical or autobiographical elements when interpreting satire and complaint, and treated the narrative voice or spokesmen of such works as that of a persona or personae.[61] Such a rigid view has long been challenged in scholarship of classical and early modern satire, and greater sensitivity is afforded to overlaps between literary conventions and personal concerns, and to representations of authors as they would like to be seen as satirists or moral commentators.[62] Both the Davy Dycar contention and *Myrrour for Man* see Churchyard exploring such overlaps and these early texts establish the pattern seen in many of his later works whereby the occasion of writing about a public issue, event, or concern also affords an opportunity to simultaneously speak about his personal situation and bids for advancement. Again, this is not the first time that personal and social motives intersect in complaint. Much of Hoccleve's prologue to the

---

[60] Churchyard, *Myrrour*, sigs. A3r–A3v.
[61] Alvin Kernan, *The Cankered Muse: Satire of the English Renaissance* (New Haven, CT, 1959).
[62] R.B. Gill, 'A Purchase of Glory: The Persona of Late Elizabethan Satire', *SP* 12 (1975), 409.

Regiment of Princes, for example, is devoted to the issue of the poet's financial distress and the means whereby writing the work in hand might elicit some relief from Prince Henry.

What distinguishes Churchyard's complaints from their medieval antecedents is not great innovation or experiments in tone or metre but the author's conceptions of the new possibilities presented in the mid-sixteenth century by popular print culture, and the way in which the publication of literary complaints revised conceptions of who was listening to or receiving them and how they might respond. The technologies of complaint available to Churchyard were obviously very different to those to which Chaucer, Langland, Gower or Hoccleve made recourse. Would the voice of one crying necessarily seem so plaintive or ineffectual if an author imagined, as Churchyard contrives in the *Playn and Fynall Confutacion*, that his words were reaching an audience of many thousands? Was Churchyard inclined to be as bold as he was in the *Dreame* because he anticipated that his words would find a receptive response from Somerset himself? And to what extent did Churchyard and his contemporaries really perceive themselves as heirs of the Langlandian tradition? Would they have considered that their texts had the potential for a greater instrumental efficacy than those of their medieval forebears? Churchyard's Edwardian complaints are preoccupied not only with the voice of one crying but with the political and social implications of what might come to pass if that voice is heard or responded to. These early satirical complaints constitute an important source for rethinking points of transition between the medieval and Renaissance periods and – crucially – the material factors that have a bearing on how genres and conventions are adapted and developed. This links of course to the bigger issue of whether the instrumental potential of medieval genres remains the same when they are adapted and employed in sixteenth-century printed books and pamphlets. Churchyard looked backwards to Langland and medieval satirical complaint to furnish himself with formal and rhetorical tools that would hopefully prove efficacious during the 'dreedfull daies' of the early 1550s. The *Dreame* itself set out a prophecy of better times for Tudor England but also made bold claims about the instrumental role that popular poetry might play in current and future political discourse.

Placing Arcadia

NANDINI DAS

Arcadia's geographical identity as a rough, inhospitable province in Greece is well known. Yet in our shared cultural memory, it is the quintessential locus of the pastoral golden world. For sixteenth-century readers, it emerged from Theocritus's bucolic *Idylls* and Virgil's *Eclogues*, although neither of them delineates a landscape that fulfils all the criteria that Arcadia suggests within the pastoral tradition. Later, it was loaded with contingent references to the real world in the hands of Petrarch and Boccaccio, and later still, it took recognisable shape in the poem that first carried its name, Jacopo Sannazaro's *Arcadia* (1504). Sannazaro's locus is dotted with verdant, jewel-like seclusions, like the one where his text opens in Prosa 1:

> There lies on the summit of Parthenius, a not inconsiderable mountain of pastoral Arcadia, a pleasant plateau, not very spacious in extent, since the situation of the place does not permit it, but so filled with tiny and deep-green herbage that, if the wanton herds with their greedy nibbling did not pasture there, one could always find green grasses in that place.[1]

This is a space that would become a commonplace. A locus of the pastoral imagination, it is a common meeting ground as much for poets as for the shepherds who inhabit their poetry, so much so that when Sir Philip Sidney began his first version of *The Countess of Pembrokes Arcadia* with the assertion that 'Arcadia among all the provinces of Greece was ever had in singular reputation', that reputation was already well-established, both for 'the sweetness of air' and the 'moderate and well tempered minds' of its inhabitants that made it the 'chiefest repairing place' for the Muses.[2]

The tense engagement that often characterises the pastoral, emerging from the marked juxtaposition of two very different views of that literary locus, has been explored before. Sidney's narrative itself, for instance, progresses through a constant dialogue between what we might call place and commonplace: historical concerns of the real world mapped onto a vaguely recognisable geopolitical entity on the one hand, and an established literary tradition of responses to the

---

[1] Jacopo Sannazaro, *Arcadia and Piscatorial Eclogues*, trans. Ralph Nash (Detroit, 1966), p. 30.
[2] Sir Philip Sidney, *The Countess of Pembroke's Arcadia (The Old Arcadia)*, ed. Jean Robertson (Oxford, 1973), p. 4.

natural world and rustic life on the other.³ That dialogue, of course, is as much a reflex of the pastoral as a genre as it is a product of Arcadia. As Helen Cooper's foundational examination in *Pastoral: Medieval into Renaissance* emphasised, 'It is in the metaphorical or ironic relationship between the world created by the poet and the real world that pastoral exists.'⁴ It is a relationship that was recognised even in its own time. In George Puttenham's *Arte of English Poesie*, we find Puttenham writing of one particular form of relationship between the 'real world' and the idyll that the pastoral enables: 'the Poet devised the Eglogue [...] not of purpose to counterfait or represent the rusticall manner of loues and communication: but under the vaile of homely persons, and in rude speeches to insinuate and glaunce at greater matters, and such as perchance had not bene safe to have bene disclosed in any other sort.'⁵

My question in returning to Arcadia, however, is less about that impulse of the pastoral to reach out to the present world around its creation to perform a kind of temporal and conceptual enfolding than it is about the making of Arcadia into a locus that fiction (and the pastoral) could inhabit in the first place. Why Arcadia? What is it about this place in particular that made it amenable to being identified as the exemplary site of pastoral fiction? Where does it come from? And what does that place allow such fiction to be?

The standard classical precedents inherited by the Renaissance offer few answers to these fundamental questions. Despite their self-consciously rustic Doric dialect, Theocritus's *Idylls*, composed largely in the urban bustle of cosmopolitan Alexandria in the mid-third century, did not mention Arcadia by name. The countryside of Cos and Syracuse in Sicily form the setting of his depiction of rustic life, although for many, even that setting remains (as Thomas Rosenmeyer puts it) 'little more than a cartographical pretence, a cypher for the *locus amoenus* with its brooks, its pastures, its groves of oaks and willows, and the occasional beach'.⁶ The closest Theocritus comes to Arcadia is when, in Idyll 1, Daphnis the shepherd calls on Pan to leave his homeland and take up the shepherd's pipe in Sicily. Even then the reference is oblique, obscured by memories of other myths:

---

[3] Blair Worden's *The Sound of Virtue: Philip Sidney's 'Arcadia' and Elizabethan Politics* (New Haven, CT, 1996) is still the most authoritative work on the *Arcadia*'s involvement in contemporary politics. On the juxtaposition of the pastoral ideal and geographical reality, see Peter Lindenbaum, *Changing Landscapes: Anti-pastoral Sentiment in the English Renaissance* (Athens, GA and London, 1986); and Elizabeth Dipple, 'Harmony and Pastoral in the Old Arcadia', *ELH* 35.3 (1968), 309–28. Constance Relihan, *Cosmographical Glasses: Geographic Discourse, Gender, and Elizabethan Fiction* (Kent, OH, 2004), explores the Turkish presence behind the geographical region of Arcadia imagined in Sidney's pastoral world.
[4] Cooper, *Pastoral*, p. 2.
[5] George Puttenham, *The Arte of English Poesie* (London, 1589), sigs. F3v–F4r.
[6] Thomas G. Rosenmeyer, *The Green Cabinet: Theocritus and the European Pastoral Lyric* (Berkeley and Los Angeles, 1969), p 232.

O Pan, Pan, whether thou art on the high hills of Lycaeus, or rangest mighty Maenalus, come to the Sicilian isle and leave the mountain peak of Helice and that high tomb of Lycaon's son wherein even the Blessed Ones delight.[7]

Other readers may understandably, then, follow Bruno Snell's claim that Arcadia 'was discovered in the year 42 or 41 BC [...] and its discoverer is Virgil'. Snell's argument, that Virgil created Arcadia as 'a landscape of the mind', itself shaped by Erwin Panofsky's references to Virgil in 'Et in Arcadia ego', was hugely influential.[8] And Virgil does mention Arcadia: imagining himself as the poet of a new golden age in Eclogue 4, he claims:

> Pan etiam, Arcadia mecum si judice certet,
> Pan etiam Arcadia dicat se judice victum.
>
> [Even were Pan to compete with me and Arcady be judge, then even Pan, with Arcady for judge, would own himself defeated.][9]

The seventh eclogue has the herdsman Meliboeus describing Thyrsis and Corydon as 'Arcades ambo' (Arcadians both). And in the tenth eclogue, the claim that 'soli cantare periti/ Arcades' (Arcadians only know how to sing) takes its familiar form.[10] Snell made a clear distinction between this literary Arcadia that is the archetypal 'spiritual landscape' and what he termed as 'humdrum' Arcadia – the geographical Arcadia described by the historian Polybius, for instance, as a place of such 'coldness and gloom' that its inhabitants were forced to practise music and dance to 'humanise their souls'.[11] Others have pointed out repeatedly that Virgil's Arcadia is hardly devoid of its share of coldness and adversity, and that in any case, the references to Arcadia in Virgil are often fleeting, appearing in only a small handful of eclogues.[12] To continue this scholarly debate on these terms seems less than useful. Regardless of whether Arcadia was conceived as congruent with the inhospitable geographical locus in the Peloponnese that Polybius described, or as a world that exists in the

---

[7] *Theocritus*, ed. and trans. A.S.F. Gow, 2nd edn., 2 vols. (Cambridge, 1952; rpt. 2008), 1: 13 (*Idylls*, I.123–6).

[8] Bruno Snell, *The Discovery of the Mind: The Greek Origins of European Thought*, trans. T.G. Rosenmeyer (Oxford, 1953), ch. 13, esp. pp. 281–309; Erwin Panofsky, 'Et in arcadia ego': Poussin and the Elegiac Tradition', *Meaning in the Visual Arts* (Garden City, NY, 1955), pp. 295–320.

[9] Virgil, *Eclogues, Georgics, Aeneid I–VI*, ed. and trans. H. Rushton Fairclough; rev. G.P. Goold (Cambridge, MA, 1999), pp. 52–3 (Eclogue 4, ll. 58–9).

[10] Virgil, *Eclogues, Georgics, Aeneid I–VI*, pp. 66–7 (Eclogue 7, l. 4); pp. 90–1 (Eclogue 10, ll. 32–3).

[11] Snell, *Discovery*, p. 280. Polybius, *The Histories of Polybius*, trans. Evelyn S. Shuckburgh (London, 1889; rpt. Cambridge, 2012), p. 297 (IV.21).

[12] For a useful review of the debate, see 'Introduction' in *Virgil's Eclogues*, ed. Katharina Volk (Oxford, 2008), pp. 1–15. Volk, for instance, cites the work of Ernst Schmidt arguing that Snell and others 'had retrojected Renaissance ideas of an idealized pastoral world onto the *Eclogues* and that the romantic notion of a Vergilian Arcadia was an anachronism' (p. 7).

imagination alone, the question remains: what was it that makes this place in particular the site that the Renaissance associated so undeniably with the pastoral, rather than Theocritus's Sicily, or Virgil's Mantua? Attending to a few less explored references in classical precedents and Renaissance texts alike, and exploring the overlaps and resonances between the literary and the historical evocations of the site, allows us to look at the Renaissance discovery of Arcadia from a somewhat different perspective. It illuminates one particular feature that appears recurrently, that may enable us to explore a different aspect to the question of what Arcadia may have offered to its Renaissance writers and readers alike: it is to do with Arcadia's relationship to memory.

We begin not in Arcadia, but in Rome, a place that is as far as possible conceptually from literary Arcadia's idyllic rural retreat. Around the year 1430, taking advantage of the comparative leisure afforded by the pope's absence, two scholars of the papal court had set out for a day's tour around Rome on horseback. At the top of the Capitoline Hill, they stopped to rest their tired horses, and sat down amid the ruins of the Tarpeian Rock. For the traveller called Antonio, the sight laid out below them offered a deeply striking emblem of the ruins wrought by time. In a practised response that one might expect from an exemplary humanist scholar, he reminded his companion of how Virgil had celebrated the Capitoline in the *Aeneid* when describing the site of Rome, and rejoiced that under Augustus Caesar it was 'Aurea nunc, olim silvestribus horrida dumis' (Golden now, then bristling with woodland thickets).[13] In Antonio's Rome, where the ruins of that classical past marked the landscape in every direction and were hardly recognisable under the overgrowth of weeds, Virgil's verse, however, would need to be rephrased: 'Aurea quondam, nunc squalida spinetis vepribusque referta' (Golden once, now massed with thorns and brambles). If Antonio's lament sounds familiar, that is because it is: it forms the opening of Poggio Bracciolini's famous mid-fifteenth-century dialogue on *The Changeability of Fortune* (*De varietate fortunae*), and the look that it casts over Rome is one that recurs throughout the period.[14]

Nearly a century before Bracciolini's excursions with Antonio Loschi, in a letter to the Dominican Giovanni Colonna di San Vito, dated 30 November 1341, Petrarch had described similar expeditions that he had undertaken with his friend in the spring of 1337:

---

[13] Virgil, *Aeneid VII–XII*, ed. and trans. H. Rushton Fairclough; rev. G.P. Goold (Cambridge, MA, 1918, rev. 2000), p. 85 (VIII.348).

[14] Giovanni Francesco Poggio Bracciolini, 'On the Inconstancy of Fortune', *The Renaissance in Europe: An Anthology*, ed. Peter Elmer et al. (New Haven, CT, 2000), pp. 6–12 (see esp. pp. 6–7).

We used to wander together in that great city, which though it appeared empty because of its vast size, had a huge population. And we would wander not only in the city itself but around it, and at each step there was something present which would excite our tongue and mind: here was the palace of Evander, there the shrine of Carmentis, here the Cave of Cacus, there the famous she-wolf and fig tree of Rumina with the more apt surname of Romulus, there the overpass of Remus, here the circus games and the rape of the Sabines, there the marsh of Capri and the place where Romulus vanished, here the conversations of Numa and Egeria, there the battle line of the *trigemini*.[15]

As Jennifer Summit has argued, the 'Letter to Colonna' introduced a 'method of reading space as a repository of history'.[16] While no doubt harking back to classical sources and challenging the precedent of the twelfth-century handbook for pilgrims that Petrarch may have consulted, the *Mirabilia Urbis Romae*, this particular excursion and its textual record combined classical and Christian perspectives on Rome into a single, resonant view. Its aim was, as Summit suggests,

> less to peel back the encrusted layers of medieval history to reach the 'authentic past' of classical Rome than to plot the city's topography in such a way as to allow the different stages of its history to become successively visible, as monuments, street names, and archaeological remains from different historical moments are brought together within the same geographical locale.[17]

It is an impetus that would continue to be replicated. In texts such as Joachim du Bellay's *Les Antiquités de Rome* (1558) or its subsequent Spenserian translation, *The Ruines of Rome* (1591), the same trick of the eye claims our attention, overlaying Rome-now with Rome-then and drawing the lesson of time from it. Rome in all such instances operates as a stable geographical and memorial locus where time can fold in on itself; it is a space that is at once very much situated in the specific historical moment of the text's creation, but at the same time, one that enables, and in fact invites, two ends of temporality to converge on it. On the one hand, there is the past – remote, multiple, and fragmented. On the other, there is a future of reception by other readers and other visitors.

That habitual trick of the eye has much in common with the particular propensity that Christopher Wood and Alexander Nagel have identified in their examination of Renaissance art. What they say about visual art, arguing against the temptation to think of the Renaissance in Panofskian terms as

---

[15] Francesco Petrarca, *Rerum familiarum libri I–VIII*, trans. Aldo S. Barnardo (Albany, NY, 1975), p. 291 (VI.2).
[16] Jennifer Summit, 'Topography as Historiography: Petrarch, Chaucer, and the Making of Medieval Rome', *JMEMS* 30.2 (2000), 218.
[17] Summit, 'Topography as Historiography', 223.

Figure 1. Etienne Dupérac, *Vestigi dell'antichita di Roma* (Rome, 1575), Plate 7. © The British Library Board. Shelfmark: General Reference Collection C.108.k.3.

an epochal view of historical consciousness that allowed for 'an intellectual distance between the present and the past', is useful in terms of thinking about Renaissance literary engagement with place as well.[18] 'The artwork', as Wood and Nagel argue, 'is made or designed by an individual or by a group of individuals at some moment, but it also points away from that moment, backward to a remote ancestral origin, perhaps, or to a prior artefact, or to an origin outside of time, in divinity.' Yet at the same time, 'it points forward to all its future recipients who will activate and reactivate it as a meaningful event'.[19] We see this in innumerable depictions of Rome, such as Figure 1 derived from Etienne Dupérac's popular and widely known pictorial records of his journey to the city, published in 1575 as *Vestigi dell'antichita di Roma* (*Remains of the Antiquity of Rome*). We see it even in the one medium that one would expect to be tied exclusively to places here and now – cartography – in the series of classical and historical maps that appeared collectively as the *Parergon* to editions of Abraham Ortelius's *Theatrum orbis terrarum* beginning in 1579. Whether it be through (as Summit writes) the 'representation of Rome as a collection of pagan buildings transformed to Christian uses' in the *Mirabilia*, that showed

---

[18] Erwin Panofsky, *Introduction to Studies in Iconology: Humanistic Themes in the Art of the Renaissance* (Oxford, 1939), p. 28; cited in Alexander Nagel and Christopher S. Wood, 'Interventions: Toward a New Model of Renaissance Anachronism', *Art Bulletin* 87.3 (2005), 409.

[19] Alexander Nagel and Christopher S. Wood, *Anachronic Renaissance* (New York, 2010), p. 9.

historical change 'to take place not through acts of destruction or repudiation of the past, but through acts of conversion that leave its subjects intact while working change within their interior parts', or in the recovery and representation of classical traces by Dupérac or in Ortelius's meticulous reconstructions that attempted to map journeys such as Aeneas's onto historical space, Renaissance representations of place are often marked by a certain temporal instability.[20] Such places resist being fitted into a linear temporal framework where the relationship between the 'past' and the 'future' is unidirectional. Like the artwork, they are able to hold apparently 'incompatible models in suspension without deciding', displaying an ability 'to "fetch" a past, create a past, perhaps even fetch the future'.[21] As artefacts, such records therefore turn what could be the site of distance and contestation or confrontation between temporal points into a meeting place, a kind of contact-zone.

What is intriguing about Arcadia is the way in which the intensity of its response to this function of the place or locus as a site of the enfolding of time influences the conception of the place itself. Despite possessing a geographical presence, its essential resonance is memorial, conditioned to be seen from a distance. In contrast to other temporally complex *loci* in the Renaissance – more than Rome itself, for instance, or Jerusalem – its perceived spatial isolation and the valorisation of memory work together to resist the layering of time in quite the same way. Looking back at some of those less explored classical precedents can help to illuminate the origins of this particular quality. In some ways, 'views' of Arcadia that the Renaissance inherited are firmly established in the central classical sources I have mentioned before: Theocritus's *Idylls*, Virgil's *Eclogues* and Polybius's *Histories*. At the same time, in the light of other ancient references, the place turns out to be oddly elusive, visible only (but insistently) out of the corner of the eye. There is the practice of singling out the Arcadians as a unique people, both spatially and temporally set apart from the rest of the world, for instance, which started with the ancient Greeks. For the sea-faring Greeks, Arcadia's defining feature was its mythography coupled with its unusual landlocked character, making it a place both of isolation and of refuge, the former strengthening its characterisation as a primitive, rural land harking back to the origins of civilisation, the latter, its identification as space redolent of the promise of past wholeness and future recovery. Even in the Hesiodic *Catalogue of Women* often attached to the end of the *Theogony* in Renaissance printed volumes, Arcadians were separated from the rest of Greece. Greek myths look back to the war-loving King Hellen and his sons

---

[20] Summit, 'Topography as Historiography', p. 228.
[21] Nagel and Wood, *Anachronic Renaissance*, p. 18. Rome of course is not the only site of such temporally complex mappings. Jerusalem and London as Troynovant illustrate exactly the same quality of temporal fluidity.

Doros, Xouthos and Aiolos as the founders of the Dorians, Acolians, Ionians and Achaians as parts of the larger Greek family, but the Arcadians were always excluded from this genealogy. Unlike Doros and his brothers, Arcadia's first king and ancestor Pelasgos was supposed to have been autochthonous, born directly from Arcadian soil.[22] His son was Lycaon, who instituted games in honour of Zeus and founded the city of Lycosoura, which Pausanias would later identify as the oldest in the world.[23] Pelasgos's grandson Arcas, son of Zeus and Callisto, and the subject of Lycaon's unfortunate challenge to Zeus which ended with Lycaon being turned into a wolf by divine wrath, would give the land and its people his name and teach them all the arts of civilisation.

In the Greek mythological and genealogical world-view, where significant emphasis was placed on primacy, such a shared history allowed Arcadians the power to claim to be the oldest and the first on multiple counts. But as Thomas Heine Nielsen notes, that reputation also meant that for the writers who discussed the land, it is Arcadia's rich and ancient mythological traditions that tended to claim attention more than its contemporaneous political reality.[24] In addition, very few of the ancient writers who write about Arcadia were actually Arcadians, with the notable exception being Polybius, although he too was an Arcadian exile in Rome. What such texts produced inevitably, therefore, is the evocation of a space that is at once present and elusive – an outsider's view of a distant point of origin, a land preserved from time, which always holds an implicit allure of *nostos* or homecoming. As Tanja Scheer has pointed out, for countless cities and groups, the claim of an Arcadian foundation became a matter of practice, with Italy, Rome, Phyrygia, Bithynia, Teuthrania, Crete, Cyprus and Pontos all at different times claiming Arcadian origins.[25] For Scheer, such claims 'were particularly attractive in areas that wanted to emphasize their Hellenicity', providing 'important elements of genealogical valorization – great age, civilizing deeds, and martial bravery – without having to resort to the famous competitors Athens and Sparta'.[26]

---

[22] Hesiod, *Hesiod*, ed. and trans. Glenn. W. Most (Cambridge, MA, 2006), pp. 157, 175, ('The Catalogue of Women', 4.30–1). Jonathan M. Hall offers a useful outline of Hellenic genealogy in *Ethnic Identity in Greek Antiquity* (Cambridge, 2000), p. 43. On Arcadians as autochthones, see Thomas Heine Nielsen, 'The Concept of Arkadia – the People, Their Land, and Their Organisation', *Defining Ancient Arkadia*, ed. Thomas Heine Nielsen and James Roy (Copenhagen, 1999), p. 35.

[23] 'Of all cities on earth, whether on the mainland or on islands, Lycosoura is the oldest, and it was the first city that ever the sun beheld. The rest of mankind learned to build cities on its model'; see *Pausanias's Description of Greece*, trans. J.G. Frazer, 6 vols. (London, 1898), 1: 423 (VIII.xxxviii).

[24] Nielsen, 'The Concept of Arkadia', pp. 16–17.

[25] Tanja Scheer, 'Ways of Becoming Arcadian: Arcadian Foundation Myths in the Mediterranean', *Cultural Identity in the Ancient Mediterranean*, ed. Erich S. Gruen (Los Angeles, 2010), p. 12.

[26] Scheer, 'Ways of Becoming Arcadian', pp. 18–19.

Partly as a result of this peculiar attraction of the Arcadian origin tale, perhaps, the Arcadians that the Renaissance inherited, be it from their classical past or medieval inheritance, are forever out of Arcadia. In the 'Catalogue of Ships' in the *Iliad*, Homer describes them as the fierce fighters hailing from the landlocked Peloponnese:

> they that held Arcadia beneath the steep mountain of Cyllene, beside the tomb of Aepytus, where are warriors that fight in close combat; and they that dwelt in Pheneos and Orchomenus, rich in flocks, and Rhipe and Stratia and wind-swept Enispe; and that held Tegea and lovely Mantineia; and that held Stymphalos and dwelt in Parrhasia, – all these were led by the son of Ancaeus, lord Agapenor, with sixty ships; and on each ship embarked full many Arcadian warriors well skilled in fight. For of himself had the king of men, Agamemnon, given them benched ships wherewith to cross over the wine-dark sea, even the son of Atreus, for with matters of seafaring had they naught to do.[27]

Incidentally, that image of the Arcadian as being always displaced, always separated from his point of origin, would continue to linger. Even in the medieval *Roman d'Alexandre*, it would appear in the form of the Arcadian fighter Emenidus, acclaimed as chief among the twelve peers of Alexander and the bearer of the royal banner.[28] Emenidus and his followers again constituted a community always on the move, traversing the far-flung corners of Alexander's empire, from Gaza to India and beyond.

It is the establishment of those tropes surrounding Arcadia – its primitivism, its attraction as a distant and secluded homeland, and the association of displacement and exile – which of course return with such enormous emotional resonance for Sannazaro and his contemporaries and successors. To understand that, however, it is to Virgil again that we need to return as the source of that phrase remembered by Antonio Loschi while looking over the ruins of the Capitoline in Rome in Poggio Bracciolini's dialogue. It appears with the introduction of another Arcadian far from home in a justly famous passage in book eight of the *Aeneid*, and it is probably the best illustration of the elusive nature of Arcadia that I am trying to describe. Evander, outcast from his Arcadian fatherland, hosts the Trojan strangers in a new Pallanteum, the rustic settlement he has created at the heart of the site of a yet-unbuilt Rome to echo the city left behind. Here, he takes Aeneas for a walk that fuses the past, present and future. Evander is described as 'Romanae conditor arcis' (founder of Rome's citadel), and his settlement is the first community in the history of

---

[27] Homer, *Iliad*, trans. A.T. Murray, 2 vols. (Cambridge, MA, 1924; rpt. 1978), 1: 95–7 (2.603–14).
[28] *The Medieval Romance of Alexander: Jehan Wauquelin's The Deeds and Conquests of Alexander the Great*, trans. Nigel Bryant (Woodbridge, 2012), p. 42.

Italy to be ruled by law.[29] As they pass the Tarpeian house and the Capitol, and Evander continues his role as guide by pointing out the 'reliquias veterumque vides monumenta virorum' (relics and memorials of men of old) for Aeneas to see, Virgil uses that phrase which Loschi had remembered, conflating the wild domain of the Arcadian then and the golden Capitol of Augustus: 'Aurea nunc, olim silvestribus horrida dumis'(Golden now, then bristling with woodland thickets). When they reach Evander's humble house, which Virgil describes as no more than a rough shelter, they see herds of cattle 'lowing in the Roman Forum and in the fashionable Carinae'.[30] The familiar conflation of the past, present and future of Rome emerges with striking clarity at such moments. If Virgil's vision of Roman national identity was entwined around Aeneas who hailed from mythical Troy, it is only to be expected that for its spiritual regeneration and awakening of a new golden age of civilisation, Rome should be linked to another ancient point of origin, Arcadia. At the same time, it is also obvious that what Virgil is offering here to Aeneas is a vision of pastoral life, a resting place reminiscent of his *Eclogues*. Evander is clearly a moral guide and a father figure, whose lesson is that of pastoral simplicity and piety combined with honest labour.[31] Yet Evander, we soon remember, is no longer in Arcadia, his lament makes him a striking predecessor of Aeneas himself:

> me pulsum patria pelagique extrema sequentem
> Fortuna omnipotens et ineluctabile fatum
> his posuere locis, matrisque egere tremenda
> Carmentis nymphaea monita et deus auctor Apollo

> [As for me, exiled from my country and seeking the very limits of the sea, almighty Fortune and inevitable Fate planted me on this soil; and the dread warnings of my mother, the nymph Carmentis, and Apollo's divine warrant, drove me here].[32]

What we have lingering as its traces behind Pallanteum is only its facsimile, a remembered, reconstructed copy made by an exile of the place he has left behind. And soon that flickers out of view too, as Evander's warriors are yet again on the move, accompanying the Trojans out of their settlement and into

---

[29] Virgil, *Aeneid VII–XII*, pp. 82–3 (8.313).
[30] Virgil, *Aeneid VII–XII*, pp. 84–5 (8.356, 348, 360–1).
[31] On Aeneas and Evander's walk, see S. Pappaioanou, 'Founder, Civilizer and Leader: Virgil's Evander and his Role in the Origins of Rome', *Mnemosyne* 56 (2003), 680–702. For Evander's kingdom as a pastoral retreat, see Michael Putnam, *Poetry of the Aeneid* (Cambridge, MA, 1965), ch. 3, esp. pp. 106–10, 121–34, which present this episode as a pastoral space where Aeneas has to retire in order to absorb new values before the culmination of his heroic action. See also D.M. Rosenberg, *Oaten Reeds and Trumpets: Pastoral and Epic in Virgil, Spenser and Milton* (East Brunswick, NJ, 1981), pp. 53–4.
[32] Virgil, *Aeneid VII–XII*, pp. 82–3 (8.333–5).

battle. What both Renaissance readers and we are left with is that very familiar memorial network of references to Roman ruins with cattle grazing on the vegetation that covers the fallen stones, evoked countlessly and memorably by Petrarch, Poggio, Dupérac and their contemporaries. There is no way for us to unsee that further layer which has been added to Virgil's text by time.[33]

The recurring occurrence of glimpses such as these unmoors Arcadia both temporally and spatially for the Renaissance. Constantly and repeatedly, from classical peregrinations to sixteenth – and seventeenth-century accounts, what we come across in references to Arcadia is a locus of absence, one that resists the kind of conflated trick-of-the-eye through which we saw Poggio and his friend 'fix' Rome as a geographical site, where temporal deposits have accreted in richly defined layers. Arcadia invites a very different kind of response, in which memory and fiction continue increasingly to fill in the gap in time and space that it has come to represent. In the section that follows, three travel texts that illuminate contemporaneous perceptions of Arcadia show us how that unmooring occurs in actual encounters with the place itself.

When we think of classical descriptions of geographical Arcadia, we tend to go to Strabo or to Polybius's Hellenistic *Histories*, in which he described his homeland of Arcadia as a rough, remote, infertile country whose people took the deliberate decision to cultivate music with the aim of 'softening and tempering [their] natural ruggedness and rusticity', since 'as a natural consequence of the coldness and gloom which were the prevailing features of a great part of the country, the general character of the people was austere.'[34] Equally familiar to Renaissance writers, although significantly less attended in current scholarship till a recent resurgence of interest, would be the second-century text we know as Pausanias's *Periegesis Hellados* (*Tour around Greece*). As a writer, Pausanias is as elusive as Arcadia itself; he mentions nothing of his parentage, origins or even his name in the *Periegesis Hellados*, which is the only surviving text by him.[35] Possibly a near contemporary of writers such as Ptolemy, Lucian of Samosata and Apuleius, and likely to be from Lydia, which

---

[33] Charles Martindale has pointed out that ambivalence or 'wavering' is inherent in Virgil's language itself, since 'olim' can refer both to the past and the future, either 'golden now, once densely wooded' or 'golden now, one day to be densely wooded'. Similarly, the 'nunc' is also ambiguous, since it could refer either to the 'now' of Aeneas's day, or of that of Virgil and Augustus; see 'Introduction', *Cambridge Companion to Virgil*, ed. Charles Martindale (Cambridge, 1997), p. 5.

[34] Polybius, *The Histories of Polybius*, p. 297 (IV.21).

[35] On dating Pausanias's text, see William Hutton, *Describing Greece: Landscape and Literature in the Periegesis of Pausanias* (Cambridge, 2005), p. 18. See also Christian Habicht, *Pausanias' Guide to Ancient Greece* (Berkeley, 1985), Maria Pretzler, *Pausanias: Travel Writing in Ancient Greece* (London, 2007), and *Following Pausanias: The Quest for Greek Antiquity*, ed. G.A. Pikoulas et al. (Athens, GA, 2007), esp. ch. 3.

he describes with great detail and accuracy, he seems to have led the life of a wealthy cosmopolitan, travelling widely through all of coastal Asia Minor and large parts of central and eastern Asia Minor, Syria, Palestine, Egypt and Byzantium. The ten books of his text are each dedicated to an area of mainland Greece, and constitute a font of geographical, mythological and historical information, yet the text remained relatively unknown and unmentioned by Pausanias's successors till the early medieval period. In 1418, a single copy from Constantinople reached the library of the humanist Niccolò Niccoli of Florence, and was stored at the library of San Marco, Venice, after his death in 1437. While this master-copy disappeared in the early sixteenth century, by that time it had generated multiple copies which form the basis of the numerous printed editions and extracts which appeared from 1516 onwards. It was translated, reprinted and adapted in various forms throughout the period and, perhaps most importantly, widely used to inform historical maps such as those of Ortelius mentioned above.

Pausanias repeats much of the mythology of Arcadia offered by Hesiod, Homer and Virgil. But for this traveller, the now familiar elusiveness of Arcadia, its identification as a site of loss, is emphasised even further by actual experience. Pausanias's visit to its main city, Megalopolis, where Polybius had been born, triggers one of the most striking *ubi sunt* meditations in his text:

> Megalopolis, the foundation of which was carried out by the Arcadians with the utmost enthusiasm, and viewed with the highest hopes by the Greeks, now lies mostly in ruins, shorn of all its beauty and ancient prosperity. I do not marvel at this, knowing that ceaseless change is the will of God, and that all things alike, strength as well as weakness, growth as well as decay, are subject to the mutations of fortune, whose resistless force sweeps them along at her will. Mycenae, which led the Greeks in the Trojan war; Nineveh, where was the palace of the Assyrian kings; Boeotian Thebes, once deemed worthy to be the head of Greece: what is left of them? [...] So transient and frail are the affairs of men.[36]

Megalopolis seems to disappear in Pausanias's lament into the line of great cities that have fallen, inevitably and inexorably, since the beginning of time. At the same time, however, those same deserted ruins that inspire this lament also re-emphasise Arcadia's identity as a land of myths and stories for Pausanias, who makes a great deal of Arcadia's antiquity and the longevity of its ancient rituals and religious cults. As Greta Hawes has pointed out, 'the Arcadians' long habitation of the same piece of land provides Pausanias with a seemingly unbroken storytelling tradition stretching from the time of myth to the present'.[37] Pausanias himself admits, 'When I began this work I used to

---

[36] *Pausanias's Description of Greece*, pp. 416–17 (VIII.xxxiii).
[37] Greta Hawes, *Rationalizing Myth in Antiquity* (Oxford, 2014), p. 216.

look on these Greek stories as little better than foolishness; but now that I have got as far as Arcadia my opinion about them is this: I believe that the Greekes who were accounted wise spoke of old in riddles, and not straight out.'[38] In Arcadia, therefore, stories gain a special resonance, crucially not because the site offers visible proofs and traces of their validity, but because of its lack of such proofs; its long-standing identity as a site of loss rather counterintuitively opens up the possibility of fiction's valorisation.

Almost fifteen hundred years later, that potential wielded by absence in Arcadia had not changed when the irascible William Lithgow undertook what he called his *Most Delectable, and True Discourse, of an Admired and Painefull Peregrination from Scotland to the Most Famous Kingdoms in Europe, Asia and Affricke* (1614). Lithgow was a staunch Scottish Protestant whose three journeys across northern Europe, the Middle East and Spain over nineteen years, according to his own calculations, 'amounteth to thirty six thousand and odde miles, which draweth neare to twice the circumference of the whole Earth'.[39] He claimed travel to be the most efficient route to the 'most necessary' of all sciences, 'the science of the world', which 'above all things [...] preferreth men to honors, and the charges that make great houses and Reipublicks to flourish; and render the actions and words of them who possesse it, agreeable both to great and small'.[40] Crucially for Lithgow, the acquisition of such knowledge was not a matter of passive, isolated absorption of information through books, but a collective, social endeavour. As he suggests in a striking defence of his second excursion, '[t]his science is onely acquisted by conversation, and haunting the company of the most experimented: by divers discourses, reports, by writs, or by a lively voyce, in communicating with strangers; and in the judicious consideration of the fashion of the living one with another. And above all, and principally by Travellers, and Voyagers in divers Regions, and remote places, whose experience confirmeth the true Science thereof; and can best draw the anatomy of humane condition.'[41]

Yet when Lithgow arrived in Arcadia during the first of his three journeys (1609–12), there was no conversation to be had, and no strangers to be interrogated. '[We] entred in the hilly and barren Countrey of Arcadia', he reports, 'where, for a dayes journey we had no village, but saw aboundance of Cattell without keepers. In this Desart way, I beheld many singular monuments, and ruinous Castles, whose names I knew not, because I had an ignorant guide.'[42] In many ways this was no different from Lithgow's experience elsewhere in

---

[38] *Pausanias's Description of Greece*, p. 382 (VIII.viii).
[39] William Lithgow, *The Totall Discourse, of the Rare Adventures, and Painefull Peregrinations of Long Nineteene Yeares Travayles* (London, 1632), p. 507.
[40] Lithgow, *Totall Discourse*, p. 341.
[41] Lithgow, *Totall Discourse*, p. 341.
[42] William Lithgow, *Most Delectable, and True Discourse*, sigs. E3r–E3v.

Greece. As he had discovered soon after his arrival, the political reality of the land under Ottoman rule was very different from the idealised image of Hellenic ancient culture. 'In all this countrey I could finde nothing', he claimed, 'to answere the famous relations, given by antient Authors, of the excellency of that land, but the name onely; the barbarousnesse of Turkes and Time, having defaced all the Monuments of Antiquity: No shew of honour, no habitation of men in an honest fashion, nor possessours of the Countrey in a Principality.'[43] Even then, however, and despite Lithgow's general disappointment with Greece and its people, the occasional courtesy and hospitality of strangers could serve to remind him of 'how curious the old Athenians were to heare of forraine newes, and with what great regard and estimation they honoured travellers'.[44] Arcadia is a different matter. For Lithgow, as for Pausanias, it is a place whose superlative barrenness, elusiveness and resistance to yielding itself to the kind of physical and temporal layering we have seen Rome undergo, for example, turn it into a purely imaginative locus, one that can be moored only in memory and the imagination. For Pausanias it became a pure *topos* of what he calls the 'mutations of fortune'. For Lithgow, those mutations of fortune breed an absence that is felt viscerally in the futile pain of the travel encounter, which, like Pausanias, he fills with the memories of inherited fiction:

> But this I remember, amongst these rockes, my belly was pinched, and wearied was my body, with the climing of fastidious mountains, which bred no small griefe to my breast. Yet notwithstanding of my distresse, the remembrance of these sweete seasoned Songs, of *Arcadian* shepherds which pregnant Poets have so well penned, did recreate my fatigated corps, with many sugred suppositions.[45]

It is not surprising, then, that this unmoored place would wander over to the New World. The name 'Arcadie' is found on many European maps of the sixteenth century. Spelt in many different ways, from 'Arcadia' and 'Archadia' to 'Arcadie', 'Acadie', and 'Cadie', it points to locations that vary from north-eastern Maine, to south-eastern Quebec to Nova Scotia, signalling not so much a place but the arrival of a memory and an idea.[46] See Figures 2 and 3. Here, for my third example, I want to focus briefly on its appearance in one particular document by the Florentine explorer Giovanni da Verrazzano, which was produced as a letter or report for Francis I of France. Verrazzano's commission from King Francis I and the merchants of Lyon was to find the fabled Northwest Passage

---

[43] Lithgow, *Most Delectable, and True Discourse*, sig. E3v.
[44] Lithgow, *Most Delectable, and True Discourse*, sig. E4r.
[45] Lithgow, *Most Delectable, and True Discourse*, sig. E3v.
[46] Richard D'Abate, 'On the Meaning of a Name: "Norumbega" and the Representation of North America', *American Beginnings: Exploration, Culture, and Cartography in the Land of Norumbega*, ed. Emerson W. Baker et al. (Lincoln, 1994), pp. 61–90; see also David Quinn, 'The Early Cartography of Maine' in the same volume, pp. 37–59.

Figure 2. Map 'Tabula Europae X' showing Arcadia in the Peloponnesus. Giacomo di Gastaldi, *La Geografia di Claudio Ptolemeo* (Venice, 1548). © The British Library Board. Shelfmark: Maps C.1.a.3.

to 'Cathay' and Asia and aid France's imperial ambitions, but the main outcome of his voyage was the charting of the Atlantic coast of northern America, approximately from present-day North Carolina to Maine. Verrazzano's letter to Francis I, dated 8 July 1524, exists in a small number of manuscript variants. A version of it would be reprinted by Giovanni Battista Ramusio in his *Navigationi et Viaggi* (1556). It was translated by Richard Hakluyt for his first publication, *Divers Voyages touching the Discoverie of America and the Ilands adjacent* (1582), which he dedicated to none other than Sir Philip Sidney, in an effort to energise English explorations of the Northwest Passage and the New World. Of the variant manuscripts, the twelve-sheet Cèllere Codex, now held at the Pierpont Morgan Library, New York, contains autograph corrections and revisions in what is now acknowledged to be Verrazzano's own hand, and offers a fuller version of the document printed by Ramusio and Hakluyt.[47]

---

[47] A full facsimile of the document is available in I.N. Phelps Stokes, *The Iconography of Manhattan Island, 1498–1909*, 2 vols. (New York, 1916), 2: 169–71 and plates 60–81. See also Lawrence C. Wroth, *The Voyages of Giovanni da Verrazzano, 1524–1528* (Paris, 1982).

Figure 3. Map 'Tierra Nueva' showing Arcadia in the New World. Gastaldi, *Geografia*. © The British Library Board. Shelfmark: Maps C.1.a.3.

It is in this document that Arcadia makes its appearance. From Verrazzano's report it appears that his first landing was made near what is now called Cape Fear in North Carolina. Travelling further along the coast, past regions he named Selva de Lauri (Woods of Laurel) and Campo di Cedri (Field of Cedars), his ship at last came to an area in what seems likely to be present-day Maryland. Describing this particular area, Verrazzano's account states:

> La terra del sito, bontà et belleza, è come l'altra; le selve rare; di vario genere d'alberi piena, ma non di tanto odore, per esser più septentrionale et fredda. Vedemmo in quella molte vite da la natura prodotte, quali alzando, s'avvoltano a li alberi, come ne la Cisalpina Gallia costumano: quali, se dagli agricoltori havessino el perfetto ordine di cultura, sanza dubio, produrebbono optimi vini, perchè più volte il frutto di quelle veggiendo suave et dolce, non dal nostro differente. Sono da loro tenute in stimatione, imperochè per tutto dove nascono lievano li arbuscelli circumstanti a causa il frutto possino germinare. Trovamo rose silvestre, viole et lilii et molte sorte d'herbe et fiori odoriferi da nostri

differenti [...] Essendo in questa dimorati tre giorni, surti a la costa, per la rarita de' porti deliberammo partire scorrendo sempre il lito.[48]

The English translation in Hakluyt's *Divers Voyages*, except for minor changes, follows this fairly closely:

> The land is in situation goodnes and fairenesse like the other: it hath woods like the other, thinne and full of divers sorts of trees: but not sweete, because the countrey is more Northerly and colde. We saw in this Countrey many Vines growing naturally, which growing up, take hold of the trees as they doe in Lombardie, which if by husbandmen they were dressed in good order, without all doubt they would yeeld excellent wines: for having oftentimes seene the fruit thereof dryed, which was sweete and pleasaunt, and not differing from ours. Wee doe thinke that they doe esteeme the same, because that in every place where they growe, they take away the under branches growing round about, that the fruit thereof may ripen the better. We found also roses, violettes, lilies, and many sorts of herbes, and sweete and odoriferous flowers different from ours [...] having made our aboade three dayes in this cuntrey, riding on the coast for want of harboroughs, we concluded to depart from thence, trending along the shore.[49]

In a striking visual illustration of the un-rooted nature of Arcadia that I have explored throughout this essay, an insertion mark in Verrazzano's hand after the word 'lito' (shore) in the Cèllere manuscript connects this to a marginal annotation, which notes, 'quale batezamo Archadia per la bellezza de li arbori' (which we named Archadia because of the beauty of the trees). (See Figure 4.) The reference is fleeting; there is only one other reference to Arcadia in a note placed at the end of the manuscript, in which Verrazzano describes an encounter with a native inhabitant ('Ne l'Arcadia trovamo un homo, el qual veneva al lito per vederce che gente eramo'; In Arcadia we found a man who came to the shore to see who we were).[50] He offers them what may have been tobacco in welcome, a gesture which Verrazzano and his men misinterpret and return by firing a shot. He responds by showing fear, then appears to pray and bless the ship. Cross-cultural misunderstandings aside, this is a different matter altogether from naming a place 'New Rome' or 'Troynovant' to give a local habitation and a name to what is otherwise strange, foreign and unfamiliar. Verrazzano's autograph note inserts Arcadia literally across the Atlantic

---

[48] Stokes, *Iconography of Manhattan Island*, plates 67–8. A conflated diplomatic transcription from all variants is available in Fabio Romanini, 'Sulla "Lettera a Francesco I re di Francia" di Giovanni da Verrazzano: con una nuova edizione', *Filologia Italiana* 9 (2012), 127–90.

[49] Richard Hakluyt, *Divers Voyages touching the Discoverie of America and the Ilands adjacent* (London, 1582), sigs. A4r–A4v.

[50] Stokes, *Iconography of Manhattan Island*, plate 80.

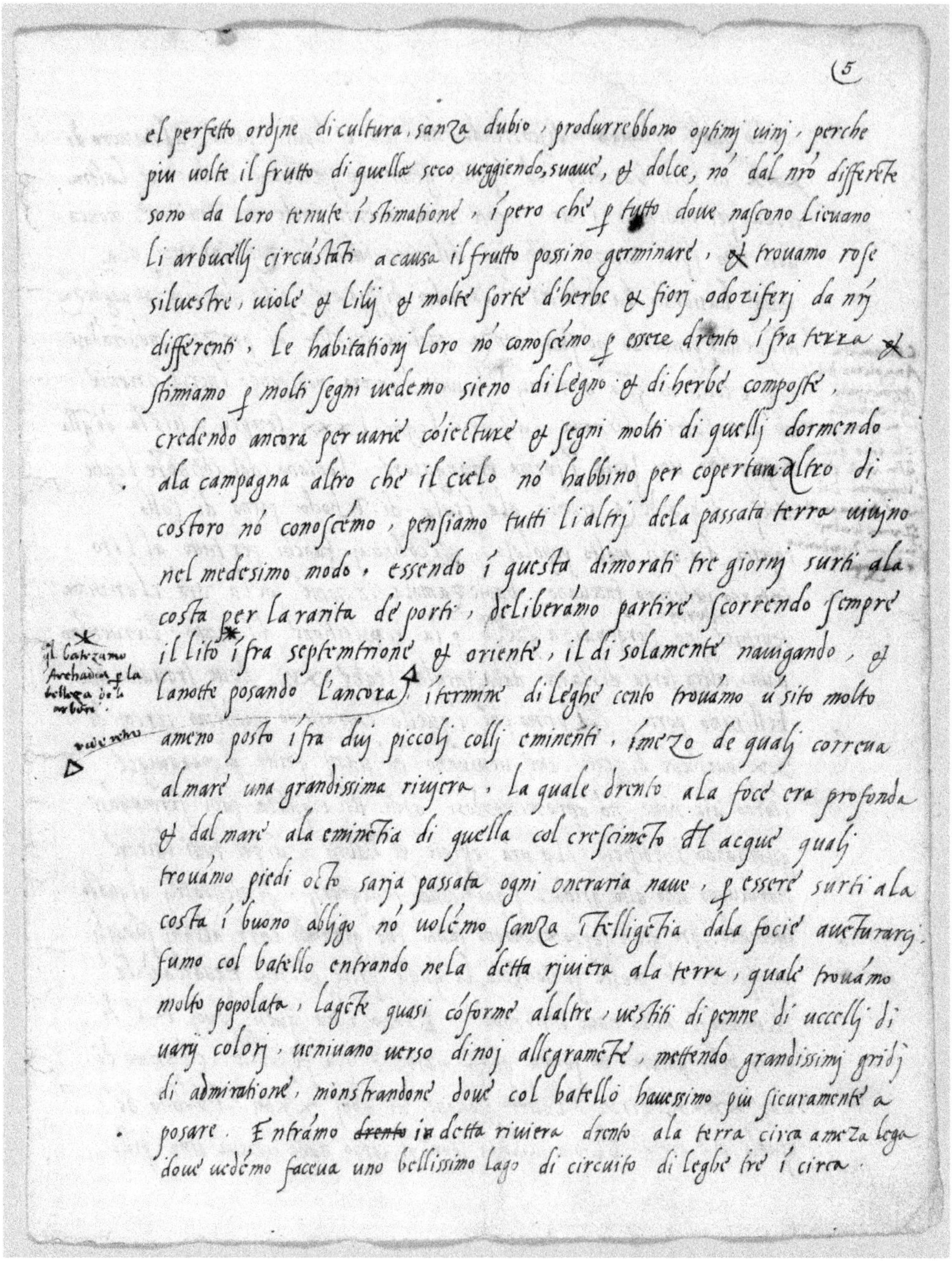
5

el perfetto ordine di cultura, sanza dubio, produrrebbono optimi uini, perche
piu uolte il frutto di quelle secco ueggiendo, suaue, et dolce, nō dal nrō differente
sono da loro tenute i stimatione, i pero che p tutto doue nascono lieuano
li arbucellj circūstanti a causa il frutto possino germinare, et trouamo rose
siluestre, uiole et lilij et molte sorte d'herbe et fiorj odoriferj da nrj
differenti. Le habitationj loro nō conoscemo p essere drento i fra terra
stimiamo p molti segni uedemo sieno di legno et di herbe composte,
credendo ancora per uarie coiecture et segni molti di quellj dormendo
ala campagna altro che il cielo nō habbino per copertura altro di
costoro nō conoscemo, pensiamo tutti li altrj dela passata terra uiuino
nel medesimo modo. essendo i questa dimorati tre giornj surti ala
costa per la rarita de porti, deliberamo partire scorrendo sempre
il lito i fra septemtrione et oriente, il di solamente nauigando, et
la notte posando l'ancora. i termine di leghe cento trouamo u sito molto
ameno posto i fra duj piccolj collj eminenti, i mezo de qualj correua
al mare una grandissima riujera, la quale drento ala foce era profonda
et dal mare ala eminentia di quella col cresciméto dl acque qualj
trouamo piedi octo sarja passata ogni oneraria naue, p essere surti ala
costa i buono abrigo nō uolemo sanza intelligentia dala focie auenturarcj.
fumo col batello entrando nela detta riuiera ala terra, quale trouamo
molto popolata, la gente quasi coforme alaltre, uestiti di penne di uccellj di
uarj colorj, ueniuano uerso di noj allegramente, mettendo grandissimj gridj
di admiratione, monstrandone doue col batello hauessimo piu sicuramente a
posare. Entramo ~~drento~~ in detta riuiera drento ala terra circa a mezza lega
doue uedemo faceua uno bellissimo lago di circuito di leghe tre i circa.

Figure 4. *Viaggio fatto nel 1524 all'America settentrionale*: copy of the long-lost Verrazano letter to Francis I, fol. 5r. Reproduced with the permission of the Pierpont Morgan Library, New York. Shelfmark: MA 776.

in this New World. While the former practice may have acknowledged the ability of certain loci to accommodate layers of time deposited across them and their ability to encourage emulative *imitatio* in a different time and space, it simultaneously confirms the spatial stability of the original locus. Arcadia is far more malleable. What Verrazzano is acknowledging in his naming is a conflation of that classically inherited Arcadia that was evoked in Aeneas's search for a new empire and its more contemporaneous, pastoral reworking by the text that reintroduced Arcadia to the Renaissance reader – Sannazzaro's pastoral poem, which was printed some twenty years before Verrazzano set off on his voyage.[51] Verrazzano's autograph insertion mark can moor that conflated Arcadia in this New World, even as Evander in Virgil's epic had done before him.

What, then, does this perception of Arcadia, the uses to which it lends itself and the ways in which it allows itself to be seen, mean for the Renaissance? Juxtaposing Arcadia with other geographical sites, such as Rome, illuminates how its function as a locus of imagination and memory is a function, in many ways, of what I have called its unmooring in time and space. As we have seen, Arcadia emerges in the Renaissance not simply as a site that accommodates memorial layering. In fact, it resists that actively through its elusiveness, its identity as a site of loss and absence. It is that same resistance, however, which allows it to become the superlative locus of the act of memory, of the activity of memorial and fictive reconstruction itself. Through that transaction, Arcadia emerges as a landscape whose true identity can be made visible only through memory and the imagination, and if, from Virgil's *Eclogues* to Sannazaro's and Sidney's respective *Arcadia*s, pastoral returns repeatedly and obsessively to 'remembrance, restless remembrance', as Sidney's shepherds put it at the opening of the *New Arcadia*, then it makes sense that such a return can be accommodated above all in this place.[52] In that respect one could see Arcadia as a 'landscape of the mind' – to use Snell's useful phrase – not in the sense that it is imaginary, but in the sense that it offers a site for imagination itself.

I will end with a moment in Renaissance English literature where this perception of the place emerges strikingly and significantly. In Sidney's revised

---

[51] Verrazano's reference to the trees and vine echoes the opening of Sannazaro's *Arcadia*, which I partly quoted in earlier in this essay, and which is followed in Sannazaro's text by a catalogue of trees. Verrazzano's text has had limited attention beyond the field of early American history; see Harry Franklin Covington, 'The Discovery of Maryland or Verrazzano's Visit to the Eastern Shore', *Maryland Historical Magazine* 10.3 (1915), 199–217; and Ernest Hatch Wilkins, 'Arcadia in America', *Proceedings of the American Philosophical Society* 101 (February 15, 1957), 4–30.

[52] Philip Sidney, *The Countess of Pembroke's Arcadia*, ed. Maurice Evans (Harmondsworth, 1987), p. 61.

version of the *Arcadia*, the beginning of Sidney's fiction merges with the hospitable Arcadian Kalander's garden, itself a concentrated example of pastoral Arcadia: 'neither field, garden, or orchard, or rather [...] both field, garden, and orchard'.[53] 'In the middest of all the place', Sidney notes:

> was a faire ponde, whose shaking christall was a perfect mirrour to all the other beauties, so that it bare shewe of two gardens; one in deede, the other in shaddowes: and in one of the thickets was a fine fountaine made thus. A naked Venus of white marble, wherein the graver had used such cunning, that the naturall blew veines of the marble were framed in fitte places, to set foorth the beautifull veines of her bodie. At her brest she had her babe Aeneas [...] who seemed [...] to looke upon her fayre eyes, which smiled at the babes follie. [...] Hard by was a house of pleasure builte for a Sommer retiring place, whether Kalander leading him, he found a square roome full of delightfull pictures, made by the most excellent workeman of Greece. There was Diana when Actaeon sawe her bathing, in whose cheekes the painter had set such a colour, as was mixt betweene shame and disdaine [...] In another table was Atalanta [...] Besides many mo, as of Helena, Omphale, [...] So then sitting downe in two chaires, and some-times casting his eye to the picture, he thus spake.[54]

Sidney's original description of Arcadia, which I cited briefly at the outset of this essay, is inserted in his revised narrative at this point. Arcadia here has become what it is: evocative of the medieval *hortus conclusus* and illuminated by the mnemonic markers of classical myth and pastoral, it is a memory theatre, the fertile 'ground-plot' from which Sidney's narrative will originate.[55] It holds not simply an enfolding of time and place, but of time and place into a third thing: the object of art, fiction per se.

---

[53] Sidney, *Countess of Pembroke's Arcadia*, p. 73.
[54] Sidney, *Countess of Pembroke's Arcadia*, p. 74.
[55] Philip Sidney, *The Defence of Poesy*, in *Sir Philip Sidney: The Major Works*, ed. Katherine Duncan-Jones (Oxford, 1989), p. 235.

Fathers, Sons and Surrogates
Fatherly Advice in *Hamlet*

⁂ JASON POWELL ⁂

The first scenes of *Hamlet* famously pose a problem of inheritance.[1] The ghost's silent appearance in full armour and the country's preparations for war in the first act recall the ancient world's most notorious assassination, when 'ere the mightiest Julius fell,/ The graves stood tenantless and the sheeted dead/ Did squeak and gibber in the Roman streets' (1.1.117–19). Recent stagings of *Julius Caesar* made these events more familiar for Shakespeare's audience, and now this ghost, so 'like the king that's dead' (1.1.44), gives 'even the like precurse of fear'd events,/ As harbingers preceding still the fates/ And prologue to the omen coming on' (1.1.124–6). Something as yet unclear threatens the kingdom. In response to this threat of historic proportions, Horatio, Marcellus, Barnardo and Francisco – all four subjects of the new king, three in his pay – choose not to bring these omens to their ruler (as two men attempt in *Julius Caesar*), but rather to approach the old king's son – 'young Hamlet' (1.1.175), a figure unmentioned up to this point and here identified only by his father's name.[2]

Denmark was, of course, an elective monarchy.[3] Nevertheless, the contrast between this final moment of scene one, when the warrior king's son seems to inherit contact with his ghost, and the next in scene two, when another

---

[1] I am grateful to András Kiséry, Ivan Lupic and Matthew Woodcock for their insightful comments on drafts of this essay. On the matter of inheritance, see also Margreta de Grazia, *Hamlet without Hamlet* (Cambridge, 2007), pp. 85–90, 143–5. For other relevant readings of this play: Stephen Greenblatt, *Hamlet in Purgatory* (Princeton, 2001); András Kiséry, '"I Lack Advancement": Public Rhetoric, Private Prudence, and the Political Agent in *Hamlet*, 1561–1609', *ELH* 81 (2014), 29–60; Aysha Pollnitz, 'Educating Hamlet and Prince Hal', *Shakespeare and Early Modern Political Thought*, ed. David Armitage, Conal Condren and Andrew Fitzmaurice (Cambridge, 2013), pp. 119–38; and David Scott Kastan, *A Will to Believe: Shakespeare and Religion* (Oxford, 2014), ch. 5.
[2] All citations from *Hamlet* are taken from Harold Jenkins, ed., *Hamlet* (1982; rpt. London, 2003). Coleridge noted the 'unobtrusive and yet fully adequate mode of introducing the main character, *young* Hamlet, upon whom transfers itself all the interest excited for the acts and concerns of the king, his father'. See Jenkins, p. 177, citing Samuel Taylor Coleridge, *Shakespearean Criticism*, ed. T.M. Raysor, 2 vols. (London, 1960), 1: 19.
[3] This fact is nevertheless sometimes brushed over by critics, as discussed in de Grazia, *Hamlet*, p. 88.

man occupies the old king's throne, is striking. No less so is the dilemma of multiple kings. The presence of the old king ('the king that's dead') silently conditions our response to Claudius in 1.2. Something is rotten long before Hamlet's 'prophetic soul' (1.5.41) learns of his uncle's crime. Yet the matter of inheritance – of sons succeeding fathers in all the ways that such succession might imply – is obviously a far broader concern in this play's first act.

Critics have long noted that Polonius speaks in the familiar discourse of fatherly advice to his son Laertes in the play's third scene. This advice was employed largely to perpetuate the father and his position through and in his children. But the scene is one of several in this act that foreground moments of fatherly instruction. Although the ghost in 1.5 sounds nothing like Polonius, Richard Helgerson is right in claiming that 'This too is a scene of paternal admonition.'[4] More recently, Reina Green has noted that act one of *Hamlet* presents 'three father-son pairings in which sons are required to listen to father-figures'.[5] Along with the instruction of Polonius to Laertes and the admonitions of the ghost, she includes the advice Claudius gives to Hamlet in 1.2. Few studies have read all three moments against the tradition of fatherly advice from which Polonius speaks, and yet the sequencing of these scenes, along with the responses of these sons, begs us to understand them together. Just as the audience's expectations related to inheritance are purposefully subverted in these first two scenes, so too are the expectations related to fathers and their advice consistently disrupted throughout the first act of *Hamlet*. These moments have significant implications for the play as a whole. If the last act insists on making Hamlet a thirty-year-old tragic hero, the first just as squarely declares him the teenage son of competing fathers. Both acts, and those in between, show Hamlet struggling, like other sons in this play, under the burden of conflicting fatherly instructions and advice.

The problem for these sons (and arguably for Ophelia as well) lies not in the advice itself, but in its infinite capacity for detachment and reuse by surrogates whose intentions are sometimes highly questionable. The common practices of imitation and commonplacing, alongside the long tradition of sententious wisdom inherited from both the ancient world and the Middle Ages, made a sort of verbal authority available to all. Brothers might sound like fathers, and bad uncles like enlightened, fatherly philosophers; a language was there to help simulate any given role. The first act's three successive scenes of fatherly instruction serve to emphasize how central the problem of surrogation and the role-playing that attended it were both for *Hamlet* and the culture of

---

[4] Richard Helgerson, 'What Hamlet Remembers', *Shakespeare Studies* 10 (1977), 79.
[5] Reina Green, 'Poisoned Ears and Parental Advice in *Hamlet*', *Early Modern Literary Studies* 11.3 (2006), 3.4.

late Elizabethan England. Following a father's commands was the duty of any child; following false fathers, however, could have dire consequences.

Critics have long sought sources for the sententious wisdom Polonius delivers to Laertes in 1.3, locating echoes behind his precepts in the *Ad Demonicum* of Isocrates, Lyly's *Euphues*, Thomas Tusser's *Five Hundereth Pointes of Good Husbandrie*, or the *Certaine Precepts* William Cecil wrote for his son Robert, among other sources.[6] But this discussion has always been something of a red herring. Polonius speaks a language recognizable to generations – indeed, centuries – of English children. The reason these parallels are so easily drawn is not because Shakespeare was reading each or any of these works as he wrote the scene; rather, the language of fatherly advice was so familiar that Shakespeare no more needed a book to hand than does the character of Polonius.

The *Ad Demonicum oratio parænetica*, perhaps the most famous source for Polonius, is an oration, in the classical sense that encompassed the letter, from Isocrates to the son of his late friend Hipponicus. Many of the Latin editions numbered the precepts within this letter, but as we shall see, the frame around these precepts is arguably more important to Shakespeare's play. The *Ad Demonicum* was only one of several collections of moral precepts familiar to readers in Tudor England and throughout the Middle Ages. These included general works of fatherly instruction such as *How the Wise Man Taught his Son*, also called *How the Good Man Taught his Son* (c.1430), which rehearsed the precepts of a 'wyse man' who taught his 'fayre man chyld [...] well in tender age'[7] in a form that varied from witness to witness between thirteen and a half and twenty-four stanzas.[8] More common still were the Latin moral sayings from antiquity that were frequently taught in medieval and Tudor grammar schools. These included the *Mimi* of Publilius Syrus and the *Disticha*, wrongly attributed to Dionysius or

---

[6] Henry Burrows Lathrop, *Translations from the Classics into English from Caxton to Chapman, 1477–1620* (1933; rpt. New York, 1967), pp. 45–6; W.L. Rushton, *Shakespeare's Euphuism* (London, 1871), pp. 44–7; Steven Doloff, 'Polonius's Precepts and Thomas Tusser's "Five Hundreth Points of Good Husbandrie"', *RES* 42 (1991), 227–8. See also Josephine Waters Bennett, 'Characterization in Polonius' Advice to Laertes', *SQ* 4 (1953), 3–9, and 'These Few Precepts', *SQ* 7.2 (1956), 275–6, as well as G.K. Hunter, 'Isocrates' Precepts and Polonius' Character', *SQ* 8.4 (1957), 501–6; Claire McGinchee, 'Still Harping ...', *SQ* 4 (1955), 362–4; Elkin Calhoun Wilson, 'Polonius in the Round', *SQ* 9 (1958), 83–5; O.B. Davis, 'A Note on the Function of Polonius' Advice', *SQ* 9 (1958), 85–6; and Charles G. Smith, *Shakespeare's Proverb Lore: His Uses of the Sententiae of Leonard Culman and Publilius Syrus* (Cambridge, MA, 1963), pp. 74, 121. For the text of Cecil's *Certaine Precepts*, which were first published only in 1617 but had circulated widely in manuscript well before that date, see Louis B. Wright, ed., *Advice to a Son: Precepts of Lord Burghley, Sir Walter Raleigh, and Francis Osborne* (Ithaca, 1962), pp. 7–13.

[7] Oxford, Balliol College MS 354, fol. 335.

[8] George Shuffelton, ed., *Codex Ashmole 61: A Compilation of Popular Middle English Verse* (Kalamazoo, 2008), p. 425.

Marcus Porcius Cato.[9] The latter was the 'most enduring of all the school texts', having been taught at least from the seventh through the sixteenth centuries.[10] Glosses by Erasmus helped give the distichs a continued currency in Tudor England. Cato advised readers to 'Drinke wine with temperatnesse', 'Tempre thine angre' and not 'dispise' 'thy inferiour', 'Love thy wife', and not make 'Many promises' if you are disposed 'to geve or lende'. The advice was often exceedingly p ractical: 'Among gestes at the table be thou of speache sobre./ Least where thou wouldest be taken manerlie, thou be called a chatter'. This was followed by a few sentences of paraphrase translated from Erasmus:

> In the courte of lawe is a place of eloquence, in the chambre of scilence in feast and at meate, it is comelie and meete to use moderate communications one with the other, and thei also pleasaunte and merie. Some men while thei goe about to bee seen curious, be troublous to the other of the geastes with their babling, to whom thei dooe leave no space and time to commune.[11]

The paraphrase works here to give contemporary resonance and immediacy to these sayings. While the *Disticha* naturally reflected the practical and secular – even pagan – tone 'of its era', this work was 'widely and [...] intensively read' in Latin as 'a first reader in the grammar course for over 1400 years'.[12]

Inattention to these and related traditions of fatherly advice has sometimes led to unhelpful misunderstandings. In depicting Polonius as 'a clear representation of the Machiavellian villain', one critic has claimed that his precepts for Laertes are 'the dangerous guide to the would-be Machiavellian', and that '[n]o better digest of *The Prince* might well be imagined'.[13] Yet as Richard Hazelton has written, a student who followed the *Disticha* closely would 'be concerned with reputation (*fama*), not honor, with the show of virtue, not virtue', that he would 'speak of service and practice profit-making', and 'lift his hands to the gods and keep his eye on the main chance'.[14] Referring more broadly to the tradition of conduct literature, John R. Woodhouse has claimed that 'every courtesy treatise which I know [...] aims to teach its reader varying degrees of dissimulation'.[15] Any

---

[9] Philippe Ariès divides the literature of medieval advice into three categories: courtesy books such as John Russell's *Book of Nurture*, morality books such as Cato's *Distichs* and writings on love such as Ovid's *Ars amoris*: *Centuries of Childhood*, trans. Robert Baldick (London, 1962), pp. 381–2.

[10] Jonathan Nicholls, *The Matter of Courtesy: Medieval Courtesy Books and the Gawain Poet* (Cambridge, 1985), p. 63.

[11] *Preceptes of Cato with annotacions of D. Erasmus of Roterodame*, trans. Robert Burrant (London, 1553), sigs. C2v, D1r, D2r, D2v, E5r, H6v.

[12] Richard Hazelton, 'The Christianization of Cato: The *Disticha Catonis* in the Light of Late Medieval Commentaries', *Mediaeval Studies* 19 (1957), 162, 157, 158n4.

[13] Myron Taylor, 'Tragic Justice and the House of Polonius', *SEL* 8.2 (1968), 275, 277.

[14] Hazelton, 'Christianization', 172.

[15] John R. Woodhouse, 'The Tradition of Della Casa's *Galateo* in English', *The Crisis of Courtesy: Studies in the Conduct-Book in Britain, 1600–1900*, ed. Jacques Carré (Leiden, 1994), p. 12.

Machiavellian resonance in the precepts of Polonius may say as much about the common tradition from which he speaks as about his character.

Nevertheless, there were some further, potentially important distinctions between the types of conduct and advice literature to which these collections belonged. Scholars often distinguish between these 'saws of moral advice' and the courtesy books that flourished in different forms in the fifteenth and sixteenth centuries.[16] A group of these from the fifteenth century and early sixteenth century are often called 'babees books', some of which sought to teach children how to behave as servants in the household of their masters. These include John Russell's *Book of Nurture*, a dialogue in rhymed couplets between a young boy, who wants to be a 'buttiler', 'pantere' or 'chamburlayne', and the usher who teaches him the skills of the household trades, covering everything from the carving of roast meat to the protocol of seating arrangements at a meal. Russell identifies himself with his profession throughout the book, claiming 'an ushere y Am' who simply 'enjoyethe to enforme and teche'. In calling his audience 'son', his language also subtly adopts the student into a filial role.[17] More general manuals included *The Boke of Curtasye* (c.1460), which advised young men to 'Clense not thi tethe at mete sittande' and 'Speke never unhonestly of woman kynde', but dealt also with the duties of household officers in the service of a noble lord.[18] This type of advice continued well into the early sixteenth century in texts such as Wynkyn de Worde's *Boke of Kervynge*, a manual about carving meat, serving meals and 'all Maner of Offyce' in 'all the Feestes in the yere', and *The Boke of Nurture* written by Hugh Rhodes 'of the Kinges Chappell' in the first half of the century.[19] More general conduct books included Thomas Elyot's *Boke Named the Governour* (1531), classical treatises such as Cicero's *De Officiis* and the continental books that were translated into English in the sixteenth century, including those by Guazzo, Della Casa and Castiglione.

More difficult to classify is Peter Idley's book-length *Instructions to His Son* (c.1450), which is initially addressed to 'the, my childe,/ That art yet yonge and somdele wylde'.[20] The *Instructions* epitomize the consistent and palpable blending of tradition, context and personality in fatherly advice and conduct

---

Woodhouse sees a possible exception in the *Galateo* by Giovanni Della Casa.

[16] Nicholls, *Matter*, p. 15.
[17] F.J. Furnivall, ed., *The Babees Book: Early English Meals and Manners*, EETS OS 32 (London, 1868), p. 3, ll. 1–83. Russell complicates the notion of his authorship, however, with an epilogue in which he claims not to have written the work, but only to have brushed up the rhyme. Yet even if the work is an adaptation of an earlier manual, the opening lines and closing mention of Duke Humphrey appear to be his, and Russell clearly inscribes himself in the role of the fatherly teacher: Furnivall, *Babees*, pp. lxxii, 82.
[18] Furnivall, *Babees*, pp. 180, 184.
[19] Furnivall, *Babees*, p. 149.
[20] Charlotte D'Evelyn, ed., *Peter Idley's Instructions to his Son* (Boston, 1935), p. 81 (Bk. I, ll. 6–7).

literature. He derives the text almost entirely by translating or reworking four popular medieval sources. His first book comes directly from two Latin treatises by Albertanus of Brescia, with the advice reordered and the narrative framework of the original text discarded. His second derives from two English texts, Robert Mannyng's *Handlyng Synne* and John Lydgate's *The Fall of Princes*. Idley maintains the general order of advice from his sources, and, while condensing the material, he 'could and did transfer whole lines', and sometimes couplets, from his sources.[21] Nevertheless, he manages to rewrite his sources, in the process turning them 'into a product of the fifteenth century' by employing the 'plain marks of fifteenth-century literary fashion' in language, diction and rhetoric.[22]

Moreover, though he aims the advice explicitly at his son, Idley's *Instructions* show evidence of a larger intended audience, particularly in the second of the two books, which deals with religious teachings such as the Ten Commandments and Seven Deadly Sins. His modern editor, Charlotte D'Evelyn, notes that after the Prologue, 'the connection with [his son] Thomas Idley is forgotten. His father, like Robert Mannyng, is addressing all the sons of Adam.'[23] Writers such as Idley and Russell were highly conscious of their roles as both public teachers and father figures and their position as inheritors of an advice tradition.

Many of these works were familiar to readers in Shakespeare's lifetime, and thus had the potential to shape the way audiences reacted to precepts at particular moments. The *Disticha* was nearly ubiquitous in Tudor England; at least thirty-four printings are recorded in the *ESTC* before 1600. The *Mimi* of Publilius Syrus appeared at least thirteen times with these in the sixteenth century. The *Ad Demonicum*, a schoolbook 'familiar to an Elizabethan audience', was printed on more than a dozen occasions in Greek, Latin and English, and sometimes with the *Disticha*.[24] *How the Wise Man* survives in at least six manuscript copies, three of which date from around 1500; another is probably from the early sixteenth century.[25] Marginalia in BL, Harley MS 2399 (one of the c.1500 copies) suggests a readership into the middle of the century: beside a line that begins 'Of my blessyng take god hete' on fol. 62r, a formal, early-to-mid-sixteenth-century secretary hand (not that of the copyist) has written 'he that in youth' in the right margin. More solid evidence of a late Tudor readership exists for Idley's *Instruc-*

---

[21] See D'Evelyn, *Instructions*, pp. 36, 46–8. The two Latin treatises are *Liber Consolationis et Consilii* and *Liber de Amore et Dilectione Dei et Proximi*. D'Evelyn discusses Idley's use of these sources at length on pp. 36–57.
[22] D'Evelyn, *Instructions*, pp. 47, 49.
[23] D'Evelyn, *Instructions*, p. 45.
[24] Waters Bennett, 'Characterization', 5. The number of printings comes from multiple searches and collations from *ESTC* listings; however, many continental editions will have escaped notice, having not been included in the *ESTC*.
[25] Eve Salisbury, ed., *The Trials and Joys of Marriage* (Kalamazoo, 2002), p. 239.

tions, which is now 'one of the best-attested vernacular poetical works of the fifteenth century', surviving in at least eleven manuscripts.[26] At least two of these date from the sixteenth century, and several contain datable marginalia suggesting continued use into or past Shakespeare's lifetime.[27] A fifteenth-century manuscript, BL, Harley MS 172, bears the late sixteenth-century hand of John Stow and the early seventeenth-century hand of Sir Simon D'Ewes,[28] as well as frequent pen trials and scribbles in late fifteenth – or early sixteenth-century hands on fols. 36v, 37v, 38r and 48r. A newly discovered fifteenth-century manuscript in the Beinecke Library at Yale has repeated sixteenth-century or early seventeenth-century inscriptions of ownership in the italic and secretary hands of one Thomas Dowse on the verso of the front pastedown, the recto of the front flyleaf, and on fol. 38v and the back pastedown. Notes in the right margin of fol. 9r in his or another sixteenth – or early seventeenth-century mixed hand have been smeared into deletion.[29] A Magdalene College, Cambridge, manuscript bears the hand of one John Bagford and the year 1682, along with a note on fol. 78r, 'tyme of Kinge henry the viii^e by me houmfri pawer'.[30] Dublin, Trinity College, MS 160, pt. 2, is also a fifteenth-century manuscript, but contains clear evidence of an Elizabethan reader who was highly engaged with the text. His adjustments at several places reveal what D'Evelyn calls a 'reformer's zeal'.[31] On fol. 25v, he deleted 'messe' (meaning 'mass') and inserted 'gospell', and 'prince' is substituted for 'pope' on fol. 56r. A more telling revision occurs on fol. 37r, where two lines reading

> And of al the sacramentis seven
> That techeth man to the blys of heven

are rewritten in the margin,

> And of the holy sacramentis twoe
> which teacheth man to heven to goe[32]

---

[26] Matthew Giancarlo notes that ten of these are independent witnesses, one being a fragment of a previously known witness. Four manuscripts – including the fragment – have been added to the seven discussed by D'Evelyn. See Matthew Giancarlo, 'Dressing up a "Galaunt": Traditional Piety and Fashionable Politics in Peter Idley's "Translacions" of Mannyng and Lydgate', *After Arundel: Religious Writing in Fifteenth-Century England*, ed. Vincent Gillespie and Kantik Ghosh (Turnhout, 2011), p. 430.
[27] BL, Additional MS 57,335 dates from the early sixteenth century, and Cambridge, Magdalene College, Pepys MS 2030 dates from perhaps later in the century; see D'Evelyn, *Instructions*, p. 62, citing M.R. James, *Bibliotheca Pepysiana, Part III, Mediæval Manuscripts* (London, 1923), pp. 67–9.
[28] D'Evelyn, *Instructions*, p. 63.
[29] Yale University, Beinecke Library, MS Osborn fa50.
[30] This is Cambridge, Magdalene College, Pepys MS 2030; see James, *Bibliotheca*, pp. 67, 69.
[31] D'Evelyn, *Instructions*, p. 66.
[32] D'Evelyn, *Instructions*, p. 66, records the same variants, but places each of them on the folio immediately preceding the one where it occurs.

The Henrician Church had varied between the Lutheran standard of three and the Catholic of seven sacraments, but with the Thirty-Nine Articles of 1563, the English Church 'for the first time stated definitely that there are two Sacraments'.[33] Taken together, these notes, revisions and ownership marks strongly suggest a continued readership for Idley's *Instructions* into the Elizabethan period.

The influence of these works is also consistently felt at moments – real or fictional – in which fathers or father-figures advised young men. As Helen Cooper ably explains, prose romances from the Middle Ages to the Elizabethan era frequently 'contained discursive passages of instruction' composed of precepts like those found in Idley, Cato, Isocrates, or *How the Wise Man*. Romances 'doubled as courtesy books, or as advice to princes – a means of training the individual in the ethics and behaviour required in order for society, one's own immediate community or the whole body politic, to function at its best'.[34] Playwrights employed similar moments of instruction on stage. So too did individual fathers borrow from this broad bank of sayings in writing to their sons. Helgerson locates ten of Sir Henry Sidney's fifteen precepts in his 1566 letter for young Philip Sidney in Cato and thirteen in Isocrates. Moreover, he finds the same *sententiae* repeated in Elizabethan prose romance: 'Six of Sir Henry's fifteen admonitions recur in *The Anatomy of Wit*, three in Greene's *Gwydonius*, four in his *Mourning Garment*, five in Lodge's *Euphues' Shadow*, and four in his *Margarite in America*'.[35] This pattern is not unique to Sidney; any number of late medieval and early Tudor works might be as plausibly identified as a source for the precepts of Polonius in the third scene of *Hamlet*. Idley's 'ffor clothyng ofte maketh man' might be glimpsed behind Polonius' 'For the apparel oft proclaims the man' (1.3.72); the old counsellor's 'Give every man thy ear, but few thy voice' (1.3.68) is a snappier version of Idley's 'Lete thy tong not clakke as a mille' or his 'Restreyne and kepe well thy tonge'. Like Polonius (and, of course, the Oracle at Delphi and the Stoics), Idley advises his son to 'Knowe thysilf'.[36] We might see William Cecil's 'Neither borrow money of a neighbor or friend'[37] directly behind Polonius's 'Neither a borrower nor a lender be' (1.3.75), but the equation is not necessary or particularly warranted. The point is not that Cato fed Sidney and Sidney in turn became a source for prose romance (though his letter was published in 1591), nor that Shakespeare

---

[33] W.H. Griffith Thomas, *The Principles of Theology: An Introduction to the Thirty-Nine Articles* (1930; rpt. Ann Arbor, 1979), p. 352.
[34] Cooper, *Romance*, p. 6.
[35] Richard Helgerson, *The Elizabethan Prodigals* (Berkeley, 1976), pp. 17–19.
[36] D'Evelyn, *Instructions*, pp. 82, 85 (Bk. I, ll. 102, 50, 69, 284). Doris Falk makes a similar point using the first of Idley's sayings in 'Proverbs and the Polonius Destiny', *SQ* 18 (1967), 27.
[37] Wright, *Advice*, p. 12.

necessarily read Idley.[38] Rather, this wisdom came from a 'common stock'[39] inherited from the Middle Ages and the late classical period.

But if this fact makes it virtually impossible to isolate a single source for any one particular precept, it cannot suggest that particular works of advice literature are irrelevant for understanding Shakespeare – in fact, quite the reverse. Precepts were everywhere: indeed, Sir Nicholas Bacon famously 'had the great chamber in his house at Gorhambury decorated with moral sayings'.[40] But they were also closely associated with particular narrative and discursive contexts. As such, their use onstage – especially in moments of fatherly instruction – was often charged with extra-textual meaning.

The first such moment comes in the second scene of *Hamlet*. The advice that Claudius delivers so publicly to his nephew there is a tissue of maxims most commonly identified, both in the sixteenth century and today, with Stoic thought. Claudius also speaks in a moment of loss familiar from Senecan *consolatio*. At the heart of this scene, the new king insists that for his nephew

> to persever
> In obstinate condolement is a course
> Of impious stubbornness, 'tis unmanly grief,
> It shows a will most incorrect to heaven,
> A heart unfortified, a mind impatient,
> An understanding simple and unschool'd;
> For what we know must be, and is as common
> As any the most vulgar thing to sense –
> Why should we in our peevish opposition
> Take it to heart? Fie, 'tis a fault to heaven,
> A fault against the dead, a fault to nature,
> To reason most absurd, whose common theme
> Is death of fathers, and who still hath cried
> From the first corse till he that died today,
> 'This must be so'. We pray you throw to earth
> This unprevailing woe, and think of us
> As of a father; for let the world take note
> You are the most immediate to our throne,
> And with no less nobility of love
> Than that which dearest father bears his son

---

[38] For this letter and its history, see Roger Kuin, ed., *The Correspondence of Sir Philip Sidney*, 2 vols. (Oxford, 2012), 1: 3–6.
[39] Helgerson, *Elizabethan Prodigals*, p. 17.
[40] Mary Thomas Crane, *Framing Authority: Sayings, Self and Society in Sixteenth-Century England* (Princeton, 1993), pp. 74–5.

> Do I impart toward you. For your intent
> In going back to school in Wittenberg,
> It is most retrograde to our desire,
> And we beseech you bend you to remain
> Here in the cheer and comfort of our eye,
> Our chiefest courtier, cousin, and our son. (1.2.92–117)

These are precepts, but they are hardly aphoristic. Claudius uses listing for emphasis: the fault is against 'heaven', 'the dead', 'nature' and 'reason'. Grief is unmanly because it shows a defect in the 'will', the 'heart', the 'mind' and the 'understanding'. Hamlet is not simply his chosen successor, but the king's 'chiefest courtier', 'cousin', and 'son'. In this context, Hamlet's earlier puns on 'sun', 'kin' and 'kind' (2.2.67, 65) work brilliantly to highlight the king's effusive style by opposing his *copia* with the condensed suggestiveness of young Hamlet's language. Both Claudius and his nephew speak in blank verse. But to the extent that Seneca's compact style (often opposed to the more florid language of Cicero) was associated with Stoic philosophy, the new king's language contrasts here with his message.

This is only one of the ways in which the king's speech clashed with what were highly familiar contexts for Shakespeare's original audiences. Benjamin Boyce long ago noted the 'ominous' gulf between the 'formal and splendid *consolatio*' Claudius delivers here and the situation of its delivery, in which Claudius violates the injunctions of both Seneca and Erasmus in flaunting his own joy while consoling another.[41] More important still is the way in which this speech flouts the pattern established by the most famous precedent for advising a son whose father had recently died. There is strong evidence in contemporary letters that advice conventions varied according to the speaker, and particularly according to whether the advisor was a father or a fatherly surrogate. William Cecil, for instance, was famously distant in his commanding precepts for Robert (1584) and even harsher in the instructions he gave to his elder son Thomas (1571).[42] But his letter to the seventeen-year-old John Harington in 1578 is much more familiar. It opens with 'I thanke you, my good Jacke, for your lettres', is signed with 'Your fathers frende that loves you' and defers at one point to 'your good father's advise'.[43]

Among the models available to fatherly surrogates, and particularly those writing after a father's death, the most important and best known was almost certainly the letter that Isocrates wrote to Demonicus. Again and again, Isocrates emphasizes the 'very hard and difficult thing for a man to finde a

---

[41] Benjamin Boyce, 'The Stoic Consolatio and Shakespeare', *Publication of the Modern Language Association* 64 (1949), 776–7.
[42] See Wright, *Advice*, pp. 3–6 and 7–13, respectively.
[43] Henry Harington, ed., *Nugæ Antiquæ* (London, 1804), pp. 131, 135.

faithfull and friendly counsayler', and the need to find 'that true friendship and familliaritie of good men' which 'no continuaunce of time can ever weare out, or by any meanes decay or infringe'.[44] Printed marginalia in a 1580 edition continually highlights the 'diffarence betwixt true and perfit friendship', noting that 'Tully [Cicero] affyrmeth true friendship to surpasse Consanguinitye, in that a man may bee a kinsman, and not a friend.' Indeed, another marginal citation of Cicero confirms that 'The grounde of true friendeship is good will born for vertues sake, and not for hope of gain, or in respecte of our owne necessity.'[45] Widely used at 'three different levels of instruction' in Tudor grammar schools,[46] the *Ad Demonicum* would have heightened an awareness in Shakespeare's early audiences of the potential for flattering kinsmen to abuse the trust of young men in precisely this moment of counsel after the father's death. Sixteenth-century editions of this text share with *Hamlet* in a common anxiety over the way that surrogate fathers might deploy and misuse advice.

Against the play's initial emphasis on the disinheritance of 'young Hamlet', and on Claudius as its cause, Isocrates stresses inheritance of two distinct but related kinds. So 'as the inheritaunce of his worldly wealth doeth of right dissend unto thee, so in my judgement also oughte the good will borne unto the Father, remayne unto his children'. As someone bearing that good will to the young boy's father, Isocrates implicitly distinguishes himself from those men 'whiche take in hand to wryte unto their friendes some exhortation' but who 'have more regarde to set oute the same in filed and figured wordes, whereby they might bring them to a flowing and eloquente phrase of speeche, then to the amending of manners, or instructing of well living'.[47] Though such men are not explicitly equated with the 'flattering kinsman'[48] against whom Isocrates also warns, they are nevertheless legitimate objects of suspicion, casting doubt upon exactly the kind of flowery speech that Claudius employs in 1.2.

Claudius departs most conspicuously from Isocrates, however, in urging Hamlet to forget his father. Just as Cecil defers to the advice of young John Harington's living father, so Isocrates exhorts Demonicus to remember his deceased father as evidence that 'only vertue remaineth unvincible':

> This my deare friende *Hipponicus* thy Father, in such sort ordered and framed his life, that he never semed in any respect, either a contemner of vertue, or lover of slouthfulnesse, but continually applying his body to travaile and paine, lodged in his brest a most willing and ready minde, alway prest to undertake

---

[44] Isocrates, *A perfite looking glasse for all estates*, trans. Thomas Forrest (London, 1580), sigs. C4v, A1r.
[45] Isocrates, *perfite looking glasse*, sigs. A1r, A3r.
[46] Waters Bennett, 'Characterization', 5.
[47] Isocrates, *perfite looking glasse*, sig. A1v.
[48] Isocrates, *perfite looking glasse*, sig. A3r.

any kinde of daunger, for the profiting of his countrey, or furtheraunce of his friendes, in nothing more waying or esteeming this worldly mucke, then that it might serve for his necessary uses, having continually such care over his Family, as though he shoulde have lived ever, and yet so using eche thing, as if he should die to morrow, only content with his owne, and not delighting in offering injury to any, or being as one greedilye coveting that which was an others. Neyther did he leade this kind of life, after a base and obscure order, but it was done with great honour, and that with the praise and commendations of all men, for he was a man both bountifull and liberall, to all his well willers, more esteeming a faithfull friend then a flattering kinsman adjudging that the confirmation and ground of true friendship did rather consist in the disposition of nature, then in ought law ordayned and constituted by mans reason, and that the lykelihoode and agreeablenesse of condicions, were of more force therein, then any bond of consanguinity, or kinred: alleaging also good will as the principall cause thereof, and not the respect of necessitye, or the hope of gaine.[49]

Demonicus is finally told to 'show thy selfe as worthy of such a Father.'[50] Whether or not this portrait of Hipponicus, 'ready minde, alway prest to undertake any kinde of daunger', fits that of Old Hamlet, it most certainly contrasts with both the advice and person of Claudius. Hipponicus rejected a 'flattering kinsman' in favour of 'a faithfull friend', knowing that 'the lykelihoode and agreeablenesse of condicions, were of more force therein, then any bond of consanguinity, or kinred'. Young Hamlet apparently carries a portrait of his father for comparison in 3.4 to that of Claudius, an act that seems to literalize a central metaphor of the *Ad Demonicum*, through which Isocrates claims to have 'showne unto thee a superficiall protracture of thy Fathers singuler disposition and nature, the which it becommeth thee to have always before thy eyes'. Indeed, thinking on their fathers, sons should consider how 'the Painter through Art, learned by dayly practise, obtayneth that skill, most lively to shadow and deliniate the perfectst shape of the bewtifulst creature' and therefore work to 'frame themselves to followe' the 'steppes' of their fathers, so as 'lively to present the worthiness of theire vertues, as children being worthy of such parents'.[51] The emphasis throughout act one on Hamlet's youth, disinheritance and the loss of his father would have conditioned original audiences to reflect upon the time-worn models designed for just such a moment. Even before the uncle-king's injunction to forget clashes with the ghost's command to remember, early audiences would have noticed the way that Claudius's advice ran counter to established patterns. Against the traditions of

---

[49] Isocrates, *perfite looking glasse*, sigs. A2v–A3r.
[50] Isocrates, *perfite looking glasse*, sigs. A3v.
[51] Isocrates, *perfite looking glasse*, sigs. A3r–A3v.

Stoic *consolatio* and the *Ad Demonicum*, the speech that Claudius gives in 1.2 would have seemed both unnerving and unnatural. Good fathers should be imitated, not forgotten.[52]

In an essay on advice in romances, Helen Cooper remarks that 'the giving of advice is not as straightforward a topos as it might appear at first sight. It is very rare, in fact, for there not to be something odd about it.' This oddness is evident in each of *Hamlet*'s successive moments of fatherly instruction. In the case of Polonius, Cooper asks

> why should Shakespeare hold up the progress of *Hamlet* for Polonius's admirable but utterly familiar advice? It consists of prescripts that the audience will know already, and Polonius is not the man to turn truism back into truth. The adviser himself, counsellor as he is, is moreover by no means exemplary; and the instruction has no obvious effect on its recipient, who goes on to raise a rebellion against the wrong man and get involved in an assassination plot. The advice is likewise useless as a rule for life within the larger context of the play. 'To thine own self be true' may be a long-established and unquestioned principle of integrity, but it is increasingly emptied of meaning when it is set against the shattering of Hamlet's own inner world. 'In my heart there was a kind of fighting': which of Hamlet's various selves is the 'true' one, and how should he recognize it? What would being true to it mean, in the circumstances in which he finds himself? Could he, or the audience, recognize if he were to reach any sort of truth to himself?

To these questions she answers that 'Polonius's advice provides the threshold from which *Hamlet*, and Hamlet, starts.' It 'does not so much signpost the way for the protagonist through the challenges to come as mark the point left behind.'[53] Helgerson similarly reads the advice in 1.3 through its relevance for the central character. In one of the seminal early discussions of *Hamlet* and memory, he identifies 'the start' of a 'prodigal son story' in the 'departure of the son, the platitudinous good counsel of the father, the talk of gaming, drinking, fencing, swearing, quarreling, and drabbing' in 1.3 and 2.1. He notes, however, that 'while these scenes suggest a prodigal son story', the prodigal is not the son at the centre of these two scenes. Instead, 'when Laertes returns two acts later, he has become a revenger', whereas 'Hamlet's behavior indicates that he may

---

[52] The injunctions of the Countess and Lafeu in the first scene of *All's Well that Ends Well* do not occasion a similar level of discomfort because the countess is respectful of Helen's father and her inheritance of virtues from him, and, unlike Claudius, she has nothing to gain from adopting Helen. Nevertheless, as in *Hamlet*, this scene quickly upends expectation when Helen reveals that she has indeed forgotten her father in her love for Bertram.

[53] Helen Cooper, 'Good Advice on Leaving Home in the Romances', *Youth in the Middle Ages*, ed. P.J.P Goldberg and Felicity Riddy (York, 2004), pp. 101, 120.

be the prodigal'.⁵⁴ As in 1.2, the play employs a familiar narrative or discursive pattern – this time from prose romance – only in order to violate precisely the expectations that pattern produces. Hamlet is not the revenger but the prodigal, Laertes not the prodigal but the revenger. These are not merely foils but shifting filial associations, matching those of the play's surrogate fathers and designed to keep the audience from locating themselves in the story just as the play's central figure struggles to find his own position.

This pattern continues in 1.5. Considering this scene, E. Pearlman sees a clear distinction in style between earlier stage ghosts, such as Don Andrea in *The Spanish Tragedy* and the ghost of Gorlois in a late 1580s play called *The Misfortunes of Arthur*, and the ghost that appears here in the revised *Hamlet*. Shakespeare's version 'speaks in a spacious dialect of his own, but one that is not nearly so swollen or purplish'. In contrast to the pale-faced ghost that Lodge ridiculed in 1596 as having 'cried so miserably at the Theatre, like an oyster-wife, Hamlet, revenge',⁵⁵ and to the customary ghost story of a classical underworld, Old Hamlet speaks 'in a diction transparent enough to have jolted audiences'.⁵⁶ 'The Ghost in *Hamlet*', Pearlman continues, 'is no longer an alien being rooted in ageless theatrical tradition; he has been reimagined as a fellow creature who just happens to be a spirit.'⁵⁷

His familiar diction here – a language so at odds with the aphoristic advice of Polonius in 1.3 and the ornate *consolatio* by Claudius – is yet another disorienting moment of disjunction between style and content. Critical debates have focused on the contradictions between the ghost's request for revenge and the inevitable outcome of that revenge (made undeniable by the Christianizing of this scene) in the damnation of his son's soul. If Hamlet's father was poisoned in the ear by Claudius, Hamlet too is infected more figuratively by the ghost's words, poured in 'the porches' of his ears (1.5.63). Though the ghost's language and advice is nothing like the old counsellor's, and thus not quite comparable to the opening of a 'prodigal son story',⁵⁸ Hamlet's response to his parting words, 'adieu, adieu, adieu. Remember me' (1.5.91), seems inserted from the context of 1.3:

> Remember thee?
> Yea, from the table of my memory
> I'll wipe away all trivial fond records,

---

⁵⁴ Helgerson, 'What Hamlet Remembers', 77–8.
⁵⁵ Jenkins, pp. 82–3.
⁵⁶ E. Pearlman, 'Shakespeare at Work: The Invention of the Ghost', *Hamlet: New Critical Essays*, ed. Arthur Kinney (New York, 2002), pp. 77–8.
⁵⁷ Pearlman, 'Shakespeare at Work', p. 80.
⁵⁸ Helgerson ('What Hamlet Remembers', 78) reads this scene through the prodigal son tales, but he does not claim similarity between this scene and those tales. Rather, he suggests that the similarity in 1.3 should carry over to 1.5. I argue here that those associations carry over, but do so primarily in Hamlet's response to what otherwise seems quite dissimilar.

> All saws of books, all forms, all pressures past
> That youth and observation copied there,
> And thy commandment all alone shall live
> Within the book and volume of my brain,
> Unmix'd with baser matter. Yes, by heaven!
> O most pernicious woman!
> O villain, villain, smiling damned villain!
> My tables. Meet it is I set it down
> That one may smile, and smile, and be a villain –
> At least I am sure it may be so in Denmark.
> So, uncle, there you are. Now to my word.
> It is 'Adieu, adieu, remember me.'
> I have sworn it. (1.5.97–112)

If 'Remember me' evokes *memento mei*, 'the most common of the many mottos that adorned sixteenth-century souvenirs of mortality', it must lead Shakespeare's audience to consider the frailty of the human condition and to think 'on last things'.[59] But what is odd here – what again defies expectations – is that Hamlet instead reacts as if his father had given him a string of *sententiae*, as if his father were Polonius. The metaphor he uses is the same one Polonius employed in comparing his son's mind to a tablet or a book: 'these few precepts in thy memory/ Look thou character' (1.3.58–9). Hamlet's response to the ghost suggests that whatever his impatience with Claudius and Polonius – whatever his dislike for his uncle and for the 'tedious old fools' with which the new king surrounds himself – Hamlet is more innately comfortable with the impulse to advise and to commonplace than he is with the command to revenge. But his unconscious confusion here of revenge command with *sententiae* also prefigures the misgivings that return at the end of the second act: his suspicion that this ghost, like Claudius, may be yet another ill-meaning false father.

To these slightly unsettled groupings of two fathers with two sons and one uncle playing 'father' (1.2.108), the first act adds another trio of father, son and kin playing the father's part in Fortinbras, Old Fortinbras and 'Norway, uncle of young Fortinbras' (1.2.28). As the play continues, allusions to other fathers and sons accumulate – first in Achilles and Pyrrhus, and then in the reference to Brutus (3.2.102–3). As Eric Rasmussen notes, this mention implicitly evokes his father, Old Brutus, who was murdered at Mutina after surrendering to Pompey in 77BC, but whom Young Brutus deliberately refrained from revenging.[60]

---

[59] Helgerson, 'What Hamlet Remembers', 88.
[60] Eric Rasmussen, 'Fathers and Sons in *Hamlet*', SQ 35 (1984), 463.

Polonius's reference to Seneca (2.2.396) may call to mind yet another famous father-son pairing associated this time both with advice and revenge. Of course, Seneca hardly needs an explicit mention to be associated with this play, as early references to the *Ur-Hamlet* make clear. The first surviving mention of a *Hamlet* play also famously refers to Seneca: Thomas Nashe wrote in the preface to Robert Greene's *Menaphon* (1589) that 'English Seneca read by candle-light yields many good sentences, as *Blood is a beggar*.' Playwrights who employ these translations, Nashe continued, 'will afford you whole Hamlets, I should say handfuls of tragical speeches'. But 'Seneca, let blood line by line and page by page, at length must needs die to our stage'.[61]

Just as the reference to Brutus unfurls under pressure to reveal yet another murdered father deep in the background of this play, the Senecan influence, too, proves more and more complicated the deeper one goes. For starters, the Shakespearean stage seemed to conceive of 'Stoicism as a *counterbalance* to the images of passionate action derived from Senecan drama'.[62] That is to say that even at its most basic, the Senecan influence on *Hamlet* was far from univocal. Modern critics have been fully attentive to these two familiar strands, but there has been less attention to the full variety of associations that Seneca might have evoked for early audiences of this play. He was not simply a tragedian for Shakespeare's contemporaries, nor even a tragedian and philosopher whose *consolatio* informed that of Claudius in 1.2. The influence of Seneca extends into the schoolboy sayings that Polonius confers in 1.3 and that Hamlet insists on recording in 1.5. A tradition of pseudo-Senecan writings, attributed to him in various forms from about the ninth through the seventeenth centuries, included a collection of precepts called the *Proverbia Senecae* and a treatise called *De moribus* (*Of Manners*). The former consisted of alphabetically arranged sentences, many taken from the aphorisms of Publilius Syrus. Though Petrarch had questioned the attribution to Seneca, his scepticism was not widely accepted. The *Proverbia* had a broad circulation in the Middle Ages – one partial survey of the manuscripts involves 143 copies – and it reappeared in the form of '*Publius's* Stage-Verses, or *Seneca's* Proverbs' in at least eleven print editions with Cato's distichs from 1659 to 1727, suggesting a continuing tradition in the interim.[63] In between, Robert Whittington published a work

---

[61] Henslowe's diary records a performance of a *Hamlet* at Newington Butts in 1594. Nashe's references to the 'kid in Aesop' and 'the trade of *Noverint*' – that is, of a scrivener – have led to the long-standing connection of this early version of *Hamlet* with the playwright Thomas Kyd: Jenkins, p. 83.

[62] Robert S. Miola, *Shakespeare and Classical Tragedy: The Influence of Seneca* (Oxford, 1992), p. 53. For more on Seneca and Shakespeare: Geoffrey Aggeler, *Nobler in the Mind: The Stoic-Skeptic Dialectic in English Renaissance Tragedy* (Newark, 1998); and Gordon Braden, *Renaissance Tragedy and the Senecan Tradition* (New Haven, CT, 1985).

[63] Quoting *Disticha de moribus* (London, 1659), sig. D5v. On the circulation of this work in manuscript during the Middle Ages, see Nicholas G. Round, 'The Medieval Reputation of

on morals (now attributed to St Martin of Braga of the sixth century) as Seneca's in 1546, as well as a translation of *De moribus* in 1547. The playwright John Marston was still using a 1547 translation by Whittington of another dubious work of Seneca's for his 1601 play *Antonio's Revenge*.[64]

Today, these works have been removed from the canon associated with Seneca, and our sense of his authorship has been further refined: we now recognize Seneca the elder as the author of writings on declamation, and Seneca the younger as the philosopher and tragedian. However, a strong and lasting tradition in Shakespeare's lifetime attributed the works of Stoic philosophy to the elder Seneca, and revenge tragedies to the younger.[65] Monsarrat notes that 'Dante, Boccaccio, Salutati, Piccolominia and Politian' all held this view, as did Petrus Crinitus, whose short essay appeared in a 1589 edition of Seneca published in London.[66]

Although the matter was far from settled by the time *Hamlet* was first performed,[67] this understanding of Seneca as a revenging poet son and a Stoic

---

the 'Proverbia Senecae': A Partial Survey Based on Recorded MSS', *Proceedings of the Royal Irish Academy. Section C: Archaeology, Celtic Studies, History, Linguistics, Literature* 72 (1972), 103–15.

[64] *A frutefull worke of Lucius Anneus Seneca named the forme and rule of honest lyvynge*, trans. Robert Whittington (London, 1546); *A frutefull worke of Lucius Anneus Senecæ. Called the Myrrour or glasse of maners and wysedome*, trans. Robert Whittington (London, 1546). The third dubious work is *Lucii Annei Senecae ad Gallioneni de remedis fortuitorum*, trans. Robert Whittington (London, 1547). The ESTC is incorrect in attributing the second of these to St Martin of Braga; it is a translation of *De moribus*. See Gilles D. Monsarrat, *Light from the Porch: Stoicism and English Renaissance Literature* (Paris, 1984), p. 31n5. On Marston's use of Whittington: Monsarrat, *Light*, p. 172n4, citing R.G. Palmer, *Seneca's 'De Remediis Fortuitorum' and the Elizabethans* (Chicago, 1953), p. 59.

[65] The *controversiae* and *suasoriae*, both now seen as belonging to the father, were attributed by Erasmus to the son. Lipsius, however, attributed them to the philosopher. On the attribution by Erasmus: Neil Rhodes, 'The Controversial Plot: Declamation and the Concept of the "Problem Play"', *Modern Language Review* 95 (2000), 612. For the attribution by Lipsius, see Lucius Annaeus Seneca, *The workes of Lucius Annæus Seneca, both morrall and naturall* (London, 1614), sig. D7r.

[66] Monsarrat, *Light*, p. 34. For the essay by Petrus Crinitus, see *L. Annæi Senecæ Cordubensis tragoediæ* (London, 1589), sig. A2rv.

[67] In his life of Seneca, printed with Seneca's prose works, Lipsius asks whether it is possible that the philosopher wrote poetry and answers that 'Oftentimes have I doubted it, and almost durst forsweare it. Howsoever he was a man, and happily that writing was enlarged and published by his enemies, and happily they corrupted it: yet note this in *Senecaes* words abovesaid; That there he delighted himselfe in more slighter studies likewise, which I suppose should be Poesie: and amongst them is *Medea*, which I am halfe assured was written in his exile, at such time as *Claudius* conquered Britanie'; see *The workes of Lucius Annæus Seneca*, sig. C8r. The question was alive even in 1674, when John Wright wrote the following in prefacing his edition of *Thyestes*: 'Whether *Seneca* the *Philosopher* (to whose Pen some abscribe Three other *Tragedy's*) was the Original *Author* of this also, or some other *Seneca*, I know not: nor is it material; since *Hensius* esteems it *Nulli caeterarum inferior*. Let it suffice that the *Author*, in many places, appears much a *Stoick*, and such was the *Philosopher*'; see *Thyestes a tragedy, translated out of Seneca* (London, 1674), sig. A3r.

father can be located much closer to Shakespeare. Defending the stage against Stephen Gosson's *School of Abuse* in 1579, the writer and playwright Thomas Lodge attempted to show 'what the learned have alwayes esteemed of poetrie'. He claimed, for instance, that '*Homer* was no les accompted then *Humanus deus*' in the ancient world. Thinking, perhaps, of Gosson's claim that 'Burrus and Seneca the schoolemaisters of Nero are flowted and hated of the people, for teaching their Scholar the song of Attis', he invoked Seneca in claiming that 'he disprayseth, who by costome hath left to speake well'. But he also enlisted the Stoic author as a father, noting that '*Seneca* theughe a stoike would have a poeticall sonne'.[68] A contemporary of Shakespeare's (born a mere six years before him), Lodge believed that the philosopher and the playwright were father and son.

Here again the play both enlists and amplifies this pairing only to unsettle it. Hamlet is placed in the revenger's role familiar from Seneca's plays. But his claim to be a 'poeticall sonne' awkwardly verges on the comic, particularly his verses for Ophelia, his instruction of the players and his 'speech of some dozen or sixteen lines' inserted within the stilted old play performed for Claudius (2.2.535). It is the false father Claudius who speaks the language of Stoic consolation, and far from seeming like a Stoic philosopher, the ghost's call for retribution runs counter to the Stoic discomfort with revenge.[69] The controlling interest behind fathers and father-figures and their precepts is to ensure that sons replicate their fathers. Against the first act's insistence that a good son must imitate his father (or his uncle, with respect to Claudius and Old Norway), the two Senecas serve as an effective counter-example: a successful son need not be the spitting image of his father. Nevertheless, the identification of yet another father-son intertext here can only emphasize the confusing layers of surrogation surrounding this play. The two Senecas, Old and Young Brutus, Pyrrhus and Achilles – even Lucianus and the Player King – are all varieties of surrogates, models through which Hamlet and the audience can choose to view the play's characters, their choices and their identities.

The net effect of the first act's repeated employment of fatherly admonition – an impact too often lost in the micro-critical early approaches to understanding

---

[68] Thomas Lodge, [*Honest Excuses*] (London, 1579), sig. A1v; Stephen Gosson, *The schoole of abuse* (London, 1579), sig. A5v. The title page of Lodge's pamphlet is lost, leading to some variation in citing it.

[69] See, for instance, Miola, *Shakespeare*, pp. 62–3. As a caveat to this, Seneca does at one point recognize the act of revenge as a duty, even in rejecting grief: 'The good man will perform his duties undisturbed and unafraid; and he will in such a way do all that is worthy of a good man as to do nothing that is unworthy of a man. My father is being murdered – I will defend him; he is slain – I will avenge him, not because I grieve, but because it is my duty'; see Seneca, *De ira* 1.12.2, in Seneca, *Moral Essays*, trans. John Basore, 3 vols. (New York, 1932) 1: 136–7, as quoted in Alan Sinfield, *Cultural Materialism and the Politics of Dissident Reading* (Berkeley and Los Angeles, 1992), p. 223.

precepts in this play – is to heighten our awareness of a dilemma that is arguably as prominent even as the call to revenge. What the ghost effectively commands is not simply vengeance, but instead that Hamlet assume the full suite of duties associated with the persona of his dead father, up to and including the instant enactment of his uncle's murder. Against the new king's injunction to forget, 'Remember me' recalls for young Hamlet and for Shakespeare's audience not only last things, but also the burden associated with the many kinds of 'inheritance' discussed in the *Ad Demonicum* and elsewhere in the many traditions of fatherly counsel: again, fathers should be imitated, not forgotten. Yet the play's persistent thwarting of easy associations between one father and one son, even as *Hamlet* repeatedly entertains implicit and explicit models for revenging sons and nephews, has the simultaneous outcome of destabilizing our understanding (and his) of the straightforward path to that inheritance. At just the moment that Hamlet searches for his own footing between successive calls to become like his uncle and to replicate his father (who may be just as falsely represented in the ghost), Shakespeare's audience is searching for a new and more secure model for understanding the inheritance of duties, of the father's friends and even of thrones in this play.

Despite his subsequent scepticism over equating the ghost with his father, Hamlet shows signs of wild and aimless imitation of the ghost in the aftermath of 1.5. He appears to Ophelia as if 'loosed out of hell' (2.1.83).[70] His famous identification of the poisoner as nephew in the Mousetrap works to suggest his own marriage to Gertrude by analogy, as if he were literally stepping into his father's position. Quite apart from whatever sexual tension exists in the closet scene, his comparison of Old Hamlet with Claudius, complete with the portraits implied metaphorically by Isocrates, seems to derive from the ghost's description of their marriage. Here is Hamlet speaking to his mother:

> See what a grace was seated on this brow,
> Hyperion's curls, the front of Jove himself,
> An eye like Mars to threaten and command,
> A station like the herald Mercury
> New-lighted on a heaven-kissing hill,
> A combination and a form indeed
> Where every god did seem to set his seal
> To give the world assurance of a man.
> This was your husband. Look you now what follows.
> Here is your husband, like mildew'd ear
> Blasting his wholesome brother. Have you eyes?

---

[70] This occurs in the first scene after we see the ghost, though clearly some time has passed that enables Polonius to speculate later that his own instructions to Ophelia had 'made him mad' (2.1.110).

Could you on this fair mountain leave to feed
And batten on this moor? Ha, have you eyes? (3.4.55–67)

These thirteen lines serve primarily to embellish and amplify the ghost's words in act one:

O Hamlet, what a falling off was there,
From me, whose love was of that dignity
That it went hand in hand even with the vow
I made to her in marriage, and to decline
Upon a wretch whose natural gifts were poor
To those of mine. (1.5.47–52)

In an insightful recent reading of the play, Timothy Hampton has even shown how Hamlet's act of killing Polonius (a name that means 'The Polish one') may reiterate, in a domestic setting, the moment in which his father 'smote the sledded Polacks on the ice' (1.1.66).[71] Yet there are problems with accepting these as figurative instances of Hamlet remembering his father. Barbara Everett has shown – and even the briefest search for 'Pollax' in Early English Books Online will confirm – how the common editorial reading of 'Polacks' for 'pollax' in the Quarto and 'Pollax' in the Folio is probably an incorrect reading for 'pole-axe', leaving young Hamlet's murder of Polonius without a clear equivalent in his father's actions.[72] His implicit threat to poison the king and marry his wife, like Lucianus in the Mousetrap, suggests a disfigured repetition of his uncle's deeds more than his father's revenge. Ophelia's description of him as 'loosed out of hell' shows him imitating not his father in life, as Isocrates instructs Demonicus, but rather following another potential false father in the ghost. His echo of the ghost in 3.4 is similarly misguided, like his failed attempt in 1.5 to distil the ghost's words into a single, short commonplace in his writing tables. The closet scene is frustrating precisely because of Hamlet's inability to report the whole of his knowledge. His claim that Gertrude's crime was to 'kill a king and marry with his brother' (3.4.29) distorts the ghost's story with impertinently spoken daggers just as his glossing of Lucianus as a 'nephew' (at 3.2.239) ultimately prevents him from knowing whether Claudius has reacted to the mirror of his crime or to the threat of the crime against him.[73] Hamlet

---

[71] See Timothy Hampton, *Fictions of Embassy: Literature and Diplomacy in Early Modern England* (Ithaca, 2009), pp. 145–53.

[72] Everett, *Young Hamlet: Essays on Shakespeare's Tragedies* (Oxford, 1989), pp. 142–5. Hampton's larger points are no less valid even if, as I believe to be the case, 'Pollax' should be read as 'pole-axe'.

[73] See the 'Longer Note' in Jenkins, p. 508. While Jenkins is lucid here, my own sense of this moment in the play differs somewhat from his. Jenkins claims 'When Lucianus becomes the image of Hamlet he does not cease to be Claudius too', but I find it crucial to note that the

is commonplacing his father, selecting phrases and parts to imitate without understanding the whole text.

These moments, rather than showing Hamlet's figurative similarity to his father, instead further signal his detachment from the task at hand (as the ghost's second appearance confirms). Hamlet is indeed 'too much in the sun' (1.2.67) even before his uncle's speech. After three successive scenes of fatherly instruction, each of which upends familiar discursive and narrative patterns, the play and its central character reveal the confusion that derives from a culture of surrogation, a world of shifting roles and authority facilitated in part by a centuries-old reverence for fatherly advice. In the play's first three acts, Hamlet rejects one false father in Claudius only to follow another in the ghost. Having falsely tested and falsely confirmed the ghost's story, he slays the wrong false father in Polonius.[74]

This confusion of roles spreads in acts four and five. In Hamlet's absence, his parts have been dispersed severally to Laertes (the revenger) and Ophelia (who goes mad and is accused of committing suicide). In 1.2, Claudius seemed bent on comforting Hamlet, offering himself as a father to a young man whose father had recently died. In act four, Claudius similarly comforts Laertes, offering fatherly care to another grieving son. Having launched a full-scale rebellion against the wrong murderer, Laertes then inherits his father's place beside the king and immediately reveals a love of poison to match that of his new false father. Perhaps more importantly, the structural parallel to Hamlet's encounter with the ghost (*memento mei*) comes in the graveyard (*memento mori*), where Hamlet discovers the memory of yet another fatherly stand-in. It is Yorick and not his father's image that finally forces Hamlet to confront last things; the fool's skull is a more effective *memento mori* even than the ghost's indisputable evidence of an afterlife. But it is haunting for another reason. Thrown from the same trap-door by which the ghost entered in 1.5, the skull is a truer mirror than his father's portrait. Yorick the court jester, who 'bore' him 'on his back a thousand times' (5.1.179–80), is the person Hamlet's actions have most resembled in this play. Hamlet finally confronts his own mortality through yet another odd surrogate.

The prince's disgust at Yorick's skull ('My gorge rises at it', 5.1.181–2),

---

mention of Lucianus further clouds his purpose, since it (as perhaps the dumb show does before this) invalidates his claim to have tested the ghost's purpose. While Claudius's guilt first becomes apparent to us at 3.1.49–54, and is reiterated at 3.3.36–72, Hamlet's glossing of Lucianus as nephew rather than brother means that he can never himself be sure based solely on the king's reaction to this play.

[74] Polonius is more than a generic father-figure in the play, as suggested by Hamlet's later reference to Laertes as 'brother' (5.2.239) and Gertrude's suggestion in the same act (however unlikely Laertes and his father consider this in 1.3) that she had hoped that Ophelia 'shouldst have been my Hamlet's wife' (5.1.237).

combined with the fact that his roles as a mad and suicidal revenger have already been usurped, may thus be seen to herald the oft-noted change in his character in act five. But the evidence for such a change is mixed at best. Upon seeing Laertes leap into Ophelia's grave, Hamlet immediately joins him there in a bizarre bout of competitive grief. The announcement 'This is I, Hamlet the Dane' (5.1.250–1) suggests a further confusion of himself with his father. Onlookers understandably describe his behaviour as 'mad', 'mere madness' and a 'fit' (5.1.267, 279, 280). Helgerson is right in claiming that 'Hamlet's remembering has evidently been a remembering of the wrong thing', and that 'The right remembering comes on the trip to England.' But there can be no genuine 'story of man's return to God'[75] embodied in the final act of this play, where murder is perceived as 'heaven ordinant' and its victims 'not near' the murderer's 'conscience' (5.2.48, 58). It is vital here to distinguish self-consciousness from self-knowledge. Hamlet everywhere considers himself, but he is rarely self-aware.

Despite a clear disjunction between his religious tone and his unconsciously darkened conscience in 5.2, this pattern does begin to change somewhat in the play's final scenes. Hamlet considers last things four acts after meeting a ghost. He stops torturing himself over his own inaction, yielding to the reality evident to the audience from act one: that Hamlet will act only in reaction. The duty of revenging a murdered father has been clouded in the play's confusing tussle of competing fathers. Hamlet's revenge is not fully his father's, nor the ghost's. Art cannot enact revenge, as it does in *The Spanish Tragedy*, but the repetition of murder onstage may compel its reiteration in life. Hamlet's revenge comes only after Claudius kills again.

In act five, Hamlet finally finds a part he can accept: his own. This role is not devoid of his father's influence, but it is not quite what the ghost required. Sealing the revised commission with his father's signet, Hamlet figuratively *re*members his father, but he does so in an act more reminiscent of the false father Claudius.[76] Hamlet is more like Claudius than he is willing to accept, even at his most self-aware. When he manages to kill the last of this play's many false fathers with both a sword and poison, he again symbolically merges the methods appropriate to his father (the sword) and his uncle (the cup). Delivering the poisoned chalice to Claudius, Hamlet finds his own 'union' of fathers and son (5.2.331). Then in giving his 'dying voice' (5.2.361) to Fortinbras, Hamlet's final act restores a kind of right inheritance – if not his own – and in so doing manages to repair at least one iteration of the play's many uncertain ties between fathers and sons. Critics have sometimes suggested that Hamlet's 'I am dead' (5.2.338, 343) may reveal 'the spirit of Hamlet's father […]

---

[75] Helgerson, 'What Hamlet Remembers', 93–4.
[76] I am grateful to Judith Owens for a conversation in which she suggested the particular phrasing of '*re*membering'.

incorporated by his son', and there is a sense that the ghost's story might 'live on' with Horatio.[77] Does Hamlet's corpse, borne 'like a soldier to the stage' (5.2.401), suggest the fulfilment of his father's legacy?

Such readings may confuse closure with redemption. Hamlet might be English literature's favourite prodigal, but he remains unredeemed. There is a soldier in the room, but it is not Hamlet. The ghost's story waits to be told, but as Hamlet's surrogate in this role, Horatio is a more fitting reporter of the prince's story than that of the ghost whose words he never heard.[78] Long before the moment of his death, Hamlet has forgotten his father. He may seem to remember in the play's final scene only by substituting one vengeance for another, mother's for father's. This failure cannot be ignored. Sons respecting parental precepts might well find success: in the late medieval romance *Melusine*, two sons well advised by their mother follow her instructions and their 'careers prosper accordingly'.[79] But advice literature is clear and consistent on the wages of forgetting. Thomas Wyatt offered blessings to his son 'apon condition that you folow my advertisment', but he also promised that 'if you answer not to that I loke for at your hands, I shal aswel studye with that that I shal leave to make sum honist man as you'.[80] William Cecil told his son Thomas that 'if you will not therein conform yourself I shall revoke you with some shame'.[81] As Idley warned generations of English sons,

> Yet may þou be hurt by a disseyte,
> As a fysshe full ofte by a swete baite
> Is lost clierely from his grete plesaunce
> And fynally put from his enheritaunse.[82]

If the ghost is truly his father's, Hamlet will suffer for his act of forgetting. Sons who ignore fatherly 'Remembraunces' (as one sixteenth-century father called his instructions for his son) will find themselves disinherited.[83] But if the ghost is in fact evil, Hamlet has been 'hurt' by the very 'disseyte' against which Isocrates warned, and is 'fynally put from his enheritaunse'. The problem of inheritance that was so repeatedly and variously emphasized in act one must now be resolved in act five. In its final drive toward closure, the play mingles

---

[77] See Greenblatt, *Hamlet*, pp. 229, 228. He argues against the second point.
[78] Greenblatt, *Hamlet*, p. 228, writes that 'Horatio, of course, never himself hears the ghost speak' and that 'the friend's narrative cannot and will not be an intimate, personal act of remembering the beloved father'.
[79] Cooper, *Romance*, p. 205.
[80] *The Complete Works of Sir Thomas Wyatt the Elder*, ed. Jason Powell, 2 vols. (Oxford, forthcoming 2016), 1: letters 1 and 2.
[81] Wright, *Advice*, p. 6.
[82] D'Evelyn, *Instructions*, p. 96 (ll. 893–6).
[83] This is the title given to a numbered list of instructions written by George Brooke, Lord Cobham, for his son upon his departure for the continent in 1541; see BL, Harley MS 283, fol. 133r.

vengeance with forgiveness and forgetting with remembrance, but it never tempers the less famous and just as persistent obsession with surrogation. Indeed, *Hamlet* achieves resolution only through yet another act of substitution: one wronged son stands in for another as Fortinbras inherits the kingdom. If the play's many rattling fathers are finally silenced, Shakespeare's audience might well have heard others pouring words in their ears. As one version of the fifteenth-century poem *How the Wise Man Taught his Son* puts it, 'That he has sparyd another wyll spende'.[84]

---

[84] Shuffelton, *Codex Ashmole 61*, p. 34, l. 76.

'To visit the sick court'
Misogyny as Disease in *Swetnam the Woman-Hater**

⇥ JOYCE BORO ⇤

Swetnam The Woman-Hater (performed 1617–19; published 1620) works very hard to publicise its connection to the eponymous character's namesake, Joseph Swetnam, and to the debate about women to which he contributed so vociferously. The paratext of the 1620 edition advertises the play's participation in contemporary discussions about the antagonism between the sexes: the complete title is *Swetnam the Woman-Hater Arraigned by Women*; the title-page engraving portrays Swetnam's trial by a female court; and the prologue foregrounds the antagonism between the sexes and the 'dayes tryall' of 'we, poore women' (pro. 4, 3).[1] Given that Swetnam only appears in six of the play's nineteen scenes, this may seem like a slightly deceptive marketing strategy intended to capitalise upon Swetnam's notoriety so that sales of printed copies and theatre admissions would increase.[2] But whereas emphasising links to Swetnam is indeed clever advertising, it is not dishonest. In this essay I contend that *Swetnam* offers a profound meditation on the context and tenor of the debate about women in which the play participates and on the type of society necessary for such debate to flourish. Drawing on a foundational principle of early modern kingship, that the monarch's vice or virtue is reflected in his subjects, and coupling this with contemporaneous medical, humoural

---

* I am very grateful to Melinda Gough, M.J. Kidnie and Valerie Wayne for their helpful comments on earlier drafts of this essay. I must also acknowledge an important debt to Jean-Francois Bernard, who inspired me to explore the role of melancholy in *Swetnam*.

[1] All quotations of the play are from Coryl Crandall, ed., *Swetnam the Woman-Hater: The Controversy and the Play* (Lafayette, 1969).

[2] As Valerie Wayne asserts, 'in a sense the text misrepresents itself by highlighting its subplot through its title and title page, but the arraignment is the play's main attraction even though it appears in its minor plot': 'The Dearth of the Author: Anonymity's Allies and *Swetnam the Woman-Hater*', *Maids and Mistresses, Cousins and Queens: Women's Alliances in Early Modern England*, ed. Susan Frye and Karen Robertson (Oxford, 1999), p. 234. Ann Rosalind Jones discusses the implications of the subordination of the Swetnam plot and 'female-voiced protest' to the conventional romance plot, which focuses on the king; see 'From Polemical Prose to the Red Bull: The Swetnam Controversy in Women-Voiced Pamphlets and the Public Theater', *The Project of Prose in Early Modern Europe and the New World*, ed. Elizabeth Fowler and Roland Greene (Cambridge, 1997), p. 134.

theory, the play demonstrates that an ill monarch results in a sick court in which ailing characters thrive and diseases proliferate. King Atticus's excessive grief unbalances his humours and his society, which is in turn afflicted by imbalances that manifest themselves most clearly in antagonism between the sexes and in misogyny, a mind-set that is pathologised as a medical condition in the play. Indeed, the king's corporeal and moral misbalance is reflected most obviously in the gender disharmony in the play. At the end of the play, Sicily's return to political stability is signalled by the restoration of balance: the king's humoural equilibrium returns; mercy and justice are balanced; and women and men, femininity and masculinity, coexist harmoniously.

After providing a brief overview of the play's sources, this essay analyses Atticus's melancholy, arguing that it is a disease with socio-political implications because it infects the king's body and the body politic. In order to demonstrate how Atticus's medical condition results in an ill court with a strong masculine bias, I investigate the aetiology and physiology of his melancholy and reveal that the dominance of harsh masculine justice unmediated by the feminised quality of mercy and the proliferation of misogyny are both symptomatic of royal melancholy. Just as Atticus's melancholy fuses the medical and the socio-political, so misogyny is reconfigured as a disease that is allowed to infiltrate the court. Turning then to Nicanor and Misogynos, I highlight how their masculinist ideology links them to Atticus and opposes them to Lorenzo and Iago, who typify equilibrium.[3] The parallels between Misogynos and the king are further developed through my analysis of Misogynos's disruptive anti-feminism, which exposes his value system as a fully developed illness of the spleen: misogyny is a medical syndrome. The final section of the essay turns to Lorenzo, who is invested with the curative powers of a skilled physician and whose exemplary, balanced androgyny enables him to cure the king and his sick court. The essay's conclusion returns to *Swetnam*'s intertextual allusions and suggests that the play re-crafts its sources in order to respond to specific Jacobean concerns. The play's arguments extend outwards, beyond the theatre, to critique the antagonistic tenor of the contemporaneous debate about women and to suggest that King James, mirroring King Atticus, may be responsible for the propagation of the debate amongst his subjects.

Swetnam is an adaptation of the late fifteenth-century Spanish romance *Grisel y Mirabella* by Juan de Flores. *Grisel* was one of the most popular vernacular texts in sixteenth-century Europe, circulating in more than sixty editions in

---

[3] In order to clearly differentiate Joseph Swetnam from his dramatic personation, I will refer to the character as Misogynos, the pseudonym he adopts in the play.

Spanish, Italian, French, Polish, German and English.[4] Five distinct English versions of the romance exist. It was translated into English twice, both anonymously: the first translation is extant in a small fragment from 1527–35, and the second forms part of the quadrilingual edition of *The Historie of Aurelio and of Isabell* (1556). *Grisel* was then adapted (again anonymously) as *A Pair of Turtle-Doves, or, The Tragical History of Bellora and Fidelio* (1606). John Fletcher dramatised the romance in *Women Pleased* at around the same time *Swetnam* was produced.[5] It is very likely that *Swetnam*'s playwright used the polyglot version of *Grisel* as his source since Princess Leonida is twice erroneously referred to as Hortensia, which is the female champion's name in that version of the romance.[6] Moreover, Queen Aurelia's name recalls the eponymous lover of *The Historie of Aurelio and of Isabell*. There are also intriguing connections between *A Pair of Turtle-Doves* and *Swetnam* that are not rooted in *Grisel* and that cannot be traced back to an earlier adaptation of the romance: both texts rely heavily on medical discourse for the purposes of characterisation, although they do so dichotomously. While *Swetnam* associates disease with men and with misogyny, *A Pair of Turtle-Doves* configures love as an illness, pathologises the female characters, and sympathetically depicts the misogynist (Agamio) as an innocent, lovesick victim.[7] These shared discursive registers and tropes firmly situate *A Pair of Turtle-Doves* within *Swetnam*'s rich intertextual web, suggesting the playwright may have read this romance adaptation even though it was not his principal source text. Furthermore, it seems *Swetnam*'s dramatist was equally familiar with *Women Pleased* and the Spanish *Grisel*. The title of Fletcher's play is twice recalled in *Swetnam*, both in prominent positions. The prologue's final tercet

> (If ever women pleased) weele please to day.
> Vouchsafe to reade, I dare presume to say,
> Yee shall be pleased; and thinke 'tis a good play

echoes the last lines of *Swetnam*: 'Come, beautyous Queene,/ We hope that all are pleased.' *Swetnam* adopts *Grisel*'s strategy of fictionalising a notorious antifeminist in order to attack him and to stake a claim in the period's ongoing debate about women. Throughout the second half of the fifteenth century,

---

[4] Joyce Boro, 'A Source and Date for the Fragment of *Grisel y Mirabella* Found in the Binding of Emmanuel College 338.5.43', *Transactions of the Cambridge Bibliographical Society* 12 (2003), 422–36.

[5] There is no clear consensus regarding *Women Pleased*'s date of composition, but the play was certainly in the King's Men's repertoire between 1619 and 1623.

[6] See 3.3.s.d. and the speaker's name at 3.3.140.

[7] Joyce Boro, 'Reading Juan de Flores's *Grisel y Mirabella* in Early Modern England', *Translation, Print and Culture in Britain, 1473–1640*, ed. S.K. Barker and B. Hosington (Leiden, 2012), pp. 50–4.

Spanish writers were preoccupied with the status and role of women in society. Unlike in early modern England, where the debate raged chiefly in pamphlets and treatises, in Spain the debate permeated the fictional realm. *Grisel* is one of the most fascinating of these *querelle*-texts since it subverts the terms of the debate, causing readers to question established gender roles. Its argumentative playfulness results in a text that can be interpreted as either proto-feminist or misogynist, and it launches an attack on the infamous Pere Torrellas, whose name was 'synonymous with misogyny' and whose text 'incited a *querelle* in its day'.[8] Following *Grisel*'s model, *Swetnam* continues to interrogate the stability of the relationship between sex and gender, and it fictionalises a contemporaneous misogynist who, like Torrellas before him, provoked an inflammatory debate about women.

Swetnam's misogynist manifesto, *The Arraignment of Lewd, Idle, Froward and Unconstant Women* (1615), prompted a textual debate about women that came to be known as the Swetnam controversy.[9] His immediately popular attack was answered in 1617 by three treatises in defence of women – *A Mouzell for Melastomas* by Rachel Speght, *Ester hath hang'd Haman* by Ester Sowernam and Constantia Munda's *The Worming of a mad dogge* – and by *Swetnam The Woman-Hater*.[10] Just as *Grisel* responds to Torrellas and the debate his texts provoked, so *Swetnam* is a reaction to its eponymous debate. The numerous allusions to the texts of the controversy equate the character Misogynos (i.e.

---

[8] Emily C. Francomano, *Three Spanish Querelle Texts: Grisel and Mirabella, The Slander Against Women, and The Defense of Ladies Against Slanderers: A Bilingual Edition and Study* (Toronto, 2013), pp. 1–2.

[9] Nineteen editions of *The Arraignment* were printed between 1615 and 1733. A Dutch translation appeared in 1641 and the text was pilfered extensively by G. Thorowgood in *Pray Be Not Angry: or, the Women's New Law*; see Cis Van Heertum, 'A Plagiarist Plagiarised: *Pray Be Not Angry: or, the Womens New Law* (1656)', *The Library* 13 (1991), 347–50. All references to Swetnam's *Arraignment* are from *A Critical Edition of Joseph Swetnam's The Arraignment of Lewd, Idle, Froward, and Unconstant Women (1615)*, ed. F.W. Van Heertum (Nijmegen, 1989).

[10] While it is likely that Sowernam and Munda are pseudonyms, Rachel Speght wrote under her real name. Earlier scholarship gendered these authors female though more recent critics discuss the implications of, and difficulties inherent in, reading these pseudonymous texts by authors of unknown genders: Diane Purkiss, 'Material Girls: The Seventeenth-Century Woman Debate', *Women, Texts and Histories 1575–1760*, ed. Clare Brant and Diane Purkiss (London, 1992), pp. 69–101; Melinda J. Gough, 'Women's Popular Culture? Teaching the Swetnam Controversy', *Debating Gender in Early Modern England, 1500–1700*, ed. Christina Malcolmson and Mihoko Suzuki (New York, 2002), pp. 79–100; Wayne, 'Dearth', pp. 221–40. For readings of Sowernam and Munda as female, see Ann Rosalind Jones, 'Counterattacks on "the Bayter of Women": Three Pamphleteers of the Early Seventeenth Century', *The Renaissance Englishwoman in Print: Counterbalancing the Canon*, ed. Anne M. Haselkorn and Betty S. Travitsky (Amherst, 1990), pp. 45–62; Elaine V. Beilin, *Redeeming Eve: Women Writers of the English Renaissance* (Princeton, 1987), pp. 247–85; Simon Shepherd, ed., *The Women's Sharp Revenge: Five Women's Pamphlets from the Renaissance* (New York, 1985); Katherine Usher Henderson and Barbara McManus, eds., *Half Humankind: Contexts and Texts of the Controversy about Women in England, 1540–1640* (Urbana, 1985), pp. 21–4.

Swetnam) with Joseph Swetnam, which enables the play to enact a powerful, symbolic defeat of Swetnam through the dramatisation of Misogynos's downfall and repentance. The references are too numerous to inventory fully here, but a few will suffice to demonstrate the dynamic allusiveness of *Swetnam*, a topic returned to in my conclusion.[11] Invoking *A Mouzell for Melastomas*, Misogynos is called by the name of Molastomus (1.2.43; 5.2.156); Atlanta suggests Misogynos wear a muzzle (5.2.328); and the latter then appears muzzled in the epilogue. Swetnam's adoption of the name Misogynos recalls Speght's text, which dismisses him and 'every such *Misogunes*'.[12] Further, Misogynos alludes to Speght's published reply in the play (1.2.43), and his inability to fight despite the fact that he is a fencing teacher evokes Speght's taunting accusations of martial incompetence.[13] Misogynos's arraignment resembles the similar trial scene in Sowernam's text. Picking up on the imagery of Munda's title and text, Misogynos is referred to as a dog on seven occasions.[14] The three writers are collectively invoked when Swash puns on Speght's name and describes how the 'two or three good wenches, in meere spight' attacked Misogynos's 'Booke' (5.2.21). Further, Misogynos speaks in passages borrowed from Swetnam's *Arraignment*,[15] the treatise is referred to abundantly, and the book is materialised as a stage property, presented as exhibit A at Misogynos's trial (5.2.291–2).[16]

Swetnam opens on a scene familiar in early modern drama: the protagonist is sad and his unhappiness is a subject of concern for those who surround him. In the tradition of Olivia in *Twelfth Night* and Antonio in *The Merchant of Venice*, in *Swetnam*, King Atticus's sadness is configured as excessive; it is emotion out of measure.[17] These surfeits of emotion were worrisome since contemporaneous medical theory pathologised excessive sadness as an illness.

---

[11] Linda Woodbridge, *Women and the English Renaissance: Literature and the Nature of Womankind, 1540–1620* (Urbana, 1984), p. 319, notes allusions to Tuvil's *Asylum veneris, or A sanctuary for ladies* in *Swetnam*. I am not including *Asylum veneris* in my discussion since, as Woodbridge explains, Tuvil's work shows knowledge of Swetnam's *Arraignment*, but is not a direct response to it (pp. 103–10).

[12] Rachel Speght, *A Mouzell for Melastomus*, in *The Women's Sharp Revenge*, ed. Shepherd, p. 37. Cf. Simon Shepherd, *Amazons and Warrior Women: Varieties of Feminism in Seventeenth-Century Drama* (New York, 1981), p. 207.

[13] Speght, *Mouzell*, p. 79.

[14] This trope occurs in 3.2.52, 64; 3.3.207; 5.2.139, 142, 329, 349. Cf. Matthew Steggle, *Wars of the Theatres: The Poetics of Personation in the Age of Jonson* (Victoria, 1998), p. 83.

[15] Compare 1.2.151–8 to 'If all the world were paper [...] crafty deceits of women', Swetnam, *Arraignment*, p. 228; 3.2.25–9, to 'they are ungratefull [...] bee avoyded', Swetnam, *Arraignment*, p. 211; 1.2.164–5, to 'If thou marriest [...] horse to the Devill', Swetnam, *Arraignment*, p. 230. Steggle, *Wars*, pp. 81–2, discusses the correspondence in 1.2.151–8 in terms of Swetnam's dramatisation as a writer.

[16] See 1.2.1, 5–7, and 45ff, 178; 5.2.267ff.

[17] *Hamlet*, John Lyly's *Endymion, the Man in the Moon* (1588) and John Ford's *The Lover's Melancholy* (1628) are crafted in the same tradition.

Atticus's, Olivia's and Antonio's gloom have varied aetiologies, yet all are manifestations of the disease of melancholy, a medical syndrome arising from a corporeal excess of black bile. Optimum health was achieved when all four humours – black bile, yellow bile, blood and phlegm – were in perfect balance. A surplus or lack of any of these four humours disturbed natural bodily harmony and resulted in illness. Not surprisingly, in plays with such melancholic characters, much of the action revolves around curing the afflicted individual by restoring their humours to a state of balance. This therapeutic process is essential to the plays' denouement, since the characters' imbalance risks upsetting or unbalancing the social order. And, the more power the characters have in their societies, the greater their effect on the individuals and social structures surrounding them. Antonio's melancholy, for example, worries his friends and they attempt to cheer him up, but his sadness does not prevent them from acting according to their desires and achieving fulfilment. At the close of *The Merchant of Venice*, he remains melancholic and, consequently, he is excluded from the final festivities. As a duchess, Olivia's excessive mourning for her brother has greater ramifications. Not only do her feelings shroud her household, but her melancholy prevents her from attending to her dynastic obligations and maintaining order, and so she must be cured. As king of Sicily, Atticus is invested with unrestrained sovereign power and so his illness infects the very fabric of society. His disease impacts his population in a very particular way: Sicily is not suffering from an epidemic outbreak of melancholy, but rather, the king's unbalanced state creates an unbalanced political state biased towards men, which enables the rise to power of other unbalanced individuals. The result is social and cultural instability; Atticus's Sicily is topsy-turvy, unbalanced, disorganised.

The king has good reason to be sad. His elder son (Lyssipus) is dead, his younger son (Lorenzo) has been missing for eighteen months, and, as Atticus opines: 'And for our daughter fayre Leonida,/ Her female Sexe cannot inherit here' (1.1.89–90). One of the unnamed nobles who opens the play evokes the surfeit of sadness: 'our sorrows still increase', he worries, 'A greater tide of woe is to be fear'd,/ The Kings decay, with grief for his two sonnes' (1.1.16–18). Atticus's 'sorrows', 'woe' and 'grief' threaten to engulf him; he is comfortless, 'in rage' and 'tread[s]' like the 'living dead'. The language of excess and repeated allusions to death alert the audience to the severity of the situation. When the king enters, he extends this lexicon of death and suffering, imagining his legacy as one of loss and sorrow:

> Death gave my sorrows life,
> For by his death my pain and grief begun,
> And in the beginning, never will have end: for though I die
> My losse will live in future memorie,

> And, I (perhaps) will be lamented too,
> And registered by some, when all shall heare
> *Sicilia* had two sonnes, yet had no heire. (1.1.29–35)

His grief is so extreme that he imagines it possessed of an independent existence and outliving him. The repetition of the terms 'death' and 'die' in conjunction with the sense of sadness he establishes in the passage through the use of terms such as 'sorrows', 'pain', 'grief' and 'losse' stresses the fact that his sorrow is out of measure. Indeed, he identifies himself as ruled by 'Griefe' and names himself 'King of all woes Monarchie' (1.1.48–9).

The destructive and harmful nature of his grief, which will eventually lead to the unduly harsh treatment of his daughter, is equally foregrounded in this opening scene. Addressing his 'sad sorrows' (1.1.57), he asks:

> Into what maze of errors will you lead mee?
> This Monster (Grief) hath so distracted mee,
> I had almost forgot mortalitie. (1.1.58–60)

Grief threatens to ruin him as it brings him to the brink of despair. His intense sadness arouses feelings of suicidal desperation; he wishes to die and ascend to heaven so he can retrieve his son. As he realises that his 'sad sorrows' have 'driven' him to contemplate the mortal sin of suicide, he breaks off his monologue. Yet, when he resumes speaking, he continues to long for death: 'I sooner looke to see me dead than hee [Lorenzo]' (1.1.71), Atticus moans, and he repeatedly forecasts his imminent death as the result of his sorrow (1.1.72–3, 82–3, 180).

Sorrow's ability to make Atticus forget himself is again invoked at the critical moment where he must decide his daughter's fate. Sicily's laws have been broken: Princess Leonida and Lisandro have been discovered together, a clear contravention of the edict stating that no man may visit her. Atticus's judges and his good advisor, the 'choric figure' Iago, urge mercy.[18] Despite their sound advice and the prevailing political tradition that urged rulers to temper justice with mercy, Atticus decides to uphold the decree rigorously. As he unflinchingly declares that his daughter must be subject to the full extent of the law, he reminds us of his 'troubled thoughts' and 'grief of mind' (3.1.15–16), which, as we have seen in the play's first scene, prevent him from assessing the situation objectively and rationally. Indeed, in his *Anatomy of Melancholy* (1621), Robert Burton explains the countless ways melancholy affects the mind, inhibiting the patient's rational faculty. In the introductory letter to the *Anatomy*, Democritus Junior declares melancholics to be 'quite mad', like 'brute beasts, and void of

---

[18] Woodbridge, *Women*, p. 307

reason', concluding that 'Where is fear and sorrow [...] wisdom cannot dwell.'[19] Burton further explains that irrationality may manifest itself in just the type of stubbornness exhibited by Atticus: 'once the melancholic be resolved [he is] obstinate, hard to be reconciled'; if melancholics 'abhor, dislike, or distaste, once [they are] settled' in their thoughts, 'no odds, counsel or persuasion' can move them.[20] Atticus himself recognises that kings must maintain justice and mercy in equilibrium and that in this particular situation he must weigh his dual roles of king and father (3.1.13–21), but while he rationally appreciates the necessity of balance, because he is suffering from an illness, a humoural imbalance, he cannot be equanimous. As a result he launches a biased, or unbalanced, legal process that will unjustly sentence his daughter to death.

Not only is the king's refusal to enact mercy a manifestation of his imbalance, but equally it highlights the masculine bias of his court. Mercy is usually configured as a feminine attribute in medieval and early modern iconography and literature, and its presentation in this play is no exception.[21] Drawing on a range of biblical and historical examples (most notably the story of Esther, and the tradition of Mary as merciful intermediary) and discourse surrounding thirteenth-century English queens, John Carmi Parsons refers to this as the typical 'king:law::queen:mercy equation'.[22] Paul Strohm describes how changes to female leadership in the early thirteenth century led to the development of the 'queen as intercessor' figure who is notable for her association with 'a range of virtues regarded as "feminine"', including mercy or compassion, and who may serve as a virtual 'allegorical figure for mercy, a figure in a psychomachia of male decision making'.[23] The conventional attribution of justice to men and mercy to women persisted through the early modern period, but rather than present mercy as a uniquely female quality to be exhibited only by women, *Swetnam* shows how this feminine trait is necessary for male rulers and for the kingdom as a whole. This is how the play illuminates the problems inherent in a society lacking in female influence and power. In her discussion of *Swetnam*, Constance Jordan defines this balance of justice and mercy as 'androgynous

---

[19] Robert Burton, *The Anatomy of Melancholy*, ed. Floyd Dell and Paul Jordan-Smith (New York, 1927), p. 61.
[20] Burton, *Anatomy*, p. 333.
[21] K.J. Kesselring, *Mercy and Authority in the Tudor State* (Cambridge, 2003), p. 143, cautiously asserts: 'Admittedly, literary treatments of pardons did offer more representations of the female than of the male intercessor, perhaps suggesting a certain tendency to see suits for mercy in gendered terms.'
[22] John Carmi Parsons, 'The Queen's Intercession', *Power of the Weak: Studies on Medieval Women*, ed. Jennifer Carpenter and Sally-Beth MacLean (Urbana, 1995), p. 154.
[23] Paul Strohm, *Hochon's Arrow: The Social Imagination of Fourteenth-Century Texts* (Princeton, 1992), pp. 96–7, 104. Cf. Parsons, 'Queen's', pp. 147–77. Lois L. Huneycutt traces this figure back to the ninth century and describes her affinities to the biblical figure of Esther; see 'Intercession and the High-Medieval Queen: The Esther Topos', *Power of the Weak*, ed. Carpenter and MacLean, pp. 126–46.

justice', arguing that the king's sense of justice 'suppresses the feminine element of society by endorsing a restrictive treatment of women; it systematically overlooks what that feminine element symbolizes in the interpretation of justice: equity or mercy'.[24]

Sicily's ruling couple exemplify the gendered dichotomy of mercy and justice: just as Atticus firmly advocates unmediated justice, Queen Aurelia campaigns incessantly for mercy. She fulfils the role typical of the 'queen as intercessor', urging the king to mercy or compassion from a place outside of the law and providing him with the opportunity for 'royal reconsideration', enabling him to do what a 'monarch cast in the mould of the "imago dei" needed on most occasions to avoid: to change his mind'.[25] But Atticus firmly resists her feminised persuasions. The king clearly articulates the contemporaneous polarisation of justice and pity, and their respective associations with masculinity and femininity, when he criticises Iago, his previously favourite counsellor:

> [He is] leniative, ore-swaid too much
> With pittie against Justice,
> He has too much of woman, otherwise
> He might be Ruler of a Monarchie,
> For policie and wisdom. (5.3.40–5)

Leniency and pity or mercy are attributes the king sorely lacks. Atticus's criticism of Iago reveals how indispensable this counsellor truly is since Iago exemplifies how best to balance 'pittie against Justice'. In recognising Iago's skills in 'policie and wisdom', the king thereby confirms that Iago is not unduly merciful; rather, we see that the king's melancholy has rendered him so hostile to pity that any display of the trait is abhorrent. He thus unwittingly affirms the importance of the equilibrium between justice and pity necessary for good kingship. Most importantly, by invoking the twinned polarities of justice and masculinity, in opposition to pity and femininity, the king reveals his aversion to both pity and the female with which it is associated. Just as there is no space for pity in his court, there is no room for women. In his eschewing of pity, Atticus creates a hyper-masculine court in which unbalanced, misogynistic characters such as Misogynos and Nicanor can thrive, as will be discussed below.

A feminised conceptualisation of mercy is essential to the king's recuperation at the play's conclusion, further demonstrating its importance to a stable

---

[24] Constance Jordan, 'Gender and Justice in *Swetnam the Woman-hater*', *Renaissance Drama* 18 (1987), 153, 161.
[25] Strohm, *Hochon's*, p. 103. On the figure of the queen as intercessor, see Strohm, *Hochon's*, pp. 95–119.

society. It is not until the last act of *Swetnam*, during the didactic morality play staged for the king's benefit, that he finally turns to mercy. The performance moves him to recognise his vice and so he calls out to Repentance – the only female character in the inset drama – for help. This signifies his willingness to accept female attributes to which he was previously entirely opposed. It also indicates he is on the path to mercy, since repentance leads to mercy within Christian doctrine. His movement from repentance to mercy is shown at the end of *Swetnam* as he forgives his evil advisor Nicanor and is reconciled with his subjects and family. He then alludes to *Women Pleased*, invoking the attribution of sovereignty to women dramatised in Fletcher's play, as he lovingly calls out to his wife, whom he previously treated with nothing but disdain: 'Come beauteous Queene,/ We hope that all are pleas'd' (5.3.12–13). These lines simultaneously recall Loretta's reference to *Women Pleased* in *Swetnam*'s prologue, which she used to welcome women to the theatre, promise them an enjoyable drama and express her disregard for the male audience members. The king's final line expresses awareness that any attempt at living without mercy and female qualities is in vain, as God wills sexual harmony: 'In vaine we strive to crosse, what Heavens decree', he acknowledges (5.3.14). The king thus places the need for mercy and repentance on a cosmic level, stressing the necessity for all individuals to live honestly, to love and respect women, to obey God, and to be merciful as well as just. The king and queen's reconciliation in the play's concluding lines represents a reunification of mercy and justice and extends a promise of a future peaceful kingdom.

The conclusion's promise of harmony and the social anarchy that permeates the drama are both equally centred on the king. Erasmus's contention that 'the life of the prince [is] mirrored in the morals of his people' was shared by political theorists from ancient Greece through the early modern period and beyond, and this idea is lucidly reflected in *Swetnam*. A peaceful king results in a harmonious court, just as an unbalanced monarch will rule over an unstable population. The latter premise is especially cogent since, as Erasmus explains, it was believed that

> The corruption of an evil prince spreads more quickly and widely than the contagion of any plague [...] No comet, no fateful power affects the progress of human affairs in the way that the life of the prince grips and transforms the moral attitudes and character of his subjects.[26]

Lorenzo observes that Atticus's court is 'sicke' (3.2.19); it is 'eclipst with clouds of discontent [...] and all hearts/ Ore-whelm'd with sorrow' (1.3.105–7). Nicanor

---

[26] Desiderius Erasmus, *The Education of a Christian Prince*, trans. Neil M. Cheshire and Michael J. Heath, ed. Lisa Jardine (Cambridge, 1997), p. 21.

clearly articulates the symbiotic relationship between king and subjects as he affirms that

> a melancholy King makes a sad Court [and] all the Court
> is clowded o'r with griefe: your sadnesse, Sir,
> Fils every Subjects heart with heavinesse. (5.3.17–19)

The mirroring of king and court is evoked in multiple ways in the play. For example, Atticus's unmitigated justice against Leonida and Lisandro directly leads to Aurelia's similarly merciless, violent treatment of Misogynos, as she abandons her pleas for mercy and she and her ladies subject Misogynos to a kangaroo court, sentencing him to bodily torture. We likewise witness the social and political unrest that arises from Atticus's behaviour. Iago observes:

> in every mouth is heard to sound,
> Nothing but murmurings and private whispers,
> Tending to severall ends: but all conclude,
> The King was too severe for such a Fact. (4.5.90–3)

Times are dangerous. Sedition swells in these murmurs and whispers. Angry women roam the streets like 'Devils in Hell' or 'Furies' in search of male victims to brutalise (1.2.16–40). But whereas conflict saturates the court, 'all' are in agreement regarding the king's injustice, which is emphasised through the paronomastic repetition of 'severall/severe'. His 'too severe' masculine comportment must be balanced by the female virtue of pity in order to calm this civil unrest.[27] Indeed, the king's medical and moral infection generates a corrupt environment of illness that leads to social anarchy and is the breeding ground in which the imbalanced Nicanor and Misogynos can flourish.

Humoural medicine provides a variety of ways to restore a patient to a balanced state but the principle underlying the practice was a doctrine of opposites: balance could be achieved by treating through contraries. As Galen writes, 'the preservation of health is through whatever is similar, whilst the cure for diseases is through whatever is opposite [...] For whatever is by nature faultless is safeguarded by what is like, whilst whatever is poorly composed is led to its proper state by what is opposite.'[28] Bloodletting, purges, emetics or poultices could be used to rid the body of an excess of a bodily fluid. The patient could ingest a medicine in the form of food, drink or herbals in order to increase the quantity of a diminished humour. Sleep, mental and physical activity, exposure to the elements and discursive techniques such as charms,

---

[27] Cf. Margaret Jane Kidnie, '"Enter [...] Lorenzo, Disguised Like an Amazon": Powerdressing in *Swetnam the Woman-Hater, Arraigned by Women*', *Cahiers Élisabéthains* 62 (2002), 38–9.
[28] Galen, *Galen on Food and Diet*, ed. and trans. Mark Grant (London and New York, 2000), pp. 42, 190.

incantations, or the contemplation of specific ideas introduced via conversation or reading material could all impact the humours and so physicians could likewise effect cures through specific recommendations in any of these areas. Melancholy – Atticus's ailment – was notoriously complex, with experts disagreeing as to its aetiologies, manifestations, typologies and effects.[29] As a result the proposed remedies were myriad, with writers acknowledging the difficulty of curing melancholy and, worryingly, the melancholic's inclination to turn to suicide before a treatment could succeed.[30] Burton notes that melancholy degenerates into other ailments and describes its spread to the patient's brain, resulting in various forms of irrationality.[31]

Rooted in grief, Atticus's melancholy was of the most common variety of the disease, and his unreasonableness and suicidal thoughts are typical symptoms.[32] However, the proliferation of auxiliary diseases stemming from melancholy is not restricted to Atticus's physical body; they also infiltrate his body politic. As previously stated, one of the main symptoms of Sicily's imbalance is the misogyny that permeates the court. While medical theorists did not classify misogyny as a humoural imbalance, if we consider the oppositional methodology of humoural therapies, then the pathology inherent in misogyny emerges clearly. In *The Literature of Misogyny in Medieval Spain*, Michael Solomon outlines the pervasive connection between misogyny and lovesickness, which is blatantly articulated in the remedies for the most acute cases. The restorative technique of *confabulatio* dominated the treatment of diseases with aetiologies rooted in mental disturbances, and thus writers including Galen, Ovid, Peter of Spain, Bernard of Gordon, Ferrand and Burton routinely propose hatred of women as the cure for love.[33] Medics prescribe insulting the beloved, reading antifeminist texts and even, in extreme cases, showing the lover the woman's bloodied menstrual towels as remedies.[34] The aim is to oppose love's desire to connect with the beloved with a dichotomous urge to flee from women. Just as cold is applied to a patient with a fever to cool the over-heated body and heat is applied to a patient who has a chill to warm the cold body, so hate can temper love and love can temper hate. The corollary, of course, is that both extremes are harmful states, symptomatic of a loss of bodily equilibrium. Indeed, medical writers highlight the dangers

---

[29] See, for example, Burton, *Anatomy*, pp. 151–5.
[30] Burton, *Anatomy*, pp. 367–74.
[31] Burton, *Anatomy*, pp. 366–7.
[32] Burton, *Anatomy*, pp. 225, 367–74.
[33] On the curative effects of reading: Mary Ann Lund, *Melancholy, Medicine and Reading in Early Modern England: Reading the Anatomy of Melancholy* (Cambridge, 2010).
[34] See Jacques Ferrand, *A Treatise on Lovesickness*, ed. Donald Beecher and Massimo Ciavolella (Syracuse, NY, 1990), pp. 315–19. For further examples, see Michael Solomon, *The Literature of Misogyny in Medieval Spain: The 'Arcipreste de Talavera' and the 'Spill'* (Cambridge, 1997), pp. 62–4.

of both hatred and love. Given that the configuration of disease is culturally and historically specific and that (Michael Solomon writes) 'since medicine is inescapably bound up in ideology it is [thus] possible to categorize any phenomenon that is deemed to disrupt the social as well as the biological order as a disease'. Or, put more simply, 'Any type of behavioral aberration, complaint, criticism, or discontent can be somatised and pathologized.'[35] Thus, although early physicians, probably due to the cultural acceptance of misogyny, do not pathologise extreme hatred of women, its existence as disease can be inferred from prevailing contemporaneous medical theory, which medicalises extreme hatred as well as the excessive love of women. Moreover, and perhaps most importantly, *Swetnam* does present misogyny as an illness that spreads from the king's melancholy throughout Sicily.

Cognisant that the king is suffering from melancholy, Iago and Nicanor act as medical confabulators, exploiting the healing properties of language since they recognise that curative power is commensurate with political power. Observing how 'despaire/ Became sole Monarke of his passions' (5.1.71–2) upon the death of Lyssipus and the disappearance of Lorenzo, Iago uses his 'relation' to 'chang[e] his countenance [and] ingender in his brest/ Some new-bred passions' (5.1.85–7). A medical context is established by the repetition of the term 'passions' alongside the affirmation of language's therapeutic ability to 'change', 'ingender', or to affect the physical body. Alarmed by the medicinal sway of Iago's counsel, Nicanor opines, 'This Physic works too strongly, and may prove a deadly potion' (5.1.111–12). He thus calls a truce with Iago and requests his assistance to 'devise/ Some pastime to supresse this heavinesse' (5.1.15–16). The political and medical coalesce, as governing the king's health is equated with governing the realm.

Nicanor and Iago's battle for Atticus's favour can be configured along the traditional lines of the evil versus the good advisor, but their feud also symbolises the tension between male and female, men and women, that permeates the court. Whereas the politic Iago is chastised by Atticus because 'He has too much of woman' in his character, Nicanor inhabits the opposite end of the spectrum. Like the king and Misogynos, Nicanor favours a court bereft of female influence. As Woodbridge argues, 'Nicanor and Misogynos [are] in the same camp: both malign women out of deprivation. [...] Atticus makes a third in an unholy trinity; amputating his sense of mercy, he forfeits all human values, even justice. All these narrowed beings are guilty of contempt for women.'[36] Nicanor feigns loyalty to Atticus and love for Leonida in order to marry the princess and inherit the kingdom as Atticus's heir. As he harshly condemns Leonida and women more generally for their 'shew[s] of dislike',

---

[35] Solomon, *Literature*, p. 18.
[36] Woodbridge, *Women*, pp. 316–17.

weak resolutions and 'seeming sanctity', he reveals an anti-female bias (2.1.103, 131). When he discovers Leonida and Lisandro together he is elated by the prospect of Leonida's impeding destruction, declaring 'Rather than lose the Royall Dignitie/ Ile strive to ruin a whole Progenie' (2.3.43–4). Leonida's 'ruin' will not prevent him from inheriting the kingdom; rather, if she is excluded from the line of descent he can inherit directly from Atticus. As he joyfully, but erroneously, boasts later in the play, 'The King alone made me the King' (4.2.45). This male-to-male passage of rule, to the exclusion of female intervention, suggests a profound disruption of natural order akin to the exclusively male mode of procreation proposed by Misogynos in act 1, scene 2 (explored below).

The parallels between Nicanor, Atticus and Misogynos are emphasised in the final exonerating lines of the play. After the morality play has worked its salutary effects on Atticus, as discussed above, with his newfound health and accurate vision he turns to Nicanor, ready to hold him legally responsible for his treachery. Whereas Iago earlier condemned Nicanor for acting 'ignobly' with 'force and tyrannie' according to the whims of his 'proud aspiring mind' (3.1.146, 149, 151), and Lorenzo censured him as a 'Tyrant', recognising his 'Serpents subtilitie' (3.2.11,13), this is the first time the king realises Nicanor is not an ideal, moral counsellor. But Nicanor escapes blame, since, like the king, he swiftly repents for his misdeeds. Not only does repentance come surprisingly quickly to both men, but their connection is further strengthened through the grammatical ambiguity in Atticus's acceptance of Nicanor's penitence: 'Well, we forgive,' he declares, 'Learne to live honest now' (5.3.211–12). The grammatical subject and object of the first sentence is clear: Atticus forgives Nicanor. Yet, uncertainty permeates the second sentence: is Atticus commanding Nicanor to learn to live honestly, or is he resolving that he himself will learn to live honestly? This slippage gestures towards the similarities between these characters and to their parallel moral trajectories. This moment is likewise imbued with thematic significance: as Atticus forgives Nicanor, he demonstrates his ability to act with clemency, which, when coupled with our knowledge of his ability to enact strict justice, illustrates his metamorphosis into a balanced ruler.

The final movement to repentance equally affects Misogynos. The epilogue sees him 'muzzled, hal'd' in by women (s.d.) as his victims prepare his second trial. Like Nicanor and Atticus before him, he speedily atones.[37] Paralleling Atticus's pardon of Nicanor that results in Nicanor's repentance, here Leonida's forgiveness precipitates Misogynos's conversion. After she 'freely pardon[s]' him, he repents, declaring, 'And here for-ever I put off this shape,/ And with it

---

[37] The rapid change in character is typical of Renaissance comedy, where conclusions often seem forced. In this case, however, when we consider Swetnam's parallel move to repentance and the joke with which it is conveyed in the epilogue we may be encouraged to read this ending against the grain.

all my spleene and malice too' (epilogue 12, 16–17). This avowal of guilt points to two important attributes of his 'malice': by configuring the transition as putting off his 'shape', the deceitful, dissembling aspect of his 'general wrong' is highlighted, and by referring to his 'spleen', his behaviour is pathologised. Of course, his declaration of repentance is comically undercut by his final words in which he invokes the familiar dichotomy of the pen and the sword, while vowing to leave the pen that he used to harm women for the sword that he will use in their defence. After witnessing his lack of skill in swordsmanship (5.2.105–7), the advantage that women may expect from his endeavours is questionable.

Misogynos blames an illness of the spleen for his misogyny. The spleen was commonly thought to be the seat of melancholy, which further emphasises affinities between Misogynos and Atticus.[38] In his *Canon of Medicine*, Avicenna enumerates 'craving of coitus', phobias of things not usually feared by others, and flatulence amongst the symptoms of melancholy.[39] Misogynos's sudden sexual desire for Lorenzo/Atlanta, his fear of women and his excessive flatulence present him as textbook patient. Iago and Lorenzo compare Mysogynos to a 'scarabee' or beetle, 'whose breeding has been [...] upon the excrement of the time', who has become so 'swolne with poisonous vapors,/ [that] He breakes wind in publique, to blast the reputation of all women' and whose 'foule breath belcht forth [slander] into the Ayre' (3.3.68). This conflation of speech with flatulence or eructation is grounded in medieval epistemologies of language, as epitomised in pseudo-Jerome's twelfth-century *Regula monachorum*:

> Wherefore as a belch bursts forth from the stomach according to the quality of the food, and the index of a fart is according to the sweetness or stench of its odor, so the cogitations of the inner man bring forth words, and *from the abundance of the heart the mouth speaks*.[40]

Misogynos expels speech, farts and burps to equal effect. Not only does Lorenzo thus reduce Misogynos's arguments to poisonous farts and foul belching, but also through invoking extreme flatulence or eructation he endorses Misogynos's self-diagnosis and aids in pathologising his misogyny. Farting and burping, as well as urination, bleeding, defecation, lacrimation and sweating,

---

[38] Quoted in Jennifer Radden, *The Nature of Melancholy: From Aristotle to Kristeva* (Oxford, 2000), p. 77.
[39] Radden, *Nature*, p. 77.
[40] Quoted in Mary Carruthers, *The Book of Memory: A Study of Memory in Medieval Culture* (Cambridge, 1990), p. 207. See also Valerie Allen, *On Farting: Laughter and Language in the Middle Ages* (New York, 2007). In 'The Miller's Tale', Chaucer humorously conflates the expulsion of air that allows words to be formed with the air of flatulence through the character of Absalon, who 'was somdeel squaymous/ Of fartyng, and of speche daungerous' (ll. 3337–8), *Riverside Chaucer*.

were modes of excreting humoural excess. Excessive flatulence is medicalised as 'ventosity' or 'internal "windiness," a condition in which the body's humours, vapours or spirits are chaotically mobile'.[41] Burton attributes 'windy melancholy', of which belching and farting are major symptoms, to the spleen, Misogynos's faulty internal organ 'that doth not his duty in purging the liver as he ought'.[42]

In addition to ridiculing Misogynos by equating his language to foul corporeal expulsions, Lorenzo further subverts Misogynos's arguments by presenting him as a 'monster' (5.2.145), a Turk (3.2.54), 'inhuman' (3.2.68) and as a beast who lives on a 'dunghill' (3.2.78). He is muzzled (5.2.328, epilogue s.d.) and likened to various animals. The comparison to a viper highlights his poisonous words (3.2.55); that to the scarab, his base nature and association with filth and excrement (3.2.33). He is as deceitful as the proverbial serpent (3.2.13, 3.3.21, 5.2.240). Lorenzo and Iago isolate deceit as his 'foule deformitie' and, indeed, his very identity is founded on falsity. He changes his name from Swetnam to Misogynos when he arrives in Sicily to disguise himself and he impersonates a fencing master, despite his lack of swordsmanship (1.2.56–61). The recurrent canine allusions provide reminders of Munda's *Worming of a mad dogge*, but also serve to emphasise Swetnam's maliciousness, spitefulness, perversity and cruelty (3.2.52, 64; 3.3.207; 5.2.140, 143, 328–9, 347).

As a result of his reprehensible nature, Misogynos had been expelled from England. His misogyny and foul behaviour rapidly earn him a similar reception amongst the Sicilians, with the exception of Atticus, Nicanor and Scanfardo (a misogynist who attends Misogynos's sham fencing school in order to learn how to master the woman he is soon to marry), who feel an affinity with Misogynos. He is also accompanied by Swash, who has followed Misogynos into exile because he desires to bear witness to Misogynos's downfall so that he can then return to England to report it, which, he hopes, will earn him the love of all Englishwomen. Misogynos does not need to win popularity contests or convince the population of Sicily to embrace him and his values. Since he has the support of the political elite, he can rise to success, and this occurs not despite but because of his unbalanced, bestial condition. His misogyny and deceit resonate with Nicanor and enable him to thrive in Atticus's male-dominated, diseased court.

Misogynos arrives in Sicily with the aim of social and sexual disruption, and as his initial speech reveals, he derives great joy from disorder:

By this, my thundering Booke is prest abroad.
I long to hear what a report it beares;

---

[41] Faith Wallis, *Medieval Medicine: A Reader* (Toronto, 2010), p. 552.
[42] Burton, *Anatomy*, p. 323.

> I know 't will startle all out Citie Dames,
> Worse then the roring Lyons, or the sound
> Of a huge double Canon; *Swetnams* name,
> Will be more terrible in womens eares,
> Then ever *Misogenysts* hath been. (1.2.7)

Misogynos's speech is loud, violent and aggressive. The noisy aural imagery is further emphasised by words like 'hear', 'sound' and 'eares'. Amidst all this clatter, we hear Misogynos's declared wish to disrupt society and create antagonism. His mission is easily accomplished because the city is already unbalanced due to Atticus's melancholy. Misogynos's rapid, unabashed success is soon revealed by Swash who rushes in fleeing the attacks of 'the women in the Towne' whom Misogynos has 'set all [...] in an uprore' (1.2.20). The cacophonous roaring and violence of his book is replicated in the women's violent actions and words.

Misogynos's disruptive agenda extends beyond angering women to the disturbance of natural and social order. Mirroring Nicanor's desire to inherit Atticus's crown without a female intermediary, Misogynos laments the necessity of women in procreation, which, in his ideal world, would be 'In man alone, without the help of woman', in the manner of a seed that can produce another or a tree that can 'revive again' (1.2.139–48). Moreover, he is elated as he recalls how his 'Bookes took effect' in England. 'O it was rare!' he exclaims

> How rife debate sprang betwixt man and wife!
> The little Infant that could hardly speake,
> Would call his Mother Whore. (1.2.47–9)

The disruption of the family unit at the heart of social order is profoundly disturbing. He descends into nihilism as he desires to exhaust all of the world's natural resources in his mission to 'make all the World/ To hate, as I doe, this affliction, Woman' (1.2.35–6). He imagines:

> That if all the World were Paper; the Sea, Inke; Trees and Plants, Pens; and every man Clarkes, Scribes, and Notaries; yet would all that Paper be scribbled over, the Inke wasted, Pens worne to the stumps, and all the Scriveners wearie, before they could describe the hunderth part of a womans wickednesse. (1.2.151–8)

Total annihilation is welcomed if it will lead to the universal hatred of women.

Misogynos's melancholy, dishonesty and disruptiveness ally him with Nicanor and Atticus while they morally and politically oppose him to Atticus's good advisor, Iago, and Lorenzo. Wise Iago is the voice of learned reason. In fact, he provides readers and spectators with a miniature *speculum principis* in the play, defining the ideal qualities of kingship. Iago's description of Atticus as the exemplary king presumably harks back to a time before his affliction with grief and, importantly, it stresses the essential attributes of balance. Iago evokes a much-beloved king who is 'just', 'equall', unmoved by emotional pleas, uninterested in harsh, punitive laws and who is 'Garded by Angels' as he straddles 'Justice and Clemencie' (1.3.14–26). Throughout the course of the play we witness Iago's attempts to cure the king and return him to this state of exemplary balance. Fulfilling the role of the ideal counsellor, Iago is unswayed by the king's tyranny and is the only courtier courageous enough to tell the king the truth despite the consequences that may befall him (5.1).

Like Iago, Lorenzo recognises the importance of the twinned virtues of mercy and justice. A ruler who combines these virtues is, according to Lorenzo, 'a worthy Prince' (1.3.27). Thus, he works to steer his father back to a *via media* that spans both pity and justice. Moreover, Lorenzo's exemplary qualities of leadership and balanced emotional state are emphasised throughout the play, thereby presenting him in the mould of the ideal ruler and differentiating him from Atticus as well as from Nicanor and Misogynos. For example, in contrast with his father, who is diseased with grief, Lorenzo offers a positive model of how to cope with loss. Upon discovering his brother's death, he declares:

> I have some tears to spend upon his Tombe
> We are the next unto the Diadem,
> That's the occasion I obscure myself. (1.3.114–17)

Tellingly, Lorenzo is reacting to the same event – Lyssipus's death – that causes Atticus's illness, but his ability to process his feelings demonstrates the emotional balance necessary in a good ruler. Lorenzo will grieve his brother and then will proceed in accordance with his newly acquired position as heir to the throne. In order to fulfil his political responsibilities, Lorenzo decides to 'obscure' himself with a disguise. Whereas disguise is linked to deceit through Nicanor's and Misogynos's dishonest uses of concealment, Lorenzo shows how disguise can be harnessed to restorative ends. Declaring, 'Happie's that Prince, that ere he rules, shall know,/ Where the chief errors of his State doe grow' (1.3.117–18), Lorenzo positions himself within an illustrious tradition of rulers who mingle with their subjects in order to improve their political acumen.[43] His nobly motivated disguise enables him to confirm Iago's loyalty and trustworthiness and then to assess the political climate, which he characterises as 'sick'. Moreover, his disguise is essential to besting Misogynos, rescuing his sister from death and curing his father.

Lorenzo is forcefully contrasted to his father and the 'sick court' since he is invested with the curative powers of a physician. His salutary powers are directly invoked as he saves Lisandro from attempted suicide: 'I have a Balme/

---

[43] See Kevin A. Quarmby, *The Disguised Ruler in Shakespeare and his Contemporaries* (Farnham, 2012).

Of knowne experience, in effecting cures/ Almost impossible' (4.5.70–2), he reveals. In early modern medical practice the application of healing balms, herbs, tinctures or purgatives was but part of the doctor's skill-set. As noted above, doctors learned to return bodily equilibrium through diverse strategies including conversation and practical experiences. Accordingly, Lorenzo also works 'by eloquence [and] by policy' to 'save' lives and cure the court (5.3.177, 176). As previously noted, he stages the play that brings the king to recognise his errors and move towards repentance and mercy, and ultimately back to health. Lorenzo mitigates Atticus's extreme sorrow by excessive joy, which results in the establishment of balance: 'The current of my joy's so violent', Atticus exclaims, 'It does o'r-come my spirits' (5.3.86–7). Recovery of his lost son is configured in medical as well as emotional terms as Lorenzo's appearance acts as the medicinal joy that brings Atticus to humoural balance and to a state of repentant clarity. Lorenzo plays an instrumental role in the morality play and in the world of the play itself, operating as *deus ex machina*. Recalling the god Hymen, he orchestrates the marriage of Leonida and Lisandro and heals Atticus. Everyone genuflects in recognition of their obligation to him as 'our Patron, and our Fames Defender': this Doctor 'Masculine Feminine' (4.3.65) is the 'Happie' prince of Sicily (1.3.116).

The exemplary coexistence of mercy and justice in Lorenzo's character is mirrored in his presentation as a man dressed as a woman. Moreover, by disguising himself as an Amazon called Atlanta, a woman who exhibits traditionally male traits, his ability to blend male and female qualities is highlighted. The ideal ruler – perhaps even the ideal individual – is presented through this Amazonian figure who combines masculine power with a sympathetic understanding of the female plight: he is 'mystically both fully man and fully woman', an 'intellectual hermaphrodite [...] the all-sided human being'.[44] His status as a brave warrior and equitable ruler is not undermined by his female self-presentation; rather, his feminine state serves to emphasise his strengths. It is as the Amazon that he can save the lovers, teach the king to shun tyranny, expose Nicanor's hypocrisy, defeat Misogynos and establish a just, harmonious kingdom.

The presentation of Lorenzo as 'Masculine Feminine' (4.3.65) is part of the play's more global methodology of subverting the essentialist dichotomy of male and female and their attendant stereotypical character traits. In texts of the *querelle des femmes*, women are usually condemned as dissembling, disloyal, lascivious and vengeful. They are deemed to be corruptors of men and incapable of keeping secrets, and they are portrayed as shrews or scolds and as prone to shed crocodile tears.[45] In *Swetnam* the men are disguised dissemblers:

---

[44] Jordan, 'Gender', 151; Woodbridge, *Women*, p. 316.
[45] Cf. Woodbridge, *Women*, pp. 304ff.

Nicanor feigns love for Leonida and pretends to be loyal to the king, Swash is disloyal to Misogynos, and Scanfardo betrays Loretta. Although their motives are not morally suspect, Lisandro and Lorenzo also use disguise to deceive others: the former masquerades as a friar, while the latter impersonates, in turn, a commoner, an Amazon and a shepherd. Loretta also deceives her mistress, showing that betrayal and duplicity are common to both sexes. Lasciviousness is treated similarly, as Loretta, Scanfardo and Misogynos all exhibit the trait. Despite the stereotype that women corrupt men, and despite the outcome of the debate, Lisandro and Nicanor pursue Leonida, and Misogynos woos Lorenzo/Atlanta. Loretta cannot keep a secret, but neither can Scanfardo. Women may be vengeful, but so are the men. Women are usually accused of shedding false tears, but here Lorenzo/Atlanta denounces the 'Crocodile tears of base dissembling men' (3.3.104) and Nicanor sheds 'tears at command' (4.2.37). Misogynos claims that tyranny is rooted in women (3.3.205ff), but all the disorder in the play stems from male action. And when Misogynos mocks Lorenzo/Atlanta, stating, 'O doe not scold, good woman!' (3.3.214), the point that men can scold as well as women is manifestly made. As Woodbridge concludes, 'The playwright is very uneasy about generalizations on men's and women's "nature".'[46] This questioning of gender-specific traits is equally visible in texts of the Swetnam controversy, but while Munda and Sowernam (as Shepherd writes) ask 'why we talk of "male" and "female" virtues, why we make assumptions about the behaviour of genders, why we extrapolate from the biological into the social', *Swetnam* moves from theory to practice and fully exposes the irrationality underlying such assumptions.[47]

The most radical disruption of the rigid gender system that characterises the formal debate about women occurs through the depiction of Lorenzo/Atlanta's androgyny and Misogynos's opposing misogyny and his exaggerated shows of masculinity. Misogynos brags about his fencing abilities, only to be easily defeated by Lorenzo/Atlanta. He attacks women, and then falls in love with the 'Masculine Feminine' Amazon (4.3.65). The fact that he lusts after a man and cannot recognise sexual difference ridicules his displays of masculinity. He pretends to be a formidable lover, but needs alcohol to bolster his courage and virility before his encounter with Lorenzo/Atlanta.[48] Misogynos's misogyny is allied to his false bravado and his exaggerated displays of masculinity, all of which are presented as injurious to social, political, natural and divine order.

It is no accident that health is restored to the court by Iago, who 'has too much of woman' in him, and Lorenzo, who is branded 'A Masculine Feminine'

---

[46] Woodbridge, *Women*, p. 309.
[47] Shepherd, *Amazons*, p. 205.
[48] Several critics allude to the possibility that repressed homosexual feelings or a lack of success with women are at the root of his misogyny: Jordan, 'Gender', 163; Kidnie, '"Enter [...] Lorenzo"', 44; Woodbridge, *Women*, pp. 314–15.

(4.3.65). These men are not afraid of the female and are, in fact, happy to embrace attributes that are traditionally gendered female and to advocate for women. This idealisation of the blending of masculine and feminine replaces the antagonism of Leonida and Lisandro's trial, and the formal debate about women with a conciliatory, harmonious approach to interactions between the sexes. Misogyny is a politically damaging disease: the king's unbalanced humours lead to illness that manifests itself in unbalanced behaviour which infects the court, enabling the rise to power of similarly imbalanced, diseased individuals and ideologies; Atticus's aversion to female attributes such as pity and mercy is pathologised and categorised as dangerous. The debate between Misogynos and Lorenzo mirrors the political reality of the play in which feminine and masculine, women and men, are at odds. It also mirrors the contemporaneous political situation in which the debate about women thrived.

By invoking its sources repeatedly, *Swetnam* gestures outwards, positioning itself at the centre of an intertextual nexus that encompasses the works of the Swetnam controversy as well as the larger debate about women in which it and *Grisel* participated. This textual locus encourages a dialogical reading of the play because the relationships that exist between *Swetnam* and its sources place it at a vantage point from which it can survey, critique and surpass previous textual traditions; they imbue *Swetnam* with the ideological and methodological force to subvert the woman debate and the hierarchical and essentialist gender norms by which it is informed. *Swetnam* thus does more than borrow a racy plot from a medieval Spanish bestseller. The thickness of the play's allusions, which extend from *Grisel* through English adaptations of *Grisel* to texts of the Swetnam controversy and debates about women more generally, enables the drama to point beyond the theatre to subtly critique the antagonistic tenor of the contemporary *querelle des femmes* and to hint at King James's moral responsibility for the popularity of misogynist texts amongst his subjects.

While Jordan argues that the play's 'larger and more imposing purpose is to expose the basis of prejudicial opinions of women, the unexamined assumptions that sustain society', Wayne connects *Swetnam* more specifically to Jacobean politics.[49] Examining the play's title-page, Wayne notes that the women depicted wear the 'brode brimd hats [and] pointed dublets' singled out for condemnation by James.[50] She further observes that the woodcut of Swetnam/Misogynos even resembles contemporary likenesses of James and that of the judge recalls Elizabeth. Wayne therefore posits that the woodcut 'may also be read as a confrontation between the misogynist James and a revived Elizabeth I, who is surrounded by female supporters for the purpose of

---

[49] Jordan, 'Gender', 149.
[50] Wayne, 'Dearth', p. 235.

arraigning the king's retrograde attitudes towards women'.[51] Shepherd reads the play as a coded battle between James's and Elizabeth's modes of enacting justice.[52] Drawing on Barbara Kiefer Lewalski's analysis of the 'subversive entertainments' patronised by Queen Anne, Ton Hoenselaars connects Aurelia and Anne's 'oppositional activities'.[53] Like many other plays performed by the Queen's Servants at the Red Bull, *Swetnam* 'provided a site for contesting the gender ideology dominant in the King's court and on the public stage – serving, perhaps, as a kind of école *des femmes*, [...] offer[ing] a patently subversive royal example to Jacobean patriarchal culture'.[54] The play thus provides a cautionary tale. If misogyny is allowed to spread unchecked, social and political disaster will ensue. By combining medical and political theory, *Swetnam* pathologises misogyny and provides a meditation on how illnesses may be transmitted from the king's body to the body politic. Whereas scholars have interpreted early modern misogyny as a scholastic game or homosocial mode of male bonding, this play reveals the darker underside of such a discourse.[55] Misogyny is not a harmless mode of entertainment or a fun intellectual exercise; *Swetnam* establishes misogyny as a disease that, if left untreated, may lead to epidemic outbreaks of extreme civil disorder.

---

[51] Wayne, 'Dearth', p. 236.
[52] Shepherd, *Amazons*, p. 215.
[53] Ton Hoenselaars, 'Joseph Swetnam, alias Misogynos, and His Women Readers (1615–1620)', *L'Auteur et Son Public au Temps de la Renaissance*, ed. M.T. Jones-Davies (Paris, 1998), p. 182.
[54] Barbara Kiefer Lewalski, *Writing Women in Jacobean England* (Cambridge, MA, 1993), p. 43. Cf. J. Leeds Barroll, *Anna of Denmark, Queen of England: A Cultural Biography* (Philadelphia, 2001), p. 97. On the Red Bull's audience: Jones, 'From Polemical Prose', pp. 122–3; Andrew Gurr, *The Shakespearean Stage, 1574–1642* (Cambridge, 2009).
[55] See Woodbridge, *Women*; R. Howard Bloch, *Medieval Misogyny and the Invention of Western Romantic Love* (Chicago, 1991); Lorna Hutson, *The Usurer's Daughter: Male Friendship and Fictions of Women in Sixteenth-Century England* (London and New York, 1994); Jonathan Goldberg, *Queering the Renaissance* (Durham, NC, 1994).

The Monument of Uncertainty
Sovereign and Literary Authority in Samuel Sheppard's *The Faerie King*

ANDREW KING

Samuel Sheppard wrote his extended poem *The Faerie King* as a tragic-epic response to the events of the English Civil War – in particular the execution of Charles I – over a period of at least five years (c.1648–54). This was a time during which, in Sheppard's words, 'violent hands have made/ *England* a Den of *Dragons*'.[1] Much of the work was composed in prison, in particular Newgate Gaol – certainly a den, for Sheppard, of disease and despair, if not quite dragons. Sheppard writes: 'I languished (surrounded with Dolour, Indigencie, Obloquie with all their Appurtenances) almost fourteene months where my best musick was the ratling of cheines the gingling of Irons, and the groanes of men destind for destruction.'[2] Elsewhere in the poem Sheppard describes his prison writing context as a place both of literal hunger and of appetite for literary fame:

> I who scarce Injoy the common ayre
> who drinke the dreggs of Want and Penurie,
> feeding on FFeare, and followd by Despaire
> exhibit songs unto Posteritie
> so Ovid neere to Isther wrapt in woe
> made better musick then the Swans of Poe. (*FK*, V.ii.4)

Literature written in exile or incarceration – such as works by Ovid, Boethius, Malory, or indeed Wilde – often combines nuanced judgement and evaluation with emotional turbulence and anxiety, and *The Faerie King* is no exception. Arguably the most striking element in this work, which certainly deserves more attention than it has received, is the poem's richly ambivalent portrait of Charles I, depicted in the figure of Ariodant, first prince and then

---

[1] Samuel Sheppard, *Epigrams Theological, Philosophical, and Romantick* (London, 1651), V.29 (pp. 135–6). All further citations from *Epigrams* are from this edition. See also 'To the Reader', sig. A3r, in the same collection.
[2] Samuel Sheppard, *The Faerie King* (c.1650), ed. P.J. Klemp (Salzburg, 1984), 'Postscript', pp. 53–8. All further citations to *The Faerie King* (*FK*) are from this edition.

briefly the contested king of Ruina. It was Sheppard's unmitigated support for Charles and the institution of monarchy in the late 1640s, expressed through underground royalist newsbooks, that landed the writer in prison on more than one occasion.[3] In *Mercurius Dogmaticus*, for instance, Sheppard inveighs against Parliament for sanctioning the imprisonment of the king: 'Where is our Great and Glorious King, whose Throne they once boasted to elevate above all his Ancestors? Now we plainly perceive, that these were only faire pretences, Syrenicall Songs, to allure us to our ruine.'[4] In a poem that prefaces this same edition of *Mercurius Dogmaticus*, Sheppard exhorts the reader:

> Haste, haste, unto the ILE OF WIGHT,
> And Rescue CHARLES from Death;
> Will NONE commisserate his plight,
> And helpe prolong his BREATH?

And yet that biased, even propagandistic journalism offers no hint of the flawed and complex portrait of Charles that he would produce in *The Faerie King* – an image of a monarch who is far from 'Great and Glorious'. The nuanced nature of Sheppard's post-regicide portrayal of Charles is a fascinating achievement, and one of the main tasks of this essay is to examine in detail that deeply ambivalent representation of the late king within the poem. Although *The Faerie King* may seem at crucial moments to uphold the authority of monarchical government, whilst demonstrating the dangers of regicide and rebellion, the poem is simultaneously painfully aware of the difficulties created by an inept or tyrannical king.

The passages quoted above, where Sheppard offers a self-portrait of his act of writing in trying circumstances, illustrate how forcefully the poet puts his own poetic persona and career ambitions into the overall narrative of *The Faerie King*. The meta-poetic dimension of the work is insistent throughout, and Sheppard's strong projection of subjectivity makes a mirror of his historical context and narrative materials in relation to his own plight. In other words, in looking at the representation of Charles as an unworthy, if also nominally legitimate, inheritor of the throne, the reader is at all times implicitly invited to consider Sheppard as a figure parallel to Charles. Expressing both ambition and fear in relation to his own poetic legitimacy, Sheppard's concern is that he

---

[3] Sheppard's longest period of incarceration was from April 1649 until at least May 1650, and it was during this confinement that he is most likely to have written much of *The Faerie King*. See further: *CSPD, 1649–1650* (London, 1875), p. 529; *CSPD, 1650* (London, 1876), p. 143. See also Jason Peacey, '"The Counterfeit Silly Cut": Money, Politics, and the Forging of Royalist Newspapers during the English Civil War', *HLQ* 67.1 (2004), 27–57; Marcus Nevitt, 'Sing Heavenly News: Journalism and Poetic Authority in Samuel Sheppard's *The Faerie King* (c.1654)', *SP* 109 (2012), 496–518.

[4] *Mercurius Dogmaticus*, Number 4, 27 January–3 February, 1648, p. 26.

too may prove unworthy to wear a (poetic) crown, despite positioning himself carefully as the heir in a complex and protracted literary dynasty with Edmund Spenser at its head. Sheppard writes to himself, in 1651, in his *Epigrams*: 'And thy new *Faerie* King shall with Queen,/ When thou art dead, still flourish ever green' (IV.28 (p. 95)). In calling his poem *The Faerie King*, Sheppard has obviously signalled or presumed a relationship both with Spenser and the Spenserian tradition and with the reception history that has intervened.[5] In many ways, that reception history makes Sheppard's use of Spenser seemingly inappropriate. David Norbrook has investigated how poets such as George Wither, William Browne, Ralph Knevett, Samuel Daniel, and Giles and Phineas Fletcher had used Spenser's pastoral poetry in particular to counter the pro-Spanish and Catholic tendencies of the Stuart courts: 'In the 1620s [...] the Spenserians frequently found themselves in opposition to royal policy. Spenser was for them a symbol of the poet's proud independence of the court.'[6] Because of the ambivalence with which Sheppard depicts Charles in *The Faerie King*, the poem partly draws upon ways that will reflect Sheppard's fundamental horror at the regicide. But however tangled this poetic family history may be, Sheppard's title proclaims an act of inheritance, placing his poem in an extended genealogical relation to Spenser's well-known poem. And the fact that it is a 'king' that inherits from a 'queen' means that this *literary* descent is inextricably linked to a *political*, specifically royal descent: the inheritance of King Charles from Elizabeth I (conveniently leaving James I to one side).

Poetry and politics co-inhabit this poem in a very specific way, and the poem's structure is built out of this large-scale analogy: the politically troubled heir Charles/Ariodant and the anxious poetic heir Sheppard. But the analogy is not perfectly parallel, and the two lines can both diverge and intertwine. Not surprisingly, crucial moments in the poem focused on the precise nature of Charles/Ariodant's failings as a ruler tend to be strongly intertextual in relation to Spenser's *Faerie Queene*. Even as Sheppard seems to be 'overgoing' Spenser in his rehandling of a key Spenserian scene, adroitly adapting its meaning to what he calls 'this transposed world' (*FK*, 'Postscript', p. 141), so this act of seemingly legitimate succession is undercut by the other parts of the analogy: the depiction in Ariodant of an unwise and incompetent successor. The varied and iconic senses of Spenser's text by the mid-seventeenth century make Sheppard's act of inheritance at once more glorious and more fraught. The poetic genealogy in which he hopes to situate himself has entertained numerous pretenders and power struggles over the decades since Spenser's death.

---

[5] See Michelle O'Callaghan, *'The Shepheards Nation': Jacobean Spenserians and Early Stuart Political Culture, 1612–1625* (Oxford, 2000).

[6] David Norbrook, *Poetry and Politics in the English Renaissance*, rev edn. (Oxford, 2002), p. 222.

Sheppard has placed himself in a literary court that is every bit as factional and unstable as that of the Stuarts. Every act that Sheppard makes to demonstrate his identity as Spenser's descendant has the potential to out him, instead, as a figure closer to the failed heir, Charles. The self-destructive potential of the poem's central analogy is not lost on Sheppard. He is banking his career and reputation on a poem written about Charles following his execution. So in a real sense, Charles's authority and reputation are nervously and irrevocably linked in the poem to Sheppard's own potential literary prestige. The narrator addresses Charles at the outset:

> thy name (Illustrious Prince) shall here subsist
> better then were the Memphian Trophies thine
> in spight of darke oblivions hyding mist
> thine bee the lustre, though the labour mine
> Let Beasts, and Bedlamers, belch as they list
> the Sun of thy cleere fame shall ever shine
> in this faire firmament drawn by my hand
> not fearing Momus bite, or Pasquills brand. (*FK*, Proem.7)

Here, the interactions and interrelations of the two heirs and would-be figures of authority – Sheppard and Charles – are particularly intricate: Charles brings the 'lustre', though Sheppard the 'labour'; Charles's 'fame shall ever shine', but that fame is 'drawn by my hand'. Agency is difficult to determine; Sheppard's poem may be, as he describes it, 'my everlasting Tombe' (Proem.2), but it is also a monument to Charles. Indeed, they seem to occupy the same grave, and Sheppard's strategy ensures that posthumous regard for Charles's authority is linked with the reading of his poem, the monument to the dead king.[7] What must lurk in the shadows, however, is fearful expectation of a 'poeticide': the completion of the analogy, achieved through the 'death' by unreading of Sheppard's poetic endeavours. Sheppard notes that Spenser's poetic authority was challenged by some, and finds little hope for himself in this:

> if *Spencer* could not scape the spite
> Of tougues [sic] malevolent [...]
> I then shall (sure) be bitt to death. (*Epigrams*, IV.10 (pp. 78–9))

Attention now turns to the poem's intriguingly ambivalent depiction of Charles/Ariodant, though the sense of Charles as an avatar for Sheppard is also insistently, if subliminally, present. Later, this essay will explore the workings

---

[7] See also *FK*, V.vi.74, where a catalogue of authors (including Spenser) who constitute the House of Eloquence culminates in Charles. The king is firmly placed in the context of a literary 'royal family', enforcing the analogy between royal and literary authority and descent at the heart of the poem.

of the central analogy as well as the poem's self-reflexiveness in greater detail. The forceful direction of the poem is not merely tragic but gesturing towards complete meaninglessness in relation to human experience. No great and 'providential' narratives are possible. Arguably, the unfinished *Faerie Queene* is moving in this direction; however, in Sheppard's work, the experience of loss – in every possible sense – is certainly more intense.

'Boundlesse Soveraignty': Ariodant, Charles, and Misguided Rule

In his complex journalistic activities, Sheppard was associated with the royalist newsbook *Mercurius Pragmaticus*, amongst others, and he may even have had some part in its description here of the impact of the regicide:

> Beware the building, for the *Foundation* is taken away, the windes begin to blow, and the waves to beate, the Restlesse *Arke* is toss'd; none but uncleane Beasts are entred into her, the *Dove* will not returne, neither will the *Olive Branch* appear. The *Axe* is laid to the *Root*, even of the *Royal Cedar*, then what can the Inferior *Tree* expect but to be crush'd and bruis'd in His fall, and afterwards hewn down and cast into the fire.[8]

The imagery in this passage of the old covenant, now sundered in the murder of the king, implicitly identifies the monarch as an instrument of divine order. Charles's authority here is clearly absolute, and the passage leaves no room for ambivalence or complexity. Turning to the first appearance of Ariodant (which is also the first representation of Charles in *The Faerie King*), however, we find not the unjustly felled '*Royal Cedar*', but rather the young prince positioned in a grove that recalls at once Spenser's Wood of Error, the opening episode of Book I of *The Faerie Queene*. Near Prince Ariodant's palace stood

> a pleasant GROVE, another TEMPE rare,
> an EDEN spared by OGYGES flood
> the POPLAR, and the gummie CEDAR, here
> mixt branches (about whom the DRYADS scud)
> the mastfull OAKE, the MAPLE and the FIRRE,
> the BOX, the ALDAR, OSYER and the WILLOW
> the HOLME, and ELME, whose Root's SYLVANUS pillow. (*FK*, 1.i.4)

The description of this grove as Edenic is carefully disingenuous: that this is a fallen rather than a 'spared' Eden must emerge from the outset through the

---

[8] *Mercurius Pragmaticus*, Number 43, 30 January–6 February, 1649, *Making the News*, ed. Joad Raymond (Moreton-in-the-Marsh, 1993), p. 249. On Sheppard's association with this newsweekly, see Sheppard, ed. Klemp, p. iv. See also *Metropolitan Nuncio*, Number 3, 6–13 June 1649, sig. C1v. On royalist writing in response to Charles's death: Robert Wilcher, *The Writing of Royalism 1628–1660* (Cambridge, 2001), pp. 287–307.

pressures created by the scene's Spenserian ancestry. Sheppard's tree-catalogue continues for another seven stanzas, and this scene's intertextual relation with Spenser's Wood of Error is firmly established in the mind of the reader through these promptings that it supplies.[9] Furthermore, since this is the grove where Paris made a judgement that culminated in 'so renowned strife [that]/ lost him all ASIA' (*FQ*, I.i.11), it has an intrinsic claim, in addition to the Spenserian palimpsest, to being a place of monumental error. Paris's position 'in state being set/ with censuring eyes' (*FQ*, I.i.11) sounds distinctly monarchical. And the destruction of Troy always carried a special threat to early modern British readers, whose imagined capital is Troynovant. Again, the darker resonance here is sounded in Spenser's text, where Paridell's flippant, half-remembered account of the sacking of Troy poses a severe challenge to Britomart's solemn assertion of her own providential quest. The fact that Ariodant makes his first appearance in such a redolent garden – positioned there from the start and not merely wandering in – is ominous. From the outset, the young prince's authority and judgement are highly suspect.

It is not just Prince Ariodant, though, who is emerging as ambivalent and thus a difficult, if compelling, subject for judgement. The wood, too, is a chiaroscuro landscape – a place that clearly requires a response, though it is challenging to see what that response should be. This wood, more than Spenser's, seems dangerously attractive, at least to the sybaritic imagination:

> the deinte APRICOCK, and astringent PEARE
> the downy QUINCE, the ORANGE (JOVES delight)
> the milkie FIG the Filbeard, Medeler
> the OLIVE, that Incends the Appetite
> the APPLE (dedicate to CUPIDS care)
> whose cheekes CYDIPPE painted red and white
> here the fine Pepper, and the Cinimon
> there dangling Nutmegs, in faire clusters hung. (*FK*, I.i.5)

As in Sir Epicure Mammon's great speeches, fetishistic cravings for food barely conceal sexual longing. Opening with the 'APRICOCK' and closing with the 'dangling Nutmegs', the stanza is genitally framed – and Cupid and 'Appetite' are in its midst. Ariodant appears to be enmeshed in a world committed to the appetites and senses – a far less stable proposition than order based on reason, rule, and dialectic. However, this wood also contains possible remedies, if the young prince could read his own context effectively:

---

[9] Cf. Spenser, *Faerie Queene*, I.i.8–9. All citations of Spenser's poem are from A.C. Hamilton's edition (abbreviated *FQ*).

> here grew those sacred SIMPLES, by whose Ayde
> beardlesse APOLLO'S son, re-joynd the bones
> of chaste HYPPOLLITUS; wee doe evade
> by you, yee plants, various Destructions
> and were your severall Virtues obvious made
> to our dull sense (your full perfections)
> Man might two hundred yeares avoyd Deaths stroke
> and have no cause to quarrell with the Oake. (*FK*, I.i.7)

The 'quarrell with the Oake' takes us from the king of trees to the king himself. Sheppard's wood embodies not merely an individual's experience of error, but the possibilities of large-scale error engulfing the nation. At the same time, the wood also holds within it the possible, if still latent, remedies against social revolution and anarchy, the destructive 'quarrell with the Oake'. Sheppard's wood is arguably more subtle, or at least ambivalent, than Spenser's; it demands from its inhabitants as well as readers a rare combination of heightened moral alertness and pragmatic response, rather than simply revulsion and escape.[10] A plant that kills in one instance may cure in another:

> here grew that Herbe, which nourishes the Asse
> but kills the Oxe, wth Oleander, that
> to Beasts is poison, but to man ere was
> a counter-poyson, thwarting his dire Fate. (*FK*, I.1.9)

Moral worth is not fixed or intrinsic, therefore, but the utility of any element depends upon the context to which it is applied. This is a rather more scientific grove than Spenser's, as befits a work from the mid-seventeenth century. And this testing, pragmatic, and experimental attitude is clearly what is needed to negotiate this context successfully. Indeed, this is not after all a wood from which to escape (unlike Spenser's) but rather one in which to seek to live profitably and astutely, so long as one can read it correctly. It is, in fact, the court, and despite all of its poison, it also embodies the potential for human and even heavenly grace:

> Saffron that wrapt about the head expells
> those fumes that BACCHUS sends up to the braine
> arming the SOULE, against all SYRENS Spells[;]
> ANGELLICA, that happy counter-bane
> sent down from Heaven, to worke miracles
> 'mongst mortalls, which into [t]he mouth being tane

---

[10] On the pragmatic goals of early modern reading strategies: Kevin Sharpe, *Reading Revolutions: The Politics of Reading in Early Modern England* (New Haven, CT, 2000), p. 87.

resists the Pestilence; the MADDER too
(that touch'd workes inward) 'mongst these rare herbs grew. (*FK*, I.1.10)

'Angellica', the heavenly messenger, recalls Spenser's Una, whose message of faith saves Redcrosse at his most calamitous moment with Error (*FQ*, I.i.19). Indeed, the 'counter-bane' that Una offers Redcrosse – 'Add faith vnto your force, and be not faint' – allows the knight to throttle Error, causing the monster to vomit:

Her vomit full of books and papers was,
With loathly frogs and toades, which eyes did lack,
And creeping sought way in the weedy gras:
Her filthie parbreake all the place defiled has. (*FQ*, I.i.20)

Sheppard's Angellica, 'which into [the] mouth being tane/ resists the Pestilence', is very specifically, and textually, 'counter'. In Sheppard's rewriting, 'Una' becomes embodied in the grove itself, and Sheppard's wood emerges as more complex and ambivalent than Spenser's, instead of wholly insidious.

The reader first views Ariodant in this redolent setting, and the possibility that error is an appropriate context for him – even one generated by his own mindset – is forceful. From the outset, Ariodant embodies the assumption of an absolute authority: a personal style that seems worthy of the most godlike of Roman emperors:

where ere this Rosey-lipt ADONIS treads
the common people of the Feild, agree
to kisse his feete, bowing their verdant heads
as homage to their Sylvan Deitie.
a civill warre upon their fragrant beds
they manage; which shall first obsequiously
present a gift. (*FK*, I.i.16)

The obsequious attentions of his followers do not so much confirm an authority based on royal descent but rather lead one to question its legitimacy – or, at least, to raise anxiety regarding the sycophantic nature of Ariodant's courtiers.[11] The 'civill warre' (line 14) in this extract hints at more than friendly jostling, and the ineluctable sway of this passage is that the particular style of Caroline kingship, exemplified here in Ariodant, encouraged a factious and insincere court. The sense of ritual in this passage – 'bowing their

---

[11] In *God and Mammon* (1646) and *The Yeare of Jubile* (1646), Sheppard represents Charles as a man of essentially good character, but surrounded by corrupt and ineffectual counsellors. Overall, this earlier work supports Fairfax, Cromwell, and Parliamentarian reforms – a position that became untenable for Sheppard after the incarceration of the king later in 1646.

verdant heads', whilst the 'fragrant beds' suggest church incense – resonates not only with the style of royal absolutism but also with the liturgical conservatism of the Arminian-Laudian theology associated with Charles and his court.[12] The illegitimacy of those rituals, from a Puritan perspective, is relevant considering that the 'Sylvan Deitie' worshipped here invokes the terminology of a false, pagan god. Sheppard's scene prompts recollection of Sylvanus and the other satyrs worshipping Una in Book I of *The Faerie Queene*, in a context where true and false religion are at the forefront; the satyrs 'worshipt her in vaine,/ And made her th'Image of Idolatryes' (*FQ*, I.vi.19). 'Image' here relates to Archimago throughout Book I, the capacity of the mind to deceive through false and beguiling mental pictures. Unlike Una, Ariodant does nothing to discourage this idolatry – this dangerously deceptive image of his own authority as god-like. Indeed, Ariodant is able, consciously or not, to generate the same compelling but misleading images created by Archimago. The eroticism of Ariodant's description here recalls Archimago's ability to create a false image of a sexually treacherous Una, 'In wanton lust and leud embracement' with a fabricated 'squire' (*FQ*, I.ii.5). Spenser's narrative of true and false holiness uses sexuality to indicate the powerful and dangerous attractions of pride; erotic attraction, as an allegory, tells the reader just how desirable and 'sexy' chivalric fame is to Redcrosse. For Sheppard, monarchical power, performed as something absolute, has the same intoxicating 'sex appeal'. In Ariodant's case, the erotic chemistry exists between the body of the young prince, 'this Rosey-lipt ADONIS', and the bower in which he is positioned, which is his courtly context. The grass 'about his body skip[s]', trying to 'taste his tempting lip' (*FK*, I.i.15). Acanthus, ivy, and vines quarrel as they all attempt 'to Intwine/ his waste, and kisse his locks' (*FK*, I.i.17). But the sense of orgy is undermined by worrying signs. 'Waste' offers a telling orthographical pun. Furthermore, 'locks', along with entwining vines, invoke subliminally the sense of the court as a prison – and Ariodant as its chief occupant; this society is captivating in the worst sense. That Ariodant's relationship with his context should be described in terms of the sexually predatory, depleting, and incarcerating seems particularly worrying in relation to his supposed control (or lack of) of that context. The narrator's outburst – 'O happy state' (I.i.18) – is deeply ironic, and Sheppard's grove seems remarkably prescient of Milton's Eden – though its ripening danger, conveyed through its literary allusiveness, is stronger.[13]

Crucially, this new Wood of Error is not simply where we first see Ariodant;

---

[12] See Nicholas Tyacke, 'Puritanism, Arminianism and Counter-Revolution', *The Origins of the English Civil War*, ed. Conrad Russell (London, 1973), p. 132.

[13] Cf. John Milton, *Paradise Lost*, ed. Alastair Fowler, 2nd edn. (Harlow, 1998), IV.773-5: 'Sleep on/ Blest pair; and O yet happiest if ye seek/ No happier state, and know to know no more'.

it is the very place and condition in which royal authority passes to him, for it is here that he learns that his father Fulgoran has died and left him the crown. Self-discovery for this new 'Redcrosse' does not occur on the Mount of Contemplation but rather emerges prematurely whilst he is still in something like the Wood of Error – with predictably disastrous results. Indeed, Spenserian pride and ambition, such as Redcrosse displays throughout much of Book I, are dangerously present in Ariodant: just prior to receiving news of his father's death, Ariodant was dreaming of sovereign rule (I.i.18). His desire seems to prompt his accession – an image of strong ambition with a barely latent suggestion of regicide, willing his father's death to enable his own succession. Like Macbeth, who envisages a dagger and then uses it, Ariodant is hungry for 'Power, and boundlesse Soveraignty' (*FK*, I.i.18); Papillio, an evil counsellor, used this same phrase, 'a boundlesse Soveraigntie' (*FK*, I.i.36), shortly after this scene, urging its attractions to Ariodant. The intensity and barely suppressed violence of his desire for succession challenge the reader's sense of its legitimacy. Despite Ariodant's legitimate inheritance from Fulgoran, the former's death, in conjunction with the latter's dream, has more than a whiff of 'murder [...] fantastical'.[14]

Ariodant is seated amidst counsellors who collectively replicate the ambivalence of the surrounding plants and trees: some offer verbal medicine, and some poison.[15] Sheppard emphasises the notion of Ariodant as an ineffectual reader of his neo-Spenserian context through a particular surprise that highlights his failure. Papillio, the bad counsellor, discusses politics and kingship as merely theatrical illusions, without moral substance, which the practitioner must employ to keep his subjects in awe. He assures Ariodant that 'the common people never see behind/ the curtaine' (*FK*, I.i.31); the sovereign should use religion as 'your cloake or crutch' (*FK*, I.i.31). The subjects are simply a means for the monarch to maintain his own power, 'like Tooles to the Mechanick' (*FK*, I.i.32), without regard to the morality of the means. The goal of monarchy is the sovereign's self-aggrandisement:

> in the worlds ETHICKS, prosperous mischeifs; still
> are Cardinall Virtues; if successe doe crowne
> your undertakings, though the worst of ill
> accomplish it; tis Glory and Renowne
> CONQUEST CONCEALES ALL GUILT; wee praise his skill
> who made so many Nations his owne. (*FK*, I.i.36)

---

[14] *Macbeth*, I.iii.138, in William Shakespeare, *The Complete Works*, ed. Stanley Wells and Gary Taylor, 2nd edn. (Oxford, 2005).

[15] Joad Raymond, 'Popular Representations of Charles I', *The Royal Image: Representations of Charles I*, ed. Thomas N. Corns (Cambridge, 1999), pp. 50–1, discusses the popular perception of Charles surrounded by bad counsellors.

Ariodant's response is interestingly measured:

> hee thanks PAPILLIO for
> his counsell, yet seemes not in every thing
> t'approve his Maximes, yea; hee does abhorre
> some parcells of his speech, as opening
> a gap to hydeous fraud, and unjust warre. (*FK*, I.i.38)

Ariodant clearly reads Papillio critically, though stops short of openly rejecting him. Indeed, in his seeming gratitude Ariodant offers here a political performance of expediency and dissimulation in the spirit of what Papillio urges, hiding his deepest thoughts and fears 'behind/ the curtaine' (*FK*, I.i.31). Later, the good counsellor, Allicandro, speaks, strongly attacking the excessive luxury and indulgence of the court; at this point, Sheppard engineers his surprise strategy. Ariodant makes no response to Allicandro's urging that princes should eschew their power 'as the meane and way/ to offer wrong, and open Violence' (*FK*, I.ii.14) or 'to stuffe his Treasurie/ [for] BANQUETS and WEOMAN, CALIDONIAN wine' (*FK*, I.ii.16). However, when the aptly named Hotspurio opposes Allicandro's speech, urging the flexing of sovereign muscle in war against the murderers of the late king, Ariodant interrupts Hotspurio's speech in fury:

> the King
> repleat with wrath, gnashing his teeth for yre
> broke off his Speech, thus (harshly) answering
> and can it bee (S^r) that you dare desire,
> (you whom I thought so Just in every thing)
> for him who caused my father to Ex[p]ire
> our Gaurd ceaze on him and convey him hence
> to Prison, till yt wee command him thence. (*FK*, I.iii.6)

The shock for the reader is to discover in the next stanza that Ariodant is condemning here not Hotspurio, but rather the good counsellor, Allicandro. Ariodant's rage has been simmering, and its sudden eruption here, involving the reader's initial misunderstanding of the target of his wrath, must provoke for the reader startled confusion at how Ariodant could be so patently wrong in his judgements. The reader's surprise recreates the experience of being within a court under volatile and erratic rule. Whatever his birthright, Ariodant here must relinquish some authority in the startled reader's eyes. Speaking in Parliament in November 1642, Sir John Evelyn depicted King Charles as duplicitous, promising Parliament he will negotiate in order to stop the war whilst intending nothing of the kind. Parliament, Evelyn said, was placated, 'thinking his Majesties heart had gone alongst with his expression, but it seems it was the least of his thoughts'.[16] James I wrote of the king as a 'speaking lawe',[17] fundamentally unassailable in his authority whatever his actions. Yet earlier in *The Faerie King*, during the funeral of King Fulgoran, the narrator meditated, Hamlet-like, on 'that Tongue the Wormes will dare to gnaw/ which once gave Oracles, was his Peoples law' (I.ii.2). Recognition of mortality and the inevitable corruption of the royal tongue hint at the fallibility of that 'speaking lawe'. Ariodant's actions here further justify that sense of royal fallibility.

Sheppard's work continues to offer moments such as this, where the reader is caught off balance in a seemingly invited reaction to a political situation, in particular in relation to sovereign authority, only to find the support of the narrative withdrawn. Reading *The Faerie King* offers an experience not dissimilar to living in what Sheppard calls 'these tumultuous times' (*FK*, 'Postscript', 133): disorienting, subtle, and necessitating frequent and rapid shifts of thought and strategy. As another instance, when, because of the misery of the war and the king's erratic manner of rule, Ariodant's troops mutiny, the reader might feel prepared to sanction their debunking of the sanctity of kingship:

> lies it in kings to cause such harme and scathe
> to those that are the Bulwarks of their state[?]
> doth not the law of Nature each man bind
> all wayes of safety for himselfe to find[?] (*FK*, III.vi.6)

The rebels echo the muscular language of Leveller tracts of the 1640s.[18] The 'Communist' Giant in Book V of *The Faerie Queene* similarly argued for the destruction of absolute monarchy: 'Tyrants that make men subject to their law,/ I will suppresse, that they no more may raine;/ And Lordings curbe, that commons over-aw' (*FQ*, V.ii.38). This episode was reprinted in 1648, with materials highlighting its topical significance, under the title *The Faerie Leveller*: the work's 'Preface' praises 'the Prince of English Poets Edmund *Spenser*, whose verses then propheticall are now become historicall in our dayes'.[19] This prefatory material imposes a crude historical allegory onto the scene, equating Artegall with a righteous Charles and the Giant with Cromwell, who is compared to 'the Traytor *Judas*'.[20] The preface fails to read into Spenser's scene the irony and tension that has been highlighted in much critical work over the last

---

[16] Raymond, ed., *Making*, p. 78.
[17] [James I and VI], *The True Lawe of Free Monarchies* (London, 1603), sig. D1r.
[18] See, for example, *Mercurius Militaris or The Armies Scout*, Number 2, 10–17 October, 1648, in Raymond, ed., *Making*, p. 178. Also rejecting the divine nature of kings is *The Moderate*, Number 11, 19–26 September, 1648: Raymond, ed., *Making*, p. 210. After the king's execution, the royalist writer John Quarles voiced the Leveller arguments, adopting the rhetorical posture of devil's advocate, in terms similar to Sheppard's rebels: John Quarles, *Regale Lectum Miseriae: or, a Kingly Bed of Misery* (London, 1649), pp. 5–6.
[19] [Anon.], *The Faerie Leveller* (London, 1648), sig. A2r.
[20] *Faerie Leveller*, sig. A2v.

few decades. And, if its author happens to be Sheppard, then this unmitigated support for Charles would be consistent with his writings in the late 1640s. However, Artegall's opposition to the Giant is arguably problematic, especially given that the Giant's justification for his levelling – 'Seest not, how badly all things present bee,/ And each estate quite out of order goth?' (*FQ*, V.ii.37) – concurs with the narrator's observation in the Proem to Book V that 'the world is runne quite out of square,/ From the first point of his appointed sourse' and that the heavenly constellations, influencing humankind, 'all range, and doe at randon rove/ Out of ther proper places farre away' (*FQ*, V.Proem.1, 6). If Sheppard (or some other) fails to recognise this complexity in 1648 in *The Faerie Leveller*, he is prepared to create a scene in *The Faerie King* that goes even further than Spenser in its depiction of troubled, but nevertheless persistent, sovereign authority.

The scene occurs when Ariodant's rebellious troops release Allicandro from prison and seek to make him their new king. Allicandro is the virtuous counsellor whom Ariodant previously imprisoned for his excessive honesty and uncompromising morality, and the reader might now expect Allicandro to become a republican figure, leading the revolt against the tyranny of kings. Indeed, Allicandro may seem to have anticipated the rebels' position when he told Ariodant earlier that kings are not above the law:

> the GODS doe not Dispense
> their Power to Princes, as the meane and way
> to offer wrong, and open Violence
> or yet in Revelling to spend the day
> the Night in Active Sweats. (*FK*, I.ii.14)

Nevertheless, Allicandro condemns utterly the rebels' attack upon the hereditary authority of kingship:

> what Devill prompts you Allicandro cries
> to these Irregularre Acts [...]
> repent ye Villaines e'r it bee too late
> and your good Prince his pardon supplicate. (*FK*, III.vi.13)

Allicandro's urging support for a king who does not seem worthy of his inherited position tells us much about the text's complex attitude towards sovereignty. Thomas Hobbes's notion of the sovereign as the instituted body comprised of the subjects' wills is perhaps too ingenious and sophisticated a piece of reasoning for this emotive moment in the text. In Hobbes's view, 'every Subject is by this Institution Author of all the Actions, and Judgments of the Soveraigne Institution'.[21] Accordingly, 'it followes, that whatsoever he [the sovereign] doth,

---

[21] Thomas Hobbes, *Leviathan*, ed. C.B. Macpherson (London, 1968), p. 232.

it can be no injury to any of this Subjects; nor ought he to be by any of them accused of Injustice'.²² But Sheppard's poem is too painfully aware of the failings of Ariodant – his inability to embody the wills of his subjects (such as the rebels here), and the suffering that his ambition and ineptitude convey upon a people. Interestingly, when Despaire persuades Ariodant to take his own life, he reminds the king: 'remember how thy Subjects did Rebell/ and spight of thee, freed ALLICANDRO too' (*FK*, IV.vi.68). Allicandro's plea to respect Ariodant's sovereignty at precisely this moment, despite the monarch's incompetence and tyranny, is surely a more desperate stand – one that can also be found in Hobbes, albeit wrested out of the larger context: whatever one might think about a tyranny, it is preferable to 'the miseries, and horrible calamities, that accompany a Civill Warre'.²³ Only in that context, made vivid as the aptly named kingdom of Ruina moves further towards apocalypse, is some sort of sovereign rule necessary. Later in the text, Ariodant himself will meditate ambiguously on the nature of sovereignty:

> why [...] are wee plac'd hie
> gaz'd at like Comets, by the vulgarre sort
> why doe all knees, bow to our Soveraigntie
> why doe wee drinke in Gold, on purple sport
> why are all Beasts, Fish, and the Fowls that flie
> serv'd up to us, and why doth FAME report
> our Acts to bee the GODS, but that above
> others, in us, Valour should live and move. (*FK*, IV.v.21)

Ariodant's intention is ultimately delivered, through a syntactically difficult and delayed meaning, in the final two lines: the series of phrases beginning 'why' were not actually questions but 'proofs' advanced to testify to his greater valour. Why else would a king have all these things, if it were not for the reason that he is more valorous? But the language works subversively, escaping the authority and control of Ariodant – in a linguistic version of the rebellious subjects just witnessed. What makes the strongest impression is the run of what appear to be genuinely interrogative challenges: why indeed should kingship enjoy these privileges? As the rebels say, 'what power is that this fond King claimes?' The answer can only be: the power to hold at bay a worse form of anarchy.

Ariodant dies in Book IV, and the character who chiefly carries the work's interest through the next two Books to the end is Olivia, a martial/marital maiden in the mode of Spenser's Britomart. Like Britomart, Olivia is dressed in male armour, and her role is to further the genealogical aspect of the epic

---

[22] Hobbes, *Leviathan*, p. 232.
[23] Hobbes, *Leviathan*, p. 238.

through marriage with Byanor. The first of two hermits who instruct the still pagan Olivia in the Christian faith says to her:

> Jove in his etern Decree
> has voted thou shallt know Christianitie
> but first thou to a Duke shallt married bee. (*FK*, III.ii.14)[24]

Despite the poem's invocation of this providential narrative, however, *The Faerie King* moves remorselessly towards tragic closure. The ending of *The Faerie King* presents a landscape that erupts with unjust and random acts of violence, comparable to the destruction of the shepherds' dwelling in Book VI of Spenser's poem (VI.x.39–44). Sheppard's world offers, especially towards its end, an even stronger sense of discrepancy between the providentially shaped patterns that should characterise the epic-romance mode and an actual narrative world that is 'runne quite out of square' (*FQ*, V.Proem.1). Recalling Merlin's prophetic mirror used by Britomart in Book III of *The Faerie Queene*, Sheppard has Olivia and Byanor look into a similar magic mirror; unlike Britomart, they see not their progeny – significantly, they are never promised any – but rather the violence and underlying greed of the Civil War. Winter has come to faerie land:

> they saw in all the struglings and dire Jarres
> that happen to this corner of the Ball
> (our present cruell, and unaturall Warres)
> though the pretence be fine and Spirituall,
> yet the true scope, the occasion of these cares
> is gold and greatnesse. (*FK*, V.v.8)

The death of Ariodant in Book IV is not climactic. Sheppard may be echoing a sense, contained in some of the royalist newsbooks, that the great event is not so much the death of the king but the repercussions that will follow. The death of Ariodant's widow, Olympia, in Book VI brings us closer to a sense of climax – of tragedy gathered and compounded. Olympia is imprisoned by a Busirane/Archimago-type enchanter, Magorto. After being raped by the enchanter (*FK*, IV.iv.33–5), Olympia escapes from him only to fall into the hands of a 'savage crew' in a forest. The scene echoes Serena's near destruction by cannibals in Book VI of *The Faerie Queene*, but with a crucial difference, highlighting Sheppard's strategic relationship to Spenser. Serena is rescued by Calepine, who finds her 'by chaunce' (*FQ*, VI.viii.46); Spenser does not obviously attribute Calepine's presence to providence, although he does allow a moral victory. When the savage crew are about to rape Olympia, Byanor is led to the scene 'by

---

[24] Cf. Merlin's words to Britomart concerning her vision of Artegall in a magic mirror (*FQ*, III.iii.24).

the will of Providence' (*FK*, VI.v.4); although he kills the attackers, he is too late to save Olympia, whom the crew kill in Byanor's ineffectual presence: 'thinking Olympia was Byanors wife/ with many wounds they first doe take her life' (*FK*, VI.v.9). Authority seems to have suffered on several counts. The authority of providence seems problematic or at best inscrutable, and the authority of royalty (here embodied in Olympia, widow of the king) also disappoints.

There is another failed authority here, however, and it is one that moves us towards the second part of my essay, with its focus on Sheppard's self-representation and his authorial anxiety in the wake of the Spenserian tradition. The invocation of the Spenserian scene and the explicit reference to the operations of providence seeking Olympia's rescue evoke for the reader expectations of a certain kind of narrative closure. When events go so shockingly wrong, it can feel as if the author has lost control of his text, lost authority. In particular, Sheppard, or his poetic persona, has failed to deliver the kind of Spenserian providential outcome (in this scene's prototype in *The Faerie Queene*) that we might reasonably expect. But 'reason' is an increasingly devalued currency in this world. Olivia expresses, at the death of Olympia, a deep sense of futility and bafflement:

> vaine, quoth the champion, vaine is our Remorse [...]
> all our contracted Dolour can't Incline
> thee too too partiall Destenies to give
> the world such blisse that shee may once more live. (*FK*, VI.v.16)

Olivia's frustration doubtless finds a counterpart in any sympathetic reader's reactions. The narrator describes Olympia's funeral as 'triviall, emptie, formlesse Exequies' (*FK*, VI.v.17) – a very different kind of funerary experience from Sheppard's initial ambitious vision of the poem as an 'everlasting Tombe' securing him a 'deathlesse date' (*FK*, Proem.2–3). Given Sheppard's tendency to relate poems to funerary monuments (a point that will be developed below), the denigration of Olympia's funeral rites threatens to undermine the poem's own achievement and substance. Of course, this 'failure' is a deliberate and intriguing artistic feature of the poem, and to understand it we must consider the extent to which Sheppard sees in Ariodant/Charles a mirror for his own condition.

Political and Poetic Authority: A Cracked Mirror

The preceding discussion of the poem's response to the regicide and Civil War has been barely able to suppress the intensity of the poet's self-reflexiveness in dealing with these events. If the reader has felt this pressure and possibly anticipated how Sheppard sees in powerful and exact terms a mirror, in the figure of Charles, of his own ambition and potential tragedy, then this essay has replicated the tension that both animates and threatens to break *The Faerie*

King. Sheppard's Spenserianism is not simply a following in the wake of a tradition. Rather, it is the literary analogy or mirror to the poem's politics: on both poetic and political levels, *The Faerie King* is anxiously parading an heir (Charles/Ariodant, as well as the poet/Sheppard) who may be unworthy or incapable of inheriting the previous generation's crown, despite all the outward signs of legitimate inheritance. The possibility of seeing Sheppard reflected in Charles/Ariodant – of comparing poetic and political authority – is strengthened by the poem's presentation of Charles himself as a literary figure. In an extended scene, Olivia and Bryanor tour 'the Sacred HOUSE OF ELOQUENCE' (*FK*, V.vi). A catalogue of writers and poets follows, starting with Old Testament figures such as David, through classical writers, Italian, French, and English (where Spenser, 'whome I doe thinke't no shame to Immitate' (*FK*, V.vi.53), gets two stanzas compared to one stanza for everyone else). The list culminates, however, in King Charles: 'last in order but the first in worth/ for ELOQUENCE, and boundlesse ORATORIE' (*FK*, V.vi.74). '[B]oundlesse Soveraignty' (*FK*, I.i.18, 36) was the earlier ambition associated with Ariodant, though Charles's 'boundlesse ORATORIE' reconstructs the potentially tyrannical king in the less threatening terms of the literary and poetic. And if Charles can be placed amongst the writers, so too the politically active Sheppard is constantly locating his career in the court – not simply its culture of patronage and artistic support, but rather seeing in courtly figures (and above all in Charles himself) a model for his own ambition to succeed and to hold literary power, as well as his anxiety about the worthiness of that succession. The political and poetic analogy working throughout *The Faerie King* is intricately bound. Not surprisingly, the most obviously Spenserian moments in the poem are also instances of acute political analysis of Ariodant's failings. As the *Faerie King*, the poem is at once about poetic tradition (faerie) and politics (kingship); the two feed off each other in a relationship that can feel more mutually parasitic than symbiotic.

The opening of *The Faerie King*, where Sheppard alludes to his movement forward on the poetic *cursus* from pastoral to epic, reveals something of his intricately complex sense of his function as an heirloom from a tradition of Spenser:

> I that was wont upon my Oaten Reede
> to chaunt the harmlesse Shepherds sweet content
> the Love that Lalus with deepe vowes decreede
> to Sylvia the Groves best ornament
> and whence the Pipe and Harpe did first proceede
> must change my peacefull lot for Mars his Tent
> adiew deare Flocks a Trumpet now must bee
> my Pipe, the sad tongu'd Fife my melodie. (*FK*, Proem.1)

Although this is a widespread *topos*, the verbal echoes with Spenser's opening are clear:

> Lo I the man, whose Muse whylome did maske,
> As time her taught, in lowly Shepards weeds,
> Am now enforst a farre vnfitter taske,
> For trumpets sterne to chaunge mine Oaten reeds:
> And sing of Knights and Ladies gentle deeds,
> Whose praises hauing slept in silence long,
> Me, all too meane, the sacred Muse areeds
> To blazon broade emongst her learned throng:
> Fierce warres and faithful loues shall moralize my song. (*FQ*, I.Proem.1)

Like Sheppard, who must 'change my peacefull lot for Mars his Tent', so too Spenser must 'for trumpets sterne [...] chaunge mine Oaten reeds'. Sheppard imitates and intensifies that Spenserian focus in his own work and developing career: Spenser's fixation on 'reeds' and 'trumpets' suggests his role as narrator, conveyed through the 'telling' function of the musical instruments. However Sheppard must move from his physical placement within an imagined pastoral landscape ('my peaceful lot') to take his place on the battlefield – in 'Mars his Tent' – not just as story-teller, but seemingly as participant. Indeed, the pun which his name invites – the Sheppard/shepherd of the pastoral world – and which he also exploits in his *Epigrams*,[25] locates him from the outset as a character *within* his own literary landscape. As 'Sheppard' in a pastoral world, he appropriately addresses directly his own charges: 'adiew deare Flocks'. And as a person caught up in the political struggles of the Civil War, writing his poem 'for the most part in severall Prisons, in the height of these tumultuos times' ('Postscript', 132–3), Sheppard is also in a real sense a 'war poet': if not quite a soldier, then at least uncomfortably close to 'Mars his Tent'. Since Sheppard is within that landscape, he also has right of access to Spenserian landscapes, the earlier or ancestral versions of his own works and worlds. Whereas for Spenser the writing of pastoral is presented as a frustrating or limiting experience of 'lowly Shepards weeds', for Sheppard his earlier work is framed positively, as 'Shepherdes sweet content'. In the reverse-engineered relationship between the openings of *The Faerie King* and *The Faerie Queene*, Sheppard appropriates

---

[25] The shepherd/Sheppard pun appears in the title of *Epigrams*, I.17 (p. 11): 'The Incarnation of Jesus Christ our blessed Redeemer, narrated by a Shepherd'. It also appears in one of the three 'pastorals' included in the 1651 *Epigrams* volume; the latter is a quintessential Sheppard passage, combining the punning on his name with the presentation of his works as a funeral monument, as well as referencing the prison context in which he seems to have written it; see 'The Third Pastoral', pp. 250–1 (quoted below p. 234). See also Anthony Davenport's verse encomium in the prefatory matter to Sheppard's *The Loves of Amandus and Sophronia* (London, 1650), sig. A4r, where the shepherd/Sheppard pun appears.

Spenser's 'shepherd', as well as the flock of the intervening Spenserian pastoralists, as if they were some earlier versions of himself. Whereas 'he' was in humble circumstances in this precursor world, he is now in a more pleasing state – at least in this imaginative, escapist construct, if not in his incarcerated reality. The effectiveness of these strategies and the concomitant possibility that a contemporary reader might 'get' them are highlighted by the fact that Sheppard does not appear to have published a major pastoral work before beginning work on *The Faerie King*; his *Epigrams*, published in 1651, contains some pastoral poetry, but one of the texts in this collection indicates that his writing of *The Faerie King* had already begun by this stage.[26] Even if he intended the three pastoral poems in *Epigrams*, along with this advertisement regarding *The Faerie King*, as a late fashioning of the Virgilian *cursus*, certainly Sheppard did not lay down the pastoral foundations of a poetic career with the exactitude and clairvoyance of Spenser.[27] The evident incongruity of *The Faerie King*'s opening to anyone reading it c.1650 and familiar with Sheppard's previous publications – compounded by the reference, in the midst of civil war, to the speaker's 'peacefull lot' – therefore demands to be reformulated in terms of Sheppard's relationship to the pastoral tradition deriving from Spenser and representing the Elizabethan poet's authority. 'Shepherds sweet content' becomes in effect the experience of Spenser's poetry assimilated from the start into *The Faerie King*, as the basis of his own authority, legacy, and poetic 'birthright' in this act of poetic succession: Samuel Sheppard's sweet contents, or inherited and enriched poetic matter and authority.

'Sweet content', in the nominal sense of contents or matter, is, however, a disingenuous description of Sheppard's reworking of the Wood of Error episode. The political implications of the scene are, as previously discussed, disturbing. And the scene's deliberate intertextuality only becomes more entangled and anxious when we reconsider the episode now in the context of the poem's concern with Sheppard's literary reputation – in which Ariodant is an avatar not merely for Charles, but for Sheppard himself. Here is the 'shepherd' poet announcing himself as one who might 'overgo' Spenser, but equally he is aware that, even as he recalls Error's wood, he might be making a big mistake. Ariodant, when first seen in the grove, is still prince and heir to the throne: 'though but young/ a Prince that must Immortall honour gaine' (I.i.1).

---

[26] Sheppard, *Epigrams*, IV.10 (pp. 78–9): '*To Clio, having but begun my Faerie King*'. Sheppard's *The Loves of Amandus and Sophronia* (London, 1650) has a short pastoral interlude, though overall the work is not pastoral.

[27] Cian O'Mahony, 'A King for the Queene: Samuel Sheppard's *The Faerie King* and his Reception of Spenser's Epic Authority' (unpublished PhD thesis, University College Cork, 2013), pp. 124–30, usefully noted Sheppard's relative lack of pastoral poetry before writing *The Faerie King* and proposes that the pastoral *Epigrams* are a retrospective fashioning of his career according to the Virgilian *cursus*.

Sheppard, who 'must change my peaceful lot for Mars his Tent', is similarly poised with expectation; and 'must' in both instances could imply the anxious expectations or constraint placed upon these novitiates rather than assurance of future success. That Sheppard should choose to start his provocatively named *Faerie King* with the reworking of a famous Spenserian episode – and then embed within that inherited landscape a young, unproven heir who must make difficult decisions if he is to survive and prosper – cannot fail to be self-reflexive in relation to Sheppard himself. Consistently throughout the poem, criticism of the monarch's competence is associated with Sheppard's self-doubt about his own poetic authority, and the glue that holds this together is strategic invocation of Spenserian moments.

Another instance that intensifies Sheppard's self-reference can be found in Book IV of *The Faerie King* where the evil enchanter Magorto constructs a demonic simulacrum of Ariodant (*FK*, IV.vi.40–1). Sheppard's passage clearly invokes Spenser's Archimago, who constructs a false Una from daemonic sprites, as well as a witch who makes a false Florimell.[28] In the context of Sheppard's poem, the possibility that a king can be successfully impersonated or replicated encourages a questioning of that figure's intrinsic authority. However false this process of replication, it implicitly involves the notion that the king is a construct – and thus can be reconstructed: 'King ARIODANT hee [i.e. the daemonic avatar] seems to mortall eyes' (*FK*, IV.vi.41). The intertextuality of this scene featuring Magorto, in its insistent connection with Spenser's poem, entails a barely suppressed anxiety: is Sheppard's work, like Magorto's, a false simulacrum, a hollow imitation of Spenser's original? To develop a strong intertextual connection with Spenser's work in a scene that focuses on false copying of an original suggests an anxiously self-aware application of the narrative to the author's own condition. Sheppard's name has the potential to be cruelly ironic: his poetic succession from Spenser might involve the kind of backwards step and disillusionment that Spenser's regression to pastoral in Book VI of *The Faerie Queene* has suggested to some readers.[29] Perhaps 'Lowly Shepards weeds' are fitting garments for our 'newer poet' after all.

Sheppard's anxiety regarding the potential questioning of the value and authority of his own work also seems to be embedded within the subjects' rebellion in Book III. Just after the subjects' rebellion, the poem's narrator addresses Clio, the muse for history, encouraging her to assume 'the choycest place of *Soveraigntie*' (*FK*, III.vi.26; my emphasis). Clio's prominence and royal status suggest that history as a subject recalls the insistence that the poem is not 'th'aboundance of an ydle braine' but rather 'matter of iust

---

[28] Cf. *FQ*, I.i.45; III.viii.5–9.
[29] Richard McCabe, *Spenser's Monstrous Regiment: Elizabethan Ireland and the Poetics of Difference* (Oxford, 2002), p. 233.

memory' (*FQ*, II.Proem.1), and Clio must present Sheppard's aspirations in turn to 'the Gubernator of my Poesie' (*FK*, III.vi.26). This figure could be either Spenser or, equally, Charles. The uncertainty here is apt, perhaps even deliberate. Sheppard's poem is a politicised realm in search of a gubernator, a figure imposing government – not dissimilar to Hobbes's state that is in peril because it lacks the leviathan leader in whom all the subjects' wills are instituted. Sheppard promises to the gubernator 'that e'r long/ Ile put a period to his Epick song' (*FK*, III.vi.26), which sounds somewhat like achieving control over a potentially anarchic situation. The quest for closure – for a safe handling of his own inheritance until its natural demise – seems daunting. Literary and political terms and values interchange, and Sheppard's act of writing epic after Spenser is equated with the inheritance of sovereign power. However, the act of inheritance is uneasy: for Sheppard to follow Spenser is like the actions of one who lights 'a Candle to the glorious Sun' (*FK*, IV.i.1). Given such a blinding contrast, Sheppard's work faces the prospect of not commanding its own readership, of failing to assert an intrinsic (rather than merely inherited) authority to a loyal following. The rebellious subjects chastised by Allicandro adumbrate the sceptical readers who challenge Sheppard's legitimacy to wear Spenser's poetic crown. Sheppard's strategy in writing an epic with a strong intertextual link to Spenser's poem requires an alert readership to make connections between the two works. (Of course, the similar titles are the starting clue.) Rather than being self-contained in its meaning, Sheppard's poem only achieves completion and something approaching coherence when a reader understands the conversation that Sheppard has created between his work and *The Faerie Queene*. The insight of the rebellious subjects – that Ariodant's kingship derives from their recognition and obedience rather than from some objective, superior force – is easily taken up by Sheppard's readers: 'Fooles that wee are, to worship that so much/ which primarily from us a being gain'd' (*FK*, III.vi.8). In reading Sheppard in the context of Spenser, not as the apprentice 'shepherd' poet but rather as the royal-epic writing overgoing Spenser, we too might be like those willing subjects who give Sheppard's inheritance 'a being'. In riposte, Sheppard might feel that his detracting readers, whom he describes 'like a broode of Frogs in a ditch' (*FK*, Postscript, 112), are rebellious subjects who deserve contempt, if not punishment, for failing to recognise his authority: 'Phaebus (on paine of his displeasure) has commanded, that I contemn and laugh at the Aguish Castigations of phrenzied Pedagogues, Censorious Cits, pit-pat Rhimers, Apoplexicall Academians, rigid Rusticks and pittifull Pedanticks' (*FK*, Postscript, 17–22). Charles I's repeated questioning of the authority (or putative lack of it) embodied in the judges at his trial – 'let me know by what lawful Authority I am seated here' – resonates with Sheppard's continuously erupting anger and anxiety regarding how his work will be judged by readers who may lack (in his view) the proper authority to appreciate his efforts.[30] Alternatively, this rebuttal has an ironic potential to unseat, or in Spenser's word, 'disthronize' (*FQ*, II.x.44), both Charles and Sheppard: what authority do *these* two men have to justify their seat or place?

Given Ariodant's analogous relationship to Sheppard, it is appropriate that he should meet a very Spenserian death. The character Despair persuades Ruina's king to take his own life (*FK*, IV.vi.63–74). Despair urges suicide to Ariodant:

> but thy condition, if thou weigh it well
> will better farre Informe thee what to doe,
> remember how thy Subjects did Rebell
> and spight of thee, free ALLICANDRO too
> that thou hast lost the DAY, I need not tell
> lift up thy eyes, thy Slaughtered Subjects view,
> swimming in Seas of blood, I neede not show
> to thee the severall Ills, that hence do grow. (*FK*, IV.vi.68)

Offered the choice of 'a loade of rustie Swords, Knives, Daggers, Ropes, boxes of Poyson, and Sharpe hookes to tare' (*FK*, IV.vi.66), Ariodant opts for the sword:

> himself hee feircely threw
> with all his might, upon the eager blade
> away, then (laughing) DESPERATION flew
> (Eclipsing PHAEBUS with her gloomie shade)
> all HELL kept Holy-day, when this they knew
> and black DESPAIRE, being pompeously Arayd,
> had a months veneration, sign'd by DIS
> with hellish Tryumph, and great Glee, for this. (*FK*, IV.vi.74)

Sheppard's Despair succeeds where Spenser's failed, but this is not simply boastful 'overgoing' of Spenser's work. Since Charles/Ariodant is such a self-reflexive figure for the author, Sheppard suggests in Ariodant's suicide his own despair, succumbing to a fear that, like Ariodant, he has 'out-liv'd my Fame' (*FK*, IV.vi.73) – or indeed that he has fallen victim to it. Interestingly, the fact that Ariodant is not deposed and executed in the text takes pressure off his role, at this moment, as a representation of Charles – and of course death by Despair intensifies his function as a Spenserian element within the text. Indeed, it is a significant change that brings Ariodant, at his demise, closer to the figure of the 'Sheppard Poet', who has been battling with Despair throughout the work. And the fact that Ariodant's death 'Eclips[es] PHAEBUS', the god

---

[30] See *The Moderate*, Number 28, 16–23 January, 1649, in Raymond, ed., *Making*, p. 229.

of poetry, makes this scene into the failure of poetry, and not just politics. Whereas Spenser could write in *Amoretti* that, after a respite, he will return to the task of writing *The Faerie Queene* – 'out of my prison I will break anew' (LXXX.6) – for Sheppard the prison is literal as well as metaphorical. And in that gaol, he tells us, he found himself in a haunted Spenserian landscape: 'feeding on FFeare, and followd by Despaire' (*FK*, V.ii.4). Not surprisingly, the start of Book V, immediately following Ariodant's suicide through the prompting of Despair, begins with another pleading invocation of Spenser's authority: 'let great Spensers melody/ ravish thy [i.e., Sheppard's muse's] Sense; o may his numbers bee/ reverberated Artfully by thee' (*FK*, V.i.2). However, the experience of Ariodant's failure of authority – in an ironically 'Spenserian' moment in Sheppard's text – overshadows this goal. Whereas *The Faerie Queene* is for Spenser 'an endlesse work' (*FQ*, IV.xii.1), Sheppard describes *The Faerie King* from its inception as 'an endlesse paine' (*FK*, I.i.1).

Reading the Remains of the Dead

Sheppard describes *The Faerie King* at the outset as 'my everlasting Tombe' (*FK*, Proem.2), and this notion of the literary works as a kind of funerary monument is the key to his intermingled aspiration and fears in relation to his work and career – as well as his ambivalent attitude towards Charles. His hope is that the poem will afford him a 'deathlesse date' (*FK*, Proem.3) – an ambiguous phrase, combining time and timelessness, but the essential sense is that the poem is a funerary monument that future generations will pause to read and admire. Sheppard clearly has this metaphor in mind, for throughout his career he is obsessed with the notion of texts as funerary monuments, even in the material sense of the appearance of the printed text or manuscript. In his *Epigrams*, Sheppard describes *The Faerie Queene* as Spenser's 'Sepulcher' (IV.28; p. 97); this volume also contains *A Mausolean Monument, Erected by a Sorrowfull Sonne over his Deceased Parents*,[31] in which the layout and topography visually recall lapidary funereal inscriptions. Given Sheppard's equation between literary works and funerary monuments, he logically expects the actual monument to Spenser in Westminster Abbey to be a corollary to his works.[32] For Sheppard, this is sadly not the case: 'Niggardly Nation be asham'd of this,/ A Tombe for thy great Poet wanting is' (*Epigrams*, IV.28; p. 97). He laments in this poem that 'fooles, not worth the naming' have impressive funerary structures that ensure 'their Names shall long outlive their dust' – though

---

[31] This work has a separate title-page and dedicatory epistle, but it is part of the continuously paginated *Epigrams* volume, beginning on p. 201.

[32] The current monument is a 1778 restoration of the original 1620 monument by Nicholas Stone. See further: Ruth Mohl, 'Spenser, Edmund', *The Spenser Encyclopedia*, gen. ed. A.C. Hamilton (Toronto, 1990), p. 671.

without such monuments they would deservedly be forgotten. 'Dust' here is not just the inevitable body's decay, but evocative of the dry or lifeless quality of the intellectual or otherwise legacy of these unworthily commemorated dead. Since Spenser does not have a fitting funereal monument, his works must fulfil that function:

> Although Great *Spencer* they did thee interre,
> Not Rearing to thy name a Sepulcher,
> Yet thou hast one shall last to the last day,
> Thy *Faerie* Queen, which never shall decay. (*Epigrams*, IV.28; p. 97)[33]

There is no dust in *that* 'sepulchre', and the literary and textual funereal monument, which is 'a Poets Priviledge' (*Epigrams*, IV.28; p. 97), is precisely Sheppard's goal in *The Faerie King*, 'my everlasting Tombe' (*FK*, Proem.2).[34]

Whether Spenser's monument, added to his burial site in 1620 by Anne, Countess of Dorset, was adequate or not, his position near Chaucer in Westminster Abbey's south transept was the final posthumous act in the Elizabethan poet's career-long alignment of his works with Chaucer's output.[35] Sheppard doubtless aspires to the same proximity to his poetic mentor, even if the tombs are only metaphorically constructed within the writings; he vows to 'ingyrt his [Spenser's] Grave with Myrtle and with Palms' (*FK*, V.vi.54). In one of the *Epigrams* focused on Spenser, Sheppard fashions his relationship to Spenser in imitation of the latter's descent from Chaucer:

> Extoll his [Spenser's] never to be equal'd Layes,
> Whom thou dost Imitate with all thy might
> As he did once in *Chawcers* veine delight. (*Epigrams*, IV.28; p. 95)

However, Sheppard's 'tomb' is not just linked with Spenser's monument but also, even more so, with Charles's. Charles was given a secluded tomb in St George's Chapel, Windsor,[36] and of course it was not accessible to the public. So if Charles's physical monument is hidden, then *The Faerie King* itself must become the monument where people can come to read about Charles's life

---

[33] Ironically, the inscription on the Spenser monument, which seems to have been part of the original 1620 monument, makes precisely this point: that Spenser's works are monument enough. His 'Divine Spirrit needs noe othir witnesse then the works which he left behind him'; see Mohl, 'Spenser', p. 671.

[34] Sheppard's descriptions of poems in terms of funerary monuments are numerous; for example, *Epigrams*, IV.30 (p. 98; Davenant); and VI.17 (p. 154; Shakespeare).

[35] See further Andrew King, 'Spenser, Chaucer, and Medieval Romance', *The Oxford Handbook of Edmund Spenser*, ed. Richard A. McCabe (Oxford, 2010), pp. 553–72.

[36] Mark A. Kishlansky and John Morrill, 'Charles I', *ODNB*, note that Charles was forbidden burial at Westminster Abbey. After its head was sewn back on, the body was buried 8 February 1649 at St George's Chapel, Windsor – 'but within the closed walls of the castle where no one could come to pray by it'.

and, in this extended funerary inscription, see both his failings and his qualities. However, the fear is that no one will want to read this monument. The post-regicide world is a hostile context for an appreciative reading of Charles's monument, fashioned by Sheppard: England is a place where 'a raging ulcer [...] like a Lernean Fen of corruption furnaceth the universall sighes and complaints of this transposed world' (*FK*, 'Postscript', 139–41).[37] The ending of *The Faerie King* is appropriately apocalyptic, and it is easy in that kind of world to imagine the monuments relating to an earlier age suffering neglect, desecration, and simply irrelevance through time. In looking at Sheppard's holograph manuscript of *The Faerie King* (Bodleian, MS Rawlinson Poet. 28), it is tempting to see there in material terms his anxious anticipation that his great poem will, like a neglected and decayed funerary monument, cease to be read or even legible. Indeed, within the poem, Sheppard nervously imagines that, 'when I'm dead', the poem will sink downwards like a partially hidden monument: 'halfe buried and halfe above the ground' (*FK*, V.v.1). And the manuscript of *The Faerie King* replicates in visual terms precisely this image of the partially sunk monument: Sheppard's signature has been torn away (almost certainly by himself) at the end of the poem's Postscript, as if the poem has subsided into the soft earth.[38] At the start of the poem, furthermore, the name 'Samuel Sheppard' written after the Proem has been scratched out – 'but so half-heartedly that is still quite legible'.[39] The poem is framed by careful, suggestive acts of erasure, and the reader is challenged to read a neglected monument, such as Charles's tomb might become in time, a stone that barely reveals the name of its occupant. If not quite acephalous, *The Faerie King* in manuscript, like Charles, loses its head, or the recognisable persona or face of its author. The ambivalence with which Sheppard has depicted Charles, the poet is all too aware, is a reaction that may haunt his own work.

Because of Charles's death, the author of *Mercurius Pragmaticus* writes '*Mutability* is but *Times* Ensigne; nothing visible is permanent, the most Glorious King, or palmed State, is but the recorded *Monument of Uncertainty*.'[40] That sense of impermanence and unstable succession clearly haunts Sheppard throughout *The Faerie King* – both in relation to his subject-matter and to his own status as 'Spenser's heir'. His tendency to conceive of his work in terms of a funerary monument or sepulchre is finally, and fortuitously, summarised by the author of this edition of *Mercurius Pragmaticus*: the neglected *Faerie*

---

[37] See also his *Epigrams*, V.29 (pp. 135–6) where 'violent hands have made/ *England* a Den of *Dragons*', and 'To the Reader' (sig. A3r) in the same collection.

[38] Bodleian, MS Rawlinson Poet. 28, fol. [81]r. Note that fol. [81]r is numbered erroneously in the manuscript as fol. 79r, but it is two folia after the correct fol. 79r.

[39] MS Rawlinson Poet. 28, fol. 4r; Sheppard, ed. Klemp, p. x.

[40] *Mercurius Pragmaticus*, Number 30 January–6 February, 1649, in Raymond, ed., *Making*, pp. 250–1.

King is, like Charles, 'but the recorded *Monument* of *Uncertainty*'. Sheppard, writing *The Faerie King* in prison at the time of Charles's execution, presents royal authority and literary authority as subject to that frightening uncertainty, however monumental and impressive their ancestry. The spectre that haunts Sheppard's work is that he, like Charles, may derive a linear authority from his 'father' poet Spenser – but he may equally prove unworthy of or unable to retain that crown.

In a pastoral poem included in his *Epigrams*, Sheppard writes his definitive self-representation, combining ambition, anxiety, and the image of the text as the funerary monument:

> There is a Shepheard cag'd in stone
>   Destin'd unto destruction,
>   Worthy of all before him were,
>   *Apollo* him doth first preferre,
>   *Renowned Lawreate be content,*
>   *Thy workes are thine own Monument.* ('The Third Pastoral', *Epigrams*, 250–1)

This 'Shepheard' resides in a nightmarish pastoral world, and the status of his monument in that world can only be ambiguous. Kevin Sharpe has written about how, from an historian's perspective, it is surprising to find in seemingly royalist literature 'evidence [of] debate and tensions, anxieties, doubts and criticisms' centred on the figure of Charles and his court.[41] *The Faerie King* is a striking instance of this, and one that deserves closer examination by both literary scholars and historians. Sheppard's poem has indeed become the sort of neglected, unread monument that its author both imagined and feared. Ironically, those fears and their realisation are now a powerful function of his own art, but the poem nevertheless deserves closer examination and new readers.

---

[41] Kevin Sharpe, *Criticism and Compliment: The Politics of Literature in the England of Charles I* (Cambridge, 1987), p. x.

Mopsa's Arcadia
Choice Flowers Gathered out of Sir Philip Sidney's Rare Garden into Eighteenth-Century Chapbooks

⊰ HELEN VINCENT ⊱

In book two of the *New Arcadia*, the ignorant peasant girl Mopsa tells a story to the royal ladies Philoclea, Pamela and Zelmane:

> In time past, […] there was a king (the mightiest man in all his country) that had by his wife the fairest daughter that ever did eat pap. Now this king did keep a great house, that everybody might come and take their meat freely. So one day, as his daughter was sitting in her window […] there came a knight into the court upon a goodly horse […]. And so, the knight, casting up his eyes to the window, did fall into such love with her that he grew not worth the bread he eat; till many a sorry day going over his head, with daily diligence and grisly groans he wan her affection.[1]

The tactful and generous Philoclea, wanting to show some appreciation for Mopsa's effort without actually bestowing undeserved praise, interrupts: 'Now good Mopsa […] I pray thee at my request keep this tale till my marriage-day, and I promise thee that the best gown I wear that day shall be thine.'[2] Such kindly patronage has generally been the lot meted out to the chapbook retellings of stories from the *Arcadia* by critics, not entirely dismissive of these Arcadian afterlives, yet conscious that they do not capture the multifaceted brilliance of the original. Dennis Kay, for instance, describes them as 'cheap and crude retellings' which, however, 'forcefully demonstrate the degree to which Sidney's stories were still read into the eighteenth century'.[3]

But these texts reveal more about how Sidney was read in the long eighteenth century than the bare fact of his being read at all. As John Simons writes

---

[1] Philip Sidney, *The Countess of Pembroke's Arcadia (The New Arcadia)*, ed. Victor Skretkowicz (Oxford, 1987, p. 214. All subsequent references to this edition will be cited as *New Arcadia*.
[2] Sidney, *New Arcadia*, p. 214.
[3] Dennis Kay, 'Sidney: A Critical Heritage', *Sir Philip Sidney: An Anthology of Modern Criticism*, ed. Dennis Kay (Oxford, 1987), p. 23.

in his edition of *Guy of Warwick and other Chapbook Romances*, 'it is true that chapbooks do not speak to a world thronged by readers who were conversant with high literary culture', but far from appealing only to the 'reader of low sophistication and intellect', these texts could 'stimulate an internal commentary and debate on the values [they] enshrined' and their producers and readers served as 'culture brokers' to their society.[4] The chapbook retellings of stories from the *Arcadia* first appeared in the late seventeenth century during a period of literary production when the prose romances which had circulated among middle-class readers 'metamorphosed' (to use Simons' word) into the histories and chapbooks that were accessible to a much broader range of readers, circulating even to the lowest households whilst still being purchased by the culturally literate.[5] In particular it was the story of Argalus and Parthenia which was most in demand. Indeed, the very phrase 'Argalus and Parthenia' became a byword for the chapbook or popular prose tale in the eighteenth century, and the text seems to have circulated until the publication format itself declined in the nineteenth century.[6] The writers who turned this particular Sidneian narrative into one of the most popular stories of the long eighteenth century altered certain elements of the story to bring it into line with the other chapbook romances, none of which exactly shared its origins in Elizabethan courtly romance. The changes they made capture the transformation of readers' appreciation of the meandering narrative of romance into a preference for the more tightly plotted novel. But they also returned to the text of the *Arcadia* as they themselves encountered it in print, and picked up on one key aspect of the story of Argalus and Parthenia: that it is a narrative of mutual desire which is transmuted into a happy marriage.

Argalus and Parthenia first appear in Sidney's revised text of the *Arcadia* in one of the many inset retrospective narratives when, in book one, Palladius (the disguised Prince Musidorus) asks Kalendar's steward why Kalendar's son Clitophon is held prisoner. In response he is told how Argalus came to Arcadia in the train of Gyneceia at her wedding, how Basilius's niece Parthenia was first courted by Demagoras, how he and her mother plotted in vain against Argalus, and how Demagoras then poisoned Parthenia so that she became like a leper. Parthenia then refused to marry Argalus and fled, after which Argalus – and Clitophon – were captured by Demagoras, in league with the revolting Helots. Several pages later, the characters become part of the main narrative. Argalus, set free thanks to Musidorus's cousin Pyrocles, is now at Kalendar's house when Parthenia, miraculously healed, reappears and is reunited with

---

[4] John Simons, ed., *Guy of Warwick and Other Chapbook Romances* (Exeter, 1998), pp. 7–8, 16.
[5] See Simons, *Guy*, pp. 6, 14–19; and Margaret Spufford, *Small Books and Pleasant Histories* (Athens, GA, 1982), ch. 3, for chapbook readers.
[6] Lori Humphrey Newcomb, *Reading Popular Romance in Early Modern England* (New York, 2001), p. 31.

him. This part of their story, the tale of their 'virtuous constancy' culminates in their marriage, after which there is no mention of Argalus and Parthenia until book three, when Basilius sends for Argalus, previously 'spared [...] in respect of his late marriage'.[7] Argalus insists on responding to Basilius's call to take up arms. He leaves Parthenia and is killed fighting the villainous Amphialus. Once again this couple's story appears to end, but several pages later a mysterious 'Knight of the Tomb' appears, insists on fighting Amphialus, is fatally wounded and is then revealed to be Parthenia. With her funeral and burial in the same tomb as her husband, the history of Argalus and Partheia is concluded.

This story was first given an independent existence by Francis Quarles, whose verse narrative *Argalus and Parthenia* was first published in 1629. Quarles's version found an audience throughout the seventeenth century, going through some twenty-one editions by 1691. There is also a play of the same title, by Henry Glapthorne, published in 1639 and revived during the Restoration; this was not reprinted and was not a textual influence on later retellings.[8] Since Quarles's poem becomes the foundation for some of the chapbook versions, how he handles the story is worth noting. As Clare Kinney has shown, in removing Argalus and Parthenia from Sidney's overarching romance, Quarles removes them from Sidney's 'larger agendas' of political and literary interrogation.[9] Instead, Quarles contextualises his story as part of the leisured recreations of the elite: it is a *'Courtier'* book, written during his 'Playday[s]'and intended for the 'silken laps' of ladies.[10] But in spite of this suggestion of a high-ranking audience, Quarles brings the story down to a more homely level, firstly in language, as when he compares Argalus wandering in search of Parthenia to a

> [m]an whose hourely wants implore
> Each meales reliefe, trudging from doore to doore,
> That heares no dialect from churlish lips,
> But newes of Beadles, and their torturing whips.[11]

Secondly, in the main incidents of his narrative, Quarles domesticates the

---

[7] Sidney, *New Arcadia*, pp. 30, 371.
[8] Pepys saw Glapthorne's play twice, on 31 January and 5 February 1661. On 31 January he wrote 'endeed it is good', but by February had changed his mind: 'Here we saw *Argalus and Parthenia* – which I lately saw. But though pleasant for the dancing and singing, I do not find good for any wit or design therein'; see *The Diary of Samuel Pepys*, ed. Robert Latham and William Matthews, 11 vols. (London, 2001), 2: 27, 31.
[9] Clare Kinney, 'Obscuring the Argument: the Seventeenth-Century Afterlife of Sidney's *Argalus and Parthenia*', unpublished conference paper given at the 37th International Congress on Medieval Studies, University of Western Michigan, Kalamazoo, 2002.
[10] Francis Quarles, *Argalus and Parthenia* (London, 1629), sigs. A3r–A3v.
[11] Quarles, *Argalus and Parthenia*, p. 89.

story, concentrating on Parthenia not as the beauty ranking with the queens of the Arcadian world, as she appears in the *Arcadia*, but as the daughter whose choice of husband is subject to her mother's approval. He expands the account that Sidney gives in a few lines of how Parthenia's mother conspired with Demagoras to murder Argalus into a whole episode where the maid Athleia, told to take what is really poison to Argalus, drinks the poison herself; the whole conspiracy is revealed and the mother dies of rage at being discovered. The other scene Quarles expands, again from a few lines of the original text, in a mingling of the courtly and the intimate, is the account of the marriage of Argalus and Parthenia, which includes the ritual itself and an elaborate masque. He then follows the couple into the marriage bed: 'And here my *Muse* bids draw our curtains too,/ 'Tis unfit to see what private Lovers do.'[12] These differences in plot, the long speeches given by Quarles to his characters throughout his version, and his leaving unnamed the disguised Parthenia called by Sidney the 'Knight of the Tomb' make it easy to tell when the prose adaptations of the story draw on his version rather than Sidney's.

At the moment in the late seventeenth century when *Argalus and Parthenia* made the transition from the culture of the educated elite to popular print, Quarles's version was still continuously in print; Sidney's own works were reprinted in 1655, 1662 and 1674, and Glapthorne's play had been performed on the Restoration stage. The story therefore did not descend to popular print because it had dropped out of elite circulation. Instead it was brought there by a combination of the increasing public demand for cheap editions of long-form fiction and the personal taste and market knowledge of the writers and printers who produced these texts.

This was a time of change in the popular print market: the ballad was being eclipsed as the dominant form by the rise of what has commonly been called the chapbook. This term has been applied to any small cheaply printed book, but a chapbook is properly a booklet printed on one single sheet of paper and then folded into a single gathering of twelve or twenty-four pages.[13] Margaret Spufford has shown – as, indeed, the title of her study *Small Books and Pleasant Histories* illustrates – how the chapbook was differentiated from other formats, with a difference in lists of publishers' stocks between the 'small book' or 'double-book', which was the chapbook proper, and the longer 'history', or piece of prose fiction, which was more complicated to produce and sold at a higher price.[14] It was common for the same story to circulate in each of these formats, and sometimes as a single-sheet ballad as well, although no single-sheet *Arcadia* adaptations are known. Gaps in the surviving evidence mean

[12] Quarles, *Argalus and Parthenia*, p. 121.
[13] See Simons, *Guy*, pp. 4–5.
[14] Spufford, *Small Books*, pp. 93, 104nn26–7.

that the history of the evolution of the chapbook during this formative period is obscure, and it is unclear to what extent the printers were producing chapbooks in response to improved literacy, to changes in production methods and paper supply, or to changes in public taste. What is clear is that it was men who already specialised in printing texts to be sold cheaply to a wide audience who were 'diversifying' into the production of longer prose fiction for this same market.[15] It was in this milieu that the chapbook editions of *Argalus and Parthenia* appeared.

The history of these editions is not complex, but for many years it has been obscured by the problem of identifying the different editions and recording them, a problem heightened by the fact that chapbooks were often undated and frequently without an imprint that is in any way useful to the bibliographical detective. Chapbook publishers issued reprint after reprint, and one chapbook printer would simply produce a straight reprint of a text published by another. Where there are edition statements, they cannot be taken as entirely reliable, since these may have simply been a marketing device used to stress that what was being sold was very new and very much in demand. Any attempt to compile a bibliography of chapbooks can therefore never claim to be definitive. All one can do is record the known information; lacunae in the dated evidence cannot be taken to imply either a continuous history of publication or a period when no editions of a particular text appeared.

It is with these caveats that the question of the different chapbook versions of *Argalus and Parthenia* must be approached. The standard starting point for most recent bibliographical discussion is B.S. Field's 1979 article 'Sidney's Influence: the Evidence of the Publication of the *History of Argalus and Parthenia*'.[16] In this article, Field describes 'two prose accounts':

> [one has] slightly varying titles such as *The Most Pleasant and Delightful History of Argalus and Parthenia, Newly Reviv'd*, in 1672, 1683, 1692, and in at least one other undated edition. The second prose account, also of varying titles, appeared throughout the eighteenth century in some eighteen editions from about 1700 to 1785, *The Unfortunate Lovers, the History of Argalus and Parthenia in Four Books, Adorn'd with Cuts*.[17]

This account, clearly delineating one seventeenth-century version and one eighteenth-century version, is followed for instance by Paul Salzman and Lori Humphrey Newcomb in their studies of early modern prose fiction.[18] Field

---

[15] Spufford, *Small Books*, p. 96.
[16] B.S. Field, 'Sidney's Influence: the Evidence of the Publication of the *History of Argalus and Parthenia*', *English Language Notes* 17 (1979), 98–102.
[17] Field, 'Sidney's Influence', p. 100.
[18] Paul Salzman, *English Prose Fiction 1558–1700* (Oxford, 1985), pp. 131–2; Newcomb, *Reading Popular Romance*, p. 31.

draws on two earlier bibliographies: Charles C. Mish's *English Prose Fiction 1661–1700* (1952) and Arundell Esdaile's *List of English Tales and Prose Romances Printed before 1740* (1912). Both of these listings, typical of their eras, do not transcribe the full titles of the works they enumerate, and confine their bibliographical descriptions to the format – two decisions which have resulted in confusion in the listing of editions of *Argalus and Parthenia*.

In fact there are not two but three discrete popular print versions of *Argalus and Parthenia*, of which a bibliography is given at the end of this essay. The earliest edition which survives, of 1672, is the one which seems to have been reprinted latest, at least to 1800 and possibly later, and it is also the one which has attracted the least attention from modern scholars.[19] The other two versions are not, strictly speaking, chapbooks, but longer narratives which fall into Spufford's category of 'history'. One only survives in two seventeenth-century editions, whereas the other, longer version seems to have been first printed in 1703 (perhaps to replace or upgrade the first), and to have remained in print until the last years of the eighteenth century. In addition to these works, there is also an adaptation of *Arcadia* itself in 'history' format: *The Famous History of Heroick Acts: or, the Honour of Chivalry. Being an Abstract of Pembroke's Arcadia*, of which only one edition survives, printed for William Spiller in 1701. In spite of its grandiloquent title, the quality of the print and illustrations and its similarity to Spiller's other publications all show that this work is an example of popular printing. However, it is indeed an 'abstract' or summary of the *Arcadia* as known to seventeenth-century readers in its printed editions, including Richard Beling's sixth book, which was first published with the 1627 edition of Sidney's *Works* and remained attached to the text for the rest of the century.

The 1672 *Argalus and Parthenia* is the earliest surviving edition, but an examination of the background to its publication suggests that it may also have been the earliest reworking of the story into chapbook format. Its full title is *The Most Excellent History of Argalus and Parthenia. Being a Choice Flower, Gathered out of Sir Philip Sydneys Rare Garden* (hereafter *The Most Excellent History of Argalus and Parthenia*). It has twenty-four octavo pages, which makes it a 'double-book' or true chapbook, and the 'T. Vere' for whom it was printed was Thomas Vere, who was one of the group of stationers identified by Cyprian Blagden and Margaret Spufford as the 'Ballad Partners' responsible for most of the ballad publication in London before the expiry of the Printing Act in 1695. Vere generally worked in partnership with a consortium which included Francis Coles, John Wright and William Gilbertson, and his career, which began in the 1640s, is used by Spufford to illustrate how these printers

---

[19] ESTC lists an edition dated to 'c.1800'; the Bodleian Library has an edition dated to 'c.1830'. See the bibliography of editions below.

were diversifying from ballads into chapbook publication during the last part of the seventeenth century.[20]

Among the prose publications Vere produced throughout his career, which began in 1646, were reprints of late Elizabethan and early Jacobean works, including Thomas Deloney's *The Noble Acts, newly found, Of Arthur of the Table Round*, Nicholas Breton's *The Soul's Harmony* and Emanuel Ford's Arcadian romance *The Most Famous, Delectable, and Pleasant History of Parismus*. In 1672 two chapbooks were printed for Vere alone, at 'the sign of the Angel without Newgate', a location identified by Spufford as prime territory for chapbook-sellers, and where chapmen congregated on the outskirts of London.[21] One chapbook is the *Most Excellent History of Argalus and Parthenia* and the other is a version of the text identified by Newcomb as the other archetypal example of popular prose fiction of the period, Robert Greene's *Pandosto*, entitled in Vere's printing *Fortunes Tennis-Ball, or, The Most Excellent History of Dorastus and Fawnia*. This is a metrical version, attributed to one 'S.S.', probably the Samuel Smithson who wrote the chapbook version of *Guy of Warwick* for Vere in the next few years. It is not impossible that Smithson may also have been responsible for the text of *The Most Excellent History of Argalus and Parthenia*.[22] Other (undated) chapbooks printed by Vere and the consortium attributed by ESTC to the period 1674–79 included *The Famous History of Guy Earl of Warwick*, *The Life and Death of the Famous Champion of England, St. George* and *The Lovers Quarrel: or, Cupids Triumph. Being the Pleasant History of fair Rosamond of Scotland*. In short, this period saw Vere publish an array of texts that were in the process of becoming the staples of popular prose fiction, both in new versions and in texts long available to other publishers. The title-pages stress that the works are 'famous', 'very delightful to read', 'pleasant' and 'worthy the pursuit of all sorts of people', but do not as a rule use authors' names to promote the books.

The strong and picturesquely worded reference to Sidney as author of the text on the title-page of *The Most Excellent History of Argalus and Parthenia*

---

[20] Cyprian Blagden, 'Notes on the Ballad Market in the Second Half of the Seventeenth Century', *Studies in Bibliography* 6 (1954), 161–80; Spufford, *Small Books*, pp. 94–8. See also the entry for Vere (under 'Veere') in Henry R. Plomer, *A Dictionary of the Booksellers and Printers who were at work in England, Scotland and Ireland from 1641 to 1667* (London, 1968), p. 186.

[21] Although the 'A.P.' who printed the book for Vere is unidentified in its entry for *The Most Excellent History*, the ESTC entry for *Fortune's Tennis-Ball* conjectures him to be A. Purslowe; see Spufford, *Small Books*, pp. 111–16.

[22] These were all printed for the consortium, not just Vere. *The Famous History of Guy Earl of Warwick* names Smithson as the author; the other chapbooks are *The Life and Death of the Famous Champion of England, St. George*, and *The Lover's Quarrel: or, Cupid's Triumph. Being the Pleasant History of Fair Rosamund of Scotland*. Newcomb, *Reading Popular Romance*, pp. 145–7, discusses *Fortune's Tennis-Ball* and attributes it to Samuel Sheppard. Andrew King's essay in this volume discusses Sheppard's identifiable publications.

is unusual in this context. Although this work does draw on Quarles's by now well-known version of the tale, in many places the text itself is clearly extrapolated from the *Arcadia*, interspersing passages which paraphrase to compress the story with passages taken almost verbatim from Sidney's original. Like Quarles's text, this version contextualises Arcadia not in Sidney's world of high politics but in the fairytale world of the other chapbook tales. For instance, in describing how Parthenia's mother 'at length finding Argalus standing between them, and that it was he that most eclipsed her affection from shining upon Demogoras, sought all means how to remove him, so much the more as he manifested himself an unremoveable suitor to her daughter, first by employing him in many dangerous enterprizes' (all of which phrasing comes almost word for word from the *Arcadia*), these enterprises, not listed by Sidney, are here given as 'desperate duels, bloody combats with Giants, Lions, Dragons, wild Boars and the like'.[23] While wild animals are certainly part of Sidney's own Arcadian landscape, the giants and dragons are mythical creatures from the popular tales of Jack the Giant Killer and St George. This whole passage does not occur at all in Quarles's text, but the next chapter of the chapbook does introduce that element of the story found only in his version, the story of the mother using the maid (here Athelia rather than Athleia) to attempt to poison Argalus. Indeed, the mother's dying line at the end of this episode, 'Welcome Death thou easer of all ills', comes from Quarles's text.[24]

Even the main storyline of the *Arcadia* is brought into this retelling. Where Quarles omits all reference to the *Arcadia*'s central characters and action, this version brings them in to chapter seven to provide the bridge between the first and second parts of the story:

> Amphialus, a Prince of Valour, being in love with Philocles [*sic*] the King's youngest daughter, who had stole her away, and kept her a strong Castle of his own; to which her father laying seige, Amphialus sent out a Challenge that if he had any knight in the Camp that durst venture himself in single Combat with him, and if he should overcome him, he would immediately set Philocles at Liberty: otherwise he was resolved to keep her: – Hereupon many Knights fought, but were slain, to the Grief of the King her Father; at last he sent a Messenger to

---

[23] *The Most Excellent History of Argalus and Parthenia* (1672), p. 5. Compare with Sidney, *New Arcadia*, p. 29: 'at length finding that Argalus standing between them was it that most eclipsed her affection from shining upon Demagoras, she sought all means how to remove him, so much the more as he manifested himself an unremovable suitor to her daughter, first by employing him in as many dangerous enterprises as ever the evil stepmother Juno recommended to the famous Hercules'.

[24] *The Most Excellent History of Argalus and Parthenia*, p. 8; Quarles, *Argalus and Parthenia*, p. 46. For the name change from Athleia to Athelia, compare the rendition of Gyneceia as Cyrecia on p.1. In both cases these may be errors of transcription or composition rather than deliberate decisions.

Argalus, desiring him to take his Quarrel in hand; who immediately granted his Desire, notwithstanding the warmest Persuasions of Parthenia to the contrary.[25]

This version also follows Sidney in naming Parthenia in disguise as the Knight of the Tomb, but where Sidney does not reveal her true identity until after the fight with Amphialus, this text explains that

> Parthenia being now weary of her Life, since Argalus was dead, and resolved that the same hand which had deprived him of Life, should also end her; whereupon she armed herself like a Man in black armour, on her shield was figured a beautiful Child with two heads whereof one was dead and the other alive, but so as necessarily to look for Death; the words were, NO WAY TO BE AIDED FROM DEATH BUT BY DEATH.[26]

The description of the *impresa* is taken verbatim from the *New Arcadia*, but the previous part of the sentence is original, giving the reader an explicit motivation for Parthenia's disguise where Sidney never gives the reader an insight into why she disguised herself, simply not mentioning her from the moment when she 'passed through the camp' at Argalus's funeral until her reappearance as the Knight of the Tomb.[27] However, the text once more returns to Sidney's words for its conclusion, ending with his eight-line epitaph on the couple.

This chapbook, therefore, is a version of the story whose fidelity is primarily to Sidney's text, as its title suggests, though deriving in part from Quarles's adaptation. Simons argues that chapbook texts may not be high culture, but this does not mean that they are written for the reader of 'low intellect': they 'do not [...] make concessions where literacy is concerned'.[28] This text may compress Sidney's text and assimilate it to the world of popular tales, but its use of his language, poetry and visual images means that it cannot just be read as a dumbing-down of Sidney's text for a popular audience.

This adaptation is really the only true chapbook version of the *Arcadia*, and as such the cheapest and easiest to produce, which perhaps explains why it was still being reprinted by chapbook publishers over one hundred years later: though no editions survive in the intervening years, there are at least five editions published after 1770, whose imprints of 'Aldermary Churchyard' and 'for the Travelling Stationers' place them firmly in the category of cheap

---

[25] *The Most Excellent History of Argalus and Parthenia*, pp. 18–19.
[26] *The Most Excellent History of Argalus and Parthenia*, p. 21. Compare with Sidney, *New Arcadia*, pp. 396-7: 'In his shield for impresa he had a beautiful child, but having two heads – whereon, the one showed that it was already dead; the other alive, but in that case looking for death. The word was, "No way to be rid from death, but by death"'.
[27] Sidney, *New Arcadia*, p. 379.
[28] Simons, *Guy*, p. 8.

print.[29] The other prose adaptations are 'histories', falling into the hinterland between chapbook and proto-novel, picking up on Quarles's domestication of Argalus and Parthenia to give readers straightforward narratives which focus on the relationship between the two central characters. Only two editions are recorded of the second version of *Argalus and Parthenia* to appear. This is a fifty-page book entitled *The Pleasant and Delightful History of Argalus and Parthenia*, and it is the version conflated with *The Most Excellent History of Argalus and Parthenia* in twentieth-century bibliographies. Once again the publishers, first Thomas Passenger and then Eben, Tracy and Blare, specialised in popular print.[30] After these two editions no further reprints are recorded, but Josiah Blare published the final, longer version, *The Unfortunate Lovers, or the Famous and Renowned History of Argalus and Parthenia*, three times the size of its immediate predecessor at approximately 150 pages in its first printings, which went on to be part of the repertoire of publishers of popular print throughout the eighteenth century.

These prose narratives are written in what Salzman describes as the 'new plain romance style' of the period – or in the words of the shorter of these versions, the *Pleasant and Delightful History*, 'a more plain and easie method, that it may universally be acceptable to all Capacities'.[31] This may be illustrated in its treatment of the letter sent by Amphialus in response to Argalus's challenge. Sidney's letter opens with a rhetorical flourish: 'Much more famous Argalus, I, whom never threatenings could make afraid, am now terrified by your noble courtesy, for well I know from what height of virtue it doth proceed, and what cause I have to doubt such virtue bent to my ruin.'[32] The *Pleasant and Delightful History* begins with the gentle politeness of a later era: 'I am sorry that your judgement should be so misinformed as to think that ever I should offer any injustice to King *Basilius*.'[33] One interesting by-product of this concern to clarify instead of complicate is that both the histories, like the chapbook, begin with the description of the country: 'In the pleasant Country of *Arcadia*, a place noted for rural delights and sweetness of air' (1672); '*Arcadia* was a Land so pleasant and delightful, that in former time it was admired in all the world' (1683); 'In *Greece*, which was once the great Theatre of Arms and Arts, there is no Province more beholden to Nature for the Fertility of the Soil, and the Pleasantness of the Air, than the Province of *Arcadia*' (1703).[34] With this,

---

[29] For the significance of Aldermary churchyard as a location for the printing of 'cheap pleasure reading', see Newcomb, *Reading Popular Romance*, p. 192.
[30] The careers of these printers are discussed in detail in Spufford, *Small Books*, ch. 4.
[31] *The Pleasant and Delightful History of Argalus and Parthenia* (n.p., 1683), p. 1.
[32] Sidney, *New Arcadia*, p. 374.
[33] *Pleasant and Delightful History*, p. 44.
[34] Salzman, *English Prose Fiction 1558–1700*, p. 132, has noted that this last text, otherwise taken mostly from Quarles, draws directly on Sidney's own words for this passage.

they return unwittingly to the way in which Sidney himself originally began his text. The *Old Arcadia*, still unpublished and unknown to the public at this time, begins 'Arcadia among all the provinces of Greece was ever had in singular reputation, partly for the sweetness of the air and other natural benefits.'[35]

These two histories acknowledge that they are working from Quarles's version, though they also refer to Sidney as the original author of the tale in their introductory matter. The *Pleasant and Delightful History* shows an awareness of Sidney's *Arcadia* text, for instance having Basilius summon Argalus because Amphialus has 'surpriz'd my only Daughter and keeps her in his Castle.'[36] However, like the earlier chapbook version, it also adds original material, with the narrator interpolating his own voice in conversation with the reader. For example, this narrator ascribes to Argalus and Parthenia a place in literary immortality, transcending their containment in the text: 'And though you find they were unfortunate unto their deaths, yet let not that affright you, for now they enjoy each other happily, where no *Demagoras* can come to trouble them.'[37] He proceeds to pick up on Quarles's account of the wedding night of Argalus and Parthenia at the point where Quarles's coy Muse 'bids draw our curtains': this author disagrees with Quarles's comment that ''Tis unfit to see what private Lovers do.'[38] His description combines the public bawdiness that was a part of contemporary weddings with attention to sensual details: the ladies 'imply their nimble hands to undress her [Parthenia's] curious Body'; the watching crowd, dismissed by Argalus, retreat downstairs to spend the night drinking; the next morning Parthenia on waking 'starts to find a man in Bed with her', and then, finally, this author evokes discretion in a manner calculated to kindle the imagination of the very reader he claims to be protecting: 'Oh then they did ——— but what they did, my pen commands me to conceal, lest some female Reader perhaps should long to taste these pleasures which this amorous couple did then enjoy.'[39]

The third adaptation was first published as *The Unfortunate Lovers, or the Famous and Renowned History of Argalus and Parthenia* in 1703. It was reprinted several times under this title, and then under the title *The Famous and Renowned History of Argalus and Parthenia* (perhaps only in later Scottish editions). It is the one which has attracted most critical attention, and it is indeed straightforwardly a prose redaction of Quarles's verse *Argalus and Parthenia*. This narrator presents his version as a return to the 'Original Soil' of Sidney's *Arcadia*, reclothing it in its 'native Garb' of prose, although he does not seem to have a

---

[35] Philip Sidney, *The Countess of Pembroke's Arcadia (The Old Arcadia)*, ed. Jean Robertson (Oxford, 1973), p. 1.
[36] *Pleasant and Delightful History*, p. 44.
[37] *Pleasant and Delightful History*, p. 2.
[38] Quarles, *Argalus and Parthenia*, p. 121.
[39] *Pleasant and Delightful History*, p. 39. This suggestive dash is at least four ems long in the text.

second thought about interposing his own words and Quarles's story between the reader and what he calls the 'original thought' of Sidney.[40] While he does, in the beginning, make an effort to depart from Quarles's language so that the text does not contain too many metrical phrases or noticeable rhyme – which may explain his beginning with Sidney's prose rather than a passage taken from Quarles – as he progresses, he more and more simply straightens out Quarles's text into prose, with the rhymes and metres once avoided now clearly visible.

How these authors translated Sidney's prose and Quarles's poetry into chapbooks and histories captures an interesting moment in the development of prose fiction, but what they adapted is the key to why this particular story, out of all the Elizabethan prose romances, became such a seminal work. The *Arcadia* is full of debates, plots and characters all wrestling with the question of how to reconcile the disruptive intensity of desire with the ordered social structure of marriage. In the story of Argalus and Parthenia, Sidney creates a story which depends on the notion that desire and emotional intimacy survive and if anything increase after marriage, as in the celebrated passage where they are discovered reading by the messenger bringing Basilius's faithful summons:

> a happy couple: he joying in her, she joying in herself (but in herself because she enjoyed him); both increasing their riches by giving to each other; each making one life double, because they made a double life one, where desire never wanted satisfaction, nor satisfaction ever bred satiety: he ruling, because she would obey – or rather because she would obey, she therein ruling.[41]

But it is not just the social control of marriage with which desire is reconciled here – and not only reconciled, but increased through being housed in this legitimate home for it. Desire is also here reconciled with the expression of religious faith. Both Argalus and Parthenia, in their dying speeches, evoke their love for each other not as part of their earthly lives to be renounced, but as something which in one sense will only be completed in the spiritual afterlife. Sidney gives to Parthenia a dying speech which moves effortlessly between desire for Argalus and the penitence of a good death according to Christian advice of the day:

> And O life! O death! answer for me that my thoughts have not so much as in a dream tasted any comfort since they were deprived of Argalus. I come, my Argalus! I come! And, O God, hide my faults in thy mercies; and grant, as I feel thou doost grant, that, in thy eternal love, we may love each other eternally.[42]

In translating this story into a prose narrative with popular appeal in late seventeenth and early eighteenth-century England, the authors of the chapbooks

---

[40] 'The Preface to the Readers', *The Unfortunate Lovers* (London, 1703), sig. A3.
[41] Sidney, *New Arcadia*, pp. 371–2.
[42] Sidney, *New Arcadia*, p. 398.

and histories bring Sidney's depiction of a marriage which reconciles virtue and desire into a world where such an ideal of romantic love as the preferred basis for a marriage and as a mode which should continue after marriage was becoming a norm in an ever-widening range of social classes.[43]

That this 'married chastity' was one aspect of the story that contemporary readers responded to may be seen from two contemporary references to *Argalus and Parthenia*. In *The Lying Lover* (1703) Richard Steele has a female character angst about 'this piteous story': 'But I hope they'll come together at the end of the Book. – And marry, and have several children.'[44] The devotional writer Elizabeth Singer Rowe, in her moral novella *Friendship in Death: in Twenty Letters from the Dead to the Living*, first published in 1728, uses the story as a marker to indicate that a character has the normal interest of a teenage girl in romance, but within the bounds of moral decency:

> The only intimacy I have contracted is with a daughter of the minister of this parish; they call her *Sally*; her conversation is perfectly innocent and agreeable, and has something in it charming beyond all the specious rules and studied elegance of the Beau-Monde; she has spent her leisure in reading, and has certainly perused all the good books in her father's study, having never opened a page on any subject but religion, except *Argalus* and *Parthenia*. Her preciseness is natural and unaffected; her looks, her words, her whole behaviour, has an air of sanctity.[45]

Although Sidney legitimises love in marriage in the story of Argalus and Parthenia, his story focuses more on their separation than their time together. Their wedding, that moment symbolical of union, is dismissed in a line. Quarles gives much more time to the courtly masque than he does to the wedding itself. But in all of the popular versions, the wedding becomes one of the most significant episodes of the story, for instance taking one fifth of the pages of *The Pleasant and Delightful History* in 1683. It is often illustrated with a woodcut of a contemporary wedding scene, with the couple clasping hands. *The Most Excellent History of Argalus and Parthenia* in 1672 accompanies the woodcut of the couple saying their vows in front of a bewigged priest with original verse giving the priest's 'benediction' at the end of the ceremony:

Now the sacred Knot is ty'd
Between the Bridegroom and the Bride.

---

[43] See Spufford, *Small Books*, pp. 156–66; Martin Ingram, 'The Reform of Popular Culture? Sex and Marriage in Early Modern England', *Popular Culture in Seventeenth-Century England*, ed. Barry Reay (London, 1985), pp. 129–65.
[44] Cited in Kay, 'Sidney: A Critical Heritage', p. 23.
[45] Elizabeth Singer Rowe, *Friendship in Death: in Twenty Letters from the Dead to the Living* (London, 1743), p. 347.

> Who are now longer two, but one,
> So to remain till Life is done.
> Still blest be they in all Affairs,
> Living in Love, and void of Cares;
> Their Children's Children for to see,
> Spring up like Branches prosperously.[46]

Along with this stress on the marriage of Argalus and Parthenia comes an invitation to the reader to share in their feelings. *The Unfortunate Lovers* begins with a poem.

> See the fond Youth! he Burns, he Loves, he Dyes,
> He Wishes as he Pines, and feeds his famish'd Eyes.
> *Parthenia* makes Returns of equal Fire,
> And Burns as well as he, with warm Desire.

The story of Argalus and Parthenia, then, appeals to the Petrarchan lover who 'burns' and 'dyes'. But it also appeals to the female reader because the story relies on Parthenia's love for Argalus being as emotionally intense as his for her: she 'Burns as well as he'. In his 'Preface to the Reader', the author of *The Unfortunate Lovers* gives a variety of practical uses for *Argalus and Parthenia*, suggesting that young men and women will be able to draw on the 'passionate Declamations' of the book in any romantic situation, whether the young man wishes to 'try the Power of his Rhetorick to his fair Mistress' or the young lady wishes to give 'a cold Entertainment to an unwelcome and importunate Lover' in return. But this is more than a conduct-book for lovers: entwined with these suggestions is an insistence on emotional identification with the story:

> In short, the various Passions of the Soul, under the strangest and most surprizing Accidents, are here express'd in the most soft and melting Accounts. So that it is impossible for one to read it, and not to make himself a Party.[47]

The author of the earlier *Pleasant and Delightful History* similarly encourages emotional identification from his readers:

> Read then this little Book at your own leisure, and if by chance you shed a tear or two, you will not be the first that have wept at these Lovers' misfortunes. The Author, as he writ it, did begin with watery Eyes to moisten what he had planted.[48]

Like Argalus and Parthenia themselves, then, the readers of these narratives are urged to experience passionate desire which, sanctioned by the religious and

---

[46] *The Most Excellent History of Argalus and Parthenia*, p. 16.
[47] *Unfortunate Lovers*, sigs. A3r–A4r.
[48] *Pleasant and Delightful History*, p. 2.

social authorities, does not diminish but persists until death. Sidney's 'happy couple', to use his own phrase, enter popular culture at a crucial moment in the development of the modern pattern of romantic love and marriage.[49] From being merely a youthful folly to be renounced before the serious business of adulthood and/or religion, the pursuit of romantic love as the natural precursor to a happy marriage became a legitimate part of the cultural landscape at every level of society, and perhaps the dominant narrative in fictional relationships on stage and in prose texts. Whether in chapbook or 'history', the story of Argalus and Parthenia both takes on the colours of contemporary conceptions of courtship and marriage and becomes an influential text in the development and propagation of those conceptions.

Known Editions of Versions of *Argalus and Parthenia* in Popular Print

1. *The Most Excellent History of Argalus and Parthenia*
Twenty-four pages; duodecimo chapbook.

The most excellent history of Argalus and Parthenia. Being a choice flower, gathered out of Sir Philip Sydneys rare garden. London: printed by A.P. for T. Vere, at the sign of the Angel without New-gate, 1672.

The history of Argalus and Parthenia. Being a choice flower gathered out of Sir Phillip Sydney's rare garden. London: Printed and sold in Aldermary Church-Yard, London, [1770?].

The history of Argalus and Parthenia. Being a choice flower gathered out of Sir Philip Sidney's rare garden. [London]: Printed and sold in Aldermary Church Yard, London, [1780?].

The history of Argalus & Parthenia: being a choice flower gathered out of Sir Philip Sidney's rare garden. [London]: [s.n.], Printed in the Year 1788.

The history of Argalus and Parthenia. Being a choice flower, gathered out of Sir Philip Sidney's rare garden. [London]: Printed and sold in London, [1800?]. *ESTC* notes 'Date a guess; bound with chapbooks which may be post-1800'.

The history of Argalus and Parthenia. Being a choice flower, gatheked [sic] out of Sir Phillip Sidney's rare garden. Warrington: printed for the travelling stationers, [1800?]. *ESTC* gives this date but a copy at the Bodleian Library is catalogued with the date 'Between ca. 1810 and 1830?'.

2. *The Pleasant and Delightful History of Argalus and Parthenia*
Fifty-six pages; quarto history.

The pleasant and delightful history of Argalus and Parthenia. [S.l.: by T.H. for T. Passenger, 1683].

---

[49] Sidney, *New Arcadia*, p. 371.

The most pleasant and delightful history of Argalus and Parthenia. Newly reviv'd. London: printed by J. M[illet]. for Eben. Tracy, and are to be sold by J. Blare, at the Looking-Glass on London-Bridge, 1691.

3. *The Unfortunate Lovers, or the Famous and Renowned History of Argalus and Parthenia*
History; 'in four books'; all but one known editions in duodecimo format; all but one consisting of more than one hundred pages.

The unfortunate lovers: or, The famous and renowned history of Argalus and Parthenia. In three [sic] books. London: printed by W[illiam]. O[nley]. and sold by J. Blare, at the sign of the Looking glass on London-bridge, [1703]. Another issue which has the same title, including erroneous 'three' for the actual four books, has a different title page which bears the imprint 'printed by W. O. and sold by C. Bates, at the Sun and Bible in Pye-corner'.

The unfortunate lovers: the history of Argalus and Parthenia. In four books. Adorn'd with cuts. London: printed by W. O. [i.e. William Onley] and sold by the booksellers, [1705?]. The only difference between this and the previous edition is that this has continuous pagination, where the previous edition begins pagination anew with each book. *ESTC* assigns 1705 as a possible date but it is not clear whether Olney printed this before or after the previous edition.

The unfortunate lovers: the history of Argalus and Parthenia. In four books. Adorn'd with cuts. 'The fourth edition'. London: printed by Tho. Norris, at the Looking-Glass on London-Bridge, [1715?].

The unfortunate lovers: or, the history of Argalus and Pathenia. In four books. Adorn'd with cuts. 'The fifth edition'. London: printed for C. Hitch and L. Hawes; S. Crowder; C. Ware; H. Woodgate and S. Brooks, [1760?].

The unfortunate lovers: the history of Argalus and Parthenia. In four books. Adorn'd with cuts. London: printed for Henry Woodgate, and Samuel Brooks, [1760?].

The Famous and renowned history of Argalus and Parthenia. In four books. Adorned with cuts. 'The seventh edition'. Glasgow: Printed by Daniel Reid, for J. Tait, Morison and M'Allum, Booksellers, in the Salt-Mercat, M,DCC,LXXII.

The famous and renowned history of Argalus and Parthenia. In four books. Adorned with cuts. 'The eighteenth edition'. Glasgow: printed for the booksellers, MDCCLXXXV. (18mo)

The unfortunate lovers; or, the tragical history of Argalus and Parthenia. Containing their great example of true love. Wolverhampton: printed by J. Smart, [1790?]. A true chapbook – twenty-four pages in duodecimo.

Bibliography

Primary

Manuscript

Cambridge
Magdalene College, Pepys MS 2030.

Dublin
Trinity College MS 160, pt. 2.

Edinburgh
National Library of Scotland, MS Advocates' 19.3.1.

London
BL, Additional MS 57,335.
BL, Harley MS 172.
BL, Harley MS 283.
BL, Harley MS 2399.
BL, MS Egerton 3132A.
BL, Royal MS 17.B.43.

New York
Pierpont Morgan Library, MS 817.

Oxford
Balliol College, MS 354.
Bodleian Library, MS Douce 261.
Bodleian Library, MS Rawlinson D82.
Bodleian Library, MS Rawlinson Poet. 28.

Yale University
Beinecke Library, MS Osborn fa50.

Printed

Agrippa, Cornelius, *Three Books of Occult Philosophy Written by Henry Cornelius Agrippa*, trans. J.F. (London, 1651).
Ascham, Roger, *The Scholemaster* (London, 1570).
[Baldwin, William], *Westerne Wyll upon the debate betweene Churchyarde and Camell* (London, [1551]).
Bourchier, John, *Duke Huon of Burdeux*, ed. S.L. Lee, EETS ES 40, 41, 43 and 50 (London, 1882–87).

Bracciolini, Giovanni Francesco Poggio, 'On the Inconstancy of Fortune', *The Renaissance in Europe: An Anthology*, ed. Peter Elmer et al. (New Haven, CT, 2000), pp. 6–12.

Brie, Friedrich W.D., ed., 'Zwei mittelenglische Prosaromane: *The Sege of Thebes* und *The Sege of Troy*', *Archiv für das Studium der neueren Sprachen und Literaturen* 130 (1913), 40–52 and 269–85.

Brinkelow, Henry, *The Complaynt of Roderyck Mors* (London, c.1542).

Bunt, G.H.V., ed., '*William of Palerne*': *An Alliterative Romance* (Groningen, 1985).

Burton, Robert, *The Anatomy of Melancholy*, ed. Floyd Dell and Paul Jordan-Smith (New York, 1927).

Calvino, Italo, *Our Ancestors*, trans. Archibald Colquhoun (London, 1980).

Camden, William, *Remaines of a greater worke, concerning Britaine* (London, 1605).

The Canterbury Tales: Fifteenth-Century Continuations and Additions, ed. John Bowers (Kalamazoo, 1992).

[Cato], *Preceptes of Cato with annotacions of D. Erasmus of Roterodame*, trans. Robert Burrant (London, 1553).

Caxton, William, *The Right Plesaunt and Goodly Historie of the Foure Sonnes of Aymon*, ed. Olivia Richardson, EETS ES 44–5 (London, 1885).

The English Poems of Charles of Orleans, ed. Robert Steele and Mabel Day, EETS OS 215, 220 (London, 1941 and 1946; rpt. 1970).

Chaucer, Geoffrey, *Works*, ed. F.N. Robinson, 2nd edn. (Oxford, 1977).

——, *The Riverside Chaucer*, gen. ed. Larry D. Benson, 3rd edn. (Oxford, 2008).

Cheke, John, *The Hurt of Sedition* (London, 1549).

Churchyard, Thomas, *Davy Dycars Dreame* (London, [1551]).

——, *A Playn and Fynall Confutacion: Of cammells corlyke oblatracion* (London, [1551]).

——, *A Myrrour for Man wherein he shall see the myserable state of thys worlde* (London, [1551–52]).

——, *The Fortunate Farewel to the most forward and noble Earle of Essex* (London, 1599).

Cicero, *De Oratore*, ed. and trans. E.W. Sutton, 2 vols. (Cambridge, MA, 1948).

Collier, Jeremy, *Ecclesiastical History of Great Britain*, 2 vols. (London, 1708–14).

Crandall, Coryl, ed., *Swetnam the Woman-Hater: The Controversy and the Play* (Lafayette, 1969).

Crowley, Robert, *Philargyrie of Great Britayne* (London, 1551).

——, *Select Works*, ed. J.M. Cowper, EETS ES 15 (London, 1872).

CSPD, 1649–1650 (London, 1875).

CSPD, 1650 (London, 1876).

Dean, James M., ed., *Medieval English Political Writings* (Kalamazoo, 1996).

D'Evelyn, Charlotte, ed., *Peter Idley's Instructions to his Son* (Boston, 1935).

Disticha de moribus (London, 1659).

Documents of the English Reformation: 1526–1701, ed. Gerald Bray (Cambridge, 2004).

Erasmus, Desiderius, *The Education of a Christian Prince*, trans. Neil M. Cheshire and Michael J. Heath, ed. Lisa Jardine (Cambridge, 1997).

The Faerie Leveller (London, 1648).

Falconer, Sheila, ed., '*Lorgaireacht an tSoidigh Naomhtha*': *An Early Modern Irish Translation of the Quest of the Holy Grail* (Dublin, 1953).

The Famous History of Heroick Acts: or, the Honour of Chivalry. Being an Abstract of Pembroke's Arcadia (London, 1701).
Ferrand, Jacques, *A Treatise on Lovesickness*, ed. Donald Beecher and Massimo Ciavolella (Syracuse, NY, 1990).
Four Middle English Romances, ed. Harriet Hudson (1996; Kalamazoo, 2006).
Foxe, John, *The Actes and Monuments* (London, 1570).
——, *A Sermon of Christ Crucified* (London, 1570).
Francomano, Emily C., *Three Spanish Querelle Texts: Grisel and Mirabella, The Slander Against Women, and The Defense of Ladies Against Slanderers: A Bilingual Edition and Study* (Toronto, 2013).
French, Walter Hoyt, and Charles Brockway Hale, eds., *Middle English Metrical Romances*, 2 vols. (New York, 1930).
Furnivall, F.J., ed., *The Babees Book: Early English Meals and Manners*, EETS OS 32 (London, 1868).
Galen, *Galen on Food and Diet*, ed. and trans. Mark Grant (London and New York, 2000).
Gascoigne, George, *The Droomme of doomesday* (London, 1576).
A godly dyalogue and dysputacyon betwene Pyers plowman and a popysh preest (London, 1550).
Gosson, Stephen, *The schoole of abuse* (London, 1579).
Gower, John, *The English Works of John Gower*, ed. G.C. Macaulay. EETS ES 81-2, 2 vols. (Oxford, 1900-01; rpt. 1969).
Green, Richard Leighton, ed., *A Selection of English Carols* (Oxford, 1962).
Hakluyt, Richard, *Divers Voyages touching the Discoverie of America and the Ilands adjacent* (London, 1582).
Hanmer, Meredith, *The Auncient Ecclesiasticall Histories of the First Six Hundred Yeares after Christ* (London, 1577).
Harington, Henry, ed., *Nugæ Antiquæ* (London, 1804).
Harvey, John, *Discoursive Probleme Concerninge Prophesies* (London, 1588).
Hesiod, *Hesiod*, ed. and trans. Glenn. W. Most (Cambridge, MA, 2006).
Heywood, John, *Works and Miscellaneous Short Poems*, ed. Burton A. Milligan (Urbana, 1956).
Hobbes, Thomas, *Leviathan*, ed. C.B. Macpherson (London, 1968).
Hoccleve, Thomas, *The Regiment of Princes*, ed. Charles R. Blyth (Kalamazoo, 1999).
Homer, *Iliad*, trans. A.T. Murray, 2 vols. (Cambridge, MA, 1924; rpt. 1978).
Hyde, Douglas, ed., *Gabháltais Shearluis Mhóir: The Conquests of Charlemagne*, ITS 19 (London, 1917).
I Playne Piers which cannot flatter (London, 1550).
[Innocent III], *The Mirror of Mans Lyfe* (London, 1576).
Isocrates, *A perfite looking glasse for all estates*, trans. Thomas Forrest (London, 1580).
[James I and VI], *The True Lawe of Free Monarchies* (London, 1603).
Juvenal and Persius, *Satires*, trans. S.M. Braund (Cambridge, MA, 2004).
Kay, John, *The siege of Rhodes* (London?, c.1482).
Keating, Geoffrey, *Foras Feasa ar Éirinn: the History of Ireland*, ed. David Comyn and P.S. Dinneen, 4 vols. (Dublin, 1902-14).

Knott, Eleanor, ed., *The Bardic Poems of Tadhg Dall Ó Huiginn*, 2 vols. ITS 22, 26 (London, 1922).
Kuin, Roger, ed., *The Correspondence of Sir Philip Sidney*, 2 vols. (Oxford, 2012).
Langland, William, *The Vision of Pierce Plowman* (London, 1550).
——, *Piers Plowman*, ed. A.V.C. Schmidt (London, 1995).
Latimer, Hugh, *Sermons*, ed. George Elwes (Cambridge, 1844).
The Lay Folks' Catechism, ed. Thomas Frederick Simmons and Henry Edward Nolloth, EETS OS 118 (London, 1901).
Leland, John, *De Viris Illustribus*, ed. and trans. James P. Carley with Caroline Brett (Toronto and London, 2010).
Lithgow, William, *Most Delectable, and True Discourse, of an Admired and Painefull Peregrination from Scotland to the Most Famous Kingdoms in Europe, Asia and Affricke* (London, 1614).
——, *The Totall Discourse, of the Rare Adventures, and Painefull Peregrinations of Long Nineteene Yeares Travayles* (London, 1632).
Lodge, Thomas, [*Honest Excuses*] (London, 1579).
——, *The famous, true and historicall life of Robert second Duke of Normandy, surnamed for his monstrous birth and behaviour, Robin the Divell* (London, 1591).
Lydgate, John, *John Lydgate: The Siege of Thebes*, ed. Robert R. Edwards (Kalamazoo, 2001).
Macalister, R.A.S., ed., *Two Irish Arthurian Romances: Eachtra an Mhadra Mhaoil, Eachtra Mhacaoimh-an-Iolair*, ITS 10 (London, 1908).
Mac Niocaill, Gearóid, ed., *Crown Surveys of Lands, 1540–41, with the Kildare Rental Begun in 1518* (Dublin, 1992).
Malory, Sir Thomas, *Works*, ed. Eugène Vinaver (Oxford, 1977).
——, *Works*, ed. Eugène Vinaver, 3rd edn., rev. P.J.C. Field, 3 vols. (Oxford, 1990).
Marlowe, Christopher, *Doctor Faustus*, ed. David Bevington and Eric Rasmussen (Manchester and New York, 1993).
Marstrander, Carl, 'Sechrán Na Banimpire', *Ériu* 5 (1911), 161–99
Melusine, ed. A.K. Donald, EETS ES 68 (London, 1895).
Mercurius Dogmaticus, Number 4 (27 January–3 February, 1648).
Metropolitan Nuncio 3 (6–13 June, 1649).
The Middle English Breton Lays, ed. Anne Laskaya and Eve Salisbury (Kalamazoo, 2001).
Milton, John, *The Minor English Poems*, ed. A.S.P. Woodhouse and Douglas Bush. Vol. 2 of *A Variorum Commentary on the Poems of John Milton*, gen. ed. Merritt Y. Hughes. 6 vols. (New York, 1970).
——, *Paradise Lost*, ed. Alastair Fowler, 2nd edn. (Harlow, 1998).
——, *The Complete Shorter Poems*, ed. Stella P. Revard (Oxford, 2009).
Müller-Lisowski, Käte, 'Stair Nuadat Find Femin', *Zeitschrift für Celtische Philologie* 13 (1921), 195–250.
Nashe, Thomas, *The Anatomie of Absurditie* (London, 1589).
Octavian Imperator, ed. Frances McSparran (Heidelberg, 1979).
O'Duffy, Richard J., ed., *Oidhe Chloinne Tuireann: The Fate of the Children of Tuireann* (Dublin, 1888).
Ó Rabhartaigh, T., and Douglas Hyde, 'An t-Amadán Mór', *Lia Fáil* 2 (1927), 191–228.

O'Rahilly, Cecile, ed., *Eachtra Uilliam* (Dublin, 1949).
——, ed. *Five Seventeenth-Century Political Poems* (Dublin, 1952).
Ovid, *Metamorphoses I*, trans. Frank Justus Miller, rev. G.P. Goold, 3rd edn., 2 vols. (Cambridge, MA, 1977).
Patrides, C.A., ed., *Milton's Lycidas: The Tradition and the Poem* (Columbia, 1983).
Pausanias, *Pausanias's Description of Greece*, trans. J.G. Frazer, 6 vols. (London, 1898).
Pepys, Samuel, *The Diary of Samuel Pepys*, ed. Robert Latham and William Matthews, 11 vols. (London, 2000).
Petrarca, Francesco, *Rerum familiarum libri I–VIII*, trans. Aldo S. Barnardo (Albany, NY, 1975).
——, *Scritti Inediti di Francesco Petrarca*, ed. Attilio Hortis (Trieste, 1874).
Pierce the Ploughmans Crede (London, 1553).
The Plowman's Tale (London, 1548).
Polybius, *The Histories of Polybius*, trans. Evelyn S. Shuckburgh (London, 1889; rpt. Cambridge, 2012).
The Praier and Complaynte of the Ploweman unto Christ (London, 1531).
Puttenham, George, *The Arte of English Poesie* (London, 1589).
Pyers plowmans exhortation unto the lordes, knightes and burgoysses of the parlyamenthouse. (London, 1550).
Quarles, Francis, *Argalus and Parthenia* (London, 1629).
Quarles, John, *Regale Lectum Miseriae: or, a Kingly Bed of Misery* (London, 1649).
Quin, Gordon, ed., *Stair Ercuil ocus a Bás: The Life and Death of Hercules*, ITS 38 (Dublin, 1939).
Raymond, Joad, ed., *Making the News* (Moreton-in-the-Marsh, 1993).
Robbins, Rossell Hope, ed., *Secular Lyrics of the XIVth and XVth Centuries* (1952; Oxford, 1955).
——, *Historical Poems of the XIVth and XVth Centuries* (New York, 1959).
Robinson, F.N., ed., 'The Irish Lives of Guy of Warwick and Bevis of Hampton', *Zeitschrift für Celtische Philologie* 6 (1908), 9–180, 273–338, 556.
Rowe, Elizabeth Singer, *Friendship in Death: In Twenty Letters from the Dead to the Living* (London, 1743).
Rowlands, Samuel, *The Complete Works of Samuel Rowlands*, ed. Edmund Gosse, 4 vols. (Glasgow, 1860).
A Ruful complaynt of the publyke weale to Englande (London, 1550).
Salisbury, Eve, ed., *The Trials and Joys of Marriage* (Kalamazoo, 2002).
Sannazaro, Jacopo, *Arcadia and Piscatorial Eclogues*, trans. Ralph Nash (Detroit, 1966).
[Seneca], *A frutefull worke of Lucius Anneus Seneca named the forme and rule of honest lyvynge*, trans. Robert Whittington (London, 1546).
——, *A frutefull worke of Lucius Anneus Senecæ. Called the Myrrour or glasse of maners and wysedome*, trans. Robert Whittington (London, 1546).
——, *Lucii Annei Senecae ad Gallioneni de remedis fortuitorum*, trans. Robert Whittington (London, 1547).
——, *L. Annæi Senecæ Cordubensis tragoediæ* (London, 1589).
——, *The workes of Lucius Annæus Seneca, both morrall and naturall* (London, 1614).
——, *Thyestes a tragedy, translated out of Seneca* (London, 1674).

——, *Moral Essays*, trans. John Basore, 3 vols. (New York, 1932).
Shakespeare, William, *Troilus and Cressida*, ed. Kenneth Palmer, The Arden Shakespeare (London, 1982).
——, *Hamlet*, ed. Harold Jenkins (1982; rpt. London, 2003).
——, *The Oxford Shakespeare: The Complete Works*, ed. Stanley Wells et al., 2nd edn. (Oxford, 2005).
——, *The Norton Shakespeare*, ed. Stephen Greenblatt et al., 2nd edn. (London, 2008).
Shepherd, Simon, ed., *The Women's Sharp Revenge: Five Women's Pamphlets from the Renaissance* (New York, 1985).
Sheppard, Samuel, *God and Mammon* (n.p., 1646).
——, *The Yeare of Jubile* (n.p., 1646).
——, *The Loves of Amandus and Sophronia* (London, 1650).
——, *Epigrams Theological, Philosophical, and Romantick* (London, 1651).
——, *The Faerie King (c.1650)*, ed. P.J. Klemp (Salzburg, 1984).
Shuffelton, George, ed., *Codex Ashmole 61: A Compilation of Popular Middle English Verse* (Kalamazoo, 2008).
Sidney, Philip, *The Countess of Pembroke's Arcadia (The Old Arcadia)*, ed. Jean Robertson (Oxford, 1973).
——, *The Countess of Pembroke's Arcadia*, ed. Maurice Evans (Harmondsworth, 1987).
——, *The Countess of Pembroke's Arcadia (The New Arcadia)*, ed. Victor Skretkowicz (Oxford, 1987).
——, *Sir Philip Sidney: The Major Works*, ed. Katherine Duncan-Jones (Oxford, 1989).
——, *Sidney's 'The Defence of Poesy' and Selected Renaissance Literary Criticism*, ed. Gavin Alexander (London, 2004).
Simons, John, ed., *Guy of Warwick and Other Chapbook Romances* (Exeter, 1998).
Sir Gawain and the Green Knight, ed. J.R.R. Tolkien and E.V. Gordon; 2nd edn., ed. Norman Davis (Oxford, 1979).
Sir Perceval of Galles and Ywain and Gawain, ed. Mary Flowers Braswell (Kalamazoo, 1995).
Six Ecclesiastical Satires, ed. James Dean (Kalamazoo, 1991).
Skelton, John, *A ryght delectable traytyse upon a goodly Garlande or Chapelet of Laurell by mayster Skelton Poete laureat* (London, 1523).
——, *Pithy pleasaunt and profitable workes of maister Skelton* (London, 1568).
——, *Complete English Poems*, ed. John Scattergood (Harmondsworth, 1983).
——, *The Latin Writings of John Skelton*, ed. David R. Carlson, *SP* 88 (1991), 1–125.
Smith, Henry, *A Treatise of the Lord's Supper* (London, 1591).
Smith, James S. Easby, ed., *The Songs of Alcaeus* (Washington, 1901).
[Smith, Thomas], *De Republica Anglorum, A Discourse on the Commonwealth of England*, ed. L. Alston. (Cambridge, 1906).
——, *A Discourse of the Common Weal of this Realm of England*, ed. Elizabeth Lamond (Cambridge, 1954).
Smithson, Samuel, *Fortunes Tennis-Ball: or, The most excellent history of Dorastus and Fawnia. Rendred in delightful English verse; and worthy the perusal of all sorts of people. By S.S. Gent.* (London, 1672).
Spenser, Edmund, *The Shorter Poems*, ed. Richard A. McCabe (New York, 1999).

———, *The Faerie Queene*, ed. A.C. Hamilton, 2nd edn., with Hiroshi Yamashita and Toshiyuki Suzuki (Harlow, 2001).
Stokes, Whitley, 'The Irish Version of *Fierabras*', *Revue Celtique* 19 (1898), 14–57, 118–67, 252–91, 364–93.
———, 'The Gaelic Maundeville', *Zeitschrift für Celtische Philologie* 2 (1899), 1–6, 226–300.
A Supplication to the Poore Commons (London, 1546).
Swetnam, Joseph, *A Critical Edition of Joseph Swetnam's The Araignment of Lewd, Idle, Froward, and Unconstant Women (1615)*, ed. F.W. Van Heertum (Nijmegen, 1989).
Theocritus, *Theocritus*, ed. and trans. A.S.F. Gow, 2nd edn., 2 vols. (Cambridge, 1952, rpt. 2008).
The Tragical History, Admirable Atchievments and various events of Guy Earl of Warwick (London, 1661).
Tyler, Margaret, *Mirror of Princely Deeds and Knighthood*, ed. Joyce Boro (London, 2014).
Tyndale, William, *The Obedience of A Christen Man* (London, 1970).
Usk, Thomas, *The Testament of Love*, ed. R.A. Shoaf (Kalamazoo, 1998).
Virgil, *Aeneid VII–XII*, ed. and trans. H. Rushton Fairclough; rev. G.P. Goold (Cambridge, MA, 1918, rev. 2000).
———, *Eclogues, Georgics, Aeneid I–VI*, ed. and trans. H. Rushton Fairclough; rev. G.P. Goold (Cambridge, MA, 1999).
Virgilius (Antwerp. 1518).
Volk, Katharina, ed., *Virgil's Eclogues* (Oxford, 2008).
Wallis, Faith, *Medieval Medicine: A Reader* (Toronto, 2010).
Warton, Thomas, *Observations on The Fairy Queene of Spenser* (London and Oxford, 1754).
Watson, Henry, *Valentine and Orson*, ed. Arthur Dickson, EETS OS 204 (London, 1937).
Wauquelin, Jehan, *The Medieval Romance of Alexander: Jehan Wauquelin's The Deeds and Conquests of Alexander the Great*, trans. Nigel Bryant (Woodbridge, 2012).
White, T.H., *The Sword in the Stone* (London, 1959).
Wright, Louis B., ed., *Advice to a Son: Precepts of Lord Burghley, Sir Walter Raleigh, and Francis Osborne* (Ithaca, 1962).
The Complete Works of Sir Thomas Wyatt the Elder, ed. Jason Powell, 2 vols. (Oxford, forthcoming 2016).

Secondary

Aers, David, 'A Whisper in the Ear of Early Modernists; or, Reflections on Literary Critics Writing the "History of the Subject"', *Culture and History, 1350–1600: Essays on English Communities, Identities and Writing*, ed. David Aers (Detroit, 1992), pp. 177–202.
Aggeler, Geoffrey, *Nobler in the Mind: The Stoic-Skeptic Dialectic in English Renaissance Tragedy* (Newark, 1998).
Alford, John A., ed., *A Companion to Piers Plowman* (Berkeley, 1988).
Allen, Valerie, *On Farting: Laughter and Language in the Middle Ages* (New York, 2007).
Archibald, Elizabeth, 'Malory's Ideal of Fellowship', *RES* NS 43 (1992), 311–28.
Armstrong, E., *A Ciceronian Sunburn: A Tudor Dialogue on Humanistic Rhetoric and Civic Poetics* (Columbia, 2006).

Ariès, Philippe, *Centuries of Childhood*, trans. Robert Baldick (London, 1962).
Arn, Mary-Jo, 'Charles of Orleans and the English Poems of Harley 682', *English Studies* 74 (1993), 222–35.
Baker, Emerson W., et al, eds., *American Beginnings: Exploration, Culture, and Cartography in the Land of Norumbega* (Lincoln, 1994).
Barnes, A.W., 'Constructing the Sexual Subject of John Skelton', *ELH* 71 (2004), 29–51.
Barney, Stephen A., 'Chaucer's *Troilus*: Meter and Grammar', *Essays on the Art of Chaucer's Verse*, ed. Alan T. Gaylord (London, 2001), pp. 163–91.
Barron, Caroline, 'Chivalry, Pageantry and Merchant Culture in Medieval London', *Heraldry, Pageantry and Social Display in Medieval England*, ed. Peter Coss and Maurice Keen (Woodbridge, 2002), pp. 219–41.
Beilin, Elaine V., *Redeeming Eve: Women Writers of the English Renaissance* (Princeton, 1987).
Benson, Larry D., *Malory's 'Morte Darthur'* (Cambridge, MA, 1976).
Blagden, Cyprian, 'Notes on the Ballad Market in the Second Half of the Seventeenth Century', *Studies in Bibliography* 6 (1954), 161–80.
Blair, Claude, *European Armour circa 1066 to circa 1700* (London, 1958).
Blake, N.F., 'Lord Berners: A Survey', *Medievalia et Humanistica* 2 (1971), 119–32.
Bloch, R. Howard, *Medieval Misogyny and the Invention of Western Romantic Love* (Chicago, 1991).
Bloom, Harold, *The Anxiety of Influence: A Theory of Poetry* (Oxford, 1973).
Bornstein, Diane, 'William Caxton's Chivalric Romances and the Burgundian Renaissance in England', *English Studies* 57 (1976), 1–10.
Boro, Joyce, 'The Textual History of *Huon of Burdeux*: A Reassessment of the Facts', *NQ* 48.3 (2001), 233–7.
——, 'A Source and Date for the Fragment of *Grisel y Mirabella* Found in the Binding of Emmanuel College 338.5.43', *Transactions of the Cambridge Bibliographical Society* 12 (2003), 422–36.
——, 'All for Love: Lord Berners and the Enduring, Evolving Romance', *Oxford Handbook of Tudor Literature, 1485–1603*, ed. Mike Pincombe and Cathy Shrank (Oxford, 2009), pp. 87–102.
——, 'Reading Juan de Flores's *Grisel y Mirabella* in Early Modern England', *Translation, Print and Culture in Britain, 1473–1640*, ed. S.K. Barker and B. Hosington (Leiden, 2012), pp. 35–59.
Boyce, Benjamin, 'The Stoic Consolatio and Shakespeare', *Publication of the Modern Language Association* 64 (1949), 771–80.
Braden, Gordon, *Renaissance Tragedy and the Senecan Tradition* (New Haven, CT, 1985).
Breathnach, Caoimhín, 'Brian Ó Corcráin and *Eachtra Mhacaoimh an Iolair*', *Éigse* 34 (2004), 44–8.
Breatnach, Pádraig A., 'The Aesthetics of Irish Bardic Composition: An Analysis of *Fuaras iongnadh, a fhir chumainn* by Fearghal Óg Mac an Bhaird', *Cambrian Medieval Celtic Studies* 42 (Winter 2001), 51–72.
Breen, Dan, 'Laureation and Identity: Rewriting Literary History in John Skelton's *Garland of Laurel*', *JMEMS* 40.2 (2010), 347–71.
Brewer, Charlotte, *Editing Piers Plowman: The Evolution of the Text* (Cambridge, 1996).

Bruford, Alan, *Gaelic Folk-Tales and Mediaeval Romances: A Study of the Early Modern Irish 'Romantic Tales' and Their Oral Derivatives* (Dublin, 1969).
Bullough, Donald, 'Recycling Charlemagne in the Fifteenth Century, North and South', *Early Medieval Europ.* 3 (2003), 389–97.
Burckhardt, Jacob, *The Civilization of the Renaissance in Italy* (London, 1990).
Burrow, John, 'The Poet as Petitioner', *Studies in the Age of Chaucer* 3 (1981), 61–75.
Byrne, Aisling, 'The Earls of Kildare and their Books at the End of the Middle Ages', *The Library* 14 (2013), 129–53.
——, 'Family, Locality and Nationality: Vernacular Adaptations of the *Expugnatio Hibernica* from Late Medieval Ireland', *Medium Ævum* 82 (2013), 101–18.
——, 'Malory's Sources for the *Tale of the Sankgreal*: Some Overlooked Evidence from *Lorgaireacht an tSoidhigh Naomhtha*', *Arthurian Literature* 30 (2013), 87–100.
——, 'A Lost Insular Version of the Romance of *Octavian*', *Medium Ævum* 83 (2014), 286–301.
——, 'The Circulation of English Romance in Medieval Ireland', *Medieval Romance and Material Culture*, ed. Nicholas Perkins (Cambridge, 2015), pp. 183–98.
Byrne, Mary E., et al., *Catalogue of Irish Manuscripts in the Royal Irish Academy*, 10 vols. (Dublin, 1926–70).
Cannon, Christopher, 'Malory's Crime: Chivalric Identity and the Evil Will', *Medieval Literature and Historical Inquiry: Essays in Honour of Derek Pearsall*, ed. David Aers (Cambridge, 2000), pp. 159–83.
Carney, Maura, 'Review of *Eachtra Uilliam*, ed. Cecile O'Rahilly', *Éigse* 6 (1948–52), 186–9.
Carpenter, Jennifer and Sally-Beth MacLean, eds., *Power of the Weak: Studies on Medieval Women* (Urbana, 1995).
Carruthers, Mary, *The Book of Memory: A Study of Memory in Medieval Culture* (Cambridge, 1990).
Chaytor, H.J., *From Script to Print: An Introduction to Medieval Vernacular Literature* (1945; London, 1966).
Chrimes, S.B., *Henry VII* (1972; London, 1977).
Coleridge, Samuel Taylor, *Shakespearean Criticism*, ed. T.M. Raysor, 2 vols. (London, 1960).
Coletti, Theresa, 'The Chester Cycle in Sixteenth-Century Religious Culture', *JMEMS* 37.3 (2007), 531–47.
Colker, Marvin L., *Trinity College Library Dublin: Descriptive Catalogue of the Medieval and Renaissance Latin Manuscripts*, 2 vols. (Dublin 1991).
Cooper, Helen, 'The Goat and the Eclogue', *Philological Quarterly* 53 (1973), 363–79.
——, 'Magic that does not work', *Medievalia et Humanistica* 7 (1976), 131–46.
——, *Pastoral: Mediaeval into Renaissance* (Cambridge, 1977).
——, *Oxford Guides to Chaucer: The Canterbury Tales*, 2nd edn. (Oxford, 1996).
——, 'Counter-Romance: Civil Strife and Father-Killing in the Prose Romances', *The Long Fifteenth Century*, ed. Helen Cooper and Sally Mapstone (Oxford, 1997), pp. 141–62.
——, 'Romance After 1400', *The Cambridge History of Medieval English Literature*, ed. David Wallace (Cambridge, 1999), pp. 690–719.
——, *The English Romance in Time: Transforming Motifs from Geoffrey of Monmouth to the Death of Shakespeare* (Oxford, 2004).

——, 'Good Advice on Leaving Home in the Romances', *Youth in the Middle Ages*, ed. P.J.P Goldberg and Felicity Riddy (York, 2004), pp. 101–121.

——, 'Thomas of Erceldoune: Romance as Prophecy', *Cultural Encounters in the Romance of Medieval England*, ed. Corinne Saunders (Cambridge, 2005), pp. 171–87.

——, 'Guy of Warwick, Upstart Crows and Mounting Sparrows', *Shakespeare, Marlowe, Jonson: New Directions in Biography*, ed. Takashi Kozuka and J.R. Mulryne (Aldershot, 2006), pp. 119–38.

——, 'Skeltonics', *LRB* 28, 14 December 2006, 32–4.

——, *Shakespeare and the Medieval World* (London, 2010).

——, 'Choosing Poetic Fathers: The English Problem', *Medieval and Early Modern Authorship*, ed. Guillemette Bolens and Lukas Erne (Tübingen, 2011), pp. 29–49.

——, Ruth Morse and Peter Holland, eds., *Medieval Shakespeare: Pasts and Presents* (Cambridge, 2013).

Covington, Harry Franklin, 'The Discovery of Maryland or Verrazzano's Visit to the Eastern Shore', *Maryland Historical Magazine* 10.3 (1915), 199–217.

Crane, Mary Thomas, *Framing Authority: Sayings, Self and Society in Sixteenth-Century England* (Princeton, 1993).

Crane, Ronald S., *The Vogue of Medieval Chivalric Romance during the English Renaissance* (1919; rpt. Norwood, PA, 1977).

Crawforth, Hannah, *Etymology and the Invention of English in Early Modern Literature* (Cambridge, 2013).

Cronin, Anne, 'The Sources of Keating's *Forus feasa ar Éirinn*', *Éigse* 4 (1945), 235–79.

Cronin, Michael, *Translating Ireland: Translation, Languages, Culture* (Cork, 1996).

Cummings, Brian, and James Simpson, eds., *Cultural Reformations: Medieval and Renaissance in Literary History* (Oxford, 2010).

Cunningham, Bernadette, *The World of Geoffrey Keating: History, Myth and Religion in Seventeenth-Century Ireland* (Dublin, 2000).

Curtius, Ernst Robert, *European Literature and the Latin Middle Ages*, trans. W.R. Trask (London, 1979).

D'Abate, Richard, 'On the Meaning of a Name: "Norumbega" and the Representation of North America', *American Beginnings: Exploration, Culture, and Cartography in the Land of Norumbega*, ed. Emerson W. Baker et al. (Lincoln, 1994), pp. 61–90.

Dane, Joseph A., 'On "*Correctness*": A Note on Some Press Variants in Thynne's 1532 Edition of Chaucer', *The Library*, 6th series 17 (1995), 156–67.

——, 'Bibliographical History versus Bibliographical Evidence: The Plowman's Tale and Early Chaucer Editions', *Bulletin of the John Rylands University Library of Manchester* 78 (1996), 47–61.

——, *Who Is Buried in Chaucer's Tomb? Studies in the Reception of Chaucer's Book* (East Lansing, 1998).

——, and Seth Lerer, 'Press-Variants in John Stow's Chaucer (1561) and the Text of "Adam Scriveyn"', *Transactions of the Cambridge Bibliographical Society* 11 (1999), 468–79.

Davies, Michael Howard, '*Fierabras* in Ireland: The Transmission and Cultural Setting of a French Epic in the Medieval Irish Literary Tradition' (unpublished PhD. thesis, Edinburgh University, 1995).

Davis, Alex, *Chivalry and Romance in the English Renaissance* (Cambridge, 2003).

Davis, O.B., 'A Note on the Function of Polonius' Advice', *SQ* 9 (1958), 85–6.
De Grazia, Margreta, *Hamlet without Hamlet* (Cambridge, 2007).
——, 'The Modern Divide: From Either Side', *JMEMS* 37 (2007), 469–91.
——, 'Anachronism', *Cultural Reformations*, ed. Cummings and Simpson, pp. 13–32.
Dillon, Myles, et al., *Catalogue of Irish Manuscripts in the Franciscan Library Killiney* (Dublin, 1969).
Dipple, Elizabeth, 'Harmony and Pastoral in the Old Arcadia', *ELH* 35.3 (1968), 309–28.
Dobin, Howard, *Merlin's Disciples: Prophecy, Poetry, and Power in Renaissance England* (Stanford, 1990).
Doloff, Steven, 'Polonius's Precepts and Thomas Tusser's "Five Hundreth Points of Good Husbandrie"', *RES* 42 (1991), 227–8.
Dooley, Ann, 'Literature and Society in Early Seventeenth-Century Ireland: The Evaluation of Change', *Celtic Languages and Celtic Peoples*, ed. Cyril J. Byrne, Margaret Harry and Pádraig Ó Siadhail (Halifax, 1992), pp. 513–34.
Driver, Martha W., and Sid Ray, eds., *Shakespeare and the Middle Ages: Essays on the Performance and Adaptation of the Plays with Medieval Sources or Settings* (London, 2009).
Edwards, A.S.G., ed., *John Skelton: The Critical Heritage* (London, 1981).
Edwards, H.L.R., *Skelton: The Life and Times of an Early Tudor Poet* (London, 1949).
Elias, Norbert, *The Civilising Process*, trans. Edmund Jephcott, 2 vols. (1939; Oxford, 1978).
Elton, G.R., 'Reform and the "Commonwealth-Men" of Edward VI's Reign', *The English Commonwealth, 1547–1640*, ed. Peter Clark et al. (Leicester, 1979), pp. 23–38.
Esdaile, Arundell, *A List of English Tales and Prose Romances Printed before 1740. Part I. 1475–1642. Part II. 1643–1739* (London, 1912).
Espie, Jeff, '(Un)couth: Chaucer, *The Shepheardes Calender* and the Forms of Mediation', *Spenser Studies*, forthcoming.
Everett, Barbara, *Young Hamlet: Essays on Shakespeare's Tragedies* (Oxford, 1989).
Falk, Doris, 'Proverbs and the Polonius Destiny', *SQ* 18 (1967), 23–36.
Ferguson, Arthur, *The Indian Summer of English Chivalry* (Durham, NC, 1960).
Field, B.S., 'Sidney's Influence: the Evidence of the Publication of the *History of Argalus and Parthenia*', *English Language Notes* 17 (1979), 98–102.
Fish, Stanley, *John Skelton's Poetry* (New Haven, CT, 1965).
Flannery, Mary C., *John Lydgate and the Poetics of Fame* (Cambridge, 2012).
Fletcher, Anthony and Diarmaid MacCulloch, *Tudor Rebellions*, 5th edn. (Harlow, 2004).
Flower, Robin, 'Ireland and Medieval Europe', *Proceedings of the British Academy* 13 (1927), 271–303.
Foucault, Michel. 'What is an Author?', *Textual Strategies: Perspectives in Post-Structuralist Criticism*, ed. Josué V. Harari (Ithaca, 1979), pp. 141–60.
Fowler, Alastair, *Kinds of Literature: An Introduction to the Theory of Genres and Modes* (Oxford, 1982).
Furrow, Melissa, *Expectations of Romance: The Reception of a Genre in Medieval England* (Cambridge, 2009).
Gans, Nathan A., 'Archaism and Neologism in Spenser's Diction', *MP* 76 (1979), 377–9.
Gellert Lyons, Bridget, *Voices of Melancholy: Studies in Literary Treatments of Melancholy in Renaissance England* (London, 1971).

Giancarlo, Matthew, 'Dressing up a "Galaunt": Traditional Piety and Fashionable Politics in Peter Idley's "Translacions" of Mannyng and Lydgate', *After Arundel: Religious Writing in Fifteenth-Century England*, ed. Vincent Gillespie and Kantik Ghosh (Turnhout, 2011), pp. 429–48.

Gill, R.B., 'A Purchase of Glory: The Persona of Late Elizabethan Satire', *SP* 12 (1975), 408–18.

Gillespie, Alexandra, *Print Culture and the Medieval Author: Chaucer, Lydgate, and Their Books 1473–1557* (Oxford, 2006).

Gillespie, Raymond, 'Print Culture 1550–1700', *The Oxford History of the Irish Book, III: The Irish Book in English 1550–1800*, ed. Raymond Gillespie and Andrew Hadfield (Oxford, 2006), pp. 17–33.

Gingerich, Owen, and Melvin J. Tucker, 'The Astronomical Dating of Skelton's *Garland of Laurel*', *HLQ* 32 (1969), 207–20.

Goldberg, Jonathan, *Queering the Renaissance* (Durham, NC, 1994).

Goodman, Anthony, *The Wars of the Roses: Military Activity and English Society, 1452–97* (London, 1981).

Gordon, Ian A., *The Movement of English Prose* (London, 1966).

Gordon, James Daniel, *The English Language: An Historical Introduction* (New York, 1972).

Gough, Melinda J., 'Women's Popular Culture? Teaching the Swetnam Controversy', *Debating Gender in Early Modern England, 1500–1700*, ed. Christina Malcolmson and Mihoko Suzuki (New York, 2002), pp. 79–100.

Gowans, Linda, 'The *Eachtra an Amadáin Mhóir* as a Response to the *Perceval* of Chrétien de Troyes', *Arthurian Literature, 19: Comedy in Arthurian Literature* (2003), 199–230.

Gray, Douglas, *Later Medieval English Literature* (Oxford, 2008).

Green, Reina, 'Poisoned Ears and Parental Advice in *Hamlet*', *Early Modern Literary Studies* 11.3 (2006).

Greenblatt, Stephen, *Renaissance Self-Fashioning: From More to Shakespeare* (Chicago, 1980).

Greene, Thomas, *The Light in Troy: Imitation and Discovery in Renaissance Poetry* (New Haven, CT, 1982).

Griffiths, Jane, 'Text and Authority: John Stow's 1568 Edition of Skelton's Works', *John Stow: Author, Editor and Reader*, ed. Ian Gadd and Alexandra Gillespie (London, 2004), pp. 127–34.

——, 'What's in a Name? The Transmission of "John Skelton, Laureate" in Manuscript and Print', *HLQ* 67 (2004), 215–35.

——, *John Skelton and Poetic Authority: Defining the Liberty to Speak* (Oxford, 2006).

Gruen, Erich S., ed., *Cultural Identity in the Ancient Mediterranean* (Los Angeles, 2010).

Gurr, Andrew, *The Shakespearean Stage, 1574–1642* (Cambridge, 2009).

Habicht, Christian, *Pausanias' Guide to Ancient Greece* (Berkeley, 1985).

Hadfield, Andrew, *Literature, Politics and National Identity: Reformation to Renaissance* (Cambridge, 1994).

Hall, Jonathan M., *Ethnic Identity in Greek Antiquity* (Cambridge, 2000).

Hamilton, A.C., 'Spenser and Langland', *SP* 55 (1958), 533–48.

Hamilton, Donna B., 'Some Romance Sources for *King Lear*: *Robert of Sicily* and *Robert the Devil*', *SP* 71 (1974), 173–91.
Hampton, Timothy, *Fictions of Embassy: Literature and Diplomacy in Early Modern England* (Ithaca, 2009).
Hamrick, Stephen, ed., *Tottel's Songes and Sonettes in Context* (Farnham, 2013).
Hardman, Phillipa, 'Popular Romances and Young Readers', *A Companion to Medieval Popular Romance*, ed. Raluca L. Radulescu and Cory James Rushton (Cambridge, 2009), pp. 150–64.
Harris, Jason, and Keith C. Sidwell, ed., *Making Ireland Roman: Irish Neo-Latin Writers and the Republic of Letters* (Cork, 2009).
Hawes, Greta, *Rationalizing Myth in Antiquity* (Oxford, 2014).
Hazelton, Richard, 'The Christianization of Cato: The *Disticha Catonis* in the Light of Late Medieval Commentaries', *Mediaeval Studies* 19 (1957), 157–73.
Heidegger, Martin, 'The Age of the World Picture', *Off the Beaten Track*, ed. and trans. Julian Young and Kenneth Haynes (Cambridge, 2002), pp. 57–85.
Helfer, Rebeca, *Spenser's Ruins and the Art of Recollection* (Toronto, 2012).
Helgerson, Richard, *The Elizabethan Prodigals* (Berkeley, 1976).
——, 'What Hamlet Remembers', *Shakespeare Studies* 10 (1977), 67–97.
——, *Self-crowned Laureates: Spenser, Jonson, Milton and the Literary System* (Berkeley, 1983).
——, *Forms of Nationhood: The Elizabethan Writing of England* (Chicago, 1992).
Henderson, Katherine Usher, and Barbara McManus, eds., *Half Humankind: Contexts and Texts of the Controversy about Women in England, 1540–1640* (Urbana, 1985).
Herron, Thomas, and Michael Potterton, eds., *Ireland in the Renaissance, c.1540–1660* (Dublin, 2007).
Hicks, Michael, *The Wars of the Roses* (New Haven, CT, 2010).
Higl, Andrew. 'Printing Power: Selling Lydgate, Gower, and Chaucer', *Essays in Medieval Studies* 23 (2006) 57–77.
Hoenselaars, Ton, 'Joseph Swetnam, alias Misogynos, and His Women Readers (1615–1620)', *L'Auteur et Son Public au Temps de la Renaissance*, ed. M.T. Jones-Davies (Paris, 1998), pp. 165–89.
Hopkins, Andrea, *The Sinful Knights: A Study of Middle English Penitential Romance* (Oxford, 1990).
Hudson, Anne, 'Epilogue: The Legacy of *Piers Plowman*', *Companion*, ed. Alford, pp. 251–66.
Huneycutt, Lois L., 'Intercession and the High-Medieval Queen: The Esther Topos', *Power of the Weak*, ed. Carpenter and MacLean, pp. 126–46.
Hunter, G.K., 'Isocrates' Precepts and Polonius' Character', *SQ* 8.4 (1957), 501–6.
Hutson, Lorna, *The Usurer's Daughter: Male Friendship and Fictions of Women in Sixteenth-Century England* (London, 1994).
Hutton, William, *Describing Greece: Landscape and Literature in the Periegesis of Pausanias* (Cambridge, 2005).
Ingram, Martin, 'The Reform of Popular Culture? Sex and Marriage in Early Modern England', *Popular Culture in Seventeenth-Century England*, ed. Barry Reay (London, 1985), pp. 129–65.

[Jaech], Sharon L. Jansen, 'British Library MS Sloane 2578 and Popular Unrest in England, 1554–56', *Manuscripta* 29 (1985), 30–41.

——, 'Politics, Protest, and a New *Piers Plowman* Fragment: The Voice of the Past in Tudor England', *RES*, n.s. 40 (1989), 93–9.

James, M.R., *Bibliotheca Pepysiana, Part III, Mediæval Manuscripts* (London, 1923).

Jones, Ann Rosalind, 'Counterattacks on "the Bayter of Women": Three Pamphleteers of the Early Seventeenth Century', *The Renaissance Englishwoman in Print: Counterbalancing the Canon*, ed. Anne M. Haselkorn and Betty S. Travitsky (Amherst, 1990), pp. 45–62.

——, 'From Polemical Prose to the Red Bull: The Swetnam Controversy in Women-Voiced Pamphlets and the Public Theater', *The Project of Prose in Early Modern Europe and the New World*, ed. Elizabeth Fowler and Roland Greene (Cambridge, 1997), pp. 122–37.

Jones, Mike Rodman, *Radical Pastoral, 1381–1594: Appropriation and the Writing of Religious Controversy* (Farnham, 2011).

Jones, Whitney R.D., *The Mid-Tudor Crisis 1539–63* (London, 1973).

Jordan, Constance, 'Gender and Justice in *Swetnam the Woman-hater*', *Renaissance Drama* 18 (1987), 149–69.

Kastan, David Scott, *A Will to Believe: Shakespeare and Religion* (Oxford, 2014).

Kay, Dennis, 'Sidney: A Critical Heritage', *Sir Philip Sidney: An Anthology of Modern Criticism*, ed. Dennis Kay (Oxford, 1987), pp. 1–41.

Kelen, Sarah A., *Langland's Early Modern Identities* (Basingstoke, 2007).

Kerby-Fulton, Kathryn, 'Langland and the Bibliographic Ego', *Written Work: Langland, Labour, and Authorship*, ed. Kathryn Kerby-Fulton and Steven Justice (Philadelphia, 1997), pp. 67–143.

Kernan, Alvin, *The Cankered Muse: Satire of the English Renaissance* (New Haven, CT, 1959).

Kerrigan, John, *Motives of Woe: Shakespeare and 'Female Complaint'* (Oxford, 1991).

Kesselring, K.J., *Mercy and Authority in the Tudor State* (Cambridge, 2003).

Kidnie, Margaret Jane, '"Enter […] Lorenzo, Disguised Like an Amazon": Powerdressing in *Swetnam the Woman-Hater, Arraigned by Women*', *Cahiers Élisabéthains* 62 (2002), 33–45.

King, Andrew, *The Faerie Queene and Middle English Romance: The Matter of Just Memory* (Oxford, 2000).

——, '*Guy of Warwick* and the *Faerie Queene*, Book II: Chivalry Through the Ages', *Guy of Warwick: Icon and Ancestor*, ed. Alison Wiggins and Rosalind Field (Cambridge, 2007), pp. 167–84.

——, 'Spenser, Chaucer, and Medieval Romance', *The Oxford Handbook of Edmund Spenser*, ed. Richard A. McCabe (Oxford, 2010).

King, John N., 'Robert Crowley's Editions of *Piers Plowman*: A Tudor Apocalypse', *MP* 73 (1976), 342–52.

——, *English Reformation Literature: The Tudor Origins of the Protestant Tradition* (Princeton, 1982).

——, 'Spenser's *Shepheardes Calender* and Protestant Pastoral Satire', *Renaissance Genres:*

Essays on Theory, History, and Interpretation, ed. Barbara Kiefer Lewalski (Cambridge, MA, 1986), pp. 369–98.
——, *Spenser's Poetry and the Reformation Tradition* (Princeton, 1990).
Kinney, Clare, 'Obscuring the Argument: the Seventeenth-Century Afterlife of Sidney's *Argalus and Parthenia*', unpublished conference paper given at the 37th International Congress on Medieval Studies, University of Western Michigan, Kalamazoo, 2002.
Kipling, Gordon, *The Triumph of Honour: Burgundian Origins of the Elizabethan Renaissance* (Hague, 1977).
Kiséry, András, '"I Lack Advancement": Public Rhetoric, Private Prudence, and the Political Agent in *Hamlet*, 1561–1609', *ELH* 81 (2014), 29–60.
Kittredge, George Lyman, 'Chaucer's Lollius', *Harvard Studies in Classical Philology* 28 (1917), 47–133.
Knight, Charles A., *The Literature of Satire* (Cambridge, 2008).
Kolve, V.A., *Telling Images: Chaucer and the Imagery of Narrative II* (Stanford, 2009).
Kuskin, William, *Symbolic Caxton: Literary Culture and Print Capitalism* (Notre Dame, 2008).
——, *Recursive Origins: Writing at the Transition to Modernity* (Notre Dame, 2013).
Lambert, Mark, *Malory: Style and Vision in 'Le Morte Darthur'* (New Haven, CT, 1975).
Lathrop, Henry Burrows, *Translations from the Classics into English from Caxton to Chapman, 1477–1620* (1933; rpt. New York, 1967).
Leeds Barroll, J., *Anna of Denmark, Queen of England: A Cultural Biography* (Philadelphia, 2001).
Leitch, Megan G., 'Thinking Twice about Treason in Caxton's Prose Romances: Proper Chivalric Conduct and the English Printing Press', *Medium Ævum* 81.1 (2012), 41–69.
——, *Romancing Treason: The Literature of the Wars of the Roses* (Oxford, 2015).
Lerer, Seth, *Chaucer and His Readers: Imagining the Author in Late-Medieval England* (Princeton, 1996).
Lewalski, Barbara Kiefer, *Writing Women in Jacobean England* (Cambridge, MA, 1993).
Lewis, C.S., *English Literature in the Sixteenth Century, Excluding Drama* (Oxford, 1954).
Lindenbaum, Peter, *Changing Landscapes: Anti-pastoral Sentiment in the English Renaissance* (Athens, GA and London, 1986).
Little, Katherine C., *Transforming Work: Early Modern Pastoral and Late Medieval Poetry* (Notre Dame, 2013).
Long, Percy W., 'Spenser and the *Plowman's Tale*', *Modern Language Notes* 28 (1913), 262.
Lounsbury, Thomas R., *Studies in Chaucer: His Life and Writings*, 3 vols. (London, 1892).
Lucas, Scott, 'Diggon Davie and Davy Dicar: Edmund Spenser, Thomas Churchyard, and the Poetics of Public Protest', *Spenser Studies* 16 (2002), 151–65.
——, *A Mirror for Magistrates and the Politics of the English Reformation* (Amherst, 2009).
Lund, Mary Ann, *Melancholy, Medicine and Reading in Early Modern England: Reading the Anatomy of Melancholy* (Cambridge, 2010).
MacCulloch, Diarmaid, *Thomas Cranmer: A Life* (New Haven, CT, 1996).
——, *Tudor Church Militant: Edward VI and the Protestant Reformation* (Harmondsworth, 1999).
MacDonald, Nicola, ed., *Pulp Fictions of Medieval England: Essays in Popular Romance* (Manchester, 2004).

Manley, Lawrence, *Literature and Culture in Early Modern London* (Cambridge, 1995).

Martin, J.W., 'The Publishing Career of Robert Crowley: A Sidelight on the Tudor Book Trade', *Publishing History* 14 (1983), 85–98.

Martindale, Charles, ed., *Cambridge Companion to Virgil* (Cambridge, 1997).

Matthews, David, 'Periodization', *A Handbook of Middle English Studies*, ed. Marion Turner (Chichester, 2013), pp. 253–66.

McCabe, Richard A., '"Little booke: thy selfe present": The Politics of Presentation in *The Shepheardes Calender*', *Presenting Poetry: Composition, Publication, Reception*, ed. H. Erskine-Hill and R.A. McCabe (Cambridge, 1995), pp. 15–40.

——, *Spenser's Monstrous Regiment: Elizabethan Ireland and the Poetics of Difference* (Oxford, 2002).

McClune, Kate, '"the vengeaunce of my brethirne": Blood Ties in Malory's *Morte Darthur*', *Arthurian Literature* 28 (2011), 89–106.

McGinchee, Claire, 'Still Harping …', *SQ* 4 (1955), 362–4.

Mentz, Steve, *Romance for Sale in Early Modern England: The Rise of Prose Fiction* (Aldershot, 2006).

Meyer-Lee, Robert, *Poets and Power from Chaucer to Wyatt* (Cambridge, 2007).

Middleton, Anne, 'Thomas Usk's "Perdurable Letters": The *Testament of Love* from Script to Print', *Studies in Bibliography* 51 (1998), 63–116.

Mills, Maldwyn, 'EB and his Two Books: Visual Impact and the Power of Meaningful Suggestion. "Reading" the Illustrations in MSS Douce 261 and Egerton 3132A', *Imagining the Book*, ed. S. Kelly and J.J. Thompson (Turnhout, 2005), pp. 173–91.

Miola, Robert S., *Shakespeare and Classical Tragedy: The Influence of Seneca* (Oxford, 1992).

Mish, Charles, *English Prose Fiction, 1600–1700: A Chronological Checklist.* (Charlottesville, 1967).

Mohl, Ruth, 'Spenser, Edmund', *The Spenser Encyclopedia*, gen. ed. A.C. Hamilton (Toronto, 1990), p. 671.

Monsarrat, Gilles D., *Light from the Porch: Stoicism and English Renaissance Literature* (Paris, 1984).

Moss, Rachel E., *Fatherhood and its Representations in Middle English Texts* (Cambridge, 2013).

Muldoon, James, ed., *Bridging the Medieval-Modern Divide: Medieval Themes in the World of the Reformation* (Farnham, 2013).

Munro, Lucy, *Archaic Style in English Literature, 1590–1674* (Cambridge, 2013).

Murphy, Gerard, *The Ossianic Lore and Romantic Tales of Medieval Ireland* (Dublin, 1961).

Nagel, Alexander, and Christopher S. Wood, 'Interventions: Toward a New Model of Renaissance Anachronism', *Art Bulletin* 87.3 (2005), 405–15.

——, *Anachronic Renaissance* (New York, 2010).

Nagy, Joseph Falaky, 'In Defense of Rómánsaíocht', *Ériu* 38 (1987), 3–19.

——, *A New Introduction to Two Irish Arthurian Romances*, ITS Subsidiary Series 7 (London, 1998).

——, 'Arthur and the Irish', *A Companion to Arthurian Literature*, ed. Helen Fulton (Malden, MA, 2009), pp. 117–27.

Nebeker, Eric, 'The Broadside Ballad and Textual Publics', *SEL* 51 (2011), 1–19.

Nevitt, Marcus, 'Sing Heavenly News: Journalism and Poetic Authority in Samuel Sheppard's *The Faerie King* (c.1654)', *SP* 109 (2012), 496–518.
Newcomb, Lori Humphrey, *Reading Popular Romance in Early Modern England* (New York, 2001).
Ní Shéaghdha, Nessa, 'Translations and Adaptations into Irish', *Celtica* 16 (1984), 107–24.
Nicholls, Jonathan, *The Matter of Courtesy: Medieval Courtesy Books and the Gawain Poet* (Cambridge, 1985).
Nielsen, Thomas Heine, 'The Concept of Arkadia – the People, Their Land, and Their Organisation', *Defining Ancient Arkadia*, ed. Thomas Heine Nielsen and James Roy (Copenhagen, 1999), pp. 16–79.
——, and James Roy, eds., *Defining Ancient Arkadia* (Copenhagen, 1999).
Nolan, Barbara, 'The *Tale of Sir Gareth* and the *Tale of Sir Lancelot*', *A Companion to Malory*, ed. Elizabeth Archibald and A.S.G. Edwards (Cambridge, 1996), pp. 153–81.
Norbrook, David, *Poetry and Politics in the English Renaissance*, rev. edn. (Oxford, 2002).
O'Callaghan, Michelle, *'The Shepheards Nation': Jacobean Spenserians and Early Stuart Political Culture, 1612–1625* (Oxford, 2000).
Ó Cuív, Brian, *Catalogue of Irish Language Manuscripts in the Bodleian Library Oxford and Oxford College Libraries* (Dublin, 2003).
O'Mahony, Cian, 'A King for the Queene: Samuel Sheppard's *The Faerie King* and his Reception of Spenser's Epic Authority' (unpublished PhD thesis, University College Cork, 2013).
Palmer, R.G., *Seneca's 'De Remediis Fortuitorum' and the Elizabethans* (Chicago, 1953).
Panofsky, Erwin, *Introduction to Studies in Iconology: Humanistic Themes in the Art of the Renaissance* (Oxford, 1939).
——, '*Et in arcadia ego*: Poussin and the Elegiac Tradition', *Meaning in the Visual Arts* (Garden City, NY, 1955), pp. 295–320.
Pappaioanou, S., 'Founder, Civilizer and Leader: Virgil's Evander and his Role in the Origins of Rome', *Mnemosyne* 56 (2003), 680–702.
Paravicini, Werner, 'The Court of the Dukes of Burgundy: A Model for Europe?', *Princes, Patronage and the Nobility: The Court at the Beginning of the Modern Age*, ed. Ronald G. Asch and Adolf M. Birke (Oxford, 1991), pp. 69–102.
Parsons, John Carmi, 'The Queen's Intercession', *Power of the Weak*, ed. Carpenter and MacLean, pp. 147–77.
Patterson, Annabel, *Reading Between the Lines* (Madison, 1993).
Patterson, Lee, 'On the Margin: Postmodernism, Ironic History and Medieval Studies', *Speculum* 65 (1990), 87–108.
——, 'The Place of the Modern in the Late Middle Ages', *The Challenge of Periodisation: Old Paradigms and New Perspectives*, ed. L. Besserman (New York, 1996), pp. 51–66.
Payne, Robert O., *The Key of Remembrance: A Study of Chaucer's Poetics* (New Haven, CT, 1963).
Peacey, Jason, '"The Counterfeit Silly Cut": Money, Politics, and the Forging of Royalist Newspapers during the English Civil War', *HLQ* 67.1 (2004), 27–57.
Pearlman, E., 'Shakespeare at Work: The Invention of the Ghost', *Hamlet: New Critical Essays*, ed. Arthur Kinney (New York, 2002), pp. 71–84.
Pearsall, Derek, *John Lydgate* (London, 1970).

——, 'The English Romance in the Fifteenth Century', *Essays and Studies* 29 (1976), 56–83.
Perkins, Nicholas, *Hoccleve's Regiment of Princes: Counsel and Constraint* (Cambridge, 2001).
Perry, Curtis, and John Watkins, eds., *Shakespeare and the Middle Ages* (Oxford, 2010).
Peter, John, *Complaint and Satire in Early English Literature* (Oxford, 1956).
Phelps Stokes, I.N., *The Iconography of Manhattan Island, 1498–1909*, 2 vols. (New York, 1916).
Pikoulas, G.A., et al., eds., *Following Pausanias: The Quest for Greek Antiquity* (Athens, GA, 2007).
Plomer, Henry R., *A Dictionary of the Booksellers and Printers who were at work in England, Scotland and Ireland from 1641 to 1667* (London, 1968).
Pollet, Maurice, *John Skelton: Poet of Tudor England*, trans. John Warrington (London, 1971).
Pollnitz, Aysha, 'Educating Hamlet and Prince Hal', *Shakespeare and Early Modern Political Thought*, ed. David Armitage, Conal Condren and Andrew Fitzmaurice (Cambridge, 2013), pp. 119–38.
Poppe, Erich, 'Stair Nuadat Find Femin: Eine irische Romanze?', *Zeitschrift für Celtische Philologie* 49–50 (1997), 749–59.
Potterton, Michael, and Thomas Herron, eds., *Dublin and the Pale in the Renaissance* (Dublin, 2011).
Pretzler, Maria, *Pausanias: Travel Writing in Ancient Greece* (London, 2007).
Purdie, Rhiannon, and Michael Cichon, eds., *Medieval Romance, Medieval Contexts* (Cambridge, 2011).
Purkiss, Diane, 'Material Girls: The Seventeenth-Century Woman Debate', *Women, Texts and Histories 1575–1760*, ed. Clare Brant and Diane Purkiss (London, 1992), pp. 69–101.
Putnam, Michael, *Poetry of the Aeneid* (Cambridge, MA, 1965).
Putter, Ad, *Sir Gawain and the Green Knight and French Arthurian Romance* (Oxford, 1995).
——, 'A Historical Introduction', *The Spirit of Medieval English Popular Romance* (Harlow, 2000), pp. 1–15.
——, and Jane Gilbert, eds., *The Spirit of Medieval English Popular Romance* (Harlow, 2000).
Quarmby, Kevin A., *The Disguised Ruler in Shakespeare and his Contemporaries* (Farnham, 2012).
Quinn, David, 'The Early Cartography of Maine', *American Beginnings: Exploration, Culture, and Cartography in the Land of Norumbega*, ed. Emerson W. Baker et al. (Lincoln, 1994), pp. 37–59.
Quitslund, Beth, *The Reformation in Rhyme: Sternhold, Hopkins and the English Metrical Psalter, 1547–1603* (Aldershot, 2008).
Radden, Jennifer, *The Nature of Melancholy: From Aristotle to Kristeva* (Oxford, 2000).
Radulescu, Raluca L., and Cory James Rushton, eds., *A Companion to Medieval Popular Romance* (Cambridge, 2009).
Rasmussen, Eric, 'Fathers and Sons in *Hamlet*', *SQ* 35 (1984), 463.

Raymond, Joad, 'Popular Representations of Charles I', *The Royal Image: Representations of Charles I*, ed. Thomas N. Corns (Cambridge, 1999), pp. 47–73.
——, *Pamphlets and Pamphleteering in Early Modern England* (Cambridge, 2003).
Relihan, Constance, *Cosmographical Glasses: Geographic Discourse, Gender, and Elizabethan Fiction* (Kent, OH, 2004).
Rhodes, Neil, 'The Controversial Plot: Declamation and the Concept of the "Problem Play"', *Modern Language Review* 95 (2000), 609–22.
Richards, Jennifer, *Rhetoric and Courtliness in Early Modern Literature* (Cambridge, 2007).
Romanini, Fabio, 'Sulla "Lettera a Francesco I re di Francia" di Giovanni da Verrazzano: con una nuova edizione', *Filologia Italiana* 9 (2012), 127–90.
Rosenberg, D.M., *Oaten Reeds and Trumpets: Pastoral and Epic in Virgil, Spenser and Milton* (East Brunswick, NJ, 1981).
Rosenmeyer, Thomas G., *The Green Cabinet: Theocritus and the European Pastoral Lyric* (Berkeley and Los Angeles, 1969).
Ross, Charles, *The Wars of the Roses: A Concise History* (London, 1976).
Rossiter, William T., *Chaucer and Petrarch* (Cambridge, 2010).
Round, Nicholas G., 'The Medieval Reputation of the 'Proverbia Senecae': A Partial Survey Based on Recorded MSS', *Proceedings of the Royal Irish Academy. Section C: Archaeology, Celtic Studies, History, Linguistics, Literature* 72 (1972), 103–15.
Rovang, Paul, *Refashioning 'Knights and Ladies Gentle Deeds': The Intertextuality of Spenser's Faerie Queene and Malory's Morte Darthur* (Madison, NJ, 1996).
Rundle, David, ed., *Humanism in Fifteenth-Century Europe* (Oxford, 2012).
Rushton, W.L., *Shakespeare's Euphuism* (London, 1871).
Rutter, Russell, 'William Caxton and Literary Patronage', *SP* 84 (1987), 440–70.
Salzman, Paul, *English Prose Fiction 1558–1700* (Oxford, 1985).
Scanlon, Larry, 'Lydgate's Poetics: Laureation and Domesticity in the *Temple of Glass*', *John Lydgate: Poetry, Culture, and Lancastrian England*, ed. Larry Scanlon and James Simpson (Notre Dame, 2006), pp. 61–97.
——, 'Langland, Apocalypse, and the Early Modern Editor', *Reading the Medieval in Early Modern England*, ed. Gordon McMullan and David Matthews (Cambridge, 2007), pp. 51–73.
Scase, Wendy, '*Dauy Dycars Dreame* and Robert Crowley's Prints of *Piers Plowman*', *YLS* 21 (2007), 171–98.
——, *Literature and Complaint in England, 1272–1553* (Oxford, 2007).
Scattergood, V.J., *Politics and Poetry in the Fifteenth Century* (London, 1971).
——, 'Skelton's *Garlande of Laurell* and the Chaucerian Tradition', *Chaucer Traditions: Studies in Honour of Derek Brewer*, ed. Ruth Morse and Barry Windeatt (Cambridge, 1990), pp. 122–38.
——, *John Skelton: The Career of an Early Tudor Poet* (Dublin, 2014).
Scheer, Tanja, 'Ways of Becoming Arcadian: Arcadian Foundation Myths in the Mediterranean', *Cultural Identity in the Ancient Mediterranean*, ed. Erich S. Gruen (Los Angeles, 2010), pp. 11–25.
Schleiner, Louise, 'Spenser's "E. K." as Edmund Kent (Kenned/ of Kent): Kyth (Couth), Kissed, and Kunning-Conning', *ELR* 20 (1990), 374–407.

Schoek, R.J., '"Go Little Book"—A Conceit from Chaucer to William Meredith', *NQ* 197 (1952), 370–2.
Schreyer, Kurt A., *Shakespeare's Medieval Craft* (Ithaca, 2014).
Sellar, W.C., and R.J. Yeatman, *1066 and All That: A Memorable History of England* (London, 1930).
Sharpe, Kevin, *Criticism and Compliment: The Politics of Literature in the England of Charles I* (Cambridge, 1987).
——, *Reading Revolutions: The Politics of Reading in Early Modern England* (New Haven, CT, 2000).
Shepherd, Simon, *Amazons and Warrior Women: Varieties of Feminism in Seventeenth-Century Drama* (New York, 1981).
Shepherd, Stephen H.A., 'The Middle English *Pseudo-Turpin Chronicle*', *Medium Ævum* 65 (1996), 19–34.
Shrank, Cathy, 'Trollers and Dreamers: Defining the Citizen-Subject in Sixteenth-Century Cheap Print', *Yearbook of English Studies* 38 (2008), 102–18.
Shuger, Debora K., *Habits of Thought in the English Renaissance* (Berkeley, 1990).
Simpson, James, *Reform and Cultural Revolution* (Oxford, 2002).
——, 'Subjects of Triumph and Literary History: Dido and Petrarch in Petrarch's *Africa* and *Trionfi*', *JMEMS* 35.3 (2005), 489–508.
Sinfield, Alan, *Cultural Materialism and the Politics of Dissident Reading* (Berkeley and Los Angeles, 1992).
Skidmore, Chris, *Edward VI: The Lost King of England* (London, 2008).
Smelik, Bernadette, 'The Intended Audience of Irish Arthurian Romances', *Arthuriana* 17 (2007), 49–69.
Smith, Charles G., *Shakespeare's Proverb Lore: His Uses of the Sententiae of Leonard Culman and Publilius Syrus* (Cambridge, MA, 1963).
Snell, Bruno, *The Discovery of the Mind: The Greek Origins of European Thought*, trans. T.G. Rosenmeyer (Oxford, 1953).
Solomon, Michael, *The Literature of Misogyny in Medieval Spain: The 'Arcipreste de Talavera' and the 'Spill'* (Cambridge, 1997).
Spearing, A.C., *Medieval Dream-Poetry* (Cambridge, 1976).
——, *Medieval to Renaissance in English Poetry* (Cambridge, 1981).
——, 'Father Chaucer', *Writing After Chaucer: Essential Readings in Chaucer and the Fifteenth-Century*, ed. Daniel J. Pinti (New York, 1998), pp. 145–66.
Spiegel, Gabrielle M., 'History, Historicism, and the Social Logic of the Text in the Middle Ages', *Speculum* 65.1 (1990), 59–86.
Spufford, Margaret, *Small Books and Pleasant Histories: Popular Fiction and its Readership in Seventeenth-Century England* (Athens, GA, 1982).
Steggle, Matthew, *Wars of the Theatres: The Poetics of Personation in the Age of Jonson* (Victoria, 1998).
Steinberg, Glenn, 'Spenser's *Shepheardes Calender* and the Elizabethan Reception of Chaucer', *ELR* 35 (2005), 31–51.
Strohm, Paul, *Hochon's Arrow: The Social Imagination of Fourteenth-Century Texts* (Princeton, 1992).
——, *Theory and the Premodern Text* (Minneapolis, 2000).

Summit, Jennifer, 'Topography as Historiography: Petrarch, Chaucer, and the Making of Medieval Rome', *JMEMS* 30.2 (2000), 211–46.

——, *Memory's Library: Medieval Books in Early Modern England* (Chicago, 2008).

Tarnoff, Maura, 'Sewing Authorship in John Skelton's *Garlande or Chapelet of Laurell*', *ELH* 75 (2008), 415–38.

Taylor, Myron, 'Tragic Justice and the House of Polonius', *SEL* 8.2 (1968), 273–81.

Thomas, W.H. Griffith, *The Principles of Theology: An Introduction to the Thirty-Nine Articles* (1930; rpt. Ann Arbor, 1979).

Tranter, Kirsten, 'Samuel Sheppard's *Faerie King* and the Fragmentation of Royalist Epic', *SEL* 49 (2009), 94–101.

Trapp, J. B., 'The Owl's Ivy and the Poet's Bays: An Enquiry into Poetic Garlands', *Journal of the Warburg and Courtauld Institutes* 21 (1958), 227–55.

Tucker, Melvin J., 'Skelton and Sheriff Hutton', *English Language Notes* 4 (1967), 245–59.

——, 'The Ladies in Skelton's "Garland of Laurel"', *Renaissance Quarterly* 22 (1969), 333–45.

Tuve, Rosemond, 'The Red Crosse Knight and Medieval Demon Stories', *Essays by Rosemond Tuve: Spenser, Herbert, Milton*, ed. Thomas P. Roche (Princeton, 1970), pp. 39–48.

Tyacke, Nicholas, 'Puritanism, Arminianism and Counter-Revolution', *The Origins of the English Civil War*, ed. Conrad Russell (London, 1973).

Vale, Malcolm, *War and Chivalry: Warfare and Aristocratic Culture in England, France and Burgundy at the End of the Middle Ages* (London, 1981).

Van Heertum, Cis, 'A Plagiarist Plagiarised: *Pray Be Not Angry: or, the Womens New Law* (1656)', *The Library* 13 (1991), 347–50.

Wakelin, Daniel, *Humanism, Reading, and English Literature 1430–1530* (Cambridge, 2007).

Walker, Greg, *John Skelton and the Politics of the 1520s* (New York, 1988).

——, *Writing Under Tyranny: English Literature and the Henrician Reformation* (Oxford, 2005).

——, 'When did "The Medieval" End? Retrospection, Foresight, and the End(s) of the English Middle Ages', *The Oxford Handbook of Medieval Literature in English*, ed. Elaine Treharne and Greg Walker (Oxford, 2010), pp. 725–38.

Wallace, David, *Chaucerian Polity: Absolutist Lineages and Associational Forms in England and Italy* (Stanford, 1997).

Walsh, Paul, 'David O Duigenan, Scribe', *Irish Men of Learning: Studies by Father Paul Walsh*, ed. Colm Ó Lochlainn (Dublin, 1947), pp. 25–33.

——, 'The Learned Family of O Duigenan', *Irish Men of Learning*, ed. Ó Lochlainn, pp. 1–12.

Wang, Yu-Chiao, 'English Romance in Print from 1473 to 1535: Reception and the History of the Book' (unpublished PhD thesis, University of Cambridge, 2008).

Warner, J. Christopher, *The Making and Marketing of Tottel's Miscellany, 1557* (Farnham, 2013).

Warner, Lawrence, 'An Overlooked *Piers Plowman* Excerpt and the Oral Circulation of Non-Reformist Prophecy, c.1520–55', *YLS* 21 (2007), 119–42.

Waters Bennett, Josephine, 'Characterization in Polonius' Advice to Laertes', *SQ* 4 (1953), 3–9.

——, 'These Few Precepts', *SQ* 7.2 (1956), 275–6.
Watkins, John, 'Bedevilling the Histories of Medieval and Early Modern Drama', *MP* 101 (2003), 68–78.
Watt, Tessa, *Cheap Print and Popular Piety, 1550–1640* (Cambridge, 1991).
Wayne, Valerie, 'The Dearth of the Author: Anonymity's Allies and *Swetnam the Woman-Hater*', *Maids and Mistresses, Cousins and Queens: Women's Alliances in Early Modern England*, ed. Susan Frye and Karen Robertson (Oxford, 1999), pp. 221–40.
Wenzel, Siegfried, *Preachers, Poets, and the Early English Lyric* (Princeton, 1986).
White, Helen C., *Social Criticism in Popular Religious Literature of the Sixteenth Century* (New York, 1965).
Wilcher, Robert, *The Writing of Royalism 1628–1660* (Cambridge, 2001).
Wilkins, Ernest H., *Studies in the Life and Works of Petrarch* (Cambridge, MA, 1955).
——, 'Arcadia in America', *Proceedings of the American Philosophical Society* 101 (February 15, 1957), 4–30.
Wilson, Elkin Calhoun, 'Polonius in the Round', *SQ* 9 (1958), 83–5.
Wittgenstein, Ludwig, *Philosophical Investigations*, trans. G.E.M. Anscombe (Oxford, 1953).
Wood, Andy, *The 1549 Rebellions and the Making of Early Modern England* (Cambridge, 2007).
Woodbridge, Linda, *Women and the English Renaissance: Literature and the Nature of Womankind, 1540–1620* (Urbana, 1984).
Woodcock, Matthew, *Thomas Churchyard: Pen, Sword, and Ego* (Oxford, forthcoming).
Woodhouse, John R., 'The Tradition of Della Casa's *Galateo* in English', *The Crisis of Courtesy: Studies in the Conduct-Book in Britain, 1600–1900*, ed. Jacques Carré (Leiden, 1994), pp. 11–26.
Worden, Blair, *The Sound of Virtue: Philip Sidney's 'Arcadia' and Elizabethan Politics* (New Haven, CT, 1996).
Wroth, Lawrence C., *The Voyages of Giovanni da Verrazzano, 1524–1528* (Paris, 1982).
Yunck, John A., 'Satire', *Companion*, ed. Alford, pp. 135–54.

Index

Agrippa, Cornelius 36
Albertanus of Brescia 168
Alcaeus 19
Alexander 151
Apuleius 96, 153
Arcadia 12, 143–6, 149–62, 235–6, 238, 242, 244–5 *see also* Sidney, Philip, *Old Arcadia* and *New Arcadia*
Archilochus 132
Ariosto, Ludovico 37, 84
armour 9, 35–54, 71, 163, 222, 243
Arthur, King 38, 43, 45–7, 49, 55, 60, 64, 66, 73–4, 82–6, 92–4, 176, 241
Ascham, Roger 6n20, 10, 92–4
Aubert, David 80
authorship 9, 17–20, 23, 27, 30, 33, 107–21, 126, 137–41, 210–11, 224–34

Bacon, Nicholas 171
Bagynon, Jean 80
Bale, John 4, 24n25, 134n42
ballads 95, 238, 241
Banyster, Edmund 95
Becon, Thomas 128
Beowulf 54n23
Berners, John Bourchier, Lord 61, 73–4
Berthelet, Thomas 25
Bevis of Hampton 10, 73–4, 76, 85, 87–8, 92–5
Bloom, Harold 72
Boccaccio, Giovanni 23, 72, 143, 179
Boethius 26, 209
Boke of Curtasye 167
Boro, Joyce 12–13
Bosworth 1, 96
Bracciolini, Giovanni Francesco Poggio 146, 151, 153

Burckhardt, Jacob 2, 107n3
Burgundy 77, 80
Burton, Robert 193–4, 198, 202
Byrne, Aisling 10, 13

Calvino, Italo 9, 37
Camden, William 75, 91
Camell, Thomas 126, 138–9
Carroll, Lewis 39
Cato 166, 168, 170
Catullus 119
Caxton, William 21, 29, 56, 60, 62, 70, 76–8, 96, 108 see also *Foure Sonnes of Aymon*
Cecil, Robert 165, 172
Cecil, Thomas 172, 185
Cecil, William 165, 170, 172–3, 185
Céilidhe Iosgaide Léithe 84–5
Cervantes, Miguel de 37, 39, 54
chapbooks 13–14, 75, 235–50
Charlemagne 61–3, 79–81, 88 see also *Huon of Burdeux*
Charles I 13–14, 209–34
Chaucer, Geoffrey 5–9, 15–33, 39–40, 49–50, 57–8, 62, 71–2, 107, 110–11, 114, 116, 121, 123–5, 132–3, 141, 232
Canterbury Tales:
  'Clerk's Tale' 58, 110
  'Franklin's Tale' 58
  'General Prologue' 29
  'Knight's Tale' 40–41
  'Man of Law's Tale' 30
  'Melibee' 30
  'Miller's Tale' 201n40
  'Parson's Tale' 30
  'Sir Thopas' 30, 40, 47, 49
  'Wife of Bath's Tale' 57–8
  see also *Plowman's Tale*

Chaucer, Geoffrey cont.
  'Complaint Unto Pity' 125
  House of Fame 30
  'Lak of Stedfastnesse' 125
  Legend of Good Women 109n9
  Troilus and Criseyde 6–7, 18, 20–26, 28, 72
Cheke, John 135–6
Chrétien de Troyes 86
Churchyard, Thomas 12, 123–41
Cicero 26–7, 93, 167, 172–3
Clanvowe, John 22
Cobham, George Brooke, Lord 185–6n83
Colonna, Giovanni 146–7
complaint 123–6, 128–30, 132, 137–41
Conway, William 129
Cooper, Helen 1, 5, 7–15, 32n45, 35, 39–41, 54–7, 75, 88, 100n29, 107, 123, 144, 170, 175
Corpus Christi plays 8n26, 12–13
courtesy books 13, 167–8, 170
Crinitus, Petrus 179
Cromwell, Oliver 220
Crowley, Robert 123, 129–30, 134–5, 137, 139
Curtius, Ernst 132

Das, Nandini 12
De Flores, Juan, *Grisel y Mirabella* 13, 188–90, 207
De Grazia, Margreta 2
Della Casa, Giovanni 167
Destruction of Troy 50
De Worde, Wynkyn 58, 82n42, 96, 102n33, 167
Donne, John 91
dream vision 109, 111–19, 121, 123, 132, 140
Du Bellay, Joachim 147
Dupérac, Etienne 148–9, 153

Eachtra an Amadáin Mhóir 84, 86
Eachtra an Mhadra Mhaoil 74, 84–5
Eachtra Mhacoimh-an-Iolair 84, 86
Eachtra Mhelóra agus Orlando 84

Eachtra Uilliam 82
Edward IV 60, 108n6
Edward VI 5, 124, 126–7, 130, 136–7, 141
Eglamour of Artois 95n17, 99
Elizabeth I 207–8, 211
Elyot, Thomas 167
Erasmus, Desiderius 166, 172, 179n65, 196
Evelyn, John 219–20

Faerie Leveller 220–21
fame 11, 16, 20, 23, 30, 107–18, 205, 209, 212, 217, 222, 230
fathers 13, 20, 37, 55–7, 62–9, 152, 163–86, 194, 234
Fierabras 10, 78–81, 83
Fish, Stanley 31–3
Flannery, Mary C. 11
Fletcher, John 189, 196
Floris and Blancheflour 35, 39
Foure Sonnes of Aymon 56, 62–3, 70, 74n7, 94n34
Foxe, John 10, 24n25, 91–3, 97, 104
Friar Daw's Reply 24

Galen 197–8
Gascoigne, George 124n6
ghosts 163–4, 174, 176–7, 180–85
Gillespie, Alexandra 9
Gilpin, Bernard 128
Glapthorne, Henry 237–8
Gosson, Stephen 180
Gower, John 9, 19, 22, 24–6, 32, 107, 111, 114, 116, 124, 135, 139–41
Greene, Robert 100n29, 170, 178, 241
Greene, Thomas 4
Guazzo, Stefano 167
Guy Earl of Warwick, Tragical History of 99–101
Guy of Warwick 10, 76, 78, 87–8, 94–6, 99

Hakluyt, Richard 157, 159
Hales, John 128
Hanmer, Meredith 93n10

Harington, John 172–3
Harvey, Gabriel 9, 15, 20
Harvey, John 94
Hegel, Georg 2–3
Heidegger, Martin 4
Helgerson, Richard 6n30, 11, 164, 170, 175, 184
Henry IV 125
Henry V 22, 125
Henry VII 1, 60, 70
Henry VIII 25, 36, 119–20, 126
Hesiod 149, 154
Heywood, John 24
Hobbes, Thomas 221–2, 229
Hoccleve, Thomas 125, 140–41
Homer 23, 119, 151, 154, 180
Horace 23
How the Wise Man Taught his Son 165, 168, 170, 186
humanism 4–5, 11, 32, 91–3, 101, 108, 146, 154
Huon of Burdeux 10, 56, 61–3, 66, 70–71, 73, 85, 94n34, 101

Idley, Peter 167–71, 185
Innocent III 124
Ireland 10, 36, 73–89
Isocrates 165, 170, 172–4, 181–2, 185

Jack Upland 24
James I 188, 207–8, 211, 220
Juvenal 126n11

Keating, Geoffrey 73–5
Kett, Robert 127, 135
Kildare Rental 76–8
King, Andrew 13–14, 96
Kyd, Thomas 178n61
  The Spanish Tragedy 176, 184

Langland, William 29–31, 123–5, 130–32, 134–5, 137, 140–41
  Piers Plowman 12, 29–31, 94, 124–5, 130–31, 133–5, 137–9
  see also ploughmen

Lanval 84
Latimer, Hugh 126–8, 135
Launcelot du Lake 94
laureates 11–12, 107–21
Lay Folks' Catechism 97–8, 106
Lefèvre, Raoul 77
Leitch, Megan G. 9–10
Leland, John 4, 29–30
Lerer, Seth 21, 108, 110, 115, 119
Lever, Thomas 128
Lewis, C.S. 2, 5–6, 8, 14, 92, 123–4
Libeaus Desconus 56–7
Lithgow, William 155–6
Lodge, Thomas 10, 95, 101–2, 104–5, 170, 176, 180
Lollardy 22, 27
Lydgate, John 19, 22, 63–4, 107, 111, 115–16, 123, 132, 135, 168
Lyly, John 165, 191n17

Mac an Bhaird, Fearghal Óg 84–5
Machiavelli, Niccolò 166–7
Malory, Thomas 9, 36, 39, 41–6, 55–7, 61–2, 64–6, 69–70, 93–4, 96, 209
  Morte Darthur 41–6, 55–7, 62n21, 64–7, 69–70, 93–4, 96
Mandeville, John 76, 86
Mannyng, Robert 166
Manso, Giovanni Battista 32–3
Marie de France 35, 39, 84
Marlowe, Christopher 12, 36–7
Marot, Clement 19
Marston, John 179
Maslen, R.W. 9
melancholy 13, 188, 191–203
Melusine 10, 56, 67–9, 185
memes 8–9, 35, 39–40, 50, 57–8
memory 6–8, 13, 37, 102, 143, 146, 149, 153, 156, 161–2, 175–7, 183
Mercurius Dogmaticus 210
Mercurius Pragmaticus 213, 233
Merlin 36, 42, 57, 94, 101, 133, 223
Milton, John 9, 31–33, 217
Mirabilia Urbis Romae 147–9
Mirror for Magistrates 5, 124

misogyny 13, 187–208
More, Thomas 132–3
Munda, Constantia 190–91, 202, 206

Nashe, Thomas 92n6, 94n34, 95, 178

Ó Duibhgeannáin, Dáibhi 81–2
Ó Huiginn, Tadhg Dall 83
Octavian 10, 61, 76, 80–81
Old English 17–18, 22, 28
Ortelius, Abraham 148–9, 154
Ovid 29, 50, 198, 209

Panofsky, Erwin 145, 147–8
pastoral 7, 12, 15–16, 27–8, 31–3, 96, 101, 143–6, 152, 156, 161–2, 211, 225–9, 234 *see also* Arcadia; Spenser, Edmund, *Shepheardes Calender*
Pausanias 150, 153–6
Peacham, Henry 51
Pepys, Samuel 237n8
Perceval 56, 86
periodisation 1–11, 14, 86–9, 91–2, 107, 121, 123, 141
Petrarch, Francesco 6–7, 26, 32n45, 91, 108, 110, 121, 143, 146–7, 153, 178, 248
Plato 133
ploughmen 12, 27, 32, 130–31, 134–5, 137 *see also Piers Plowman*; *Plowman's Tale*
Plowman's Tale 9, 27–32, 130n26
Polybius 145, 149–50, 153–4
Powell, Jason 12–13
Prayse and Commendacion of Suche as Sought Comen Welthes 128–9
prophecy 94, 131, 133–5, 137, 141
prose romance
    Elizabethan 170, 236, 246 *see also* Sidney, Philip, *Old Arcadia* and *New Arcadia*
    fifteenth-century 9–10, 55–72, 96, 170, 176 *see also under individual entries*
Pseudo-Turpin Chronicle 79–80, 83

Publilius Syrus 165, 168, 178
Puttenham, George 11, 144

Quarles, Francis 242–7
Queste del Saint Graal 83–4

Recuyell of the Historyes of Troye 76–8, 87
Reformation 2, 4, 10–11, 22, 28, 30, 91–106, 127–8, 130–31, 169
Rhodes, Hugh 167
Richard II 125, 130
Richard III 91
Robert of Cisyle 95n16, 99, 105
Robert the Devil 70, 95, 101, 104–5 *see also* Lodge, Thomas
Rogers, Owen 139
Roman d'Alexandre 151
romance
    condemnation of 92–4
    dramatised 10–11, 13, 99–101, 104, 188–208
    in Ireland 10, 74–89
    penitential 10–11, 95–101, 105
    see also prose romance; *individual entries*
Rome 29, 98, 103–4, 110, 118n30, 146–53, 156, 159, 161
Rowe, Elizabeth Singer 247
Rowlands, Samuel 74
Ruful complaynt 129, 136
Russell, John 165n9, 167–8

St Patrick's Purgatory 104
Sannazaro, Jacopo 143, 151, 161
satire 12, 74, 119, 123–6, 129, 132, 140–41
Scattergood, John 115, 132
Sellar, W.C. 1
Seneca 171–2, 178–80
Shakespeare, William 8n26, 12–13, 50–51, 95, 100, 105–6, 163, 165, 168–81, 186, 232n34
    All's Well That Ends Well 175n52
    Hamlet 13, 163–86, 191n17, 220
    Henry V 51

Julius Caesar 163
King Lear 11, 104–6, 133n40
Macbeth 218
Merchant of Venice 191–2
Titus Andronicus 51
Troilus and Cressida 9, 50–54
Twelfth Night 191–2
Sheppard, Samuel 13–14, 209–34, 241n22
Sidney, Henry 170
Sidney, Philip 5, 13–14, 96, 143, 157, 170
  Defence of Poesy 5, 162
  Old Arcadia 143, 245
  New Arcadia 13, 50, 96, 161–2, 235–50
    'Argalus and Parthenia' 13–14, 236–50
Siege of Thebes, prose 10, 56, 63–6, 69–70
Siege of Troy, prose 56, 69–70
Simpson, James 2–4, 6, 14–15
Sir Gawain and the Green Knight 9, 47–8, 95
Sir Gowther 10, 68, 70, 95, 98–9, 101–4
Sir Isumbras 10, 95, 99
Sir Launfal 42
Sir Perceval of Galles 37–8, 59–60, 86
Sir Tristram 94
Skelton, John 11–12, 14, 19, 107–21, 123, 133, 136, 139
  Bowge of Court 136
  Collyn Clout 133, 139
  Garland of Laurel 11–12, 14, 107–21
Smith, Thomas 16–17, 127
Smithson, Samuel 241
Somerset, Edward Seymour, Duke of 126–9, 131, 136–7, 141
Sowernam, Ester 190–1, 206
Spearing, A.C. 4–6, 11, 57, 111–12, 115
Speght, Rachel 190–1
Spenser, Edmund 8, 12, 14, 33, 36–7, 49, 75–6, 96–8, 147, 211–34
  Amoretti 231
  Faerie Queene 8–9, 13, 36–7, 49–50, 96–8, 211–31
  Ruines of Rome 147
  Shepheardes Calender 9, 15–32

Spufford, Margaret 238, 240–1
Stair Nuadat Find Femin 87–8
Steele, Richard 247
Stoicism 170–2, 175, 178–80
Stow, John 21–2, 32n45, 120, 133n39, 169
Summit, Jennifer 4, 147–8
Surrey, Henry Howard, Earl of 11
Swetnam, Joseph 13, 187, 189–91, 206–7
Swetnam the Woman-Hater 13, 187–208

Theocritus 14–16, 149
Thynne, John 22, 29
tragedy 14, 99–100, 223
Troy 50, 149n21, 152, 159, 214
Tudor dynasty 1, 5, 70–71, 91, 126, 136–7
Turk and Sir Gawaine 86
Tusser, Thomas 165
Tyler, Margaret 74
Tyndale, William 92–4

Ur-Hamlet 178
Usk, Thomas 22, 24, 32

Valentine and Orson 10, 56, 58–61, 63, 71, 95, 99
Vere, Thomas 240–41
Verrazzano, Giovanni da 156–61
Vincent, Helen 13–14
Virgil 12, 15, 19, 29, 143, 145–6, 149, 151–4, 161, 227
Virgilius 36–7
Vision of Tundale 104

Wade, James 3, 10–11, 13, 107
Warwick, John Dudley, Earl of 136–7
Webster, John, *The White Devil* 50
White, T.H. 9, 38
William of Palerne 10, 82, 86
Wolsey, Thomas 119–20, 133
Woodcock, Matthew 12
Wyatt, Thomas 11, 185
Wycliffe, John 24n25, 28

Yeatman, R.J. 1

A Bibliography of Helen Cooper's Published Works[1]

Books

Pastoral: Mediaeval into Renaissance (Ipswich, 1977).
Great-Grandmother Goose (London, 1978).
The Structure of the Canterbury Tales (London, 1983; rpt. 1992). 'An Opening: The Knight's Tale', reprinted in *Geoffrey Chaucer, The Knight's Tale: Modern Critical Interpretations*, ed. Harold Bloom (New York, 1988).
Oxford Guides to Chaucer: The Canterbury Tales (Oxford, 1989; rev. paperback edn., 1991; second rev. edn., 1996).
The Long Fifteenth Century: Essays for Douglas Gray, co-edited with Sally Mapstone (Oxford, 1997).
Sir Gawain and the Green Knight, introduction and commentary to a translation by Keith Harrison. Oxford World's Classics (Oxford, 1998).
Sir Thomas Malory: Le Morte Darthur – The Winchester Manuscript, a new edition (modern spelling, slightly abridged), with introduction and commentary. Oxford World's Classics (Oxford, 1998).
Playing with Fire: The Cycle Plays and the Reformation Stage, The William Matthews Lectures 2003 (London, 2003).
The English Romance in Time: Transforming Motifs from Geoffrey of Monmouth to the Death of Shakespeare (Oxford, 2004).
Shakespeare and the Middle Ages: Inaugural Lecture Delivered at the University of Cambridge, 29 April 2005 (Cambridge, 2006).
Shakespeare and the Medieval World (London, 2010; paperback rpt. 2012).
Medieval Shakespeare: Pasts and Presents, co-edited with Ruth Morse and Peter Holland (Cambridge, 2013).

Articles

'A Note on the Wakefield "Prima Pastorum"', *NQ* 20 (1973), 326.
'The Scales of Justice and "The Woman Taken in Adultery"', *Parergon* 5 (1973), 16–20.
'The Goat and the Eclogue', *Philological Quarterly* 53 (1974), 363–79.
'Magic that does not work', *Medievalia et Humanistica* 7 (1976), 131–46.

---

[1] We are grateful to Helen herself for providing us with information that enabled this bibliography to be as comprehensive, accurate and up-to-date as possible.

'The Girl with Two Lovers: Four Canterbury Tales', *Medieval Studies for J.A.W. Bennett*, ed. P.L. Heyworth (Oxford, 1981), pp. 65–79.

'Wyatt and Chaucer: A Reappraisal', *Leeds Studies in English* 13 (1982), 104–23.

'Locality and Meaning in Masque, Morality and Royal Entertainment', *The Court Masque*, ed. David Lindley (Manchester, 1984), pp. 135–48.

'Chaucer and Joyce', *Chaucer Review* 21 (1986), 142–54.

'Chaucer and Ovid: A Question of Authority', *Ovid Renewed*, ed. C.A. Martindale (Cambridge, 1987), pp. 71–81.

'Langland's and Chaucer's Prologues', *YLS* 1 (1987), 71–81.

'Mantuan', 'Pastoral' and 'Satire', *The Spenser Encyclopedia*, ed. A.C. Hamilton (Toronto, 1990), pp. 452–3, 529–32 and 626–8.

'The Shape-shiftings of the Wife of Bath, 1395–1670', *Chaucer Traditions*, ed. Ruth Morse and B.A. Windeatt (Cambridge, 1990), pp. 168–84.

'Gender and Personification in *Piers Plowman*', *YLS* 5 (1991), 31–48.

'Generic Variations on the Theme of Poetic and Civil Authority', *Poetics: Theory and Practice in Medieval English Literature*, ed. Piero Boitani and Anna Torti (Cambridge, 1991), pp. 83–103.

'"God grant mercy!" A Pun in Malory?', *NQ* 237 (1992), 24–5.

'"Peised evene in the balance": A Thematic and Rhetorical Topos in Gower', *Mediaevalia* 16 (1993), 113–39.

'Literary and Symbolic Inspiration in "The Pardoner's Prologue" 1924', *Harry Mileham 1873–1957: A Catalogue*, ed. Patrick Mileham (Paisley, 1995), pp. 45–7.

'The Order of Tales in the Ellesmere Manuscript', *The Ellesmere Chaucer: Essays in Interpretation*, ed. Martin Stevens and Daniel Woodward (San Marino and Tokyo, 1995), pp. 245–61.

'Prospero's Boats: Magic, Providence and Human Choice', *Renaissance Essays for Kitty Scoular Datta*, ed. Sukanta Chaudhuri (Calcutta and Oxford, 1995), pp. 160–75.

'*The Book of Sir Tristram de Lyones*', *A Companion to Malory*, ed. A.S.G. Edwards and Elizabeth Archibald (Cambridge, 1996), pp. 183–201.

'*Hamlet* and the Invention of Tragedy', *Writing Over: Medieval to Renaissance*, ed. Supriya Chaudhuri and Sukanta Chaudhuri (Calcutta, 1996), pp. 97–112; revised version published in *SEDERI* 7 (Coruna, 1996), 189–99; further version published in *Literary Research* (Tbilisi, 2008).

'Shakespeare's Comedy of *King Lear*', *Visva-Bharati Quarterly* NS 5 (1996 for 1994–95), 103–21.

'Introduction' and 'Counter-Romance: Civil Strife and Father-killing in the Prose Romances', *The Long Fifteenth Century: Essays for Douglas Gray*, co-edited with Sally Mapstone (Oxford, 1997), pp. 1–14, 141–62. 'Counter-Romance' reprinted in the Norton edition of Malory's *Morte Darthur*.

'M for Merlin: The Case of the Winchester Manuscript', *Medieval Heritage: Essays in Honour of Tadahiro Ikegami*, ed. M. Kanno et al. (Tokyo, 1997), pp. 1–15.

'Romance after Bosworth', *The Court and Cultural Diversity: Selected Papers from the Eighth Triennial Congress of the International Courtly Literature Society 1995*, ed. Evelyn Mullally and John Thompson (Cambridge, 1997), pp. 149–57.

'Sources and Analogues of Chaucer's *Canterbury Tales*: Reviewing the Work', *Studies in the *Age of Chaucer* 19 (1997), 183–210. Reprinted as 'The Frame', *Sources and Analogues of the Canterbury Tales*, vol. 1, ed. Robert M. Correale and Mary Hamel (Cambridge, 2002), pp. 1–22.

'The Supernatural', *A Companion to the Gawain-poet*, ed. Derek Brewer and Jonathan Gibson (Cambridge, 1997), pp. 277–91.

'Averting Chaucer's Prophecies: Miswriting, Mismetering, and Misunderstanding', *A Guide to Editing Middle English Texts*, ed. V.P. McCarren and D. Moffatt (Ann Arbor, 1998), pp. 79–93.

'Chaucer', in the *Garland Encyclopedia of Medieval England*, ed. Teresa Tavormina et al. (New York, 1998).

'Jacobean Chaucer: *The Two Noble Kinsmen* and other Chaucerian Plays', *Refiguring Chaucer in the Renaissance*, ed. T.M. Krier (Gainesville, 1998), pp. 189–209.

'Romance after 1400', *The Cambridge History of Medieval English Literature*, ed. David Wallace (Cambridge, 1998), pp. 690–719.

'The Four Last Things in Dante and Chaucer: Ugolino in the House of Rumour', *New Medieval Literatures* 3 (1999), 39–66.

'The Strange History of *Valentine and Orson*', *Tradition and Transformation in Medieval Romance*, ed. Rosalind Field (Cambridge, 1999), pp. 153–68.

'The Elizabethan *Havelok*: William Warner's First of the English', *Medieval Insular Romance: Translation and Innovation*, ed. Judith Weiss (Cambridge, 2000), pp. 169–83.

'Opening up the Malory Manuscript', *The Malory Debate: Essays on the Text*, ed. Bonnie Wheeler, Robert L. Kindrick and Michael N. Salda (Cambridge, 2000), pp. 255–84.

'Responding to the Monk', in 'Colloquium on *The Monk's Tale*', *Studies in the Age of Chaucer* 22 (2000), 425–33.

'Welcome to the House of Fame', *TLS* 5091 (27 October 2000), 3–4 (cover/lead article: Chaucer 600th Centennial lecture).

'Chaucerian Self-Fashioning', *Poetica* 55 (2001), 55–74.

'Did Shakespeare play the Clown?', *TLS* 5116 (20 April 2001), 26–7.

'Joyce's Other Father: The Case for Chaucer', *Medieval Joyce*, ed. Lucia Boldrini, European Joyce Studies 13 (Amsterdam, 2002), pp. 143–63.

'After Chaucer' (the Presidential Address to the New Chaucer Society, 2002), *Studies in the Age of Chaucer* 25 (2003), 3–24.

'Chaucerian Representation' and 'Chaucerian Poetics', *New Readings of Chaucer's Poetry*, ed. Robert G. Benson and Susan J. Ridyard, Chaucer Studies 31 (Cambridge, 2003), pp. 7–50.

'The *Lancelot-Grail Cycle* in England: Malory and his Predecessors', *A Companion to the Lancelot-Grail Cycle*, ed. Carol Dover (Cambridge, 2003), pp. 147–62.

'Good Advice on Leaving Home', *Youth in the Middle Ages*, ed. Felicity Riddy and Jeremy Goldberg (York, 2004), pp. 101–21.

'Malory and the Early Prose Romances', *The Blackwell Companion to Romance*, ed. Corinne J. Saunders (Oxford, 2004), pp. 104–20.

'Malory's Language of Love', *Arthurian Studies in honour of P.J.C. Field*, ed. Bonnie Wheeler (Cambridge, 2004), pp. 297–306.

'Prose Romances', *A Companion to Middle English Prose*, ed. A.S.G. Edwards (Cambridge, 2004), pp. 215–29.

'Speaking for the Victim', *Writing War: Medieval Literary Responses to Warfare*, ed. Corinne Saunders, Françoise le Saux and Neil Wright (Cambridge, 2004), pp. 213–31.

'Textual Variation and the Alliterative Tradition: *Canterbury Tales* I.2602–2619, the D Group and Takamiya MS 32', *The Medieval Book and a Modern Collector: Essays in Honour of Toshiyuki Takamiya*, ed. Takami Matsuda, Richard A. Linenthal and John Scahill (Cambridge, 2004), pp. 71–80.

'"This worthy olde writer": *Pericles* and other Gowers, 1592–1640', *A Companion to Gower*, ed. Sian Echard (Cambridge, 2004), pp. 99–114.

'Thomas of Erceldoune: Romance as Prophecy', *Cultural Encounters in Medieval English Romance*, ed. Corinne J. Saunders (Cambridge, 2004), pp. 171–87.

'The Classical Background', *Chaucer: An Oxford Guide*, ed. Steve Ellis (Oxford, 2005), pp. 255–71.

'Lancelot, Roger Mortimer, and the Date of the Auchinleck Manuscript', *Studies in Late Medieval and early Renaissance Texts in Honour of John Scattergood: The Key of All Good Remembrance*, ed. A.J. Fletcher and A.-M. D'Arcy (Dublin, 2005), pp. 91–9.

'Guy of Warwick, Upstart Crows and Mounting Sparrows', *Shakespeare, Marlowe, Jonson: New Directions in Biography*, ed. J.R. Mulryne and Takashi Kozuka (Aldershot, 2006), pp. 119–38.

'Lancelot's Wives', *Arthuriana* 16.2 (2006), 1–4.

'London and Southwark Poetic Companies: "Si tost c'amis" and the *Canterbury Tales*', *Chaucer and the City*, ed. Ardis Butterfield (Cambridge, 2006), pp. 109–25.

'Love before *Troilus*', *Writings on Love in the English Middle Ages*, ed. Helen Cooney, Studies in Arthurian and Courtly Culture (London, 2006), pp. 25–43.

'Shakespeare and the Mystery Plays', *Shakespeare and Elizabethan Popular Culture*, ed. Stuart Gillespie and Neil Rhodes, Arden Companions to Shakespeare (London, 2006), pp. 18–41, 222–6.

'*A Tale of Robin Hood*: Robin Hood as Bishop', *Medieval Cultural Studies: Essays in Honour of Stephen Knight*, ed. Ruth Evans, Helen Fulton and David Matthews (Cardiff, 2006), pp. 75–90.

'Guy as Early Modern Hero', *Guy of Warwick: Icon and Ancestor*, ed. Rosalind Field and Alison Wiggins (Cambridge, 2007), pp. 185–99.

'Honour and Sexuality in Three Shakespeare Plays', *Shakespeare between the Middle Ages and Modernism: From Translator's Art to Academic Discourse*, ed. Martin Procházka and Jan Cermák (Prague, 2008), pp. 77–94.

'Epilogue: Edmund Spenser and the Passing of Tudor Literature', *The Oxford Handbook of Tudor Literature 1485–1603*, ed. Mike Pincombe and Cathy Shrank (Oxford, 2009), pp. 749–66.

'Translation and Adaptation', *A Concise Companion to Middle English Literature*, ed. Marilyn Corrie (Oxford, 2009), pp. 166–87.

'Chaucer', in *The Oxford Dictionary of the Middle Ages*, ed. Robert Bjork (Oxford, 2010).

'The Immortal Memory: Pepys and the Wife of Bath', *Magdalene College Record* (2010), 71–6.

'Introduction', *Chaucer and Religion*, ed. Helen Phillips (Cambridge, 2010), pp. xii–xix.

'Introduction', *Romance and Christianity in Medieval England*, ed. Rosalind Field, Phillipa Hardman and Michaela Sweeney (Cambridge, 2010), pp. xiii–xxi.

'Poetic Fame', *Cultural Reformations: Medieval and Renaissance in Literary History*, Twenty-First-Century Approaches to Literature, ed. Brian Cummings and James Simpson (Oxford, 2010), pp. 361–78.

'Choosing Poetic Fathers: The English Problem', *Medieval and Early Modern Authorship*, ed. Guillemette Bolens and Lukas Erne (Tübingen, 2011), pp. 29–49.

'Going Native: The Caxton and Mainwaring Versions of *Paris and Vienne*', *Travel and Prose Fiction in Early Modern England*, ed. Nandini Das, special number of *The Yearbook of English Studies* 41.1 (2011), 21–34.

'In Memoriam Derek Brewer', *Chaucer Review* 45.3 (2011), 241–7.

'Literary Reformations of the Middle Ages', *The Cambridge Companion to Medieval England*, ed. Andrew Galloway (Cambridge, 2011), pp. 261–78.

'The Ends of Storytelling', *Traditions and Innovations in the Study of Middle English Literature: The Influence of Derek Brewer*, ed. Charlotte Brewer and Barry Windeatt (Cambridge, 2013), pp. 188–201.

'Introduction' and 'The Afterlife of Personification', *Medieval Shakespeare: Pasts and Presents*, ed. Ruth Morse, Helen Cooper and Peter Holland (Cambridge, 2013), pp. 1–16, 98–116.

'Milton's King Arthur', *RES* NS 65 (2013), 252–65.

'The Origins of the Early Modern', *Journal for Early Modern Cultural Studies* 13.3 (2013), 133–7.

'C.S. Lewis as Medievalist', *Linguaculture* 5.2 (2014), 45–56.

'Finishing the Unfinished', *Emprynted in thys manere: Early Printed Treasures from Cambridge University Library*, ed. Ed Potten and Emily Dourish (Cambridge, 2014), pp. 90–1.

'Medieval Drama in the Elizabethan Age', *SELIM* 20 (2014), 1–23.

'Romance Patterns of Naming in *Piers Plowman*', *'Truthe is the beste': A Festschrift in Honour of A.V.C. Schmidt*, ed. Nicolas Jacobs and Gerald Morgan (Oxford and Bern, 2014), pp. 37–63.

'Valerius', in *The Virgil Encyclopedia*, ed. Richard F. Thomas and Jan M. Ziolkowski (Oxford, 2014).

'Afterword: Malory's Enigmatic Smiles', *Emotions in Medieval Arthurian Literature: Body, Mind, Voice*, ed. F. Brandsma, Carolyne Larrington and Corinne Saunders (Cambridge, 2015), pp. 181–8.

'Arthur in Transition: Malory's *Morte Darthur*', *Romance and History: Imagining Time from the Medieval to the Early Modern Period*, ed. Jon Whitman (Cambridge, 2015), pp. 120–36.

'Pastoral and Georgic, 1558–1660: Greek and Roman', *The Oxford History of Classical Reception in English Literature, Vol. 2, 1558–1660*, ed. Patrick Cheney and Philip Hardie (Oxford, 2015), pp. 201–24.

'Chaucer: *The Canterbury Tales*' and 'Romance', *The Encyclopedia of British Medieval Literature*, ed. Sian Echard and Robert Rouse (Oxford, 2016).

'Dramatizing the Tudors', *1616: Shakespeare and Tang Xianzu's China*, ed. Tian Yuan Tan, Paul Edmondson and Shih-pe Wang (London, 2016), pp. 76–94.

'Gower and Mortality: The Ends of Storytelling', *John Gower: Others and the Self*, ed. R.F. Yeager (Cambridge, 2016).

'"The most excellent creatures are not ever born perfect": Early Modern Attitudes to Middle English', *Imagining Medieval English: Language Structures and Theories, 500–1500*, ed. Tim Machan (Cambridge, 2016), pp. 241–60.

Review articles

'The Age of Anxiety', *TLS* 4317 (27 December 1985).
'Louis MacNeice: A Double Anniversary', *Cambridge Review* 109 (1988), 171–2.
'Why the Vice-Chancellor Hanged Himself and Other Stories', *Cambridge Review* 110 (1989), 188–9.
'A Thing *varium et mutabile*', *TLS* 4607 (19 July 1991), 5 (cover article).
'Visions of Women', *TLS* 4689 (12 February 1993), 5–6.
'Through the Gullet', *LRB* 20.8 (16 April 1998), 26; reprinted in *Australian Financial Review*.
'Surviving the Reformation', *LRB* 20.20 (15 October 1998), 20–1.
'A Glimpse of Paradise', *TLS* 5007 (18 March 1999), 3–4 (cover/lead article).
'M for Merlin', *LRB* 21.23 (25 November 1999), 32–3.
'Blood Running Down,' *LRB* 23.15 (9 August 2001), 13–14.
'Fill it with Fish', *LRB* 24.1 (6 June 2002), 34–5.
'Queen's Moves', *TLS* 5291 (27 August 2004), 8.
'Family Fortunes', *LRB* 27.15 (4 August 2005), 12–13.
'Skeltonics', *LRB* 28.24 (14 December 2006), 32–4.
'The Word and the World', *Essays in Criticism* 59 (2009) 59–65.
'Malorys for Teaching and Reading', *Arthuriana* 20.1 (2010), 95–9.
'Writing French in English', *LRB* 32.19 (7 October 2010), 9–11.
'A Right Herbert', *The Guardian Review* (17 August 2013), 5.
'Such Werkes', *Cambridge Quarterly* 43.4 (2014), 384–9.

Tabula Gratulatoria

Gavin Alexander
Gillian Austen
Anthony Bale
Helen Barr
Joanna Bellis
Joyce Boro
Ardis Butterfield
Aisling Byrne
Nandini Das
Susanna Fein
Mary C. Flannery
Victoria Flood
Helen Fulton
Alexandra Gillespie
Jane Grogan
D. Thomas Hanks, Jr.
Phillipa Hardman

Paulina Kewes
Andrew King
Hester Lees-Jeffries
Megan G. Leitch
Scott C. Lucas
Andrew L. Lynch
Raphael Lyne
Sally Mapstone
R. W. Maslen
Richard McCabe
Nicola McDonald
Helen Moore
David Norbrook
Bernard O'Donoghue
Cian O' Mahony
Derek Pearsall
Nicholas Perkins

Helen Phillips
Jason Powell
Rhiannon Purdie
Ad Putter
Raluca Radulescu
David Raybin
Gillian Rogers
Robert Allen Rouse
Laura Varnam
Helen Vincent
James Wade
David Wallace
Carl Watkins
Jocelyn Wogan-Browne
Matthew Woodcock
Andrew Zurcher